POPULAR TALES

OF

THE WEST HIGHLANDS

POPULAR TALES

OF

THE WEST HIGHLANDS

ORALLY COLLECTED

With a Translation

BY THE LATE J. F. CAMPBELL

NEW EDITION

VOLUME II

WILDWOOD HOUSE

1983

First published in 1860 by Edmonston and Douglas of Edinburgh.

Second corrected edition published in 1890 by Alexander Gardner of Paisley and London.

This facsimile paperback of the second edition first published in 1983 by

Wildwood House Ltd.,
Jubilee House,
Chapel Road,
Hounslow,
Middlesex
TW3 1TX

Campbell, J.F.
Popular tales of the West Highlands. —
(Wildwood rediscoveries)
Vol. 2
1. Tales — Scotland — Highlands of Scotland
I. Title
398.2'5'094118 GR142.W./

ISBN 0 7045 0491 X Paperbound

The Publishers gratefully acknowledge the financial assistance given by the Scottish Arts Council.

Printed and bound by The Guernsey Press Company Limited in the Channel Islands.

CONTENTS.

POPULAR TALES

OF

THE WEST HIGHLANDS.

XVIII.

THE CHEST.

From Mrs MacGeachy, Islay.

BEFORE this there was a king, and he wished to see his son with a wife before she should depart. His son said he had better go for a wife; and he gave him half a hundred pounds to get her. He went forward in to a hostelry to stay in it. He went down to a chamber with a good fire in front of him; and when he had gotten meat, the man of the house went down to talk to him. He told the man of the house the journey on which he was. The man of the house told him he need not go further; that there was a little house opposite to his sleeping chamber; that the man of the house had three fine daughters; and if he would stand in the window of his chamber in the morning, that he would see one after another coming to dress herself. That they were all like each other, and that he could not distinguish one from the other, but that the eldest had a mole. That many were going to ask for them, but that none got them, because whoever wished for one, must tell whether the one he liked best was younger or older; and if he made her out, that she would cost him a hundred pounds. "I have but half a hundred," said the king's son. "I will give thee another half hundred," said the man of the house, "if thou wilt pay me at the end of a day and a year; and if thou dost not pay me, a strip of skin shall come from the top of thy head to the sole of thy foot."

On the morrow when he rose he went to the window; he saw the girls coming to dress themselves; and after meat in the morning, he went over to the house of their father. When he went in he was taken down to a chamber, and the man of the house went down to talk to him. He told the journey on which he was, and he said to him, "They tell me that thou hast three fine daughters." "I have that same, but I am afraid that it is not thou who wilt buy them." "I will give them a trial, at all events," said he. The three were sent down before him, and it was said to him "Whether she, the one he liked best, was the elder or younger." He thought he would take the one with the mole, because he knew she was the eldest. She then was much pleased that it was she herself he was for. He asked her father how much she would be, and her father said she would be a hundred pounds. He bought her, and he took her to the house of his father, and they married. Shortly after they married his father departed.

A day or two after the death of the old king, the young king was out hunting; he saw a great ship coming in to the strand; he went down to ask the captain what he had on board. The captain said,

"That he had a cargo of silk." "Thou must," said he, "give me a gown of the best silk thou hast for my wife." "Indeed!" said the captain, "thou must have an exceedingly good wife when thou must have a gown of the best silk I have on board." "I have that," said the king, "a wife many of whose equals are not to be got." "Wilt thou lay a wager," said the captain, "that with all her goodness I will not get leave to enter thy chamber?" "I will lay a wager, anything thou desiredst, that thou wilt not." "What wager wilt thou lay?" said the captain. "I will put the heirship in pledge," said the king. Said the captain: "I will put all the silk in ship in pledge to thee that I will." The captain came on shore and the king went on board.

The captain went where the hen-wife was, to try if she could make any way to get in with to king's chamber that night. The hen-wife thought a while, and she said "That she did not think that there was any way that would succeed." The captain rose here, and he was going. "Stop thou!" said she, "I have thought on a way: her maid servant and I are well with each other; I will say to her that I have got word from a sister of mine that I will scarce find her alive; I will say to the king's wife that I must go to see my sister; that I have a big kist, of good worth, and I should like if she would oblige me and let it into her own sleeping chamber till I come back." She went where the queen was, she asked her this, and she got leave. Here the captain was put into the kist, and the king's gillies were gathered, and the kist put in the chamber. The king's wife was within by herself wearying, for the king was not coming home. At last she went to bed; when she was going to bed she put a gold ring that was on her finger, and a gold chain that was about her neck, on a board that was opposite to the bed. When the man who was in the kist thought that she had time to be asleep, he rose and he took with him the chain and the ring, and he went into the kist again. At the mouth of day came the hen-wife to ask for the kist; the gillies were gathered, and the kist was taken down. When every one went from the house, as soon as he could, the captain rose and he went down to the ship; he shook the chain and the ring at the king. Then the king thought that the captain had been with his wife, or that he could not have the chain and ring. He said to the captain, "Would he put him over to the other side of the loch?" The captain said, "That he would." When the captain got him over he returned himself, and he went to dwell in the king's house. Then the king's wife did not know what to do with herself, for that the king had not come home. She went that day and she dressed herself in man's clothes, and she went down to the strand; she met with a boat, and she said to them, "Would they put her over on the other side?" They put her over, and she went on forward till she reached the house of a gentleman; she struck in the door, and the maid servant came down. She said to her, "Did she know if her master wanted a stable gillie?" The maid servant said, "That she did not know, but that she would ask." The maid servant went and she asked her master if he wanted a stable gillie. He said, "He did;" and he asked that he should come in; he engaged her, and she stayed working about the stable. There was a herd of wild beasts coming every night, and going into an empty barn that the gentleman had; a wild man after them, and his face covered with beard. She kept asking her master to send a man with her, and that they would catch him. Her master said, "That he would not; that they had no business with them; and that he had not done any harm to them." She went out one night by herself, and she stole with her the key of the barn door; she lay hid in a hole till the wild man and the beasts went in; she took with her the gillies, and they caught the wild man. They brought him in and they took off his beard; when the beard came off him she knew him, but she took no notice; and he did not know her. On the morrow he was about to go, but she spoke to her master to keep him; that the work was too heavy on her, and that she needed help. Her master ordered her to keep him. She kept him with her, and he himself and she were cleaning the stable.

A short time after this she spoke to her master for leave to go home on a trip to see her friends. Her master gave her leave. She said she would like well to have her gillie with her, and the two best horses that were in the stable.

When they went, she was questioning him by the way what had made him go with these wild beasts; or what he was at before the day. He would not tell her anything. They went on forward till they came to the hostelry where he had got the half hundred pounds. When she set her face down to the house, he refused to go into it. She said to him, "Did he do anything wrong, as he was refusing to go into it." He said, "That he had got half a hundred pounds from the man of the house." She said to him, "Had he paid them;" and he said, "That he had not paid, and that a strip of skin was to come from the top of his head to the sole of his foot, if it was not paid at the end of a day and a year." She said, "It would be well deserved; but that she was going to stay the night in the hostelry, and that she must go down." She asked him to put the horses into the stable, and they went in to the hostelry. He was standing in the door of the stable, and his head was bent. The man of the house came out, and he saw him. "My big gillie, I have thee here," said the man of the house; "art thou going to pay me to-day?" "I am not," said he. Then he went in, and they were going to begin to cut the strip of skin. She heard the noise, and she asked what they were going to do to her gillie. They said, "They were going to cut a strip of skin off him from his crown to his sole." "If that was to be done," said she, "he was not to lose a drop of blood; send up here a web of linen, let him stand on it, and if a drop of blood comes out of him, another strip of skin shall come off thee." Here there was nothing for it but to let him go; they could not make anything of it. Early on the morrow she took him over with her to the house of her father. If he was against going to the hostelry the night before, he was seven times as much when going to her father's house. "Didst thou do harm here too, as thou art against going in?" "I got a wife here such a time since." "What came of her?" "I don't know." No wonder whatever happens to thee, thou hast only to put up with all that comes thy way." When her father saw him, he said: "I have thee here! Where is thy wife?" "I don't know where she is." "What didst thou to her?" said her father. He could not tell what he had done to her. Now there was nothing to be done but to hang him to a tree. There was to be a great day about the hanging, and a great many gentlemen were to come to see it. She asked her father what they were going to do to her gillie. Her father said, "That they were going to hang him; he bought a wife from me, and he does not know what has happened to her." She went out to see the gentles coming in to the town; she asked of the one of the finest horse, what was his worth. "Five score," said he. "Though he were five hundreds, he's mine," said she. She told her servant to put a shot in the horse. She asked her father if he had paid for his wife. He said he had paid. "If he paid," said she, "thou hast no business with him, he might do what he liked with her; I bought the finest horse that came into the town to-day; I made my gillie put a shot in him, and who dares to say that it is ill." Here there was nothing to be done but to let him loose. They could do nothing to him because he had bought her.

Here she went in to her father's house, and she told one of her sisters to give her a gown. "What art thou going to do with a gown?" said she. "Never mind, if I spoil it I'll pay for it." When she put on the gown her father and sisters knew her. Her father and sisters told him that it was she was with him, and he did not believe them. She put off the woman's clothes and put on the man's clothes again. They went, herself and he; they went on forward till they were near his own old house. "Now," said she, "we will stay here to-night; do thou sit at the top of the stair, and thou shalt set down all the talk that I and the man of the house will have." When they went in and sat, she and the man of the house began to talk together. "I thought," said she to the captain, "that a king was dwelling here; how didst thou get it?" He was that who was here before; but I am thinking, as thou art a stranger, that I may tell thee how I got it." "Thou mayest," said she, "I will not make a tale of thee, the matter does not touch me." He told her every turn, how the hen wife had put him in the kist, and the rest of the matter, to the going of the king on the morrow.

Very early on the morrow the man of the house was going to court: he said to her "That if she was not in a hurry to go away, that she might go with him to listen to the court." She said "she would be willing, and she would like well that her gillie should be with her." She went in the coach with the captain, and her gillie rode after her. When the court was over she said, "That she had got a word or two to say, if it were their pleasure to let her speak." They said to her, "To let them hear what she had to say." She said to her gillie, "Rise up and give them the paper thou wrotest last night." When they read the paper, she said, "What should be done to that man?" "Hang him, if he were here," said they.

"There you have him," said she, "do with him what you will." Herself and the king got back to their own house, and they were as they were before.

URSGEUL.

BHA rìgh ann roimhe so, 's bha toil aige bean fhaicinn aig a mhac ma'n siùbhladh e. Thuirt e r'a mhac gum b' fheàrra dha folbh airson mnatha, 's thug e dha leith chiad punnd airson a faotainn. Choisich e air aghaidh fad latha; 's nur a thàinig an oidhche chaidh e stigh do thigh òsd' airson fantainn ann. Chaidh e sios do sheombar, 's gealbhan math air a bheulthaobh; 's nur a fhuair e 'bhiadh chaidh fear an tighe sios a chomhnadal ris. Dh' innis e do' dh' fhear an tighe an turas air an robh e. Thuirt fear an tighe ris nach ruigeadh e leas dol na b' fhaide ; gu' robh tigh beag ma choinneamh an t-seombair chadail aige ; gu robh tri nigheanan gasd' aig fear an tighe ; agus na 'n seasadh e 'n uinneag a sheombair anns a' mhadainn, gu' faiceadh e te an déigh te 'tighinn a 'h-éideadh féin. Gu' robh iad air fad cosmhuil r'a' chéile, 's nach aithneachadh e eadar te seach te ; ach an te 'bu shine, gu' robh ball dòrain urra. Gu robh móran a' dol g'an iarraidh, ach nach robh gin 'gam faotainn ; a thaobh gu' feumadh neach a bhiodh air son h-aon diu innseadh co dhiu a b'i an te d'an robh taitneachd aige b' òige na' bu shine ; 's na'n déanadh e mach i gun cosdadh i dha ciad punnd. "Cha 'n 'eil agams' ach leith chiad," ursa mac an rìgh. "Bheir mise dhuit leith chiad eile," ursa fear an tighe, "ma phàigheas thu mi 'n ceann la is bliadhna ; 's mar am pàigh thig iall o mhullach do chinn gu bonn do choise." Nur a dh' éiridh e 'n la 'r na mhàireach chaidh e gus an uinneig. Chunnaic e na nigheanan a' tighinn a'n éideadh fein, 's an déigh a bhìdh 'sa mhadainn chaidh e nunn gu tigh an athar. Nur a chaidh e stigh chaidh a thoirt sios do sheombar, 's chaidh fear an tighe sìos a chomhnadal ris. Dh' innis e 'n turus air an robh e, 's thuirt e ris, "Tha iad ag ràdh rium gu' bheil tri nigheanan bréagh agad." "Tha sin féin agam ; ach tha eagal orm nach tusa 'cheannaicheas iad." "Bheir mi feuchainn dhaibh," urs' esan. Chaidh an tri chuir sìos ma 'choinneamh, 's a ràdh ris, cò'ca a b'i 'n te d'an gabhadh e taitneachd an te bu shine na 'n te b' òige. Smaoinich e gu'n gabhadh e té a' bhall dòrain ; o'n a bha fhios aige gur h-i 'bu shine. Ghabh ise an sin toil-inntinn mhòr gur h-i féin a bha e air a shon. Dh' fheòraich e d'a h-athair co mhìod a bhitheadh i, 's thuirt a h athair gum biodh i ciad punnd. Cheannaich e i, 's thug e leis i gu tigh athar, 's phòs iad. Goirid an déigh dhaibh pòsadh shiubhail athair.

Latha na dha an déigh bàs àn t-sean rìgh, bha 'n rìgh òg a mach a' sealgaireachd. Chunnaic e long mhòr a' tighinn a stigh thun a' chladaich. Chaidh e sìos a dh' fheòraich de 'n chaibhtinn de 'bha aige air bòrd. Thuirt an caibhtinn gu' robh luchd sìoda. "Feumaidh tu," urs' esan, "guthann de 'n t-sìoda 's fheàrr a th' agad a thoirt dhòmhsa airson mo mhnatha." "Seadh," urs' an caibhtinn, "feumaidh gu' bheil bean fhuathasach mhath agadsa, nur a dh' fheumas i guthann de'n t-sìoda is fheàrr a th' agamsa air bòrd." "Tha sin agam," urs' an rìgh, "bean nach 'eil mòran d'a leithidean r'a fhaotainn." "An cuir thu geall," urs' an caibhtinn, "a' h-uile mathas a th' urra, nach fhaigh mise dol a laidhe leatha nochd?" "Cuiridh mi geall, ni 'sam bith a shannt-aicheas thu, nach fhaigh." "Dé 'n geall a chuireas tu?" urs' an caibhtinn. "Cuiridh mi 'n oighreachd an geall," urs' an rìgh. Urs' an caibhtinn, "Cuiridh mise na bheil de shìoda 'san long an geall riutsa gu'm faigh." Thàinig an caibhtinn air tír, 's chaidh an rìgh air bòrd. Chaidh an caibhtinn far an robh cailleach nan cearc feuch an dèanadh i dòigh 'sam bith air 'fhaotainn a stigh le bean an rìgh an oidhche sin. Smaointich cailleach nan cearc tacan, 's thuirt i nach robh dùil aice gu' robh dòigh 'sam bith a dhéanadh feum. Dh' éirich an caibhtinn an sin, 's bha e 'falbh. "Stad ort," urs' ise, "smaointich mi air dòigh." Tha 'n searbhannt aice 's mi féin gu math mòr. Their mi rithe gu'n d' fhuair mi fios o phiuthar dhomh nach beirinn beò urra. Their mi ri bean an rìgh gu' feum mi folbh a dh' fhaicinn mo pheathar; gu 'bheil cisde mhòr agam gu math luachar, a bu mhath leam, na'n lughasachadh i dhomh, a leigeil d'a seombar-cadail féin gus an till mi." Chaidh i far an robh 'bhanrighinn; dh' fheòraich i so dhi, 's fhuair i cead. Chaidh an so an caibhtinn a chur a stigh do'n chisde, 's gillean an righ a chruinneachadh, 's a' chisde' chur do 'n t-seombar. Bha bean an rìgh a stigh leatha féin, 's fadal urra nach robh an rìgh a' tighinn dachaidh. Ma dheireadh chaidh i 'laidhe. Nur a bha i 'dol a laidhe chuir i fainne òir a bha air a meur, agus slabhraidh òir a bha ma 'muineal, air bòrd a bha ma choinneamh na leapa. Nur a smaointich am fear a bha 's a' chisde gu' robh ùine aice 'bhi 'na cadal, dh' éirich e, s thug e leis an t-slabhraidh 's am fainne, 's chaidh e stigh do'n chisde a rithisd. Am beul an latha thàinig cailleach nan cearc a dh' iarraidh a cisde. Chaidh na gillean a chruinneachadh 's a' chisde 'thoirt a nuas. Nur dh' fholbh a' h-uile duine o'n tigh, cho luath sa' bu leur dha, dh' éirich an caibhtinn, 's dh' fholbh e sìos thun na luinge. Chrath e'n t-slabhraidh 's am fainne ris an rìgh. Smaointich an rìgh an sin gun d'fhuair an caibhtinn a stigh le a bhean, no nach biodh an t-slabhraidh 's am fainne aige. Thuirt e ris a' chaibhtinn an cuireadh e nunn e gus an taobh eile de'n loch. Thuirt an caibhtinn gun cuireadh. Nur a fhuair an caibhtinn thairis e, thill e féin 's chaidh e 'chòmhnuidh do thigh an rìgh.

Bha bean an rìgh an sin 's gun fhios aice dé a dhèanadh i rithe féin, o'n nach d' thàinig an rìgh dhachaidh. Dh' fholbh i 'n latha sin, 's dh' éid i i féin ann an aodach fir, 's chaidh i sìos thun a' chladaich. Thachair bàta urra, 's thuirt i riu an cuireadh iad ise a nunn air an taobh eile. Chuir iad a nunn i, 's ghabh i air a h-aghaidh gus an d' ràinig i tigh duine uasail. Bhuail i 'san dorus, 's thàinig an searbhannt' a nuas. Thuirt i rithe an robh fhios aice an robh gille stàbuill a dhìth air a maighstir. Thuirt an searbhannta nach robh fhios aice, ach gu 'foighneachdadh i. Chaidh an searbhanta 's dh' fheòraich i d'a maighstir, an robh gille stàbuill a dhìth air. Thuirt e gun robh, agus dh' iarr e e 'thighinn a stigh. Dh' fhasdaidh e i, 's dh' fhan i 'g obair ma'n stàbull. Bha 'n sin treud de bheathaichean fiadhaich a' tighinn a' h-uile h-oidhche, 's a' dol a stigh do shabhal fàs a bha aig an duine uasal, 's duine fiadhaich as an déigh, 's aodann còmhdaichte le feusaig. Bha ise ag iarraidh air a maighstir na'n cuireadh iad duine leatha, gum beireadh iad air. Thuirt a maighstir nach cuireadh, nach robh gnothach aca ris, 's nach d' rinn e coire 'sam bith orra. Dh' fholbh ise mach oidhche leatha féin, 's ghoid i leatha iuchair doruis an t-sabhail. Laidh i 'm falach ann an toll gus an deachaidh an duine fiadhaich agus na beathaichean a stigh. Thug i leatha na gillean, 's rug iad air an duine fhiadhaich. Thug iad a stigh e, 's thug iad dheth an fheusag. Nur a thàinig an fheusag dheth dh' aithnich ise e, ach cha do leig i rud sam bith urra, 's cha d' aithnich esan ise. An la 'r na mhàireach bha e' dol a dh' fholbh, ach bhruidhinn ise r'a maighstir airson a ghleidheadh, gu'n robh an obair tuillidh is trom urra, 's gu 'feumadh i cuideachadh. Dh' òrduich a maighstir dhi 'ghleidheadh. Ghléidh i leath' e, 's bha e fein agus ise a' glanadh an stàbuill.

Beagan ùine 'na dhéigh so bhruidhinn i r'a maighstir, airson cead a dhol dhachaidh air sgrìob a dh' fhaicinn a càirdean. Thug a maighstir cead dhi. Thuirt i gu'm bu mhath leatha a gille, 's an da each a b' fheàrr a bh' ann 's an stàbull a bhi leatha. Nur a dh' fholbh iad bha i 'ga cheasnachadh air an rathad ; dé thug dha bhi folbh leis na beathaichean ud, na de bha e ris an toiseach a latha. Cha 'n innseadh e ni sam bith dhi. Ghabh iad air an aghaidh gus an d' thàinig iad gus an tigh òsda far an d' fhuair esan an leith chiad punnd. Nur a thug ise a h-aghaidh sìos gus an tigh, dhiult esan a dhol ann. Thuirt i ris an d' rinn e ni sam bith ceàrr, nur a bha e diùltainn dol ann. Thuirt e gun d' fhuair e leith chiad punnd o fhear an tighe. Thuirt i ris an do phaigh e iad, 's thuirt e nach do phàigh, 's gu'n robh iall ri tighinn o mhullach a chinn gu bonn a choise, mar am biodh e pàighte an ceann la is bliadhna. Thuirt i gum bu mhath an airidh ; ach gu' robh ise a' dol a dh' fhantainn 's an tigh òsda 'san oidhche, 's gu' feumadh e dol sìos. Dh' iarr i air na h-eich a chur a stigh 'san stàbull, 's chaidh eud a stigh do 'n tigh òsda. Bha esan na sheasamh ann an dorus an stàbuill, 's a cheann crom. Thàinig fear an tighe mach 's chunnaic e e. "Mo ghille mòr tha thu an so agam," ursa fear an tighe. "Am bheil thu' dol am' phàigheadh an diugh?" "Cha 'n 'eil," urs' esan. Chaidh e 'sin a stigh, 's bha iad a' dol a thòiseachd air an iall a ghearradh. Chual ise an fhuaim, 's dh' fheòraich i gu dé 'bha iad a' dol a dhèanadh air a gille. Thuirt iad gun robh iad a' dol a ghearradh iall deth o mhullach gu bonn. "Ma bha sin r'a dhèanadh," urs' ise, "cha robh e ri deur fola a chall." "Cuir an nuas an so lìon aodach, a's seasadh e air, 's ma thig deur fola as thig iall eile dhìotsa." Cha robh an so ach a leigeil ma sgaoil. Cha b' urrainn iad stugh a dhèanadh dheth. Mochthradh an la'r na mhàireach thug i leatha nunn e gu tigh a h-athar. Ma bha e 'n aghaidh dol a'n tigh òsda an oidhche roimhid, bha e seachd uairean na bu mhotha 'n aghaidh dol do thigh a h-athar. "An do rinn thu cron an so cuideachd nur a tha thu 'n aghaidh dol ann?" "Fhuair mi bean an so o cheann a leithid do dh' ùine." "De 'thàinig urra?" "Cha 'n 'eil fhios'am." "Cha 'n iongantach dé dh' éireas duit! cha 'n 'eil agad ach gabhail ris na thig a'd' rathad!" Nur a chunnaic a h-athair e thuirt e, "Tha thu 'so agam; càit a' bheil do bhean?" "Cha 'n 'eil fhiosam càit' a' bheil i." "Dé a rinn thu rithe?" urs' a h-athair. Cha b' urrainn e innseadh dé a rinn a rithe. Cha robh 'nis ach a chrochadh ri craoibh. Bha latha mòr ri 'bhi timchioll a chrochaidh, 's bha mòran de dhaoine uaisle ri tighinn a 'fhaicinn. Dh' fheòraich ise d'a h-athair dé 'bha iad a dol a dhèanadh r'a gille. Thuirt a h-athair gu'n robh iad a' dol da chrochadh. "Carson," urs' ise, "a tha e r'a chrochadh." "Cheannaich 'e bean uamsa, 's cha 'n 'eil fhios aige dé 'thàinig rithe. Dh' fholbh i 'mach a dh' fhaicinn nan uaislean a' tighinn a stigh do'n bhaile. Dh' fheòraich i de 'n fhear a bu chiataich' each de 'b' fhiach dha." "Coig fichead," urs' esan. "Ged a bhiodh e coig ciad 's leamsa e," urs' ise. Thuirt i r'a gille urchair a chur 'san each. Dh' fheòraich i d'a h-athair an do phàigh e 'bhean. Thuirt e gun do phàigh. "Ma phàigh," urs' ise, "cha 'n 'eil gnothach agadsa ris; dh' fhaodadh e 'roighinn a dhèanadh rithe. Cheannaich mise an t-each a bu chiataiche a thàinig a stigh do 'n bhaile an diugh. Thug mi air mo ghille urchair a chur ann, 's co aig a' bheil a chridhe a ràdh gur olc. Cha u robh 'so ach a leigeil ma sgaoil. Cha b' urrainn iad stugh a dhèanadh air o'n a cheannaich e i.

Chaidh i an sin a stigh do thigh a h-athar, 's thuirt i ri h-aon d'a peathraichean guthann a thoirt dhi. "De 'tha thusa 'dol a dhèanadh do ghuthann?" urs' ise. "Nach coma leatsa. Ma ni mi milleadh air pàighidh mi e." Nur a chuir i urra an guthann dh' aithnich a h-athair's a peathraichean i. Dh' innis a h-athair 's a peathraichean dha gur h-i 'bha leis, 's cha robh e gan creid-sinn. Chuir i dhi an t-aodach mnatha, 's chuir i urra an t-aodach fir a rithisd. Dh' fholbh i féin is esan, 's ghabh iad air an aghaidh gus an robh iad dlùth air a shean tigh féin. "Nis," urs' ise, "feumaidh sin fuireachd an so an nochd. Suidhidh tusa air bràigh na staighreach, agus cuirridh tu sìos gach comhnadal a bhios agams' agus aig fear an tighe. Nur a chaidh iad a stigh 's a shuidh iad, thòisich i fein agus fear an tighe air comhradh. "Shaoil mi," urs' i ris a' chaibhtinn, "gum b' e rìgh a bha 'chòmhnuidh an so. Démur 'fhuair thusa e?" "'Se sin a bha roimhid an so; ach tha mi smaointeachadh, o'n a tha thusa a'd' choigreach, gum faod mi innseadh dhuit démur a fhuair mi e." "Faodaidh," urs' ise, "cha dèan mise sgeul ort; cha bhoin an gnothach dhomh." Dh' innis e dhi 'h-uile car mar a chuir cailleach nan cearc a stigh 'sa chisd' e, 's a' chuid eile de'n chùis; 's gun d' fholbh an rìgh an la 'r na mhàireach.

Mochthrath an la 'r na mhàireach bha fear an tighe 'dol gu cùirt. Thuirt e rithese, mar an robh deifir urra a dh' fholbh, gum faodadh i dol leisean a dh' éisdeachd na cùirt. Thuirt i gum biodh i toileach, 's gum bu mhath leatha a gille 'bhi leatha. Chaidh ise anns a' charbad leis a chaibhtinn, 's mharcaich a gille 'na déigh. Nur a bha 'chùirt seachad, thuirt i gun robh facal na dha aicese r'a ràdh, n'am b' e'n toil leigeil leatha bruidhinn. Thuirt iad rithe leigeil a chluinntinn daibh gu dé 'bha aice r'a ràdh. Thuirt i r'a gille. "Eiridh suas 's thoir dhaibh am paipeir sin a sgriobh thu 'rair." Nur a leubh iad am paipeir, thuirt i dé 'bu chòir a dhèanadh air an fhear sin. "A chrochadh na'm biodh e 'n so," urs' iadsan. "Sin agaibh e," urs' ise, 's deanaibh bhur roighinn ris." Fhuair i féin 'san rìgh tilleadh air an ais d'an tigh féin, 's bha iad mar a bha iad roimhid.

This was written, April 1859, by Hector MacLean, "from the dictation of Catherine Milloy, a Cowal woman, married to a farmer at Kilmeny, Islay—one Angus MacGeachy. Mrs.

MacGeachy learned the story from a young man who resides in Cowal, Robert MacColl."

May 1860.—No other version of this story has come to me as yet. It resembles Cymbeline in some of the incidents; and one incident, that of the blood, is like Portia's defence in the Jew of Venice. It is worth remark that the scene of Cymbeline is partly laid in Britain, partly in Italy.

In the Decameron, 2nd day, novel 9, is the Italian story from which Cymbeline is supposed to have originated. "Bernard of Genoa is imposed upon by one Ambrose, loses his money, and orders his wife, who is quite innocent, to be put to death. She makes her escape, and goes in man's dress into the service of the Sultan; there she meets with the deceiver, and, sending for her husband to Alexandria, has him punished; she then resumes her former habit, and returns with her husband rich to Genoa."

In the Decameron, the Italian merchants dispute at Paris, and lay a bet. "A poor woman who frequented the house," replaces the Gaelic "Hen wife." The man who was hid in the chest took a ring, a girdle, a purse, and a gown, and in the Gaelic he takes a ring and a chain. The wife disguises herself as a man in both, but the service which she undertakes is different; and "the Sultan" is replaced by "a gentleman." In both stories she discloses the cheat in open Court,—in the one, before "the Sultan's court;" in the other, "in a court"—"to them." But though there are such resemblances, the two stories differ widely in spirit, in incident, in scene, and in detail. Those who hold that old stories are handed down traditionally, will probably consider this to be one of the kind; and if so, Shakspeare *may* have gathered his incidents at home. On the other hand, so well known a book as the Decameron, translated into English, 1566, might well account for part of the story.

In either case it is curious to trace the resemblance and the difference in these three versions of what appears to be the same popular tale; told by Boccaccio, Shakspeare, and a farmer's wife in the Highlands. If traditional, the story would seem to belong to a forgotten state of society. It is not *now* the custom to buy a wife, and thereby acquire the right to shoot her; and yet this right is insisted on, and acknowledged, and the story hinges on it. It seems that the Gauls had the power of life and death over their families, and that there was a custom very like the purchase of a wife among the old Icelanders.

There used to be, and probably there still are, certain ceremonies about betrothals, both in Norway and in the Highlands, which look like the remains of some such forgotten practice.

In the Highlands, a man used to go on the part of the bridegroom to settle the dower with the bride's father, or some one who acted for him. They argued the point, and the argument gave rise to much fun and rough wit. For example, here is one bit of such a discussion, of which I remember to have heard long ago.

"This is the youngest and the last, she must be the worst; you must give me a large dower, or I will not take her."

"Men always sell the shots first when they can; this is the best—I should give no dower at all."

The first knotty point settled, and the wedding day fixed, the bridegroom, before the wedding day, sent a best man and maid to look after the bride, and gathered all his friends at home. The bride also gathered her friends, and her party led the way to church, the bride was supported by the best-man and best-maid, and a piper played before them. The bridegroom's party marched first on the way home; and then there was a jollification, and a ball, and some curious ceremonies with a stocking.

The strip of skin to be cut from the debtor is mentioned in other stories; and I believe such a mode of torture can be traced amongst the Scandinavians who once owned the Western Islands.

In another story which I have heard, a man was to be punished by cutting IALL, a thong, from his head to his heels, another from his forehead to his feet, a thong to tie them, and a thong to make all fast.

TIGH-OSDA' is the word commonly used for an inn. It is probably derived from the same root as Hostelry; Spanish, Osdal; French, Hôtel.

SEOMBAR is pronounced almost exactly like the French chambre—the only difference being that between the French *a* and the Gaelic *o*.

SEARBHANNT is very near the French servante.

XIX.

THE INHERITANCE.

From Donald Macintyre, Benbecula.

THERE was once a farmer, and he was well off. He had three sons. When he was on the bed of death he called them to him, and he said, "My sons, I am going to leave you: let there be no disputing when I am gone. In a certain drawer, in a dresser in the inner chamber, you will find a sum of gold; divide it fairly and honestly amongst you, work the farm, and live together as you have done with me;" and shortly after the old man went away. The sons buried him; and when all was over, they went to the drawer, and when they drew it out there was nothing in it.

They stood for a while without speaking a word. Then the youngest spoke, and he said—"There is no knowing if there ever was any money at all;" the second said—"There was money surely, wherever it is now;" and the eldest said—"Our father never told a lie. There was money certainly, though I cannot understand the matter." "Come," said the eldest, "let us go to such an old man; he was our father's friend; he knew him well; he was at school with him; and no man knew so much of his affairs. Let us go to consult him."

So the brothers went to the house of the old man, and they told him all that had happened. "Stay with me," said the old man, "and I will think over this matter. I cannot understand it; but, as you know, your father and I were very great with each other. When he had children I had sponsorship, and when I had children he had gostji. I know that your father never told a lie." And he kept them there, and he gave them meat and drink for ten days.

Then he sent for the three young lads, and he made them sit down beside him, and he said—

"There was once a young lad, and he was poor; and he took love for the daughter of a rich neighbour, and she took love for him; but because he was so poor there could be no wedding. So at last they pledged themselves to each other, and the young man went away, and stayed in his own house. After a time there came another suitor, and because he was well off, the girl's father made her promise to marry him, and after a time they were married. But when the bridegroom came to her, he found her weeping and bewailing; and he said, 'What ails thee?' The bride would say nothing for a long time; but at last she told him all about it, and how she was pledged to another man. 'Dress thyself,' said the man, 'and follow me.' So she dressed herself in the wedding clothes, and he took the horse, and put her behind him, and rode to the house of the other man, and when he got there, he struck in the door, and he called out, 'Is there man within?' and when the other answered, he left the bride there within the door, and he said nothing, but he returned home. Then the man got up, and got a light, and who was there but the bride in her wedding dress.

"'What brought thee here?" said he. 'Such a man,' said the bride. 'I was married to him to-day, and when I told him of the promise we had made, he brought me here himself and left me.'

"'Sit thou there,' said the man; 'art thou not married?' So he took the horse, and he rode to the priest, and he brought him to the house, and before the priest he loosed the woman from the pledge she had given, and he gave her a line of writing that she was free, and he set her on the horse, and said, 'Now return to thy husband.'

"So the bride rode away in the darkness in her wedding dress. She had not gone far when she came to a thick wood where three robbers stopped and seized her. 'Aha!' said one, 'we have waited long, and we have got nothing, but now we have got the bride herself.' 'Oh,' said she, 'let me go: let me go to my husband; the man that I was pledged to has let me go. Here are ten pounds in gold--take them, and let me go on my journey.' And so she begged and prayed for a long time, and told what had happened to her. At last one of the robbers, who was of a better nature than the rest, said, 'Come, as the others have done this, I will take you home myself.' 'Take thou the money,' said she. 'I will not take a penny,' said the robber; but the other two said, 'Give us the money,' and they took the ten pounds. The woman rode home, and the robber left her at her husband's door, and she went in, and showed him the line—the writing that the other had given her before the priest, and they were well pleased."

"Now," said the old man, "which of all these do you think did best? So the eldest son said, "I think the man that sent the woman to him to whom she was pledged, was the honest, generous man: he did well." The second said, "Yes, but the man to whom she was pledged did still better, when he sent her to her husband." "Then," said the youngest, "I don't know myself; but perhaps the wisest of all were the robbers who got the money." Then the old man rose up, and he said, "Thou hast thy father's gold and silver. I have kept you here for ten days; I have watched you well. I know your father never told a lie, and thou hast stolen the money." And so the youngest son had to confess the fact, and the money was got and divided.

I know nothing like No. 19. No. 20 begins like a German story in Grimm; but the rest is unlike anything I have read or heard. The first part has come to me in another shape, from Ross-shire; and some men whom I met in South Uist seemed to know these incidents.

The two belong to the class referred to in the Introduction, page xxxv. as fourth. Many of the novels in Boccaccio might be ranked with the same class; they are embryo three-volume novels, which only require nursing by a good writer to become full-grown books. There are plenty of the kind throughout the Highlands, and, as it seems to me, they are genuine popular traditions, *human* stories, whose incidents would suit a king or a peasant equally well. Without a wide knowledge of books, it is impossible to say whence these stories came; or whether they are invented by the people. MacIntyre said he had learned those which he told me from old men like himself, in his native island; and all others whom I have questioned say the same of their stories.

XX.

THE THREE WISE MEN.

From Donald MacIntyre, Benbecula.

THERE was once a farmer, and he was very well off, but he had never cast an eye on the women, though he was old enough to be married. So one day he took the horse and saddle, and rode to the house of another farmer, who had a daughter, to see if she would suit him for a wife, and when he got there the farmer asked him to come in, and gave him food and drink, and he saw the daughter, and he thought she would suit him well. So he said to the father, "I am thinking it is time for me to be married, I am going to look for a wife"—(here there was a long conversation, which I forget). So the man told his wife what the other had said, and she told her daughter to make haste and set the house in order, for that such a man was come and he was looking for a wife, and she had better show how handy she was. Well never mind, the daughter was willing enough, so she began to set the house in order, and the first thing she thought of was to make up the fire, so she ran out of the house to the peat-stack. Well, while she was bent down filling her apron with peats, what should fall but a great heap from the top of the stack on her head and shoulders. So she thought to herself, "Oh, now, if I were married to that man, and about to be a mother, and all these peats fallen on my head, I should now be finished and all my posterity;" and she gave a great burst of weeping, and sat down lamenting and bewailing. The mother was longing for her daughter to come back, so she went out and found her sitting crying in the end of the peat-stack, and she said, "What is on thee?" and the daughter said, "Oh, mother, the peat-stack fell on my head, and I thought if I were now married to that man, and about to be a mother, I was done, and all my posterity;" and the mother said, "That is true for thee, my daughter; that is true, indeed," and she sat down and cried too. Then the father was getting cold, so he too went out, wondering what kept the women, and when he found them, they told him what happened, and he said, "That would have been unfortunate indeed," and he began to roar and cry too. The wooer at last came out himself, and found them all crying in the end of the peat-stack, and when they had told him why they were lamenting, he said, "Never you mind. It may be that this may never happen at all. Go you in-doors, and cry no more." Then he took his horse and saddle, and rode home; and as he went, he thought, "What a fool I am to be stopping here all my life. Here I sit, and know no more of the world than a stock. I know how to grow corn, and that is all I know. I will go and see the world, and I will never come home till I find thee as wise as those were foolish whom I left crying in the peat-stack." And so when he got home, he set everything in order, and took the horse and went away. And he travelled the Gældom and the Galldom Highlands and strange lands for many a day, and got much knowledge. At last, one fine evening he came to a pretty plot of green ground in a glen, by a river; and on it there were three men standing. They were like each other, and dressed alike. Their dress was a long coat with short brigis, and a broad belt about the middle, and caps on their heads. (What dress is that? That is the dress they used to wear here. I remember my father well; he always wore it.) So he put Failte on them (saluted them). The three men never answered a word. They looked at him, and then they bent their heads slowly towards each other—(here the narrator bent his own head, and spoke solemnly)—and there they staid with their heads bowed for ten minutes. Then they raised their heads, and one said, "If I had without what I have within, I would give thee a night's share;" the second said, "If I had done what is undone, I would give thee a night's share;" and the third said, "I have nothing more than usual, come with me." So the farmer followed the old man to his house, wondering what all this should mean. When they had gone in and sat down, he wondered still more, for his host never offered him a drink till he had told him all about his journey. Then he said, "Quicker is a drink than a tale;" and the old man gave a laugh, and struck the board, and a fine woman came and gave him a great cup of ale, and that was good. And he drank it, and thought to himself, "If I had that woman for my wife, she would be better than the one I left weeping in the peat-stack." The old man laughed again, and he said, "If two were willing that might be." The farmer wondered that this old man should know his thoughts, and answer them, but he held his tongue. Then the old man struck the board, and a girl came in, and he thought, "If I had that one for my wife, she would be better than the girl I left howling in the peat-stack." The old man gave another little laugh, and he said, "If three were willing that might be too," and the girl set a small pot on the fire. The farmer looked at it, and thought, "This man must have a small company." "Ah," said the man, "it will go about."

"Now," said the farmer, "I *must* know what all this means. I will neither eat nor drink in this house unless you tell me. I saluted you, and you bent your heads, and never answered for ten minutes. When you did speak, I could not understand you, and now you seem to understand my thoughts." Then the old man said, "Sit down, and I will explain it all. Our father was a very wise man. We never knew how wise he was till long after he went away. We are three brothers, and on the bed of death our father left us this pretty place, and we have it amongst us, and plenty besides. Our father made us swear that we would never talk on important matters but in whispers. When thou camest, we bent our heads and whispered, as we always do, for men cannot dispute in a whisper, and we never quarrel. My first brother had the corpse of his mother-in-law within; he was unwilling to ask a stranger to a house of sorrow. She is to be buried to-morrow—If that were out which he had within, he had given thee a night's share. My second brother has a wife who will do nothing till she gets three blows of a stick. Then she is like other women, and a good wife; he did not like a stranger to see the blows given, and he knew she would do nothing without them—If he had done what was undone, he had given thee a night's share. I had nothing to do more than usual. Thou didst tell thy news, and when my wife came in, I knew thy thought. If I were dead, and thou and she were willing, you might be married. So if I, and thou, and my daughter were willing, you might be married too. Now, then, said the old man, sit and eat. The little pot will go about; it will serve for us. My company eat without." On the morrow, the old man said, "I must go to the funeral to my brother's house, do thou stay here." But he said, "I will not stay in any man's house when he is away. I will go with you to the funeral." When they came back he staid some time in the old man's house. He married the daughter, and got a good share of the property. And, now, was not that a lucky peat-stack for the farmer.

This story and No. 19 were told to me on the 6th of September 1859, in the inn at the Sound of Benbecula, by a man whose name would sound to Saxon ears like Dolicolichyarlich; a Celt would know it for Donald MacDonald MacCharles, and his surname is MacIntyre; he is a cotter, and lives in Benbecula.

Donald is known as a good teller of tales, so I walked six miles to his house and heard him tell a long version of the tale of Conal Gulbanach.

It lasted an hour, and I hope to get it written some day; I have other versions of the same incidents. There was an audience of all the people of the village who were within reach, including Mr. Torrie, who lives there near Baile nan Cailleach, which is probably so called from an old nunnery. After the story, the same man recited a fragment of a poem about Fionn and his companions. A man returning from battle with a vast number of heads on a withy, meets a lady who questions him, he recites the history of the heads, and how their owners died. The poem was given rapidly and fluently. The story was partly told in measured prose; but it was very much spun out, and would have gained by condensation.

I told the old man that he had too many leaves on his tree, which he acknowledged to be a fair criticism. He followed me to the inn afterwards, and told me other stories; the household being assembled about the door, and in the room, and taking a warm interest in the proceedings. After a couple of glasses of hot whisky and water, my friend, who was well up in years, walked off home in the dark; and I noted down the heads of his stories in English, because my education, as respects Gaelic writing, was never completed. They are given as I got them, condensed, but unaltered. Donald says he has many more of the same kind.

XXI.

A PUZZLE.

From Kenneth M'Lennan, Turnaid, Ross-shire.

THERE was a custom once through the Gældom, when a man would die, that the whole people of the place would gather together to the house in which the dead man was—Tigh aire faire (the shealing of watching), and they would be at drinking, and singing, and telling tales, till the white day should come. At this time they were gathered together in the house of watching, and there was a man in this house, and when the tale went about, he had neither tale nor song, and as he had not, he was put out at the door. When he was put out he stood at the end of the barn; he was afraid to go farther. He was but a short time standing when he saw nine, dressed in red garments, going past, and shortly after that he saw other nine going past in green dresses; shortly after this he saw other nine going past in blue dresses. A while after that came a horse, and a woman and a man on him. Said the woman to the man, "I will go to speak to that man who is there at the end of the barn." She asked him what he was doing standing there? He told her? "Sawest thou any man going past since the night fell?" said she. He said that he had; he told her all he had seen. "Thou sawest all that went past since the night fell," said she. "Well then," said she, "the first nine thou sawest, these were brothers of my father, and the second nine brothers of my mother, and the third nine, these were my own sons, and they are altogether sons to that man who is on the horse. That is my husband; and there is no law in Eirinn, nor in Alaba, nor in Sasunn that can find fault with us. Go thou in, and I myself will not believe but that a puzzle is on them till day;" and she went and she left him.

TOIMHSEACHAN.

Bha cleachdadh aon uair air feadh na Gaeltachd, dar a Bhasaicheadh duine, gu tionaladh sluagh a' bhaile uile gu leir, dho'n tigh sam bitheag an duine marbh, tigh *aire faire*, agus bhithag iad ag' òl 's ag òran 's aginnse sgeulachdan, gus an digadh, an latha geal. Air an am so bha iad cruinn 'san tigh fhaire, agus bha duine anns an tigh so, agus dar a chaidh an sgeulachd mu 'n cuairt cha robh aon chuid aige, sgeulachd, na òran, agus bho'n nach robh chaidh a chur a mach air an dorus. Dar a chaidh, sheas e aig ceann an t-sabhail, bha eagal air dol ni b' fhaide. Cha robh e ach goirid na sheasaidh dar a chunnaic e naodhnar air an sgeadachadh ann an trusgain dhearga a' dol seachad, agus goirid na dheighe sin chunnaic e naodhnar eile a' dol seachad ann an deiseachan uaine; began an deighe so chunnaic e naodhnar eile a' dol seachad ann an deiseachan gorma; tacan an déigh so thàinig each, 's bean 's duine air a mhuin. Thuirt a' bhean ris an duine, "Théid mi 'bhruidhinn ris an fhear a tha 'siud, aig ceann an t-sabhail." Dh' fhoighnichd i ris dé bha e dianamh an siud 'na sheasamh. Dh' innis e dhi. "Am faca tu duine air bhith a' dol seachad bho thuit an oidhche?" os ise. Thuirt gu 'fac. Dh' innis e dhi na chunnaic e. "Chunna tu na chaidh seachad bho thuit an oidhche," os ise. "Mata," os ise, "na ceud naodhnar a chunna tu 'se sin bràithrean m' athar, agus an darna naodhnar bràithrean mo mhàthair, agus an treas naodhnar 'se sin mo mhic fhéin; agus 's mic dha n' duine ud a tha air muin an eich iad uile gu léir. 'Se sin an duine agamsa; agus cha 'n 'eil lagh ann an Eirinn, na 'n Allaba, na 'n Sasunn a's urrainn coir' fhaotainn dhuinn.

Folbh thusa a nis a steach ; 's cha chreid mise nach 'eil toimhseachan orra gu latha." 'S dh' fholbh i 's dh' fhàg i e.

Written by Hector Urquhart. The answer is founded on a mistaken belief that it is lawful for a woman to marry her grandmother's husband. I am told that there are numerous puzzles of the same kind now current in India.

XXII.

THE RIDERE (KNIGHT) OF RIDDLES.

From John Mackenzie, fisherman, near Inverary.

THERE was a king once, and he married a great lady, and she departed on the birth of her first son. And a little after this the king married another one, and he had a son by this one too. The two lads were growing up. Then it struck in the queen's head that it was not her son who would come into the kingdom; and she set it before her that she would poison the eldest son. And so she sent advice to the cook that they would put poison in the drink of the heir; but as luck was in it, so it was that the youngest brother heard them, and he said to his brother not to take the draught, nor to drink it at all; and so he did. But the queen wondered that the lad was not dead; and she thought that there was not enough of poison in the drink, and she asked the cook to put more in the drink on this night. It was thus they did: and when the cook made up the drink, she said that he would not be long alive after this draught. But his brother heard this also, and he told this likewise. The eldest thought he would put the draught into a little bottle, and he said to his brother—"If I stay in this house I have no doubt she will do for me some way or other, and the quicker I leave the house the better. I will take the world for my pillow, and there is no knowing what fortune will be on me." His brother said that he would go with him, and they took themselves off to the stable, and they put saddles on two horses and they took their soles out of that.

They had not gone very far from the house when the eldest one said—"There is no knowing if poison was in the drink at all, though we went away. Try it in the horse's ear and we shall see." The horse went not far when he fell. "That was only a rattle-bones of a horse at all events," said the eldest one, and together they got up on the one horse, and so they went forwards. "But," said he, "I can scarce believe that there is any poison in the drink, let's try it on this horse." That he did, and they went not far when the horse fell cold dead. They thought to take the hide off him, and that it would keep them warm on this night for it was close at hand. In the morning when they woke they saw twelve ravens coming and lighting on the carcase of the horse, and they were not long there when they fell over dead.

They went and lifted the ravens, and they took them with them, and the first town they reached they gave the ravens to a baker, and they asked him to make a dozen pies of the ravens. They took the pies with them, and they went on their journey. About the mouth of night, and when they were in a great thick wood that was there, there came four and twenty robbers out of the wood, and they said to them to deliver their purses; but they said that they had no purse, but that they had a little food which they were carrying with them. "Good is even meat!" and the robbers began to eat it, but they had not eaten too boldly when they fell hither and thither. When they saw that the robbers were dead, they ransacked their pockets, and they got much gold and silver on the robbers. They went forward till they reached the Knight of Riddles.

The house of the Knight of Riddles was in the finest place in that country, and if his house was pretty, it was his daughter was pretty (indeed). Her like was not on the surface of the world altogether; so handsome was she, and no one would get her to marry but the man who would put a question to this knight that he could not solve. The chaps thought that they would go and they would try to put a question to him; and the youngest one was to stand in place of gillie to his eldest brother. They reached the house of the Knight of Riddles with this question—"One killed two, and two killed twelve, and twelve killed four and twenty, and two got out of it;" and they were to be in great majesty and high honour till he should solve the riddle.

They were thus a while with the Ridere, but on a day of days came one of the knight's daughter's maidens of company to the gillie, and asked him to tell her the question. He took her plaid from her and let her go, but he did not tell her, and so did the twelve maidens, day after day, and he said to the last one that no creature had the answer to the riddle but his master down below. No matter! The gillie told his master each thing as it happened. But one day after this came the knight's daughter to the eldest brother, and she was so fine, and she asked him to tell her the question. And now there was no refusing her, and so it was that he told her, but he kept her plaid. And the Knight of Riddles sent for him, and he solved the riddle. And he said that he had two choices: to lose his head, or to be let go in a crazy boat without food or drink, without oar or scoop. The chap spoke and he said—"I have another question to put to thee before all these things happen." "Say on," said the knight. "Myself and my gillie were on a day in the forest shooting. My gillie fired at a hare, and she fell, and he took her skin off, and let her go ; and so he did to twelve, he took their skins off and let them go. And at last came a great fine hare, and I myself fired at her, and I took her skin off, and I let her go." "Indeed thy riddle is not hard to solve, my lad," said the knight. And so the lad got the knight's daughter to wife, and they made a great hearty wedding that lasted a day and a year. The youngest one went home now that his brother had got so well on his way, and the eldest brother gave him every right over the kingdom that was at home.

There were near the march of the kingdom of the Knight of Riddles three giants, and they were always murdering and slaying some of the knight's people, and taking the spoil from them. On a day of days the Knight of Riddles said to his son-in-law, that if the spirit of a man were in him, he would go to kill the giants, as they were always bringing such losses on the country. And thus it was, he went and he met the giants, and he came home with the three giants' heads, and he threw them at the knight's feet. "Thou art an able lad doubtless, and thy name hereafter is the Hero of the White Shield." The name of the Hero of the White Shield went far and near.

The brother of the Hero of the White Shield was exceedingly strong and clever, and without knowing what the Hero of the White Shield was, he thought he would try a trick with him. The Hero of the White Shield was now dwelling on the lands of the giants, and the knight's daughter with him. His brother came and he asked to make a comhrag (fight as a bull) with him. The men began at each other, and they took to wrestling from morning till evening. At last and at length, when they were tired, weak, and given up, the Hero of the White Shield jumped over a great rampart, and he asked him to meet him in the morning. This leap put the other to shame, and he said to him "Well may it be that thou wilt not be so supple about this time to-morrow." The young brother now went to a poor little bothy that was near to the house of the Hero of the White Shield tired and drowsy, and in the morning they dared the fight again. And the Hero of the White Shield began to go back, till he went backwards into a river. "There must be some of my blood in thee before that was done to me." "Of what blood art thou?" said the youngest. "'Tis I am son of Ardan, great King of the Albann." "'Tis I am thy brother." It was now they knew each other. They gave luck and welcome to each other, and the Hero of the White Shield now took him into the palace, and she it was that was pleased to see him—the knight's daughter. He stayed a while with them, and after that he thought that he would go home to his own kingdom; and when he was going past a great palace that was there he saw twelve men playing at shinny over against the palace. He thought he would go for a while and play shinny with them; but they were not long playing shinny when they fell out, and the weakest of them caught him and he shook him as he would a child. He thought it was no use for him to lift a hand amongst these twelve worthies, and he asked them to whom they were sons. They said they were children of the one father, the brother of the Hero of the White Shield, but that no one of them had the same mother. "I am your father," said he; and he asked them if their mothers were all alive. They said that they were. He went with them till he found the mothers, and when they were all for going, he took home with him the twelve wives and the twelve sons; and I don't know but that his seed are kings on Alba till this very day.

RIDERE NAN CEIST.

Bha righ ann uair, 's phòs e ban-tighearna mhòr, agus shiubhail i air a cheud mhac, ach bha am mac bèo; agus beagan na dhéigh so, phòs an rìgh tè eile, 's bha mac aige rithe so cuideachd. Bha 'n dà ghille cinntinn suas. An sin bhuail an ceann na banrigh, nach b'è macse a thigeadh a stigh air an rìoghachd, agus chuir i roimpe gu 'm puinseanaicheadh i 'm mac bu shine, agus mar so chuir i comhairle ris a chòcaire, gu 'n cuireadh iad pùinsean ann an deoch an oighre; ach mar bha sonas an dàn, chual' am bràthair a b' òige iad, agus thubhairt e ri 'bhràthair, gun an deoch a ghabhail na idir a h-òl; agus mar so rinn e. Ach bha iongontas air a bhan-righ nach robh an gille marbh, agus smaoinich i nach robh na leòir a phùinsean anns an deoch, 's dh' iarr i air a chòcaire tuillidh a chuir 'san deoch air an oidhche so. Is ann mar so a rinn iad, agus a nuair a rinn an còcaire suas an deoch, thubhairt i nach bitheadh e fada beo an déigh na dibhe so; ach chual' bhràthair so cuideachd 's dh' innis e so mar an ceudna. Smaoinich e gu' cuireadh e 'n deoch ann am botul beag, agus thubhairt e ri' bhrathair, "Ma dh' fhanas mi 'san tigh cha 'n 'eil teagamh agam nach cuir i as domh dòigh a thaobhaigin, 's mar is luaithe dh' fhàgas mi 'n tigh, 'se is feàrr. Bheir mi an saoghal fo' m' cheann, 's cha 'n 'eil fios de 'm fortan a bhitheas orm." Thubhairt a bhràthair gu' falbhadh e leis, 's thug iad orra do 'n stàbull, 's chuir iad dìollaid air dà each, 's thug iad na buinn asda. Cha deach iad glé fhad' o'n tigh, dur a thubhairt am fear bu shine, "Cha 'n 'eil fios an robh puinsean idir san deoch ged a dh' fhalbh sinn; feuch ann an cluais an eich e, 's chì sinn." Cha b' fhada chaidh an t-each dur a thuit e. "Cha robh an sud, ach gliogaire do dh' each co dhiu," thubhairt am fear bu sine, agus le' chéile ghabh iad air muin an aoin eich 's mar so chaidh iad air an aghaidh. "Ach," ars' esan, "'s gann orm a chreidsinn, gu' bheil pùinsean sam bith 'san deoch; feucham i air an each so." Sinn a rinn e, agus cha deach iad fada nuair a thuit an t-each fuar, marbh. Smaonich iad an t-seiche 'thabhairt dheth 's gu cumadh i blàth iad air an oidhche oir bha i dlùth làimh. 'Sa' mhaduinn, 'n uair a dhùisg iad, chunnaic iad dà fhitheach dheug a tighinn, 's laidh iad air closaich an eich. Cha b' fhada' bha iad an sin, 'n uair a thuit iad thairis marbh. Dh' fhalbh iad 's thog iad na fithich, 's thugar leo iad, agus a cheud bhaile a ràinig iad, thug iad na fithich do dh' fhuineadair 's dh' iarr iad air dusan pìth a dheanamh do na fithich. Thug iad leo na pithean, 's dh' fhalbh iad air an turus. Mu bheul na h-oidhche, 's iad ann an coille mhòr dhùmhail a bha sin thàinig ceithir thar fhichead do robairean a mach as a choille, 's thubhairt iad riu, "Iad a liobhairt an sporain;" ach thubhairt iadsan, "Nach robh sporan aca, ach gu 'n robh beagan bìdh a bha iad a giulan leo." "'S maith biadh f héin," agus thoisich na robairean air itheadh. Ach cha deach iad ro dhàna 'n uair a thuit fear thall sa bhos dhiubh. A nuair a chunnaic iad gu'n robh na robairean marbh, rannsaich iad na pocaichean aca, 's fhuair iad mòran òr 's airgiod air na robairean. Dh' fhalbh iad air an aghaidh gus an dràinig iad Ridire nan Ceist. Bha tigh Ridire nan Ceist anns an àite bu bhrèagha san dùthaich sin, agus ma bha 'n tigh bòidheach, 'se bha bòidheach a nighean. Cha robh a leithid air uachdar an t-saoghail gu léir, co maiseach rithe. 'S cha 'n fhaigheadh a h-aon ri phòsadh i, ach fear a chuireadh ceist air an ridire so nach b'urrainn da fhuasgladh. Smaonich na fleasgaich gu 'n rachadh iad 's gu feuchadh iad ceist a chuir air; agus bha 'm fear a b' òige gu seasadh an àite gille d'a bhràthair bu sine. Ràinig iad tigh Ridire nan Ceist, leis a cheist so, "Mharbh a h-aon, dithis, 's mharbh dithis a dha-dheug 's marbh dha-dheug, ceithir thar-fhichead, 's thàinig dithis as; 's bha iad gu bhi air bhòrt mòr 's àirde onair gus am fuasgladh e a cheist. Bha iad greis mar so leis an ridire; ach oidhche do na h-oidhchean, thàinig te do na maighdeannan coimhideachd aig nighean an ridire, gu leaba 'ghille, 's thubhairt i ris, "N' an innseadh e à cheist dhith gu' rachadh i luidhe leis, agus mar sin fhéin rinn i; ach mu 'n do leig e air falbh i, thug e a léine dhi, ach cha do dh' innis e dhi a cheist; agus mar sin rinn an da mhaighdean dhèug, oidhch' an déigh oidhche agus thubhairt e ris an te mu dheireadh, "Nach robh fios an toimhseachan aig neach air bith ach aig a mhaighstir san a mhàin." Coma co-dhiù dh' innis an gille gach ni mar a bha' tachairt da mhaighstir; ach aon oidhch' an déigh so, thàinig nighean an ridire do sheòmar a bhrathair bu sine, 's thubhairt i gu'n rachadh i luidhe leis na 'n innseadh e a' cheist dhi. Nise cha robh na chomas a diùltadh, agus 's ann mar so a bha, chaidh i luidhe leis, ach anns a mhaduinn, thug e a léine dhi, 's leig e air falbh i, 's co luath 'sa dh'éirich Ridire nan Ceist, chuir e fios air, 's dh' fhuasgail e a' cheist, 's thubhairt e ris, "Gun robh a dha roghainn aige, an ceann a chall, na' leigeil air falbh ann an eithear, gun bhiadh gun deoch, 's gun ràmh na taoman." Labhair am fleasgach, 's thubhairt e, "Tha ceist eil agam ri chuir ort mu 'n tachair na h-uile nithibh so." "Abair romhad," thuirt an ridire. "Bha mi fein 's mo ghille, latha ann am frìdh a' sealg; loisg mo ghille air maigheach 's thuit i; thug e 'n craiceann dhi, 's leig e air falbh i. Rinn e mar sin air a dha-dheug; thug e 'n craiceann diubh 's leig e air falbh iad, agus mu dheireadh, thainig maigheach mhòr bhrèagha, 's loisg mi féin oirre, 's thug mi 'n craiceann dhi, 's leig mi air falbh i." "Moire, cha 'n 'eil do cheist duillich fhuasgladh òganaich," thirt an ridire, "tha sin ag innseadh gu'n do luidh do ghille le dà mhaighdean dheug mo nighinn-sa, agus thu fein le mo nighean 's gu'n d' thug sibh na léintean dhiubh. Sin agad do thoimhseachain mo ghille maith, agus feuma tu 'pòsadh." Agus se sin a rinn iad 's banais mhòr, ghreadhnach a mhair latha 's bliadhna. Dh' fhalbh am fear a b-òige dhachaidh an so, 'n uair a fhuair e a bhràthair co maith air a dhòigh, 's thug am bràthair bu sine dha na h-uile còir air an rìoghachd a bha aig an tigh. Bha dlùth do dh' fhearann Ridire nan Ceist triùir fhamhairean, agus iad daonnan a' mort 'sa' marbhadh cuid do dhaoine an Ridire, 'sa tabhairt uapa spùill. Latha do na laithean, thuirt Ridire nan Ceist ri chliamhuinn, na 'm biodh spiorad duin' ann, gu'n rachadh e a mharbhadh nam famhairean. Agus 's ann mar so a bha, dh' fhalbh e, 's choinnich e na famhairean agus thainig e dhachaidh le ceann nan tri famhairean, 's thilg e iad aig casan an ridire. "'S òlach tapaidh thu gun teagamh, agus 'se is ainm dhuit na dheigh so, Gaisgeach na sgiath bàine." Chaidh ainm Gaisgeach na sgiath bàine am fad 's an goirid. Bha bràthair Gaisgeach na sgiath bàine anabarrach laidir, tapaidh, agus gun fhios aige co e Gaisgeach na sgiath bàine, smaoinich e gun rachadh e dh' fheuchainn cleas ris. Bha Gaisgeach na sgiath-bàine a' gabhail còmhnuidh air fearann an fhamhair a nis, 's nighean an ridire leis. Thàinig a bhràthair 's dh' iarr e còmhrag a dhèanamh ris. Thòisich na fir air a' chéile, agus thug iad air gleachd bho mhaduinn gu feasgar. Mu dheireadh thall 'n uair a bha iad sgìth, fann, 's air toirt thairis, leum Gaisgeach na sgiath bàine am Baideal mòr, 's dh' iarr e air coinneachainn ris sa mhaduinn. Chuir an leum so am fear eile fuidh sprochd, 's thubhairt e, "Math dh' fhaoidte nach bi thu co subailte mu 'n am so am màireuch." Chaidh am bràthair òg a nise do bhothan beag, bochd a bha dlùth do thigh Gaisgeach na sgiath-bàine, gu sgith, airsnealach; agus anns a mhaduinn, dh' ùraich iad an tuasid agus thòisich Gaisgeach na sgiath-bàine air dol air ais, gus an deach e 'n coimhir a chùil ann an abhuinn. "Feumaidh e gu' bheil cuid do m' fhuil annad mu 'n deanadh tu so ormsa." "Co 'n fhuil da 'm bheil thu?" thuirt am fear a b' òige. "'S mise mac [?] Ardan rìgh mòr na h-Albann." "'S mise do bhràthair." 'S ann an so a dh' aithnich iad a' chéile. Chuir iad fàilte 's furan air a chéile, 's thug Gaisgeach na sgiathe-bàine an so a stigh e do 'n lùchairt, agus 's e 'bha toileach fhaicinn nighean an ridire. Dh' fhan e car tamull maille riu, agus 'na dheigh sin, smaoinich e gun rachadh e dhachaidh d'a rìoghachd féin, agus a nuair a bha e gabhail seachad air pàileas mòr a bha' sin, chunnaic e dà fhear dheug a' camanachd fa chomhair a phàileis. Smaoinich e gun rachadh e greis a chamanachd leo, ach cha b' fhad' a bha iad a' camanachd 'n uair a chaidh iad a mach air a' chéile, agus rug am fear bu suarraiche dhiubh air, agus chrath 'se e mar gu'n deanadh e air pàisde. Smaoinich e nach robh math dha' làmh a thogail, am measg an dà cheathairneach dheug so, agus dh' fheoraich e dhiubh, co dha bu mhic iad? Thubhairt iad, "Gu 'm b'e clann aon athar iad, bràthair do Ghaisgeach na sgiath-bàine, agus nach b'e an aon mhàthair a bh' aig a h-aon dhiubh." "'S mise bhur n-athair," thubhairt esan; is dh' fharraid e dhiubh, "An robh am màthraichean, uile beo?" Thuirt iad gu 'n robh. Chaidh e leo gus an d'fhuair e na màthraichean, agus a nuair a bha iad uile gu falbh thug e leis dhachaidh an dà bhean dèug 's a' dhà mhac dhèug, agus cha 'n 'eil fios agamsa nach e 'n sliochd a tha 'nan righrean air Alba gus a' latha 'n diugh.

Written down from the recitation of John Mackenzie, fisherman at Inverary, who says that he learned the tale from an old man in Lorn many years ago. He has been thirty-six years at Inverary. He first told me the tale fluently, and afterwards dictated it to me; and the words written are, as nearly as possible, those used by Mackenzie on the first occasion.

April, 1859. HECTOR URQUHART.

The word pronounced Rēēt-djĕ-rĕ, and variously spelt Ridir, Righdir, and Righdeire, is explained in a manuscript history of the Campbells, written about 1827, as Righ, king—dei, after—Ri, king. If this be correct, the word would mean a following or minor king. It may equally be a corruption of Ritter, or Reiter; and I have translated it by *knight*, because it is now applied to all knights.

The author of the manuscript says :—The term is handed down even in Gaelic tales, and mentions several which were then current, Righdiere nan Spleugh, and an Righdeiri Ruadh; he adds, that Righdeirin dubh Loch Oigh (the Black Knights of Loch Awe) was the name then used by old Highlanders in mentioning the chiefs of the Duin (Campbells), and that the ruins of Eredin Castle were then known by no other name than Larach tai nan Righdeirin—the ruins of the house of the knights.

The writer argues from old manuscript histories, charters, etc., that the term was brought from Ireland by the colony who settled in Cantire at a very early period, and who spread thence over Argyllshire, and founded a kingdom, of which frequent mention is made in Irish annals as the Dalreudinan, or Scoto-Irish colonization of Argyll, Cantire, Lorn, and Islay. It is supposed to have taken place about A.D. 503, under Laorn, Fergus, and Angus, three sons of Eric, the descendant of Cairbre Ruadh, a son of Conary II., who ruled as chief king of Ireland A.D. 212. Be that as it may, all the Gaelic traditions now current in the Isles point at an Irish migration which took place in the year of grace *once upon a time*, and the word Righdeire occurs continually, where it seems to mean a small king, and a king of Erin; for example, "there was a king (Ree) and a Reet-djer—as there was and will be. and, as grows the fir-tree, some of them crooked and some of them straight—and he was a king of Erin." Even the word Albanach, now used for Scotchman, means Wanderer. When the king's son changes his name, after killing the giants, it seems as if he were made a knight.

This tale, then, would seem to be some mythological account of events which may be traced in Grimm's stories, in the Classics, and elsewhere, mixed up with names and titles belonging to the colonization of Argyllshire by Irish tribes, and all applied to the kings of Scotland in the last sentence. It is a fair representation of the strange confusion of reality and fancy, history and mythology, of which I believe these stories to be composed.

The nearest story to it which I know is Das Räthsel, in Grimm, No. 22. Several versions are given in the third volume, which seem to vary from each other, about as much as this Gaelic version varies from them all.

There is something like the fight between Romulus and his brother. Alba means Scotland.

XXIII.

THE BURGH.

From Alexander M'Donald, tenant, and others, Barra, July 1859.

FOUR were watching cattle in Baileburgh (Burgh Farm). They were in a fold. The four were Domhnull MacGhilleathain, Domhnull Mac-an-t-Saoir, Calum MacNill, and Domhnull Domhnullach. They saw a dog. Calum MacNill said that they should strike the dog. Said Domhnull MacGhilleathain, "We will not strike. If thou strikest him thou wilt repent it." Calum MacNill struck the dog, and his hand and his arm lost their power. He felt a great pain in his hand and his arm, and one of the other lads carried his stick home; he could not carry it himself. He was lamenting his hand, and he went where there was an old woman, Nic a Phi, to get knowledge about his hand. She said to him that he would be so till the end of a day and a year; and at the end of a day and year, to go to the knoll and say to it, "If thou dost not let with me the strength of my hand, I or my race will leave neither stick nor stone of thee that we will not drive to pieces."

At the end of a day and year his comrades said, "There is now a day and year since thou hast lost the power of thy hand, come to the knoll till thy hand get its power, as the woman said." He went himself and his comrades. They reached the hill. He drew his stick, and he said to the knoll, "If thou dost not let with me the strength of my hand, I myself or my race will leave neither stick nor stone of thee that we will not drive to pieces." And he got the power of his hand.

BAILE BHUIRGH.

BHA ceathrar a' faire cruidh ann am Baile bhuirgh. Bha iad ann an cuidh. B'e 'cheathrar Domhnull MacGhilleathain, Domhnull Man-an-t-Saoir, Calum MacNill, agus Domhnull Domhnullach. Chunnaic iad cù. Thuirt Calum MacNill gum buaileadh eud an cù. Thuirt Domhnull MacGhilleathain. "Cha bhuail, ma bhuaileas tu e bidh aithreachas ort." Bhuail Calum MacNill an cù agus chaill a làmh agus a ghàirdean an lùgh. Bha e mothachainn cràdh mòr 'na làimh agus 'na ghàirdean, agus ghiùlain h-aon de na gillean eile dachaidh am bata, cha b' urrainn e fhìu a ghiùlan. Bha e 'gearan a làimhe, 's chaidh e far an robh seana bhean, Nic a Phì, airson eolas fhaotainn ma làimh. Thuirt i ris gum biodh e mur sin gu ceann la as bliadhna, 's an ceann la a's bliadhna e dhol gos a' chnoc, 's a radh ris "Mar an lig thu leamsa lùgh mo làimhe cha n fhag mise, na mo shliochd, clach na crann diot nach cuir sin as a chéile." An ceann la a's bliadhna thuirt a chompanaich ris, "Tha nis la a's bliadhna o'n a chaill thu lùgh na làimhe, thalla gos a' chnoc, 's go'm faigheadh do làmh a lùgh mar a thuirt a' bhean." Dh' fholbh e fhìn 's a chompanaich, 's ràinig eud an cnoc. Tharruinn e'm bata 's thuirt e ris a' chnoc, "Mar an lig thu leamsa lùgh mo làimhe cha 'n fhàg mi fhìn, na mo shliochd, clach na crann diot nach d' thoir sin as a cheile." Fhuair e lùgh na làimhe.

Written by Hector MacLean, from the telling of a man in Barra. This may be compared with the Manks tradition about the Black Dog, at Peel Castle.

XXIV.

THE TULMAN.

From Alexander M'Donald, tenant, and others, Barra. July 1859.

THERE was a woman in Baile Thangusdail, and she was out seeking a couple of calves; and the night and lateness caught her, and there came rain and tempest, and she was seeking shelter. She went to a knoll with the couple of calves, and she was striking a tether-peg into it. The knoll opened. She heard a gleegashing as if a pot-hook were clashing beside a pot. She took wonder, and she stopped striking the tether-peg. A woman put out her head and all above her middle, and she said, "What business hast thou to be troubling this tulman in which I make my dwelling?" "I am taking care of this couple of calves, and I am but weak. Where shall I go with them?" "Thou shalt go with them to that breast down yonder. Thou wilt see a tuft of grass. If thy couple of calves eat that tuft of grass, thou wilt not be a day without a milk cow as long as thou art alive, because thou hast taken my counsel."

As she said, she never was without a milk cow after that, and she was alive fourscore and fifteen years after the night that was there.

AN TULMAN.

BHA boireannach ann am Baile Thangasdail, 's bha i mach aig iarraidh caigionn laogh, agus rug an oidhche 'san t-anmoch urra, agus thàinig sileadh agus sìon, 's bha i 'g iarraidh fasgaidh. Chaidh i go cnoc leis a' chaigionn laogh 's bha i 'bualadh a' chipein ann. Dh' fhosgail an cnoc. Chual i gliogadaich, mar go'm biodh buthal a' gleadhraich taobh poite. Ghabh i ionghantas. Stad i 'bhualadh a' chipein. Chuir boireannach a mach a ceann, 's na robh as cionn a miadhoin, 's thuirt i rithe. "Dé 'n gnothach a th' agad a bhi 'cur dragh air an tulman so 's a' bheil mise 'gabhail comhnuidh?" "Tha mi 'toirt an air' air a' chaigionn laogh so, 's cha 'n 'eil mi ach lag, ca' n d' théid mi leo?" Théid thu leo 'ionnsuidh an uchd 'ud shias, chi thu bad feoir an sin. Ma dh' itheas do chaigionn laogh am bad feoir sin cha bhi thu latha gun mhart bainne fhad 's is beo thu, o'n a ghabh thu mo chomhairle." Mar a thubhairt i, cha robh i riabh gun mhart bainn' as a dhéigh so, 's bha i beò còig deug agus ceithir fichead bliadhna 'n déigh na h' oidhche 'bha 'n siod."

Written by Hector MacLean, from the dictation of a man in Barra

XXV.

THE ISLE OF PABAIDH.

From Alexander M'Donald, tenant, and others, Barra. July 1859.

THERE came a woman of peace (a fairy) the way of the house of a man in the island of Pabaidh, and she had the hunger of motherhood on her. He gave her food, and that went well with her. She staid that night. When she went away, she said to him, "I am making a desire that none of the people of this island may go in childbed after this." None of these people, and none others that would make their dwelling in the island ever departed in childbed from that time.

EILEAN PHABAIDH.

THAINIG boireannach sìth rathad tigh duin' ann an eilean Phabaidh, agus acras na laidhe shiùbhl' ùrra. Thug e biadh dhi, 's ghabh sin go math aice. Dh' fhan i 'n oidhche sin. Nur a dh' fhalbh i thuirt i ris, "Tha mise deanadh iarrtas nach fhalbh gin de dhaoin' an eilean so ann an leaba na siùbhla as a dhéigh so." Cha d' fhalbh gin riabh de na daoine sin, 'na gin eile bhiodh a' gabhail comhnuidh 'san eilean uaidhe sin, ann an leaba na siùbhla.

Written by Hector MacLean, from the telling of a man in Barra.

XXVI.

SANNTRAIGH.

From Alexander M'Donald, tenant, and others, Barra. July 1859.

THERE was a herd's wife in the island of Sanntraigh, and she had a kettle. A woman of peace (fairy) would come every day to seek the kettle. She would not say a word when she came, but she would catch hold of the kettle. When she would catch the kettle, the woman of the house would say—

A smith is able to make
Cold iron hot with coal.
The due of a kettle is bones,
And to bring it back again whole.

The woman of peace would come back every day with the kettle and flesh and bones in it. On a day that was there, the housewife was for going over the ferry to Baile a Chaisteil, and she said to her man, "If thou wilt say to the woman of peace as I say, I will go to Baile Castle." "Oo! I will say it. Surely it's I that will say it." He was spinning a heather rope to be set on the house. He saw a woman coming and a shadow from her feet, and he took fear of her. He shut the door. He stopped his work. When she came to the door she did not find the door open, and he did not open it for her. She went above a hole that was in the house. The kettle gave two jumps, and at the third leap it went out at the ridge of the house. The night came, and the kettle came not. The wife came back over the ferry, and she did not see a bit of the kettle within, and she asked, "Where was the kettle?" "Well then I don't care where it is," said the man; "I never took such a fright as I took at it. I shut the door, and she did not come any more with it." "Good-for-nothing wretch, what didst thou do? There are two that will be ill off—thyself and I." "She will come to-morrow with it." "She will not come."

She hasted herself and she went away. She reached the knoll, and there was no man within. It was after dinner, and they were out in the mouth of the night. She went in. She saw the kettle, and she lifted it with her. It was heavy for her with the remnants that they left in it. When the old carle that was within saw her going out, he said,

> Silent wife, silent wife,
> That came on us from the land of chase,
> Thou man on the surface of the "Bruth,"
> Loose the black, and slip the Fierce.

The two dogs were let loose; and she was not long away when she heard the clatter of the dogs coming. She kept the remnant that was in the kettle, so that if she could get it with her, well, and if the dogs should come that she might throw it at them. She perceived the dogs coming. She put her hand in the kettle. She took the board out of it, and she threw at them a quarter of what was in it. They noticed it there for a while. She perceived them again, and she threw another piece at them when they closed upon her. She went away walking as well as she might; when she came near the farm, she threw the mouth of the pot downwards, and there she left them all that was in it. The dogs of the town struck (up) a barking when they saw the dogs of peace stopping. The woman of peace never came more to seek the kettle.

SEANNTRAIGH.

Bha bean fir coimhead ann an eilean Shanntraigh agus bha coir' aice. Thigeadh bean shìth h-uile latha dh' iarraidh a' choire. Cha chanadh i smid nur a thigeadh, i ach bheireadh i air a' choire. Nur a bheireadh i air a' choire theireadh bean an tighe.

'S treasaiche gobha gual
Go iarrunn fuar a bhruich ;
Dleasnas coire cnàimh
'Sa thoirt slàn go tigh.

Thigeadh a' bhean shìth air a h-ais 'h-uile latha leis a' choire, agus feoil as cnàmhan ann. Latha bha 'n sin bha bean an tighe airson dol thar an aiseig do Bhail' a Chaisteil, agus thuirt i r'a fear, "Ma their thusa ris a' bhean shìth mar a their mise, falbhaidh mi 'Bhaile Chaisteil." "U ! their," urs' esan, "'s cinnteach gur mi 'their." Bha e sniamh siamain fraoich gos a chur air an tigh. Chunnaic e bean a' tighinn 's faileas as a casan, 's ghabh e eagal roimhpe. Dhruid e 'n dorusd as stad e d'a obair. Nur a thàinig ise do 'n dorusd cha d' fhuair i 'n dorusd fosgailte, 's cha d' fhosgail esan di e. Chaidh i as cionn toll a bha 's an tigh. Thug an coire da leum as, agus air an treas leum dh' fhalbh e mach air drìom an tighe. Thàinig an oidhche, 's cha d' thàinig an coire. Thill a' bhean thar an aiseig, 's cha 'n fhac i dad de 'n choire stigh, agus dh' fhoighnichd i ca 'n robh 'n coire. "Mata 's coma leam ca' bheil e," urs' a fear, "cha do ghabh mi riabh a leithid de dh' eagal 's a ghabh mi roimhe. Ghabh mi eagal, 's dhùin mi 'n dorusd, 's cha d' thàinig i tuillidh leis. "A dhonain dhona, dè rinn thu? 's dithisd a bhios gu don' thu fhìn agus mise." "Thig i 'm màireach leis." "Cha d' thig."

Sgioblaich i i fhìn, 's dh' fhalbh i 's ràinig i 'n cnoc, 's cha robh duine stigh. Bha e 'n déigh na dinnearach, 's bha eud a mach am bial na h-oidhche. Ghabh i stigh. Chunnaic i 'n coire 's thog i leath' e. Bha e trom aice, 'san còrr a dh' fhag eud ann. Nur a chunnaic am bodach a bha stigh i dol amach, thuirt e,

A bhean bhalbh, a bhean bhalbh,
A thàinig oirnn a tir nan sealg ;
Fhir a tha 'n uachdar a' bhruth,
Fuasgail an Dugh 's lig an Garg.

Ligeadh an da chù ma sgaoil, 's cha b' fhada bha is' air falbh nur a chual i strathail nan con a' tighinn. Ghléidh i 'n còrr a bha 's a' choire air alt 's na 'm faigheadh i leath' e gum bu mhath, 's na 'n d' thigeadh na coin gun tilgeadh i orr' e. Dh' fhairich i na coin a' tighinn, 's chuir i làmh sa' choire, 's thug i 'm bòrd as, 's thilg i orra ceathra de na bh' ann. Thug eud an aire treis air an siud. Dh' fhairich i rìs eud, 's thilg i pìos' eil' orra nur a chas eud urra. Dh' fhalbh i coiseachd cho math 's a dh' fhaodadh i. Nur thàinig i dlùth air a' bhaile thilg i 'bhial fodha, 's dh' fhàg i 'n siud aca na bh' ann. Bhuail coin a' bhail' air comhartaich nur a chunnaic eud na coin shith 'stad. Cha d' thàinig a' bhean shìth riabh tuillidh a dh' iarraidh a' choire.

Written by Hector MacLean, from the telling of a man in Barra.

XXVII.

CAILLIACH MHOR CHLIBHRICH.

From W. Ross, stalker.

THIS celebrated witch was accused of having enenchanted the deer of the Reay forest, so that they avoided pursuit. Lord Reay was exceedingly angry, but at a loss how to remedy the evil. His man, William (the same who braved the witch and sat down in her hut) promised to find out if this was the case. He watched her for a whole night, and by some counter enchantments managed to be present when in the early morning she was busy milking the hinds. They were standing all about the door of the hut till one of them ate a hank of blue worsted hanging from a nail in it. The witch struck the animal, and said, "The spell is off you; and Lord Reay's bullet will be your death to-day." William repeated this to his master to confirm the tale of his having passed the night in the hut of the great hag, which no one would believe. And the event justified it, for a fine yellow hind was killed that day, and the hank of blue yarn was found in its stomach.

This is one of nearly a hundred stories, gathered amongst the people of Sutherland by a very talented collector, whose numerous accomplishments unfortunately do not include Gaelic. This resembles an account of a Lapp camp (see Introduction). It also bears some affinity to a story published by Grant Stewart, in which a ghost uses a herd of deer to carry her furniture.

XXVIII.

THE SMITH AND THE FAIRIES.

From the Rev. Thomas Pattieson, Islay.

YEARS ago there lived in Crossbrig a smith of the name of MacEachern. This man had an only child, a boy of about thirteen or fourteen years of age, cheerful, strong, and healthy. All of a sudden he fell ill; took to his bed and moped whole days away. No one could tell what was the matter with him, and the boy himself could not, or would not, tell how he felt. He was wasting away fast; getting thin, old, and yellow; and his father and all his friends were afraid that he would die.

At last one day, after the boy had been lying in this condition for a long time, getting neither better nor worse, always confined to bed, but with an extraordinary appetite,—one day, while sadly revolving these things, and standing idly at his forge. with no heart to work, the smith was agreeably surprised to see an old man, well known to him for his sagacity and knowledge of out-of-the-way things, walk into his workshop. Forthwith he told him the occurrence which had clouded his life.

The old man looked grave as he listened; and after sitting a long time pondering over all he had heard, gave his opinion thus—"It is not your son you have got. The boy has been carried away by the 'Daoine

Sith,' and they have left a *Sibhreach* in his place." "Alas! and what then am I to do?" said the smith. "How am I ever to see my own son again?" "I will tell you how," answered the old man. "But, first, to make sure that it is not your own son you have got, take as many empty egg shells as you can get, go with them into the room, spread them out carefully before his sight, then proceed to draw water with them, carrying them two and two in your hands as if they were a great weight, and arrange when full, with every sort of earnestness round the fire." The smith accordingly gathered as many broken egg-shells as he could get, went into the room, and proceeded to carry out all his instructions.

He had not been long at work before there arose from the bed a shout of laughter, and the voice of the seeming sick boy exclaimed, "I am now 800 years of age, and I have never seen the like of that before."

The smith returned and told the old man. "Well, now," said the sage to him, "did I not tell you that it was not your son you had: your son is in Brorra-cheill in a digh there (that is, a round green hill frequented by fairies). Get rid as soon as possible of this intruder, and I think I may promise you your son."

"You must light a very large and bright fire before the bed on which this stranger is lying. He will ask you 'What is the use of such a fire as that?' Answer him at once, 'You will see that presently!' and then seize him, and throw him into the middle of it. If it is your own son you have got, he will call out to save him; but if not, this thing will fly through the roof."

The smith again followed the old man's advice; kindled a large fire, answered the question put to him as he had been directed to do, and seizing the child flung him in without hesitation. The "Sibhreach" gave an awful yell, and sprung through the roof, where a hole was left to let the smoke out.

On a certain night the old man told him the green round hill, where the fairies kept the boy, would be open. And on that night the smith, having provided himself with a bible, a dirk, and a crowing cock, was to proceed to the hill. He would hear singing and dancing and much merriment going on, but he was to advance boldly; the bible he carried would be a certain safeguard to him against any danger from the fairies. On entering the hill he was to stick the dirk in the threshold, to prevent the hill from closing upon him; "and then," continued the old man, "on entering you will see a spacious apartment before you, beautifully clean, and there, standing far within, working at a forge, you will also see your own son. When you are questioned, say you come to seek him, and will not go without him."

Not long after this, the time came round, and the smith sallied forth, prepared as instructed. Sure enough as he approached the hill, there was a light where light was seldom seen before. Soon after a sound of piping, dancing, and joyous merriment reached the anxious father on the night wind.

Overcoming every impulse to fear, the smith approached the threshold steadily, stuck the dirk into it as directed, and entered. Protected by the bible he carried on his breast, the fairies could not touch him; but they asked him, with a good deal of displeasure, what he wanted there. He answered, "I want my son, whom I see down there, and I will not go without him."

Upon hearing this, the whole company before him

gave a loud laugh, which wakened up the cock he carried dozing in his arms, who at once leaped up on his shoulders, clapped his wings lustily, and crowed loud and long.

The fairies, incensed, seized the smith and his son, and throwing them out of the hill, flung the dirk after them, "and in an instant a' was dark."

For a year and a day the boy never did a turn of work, and hardly ever spoke a word; but at last one day, sitting by his father and watching him finishing a sword he was making for some chief, and which he was very particular about, he suddenly exclaimed, "That is not the way to do it;" and taking the tools from his father's hands he set to work himself in his place, and soon fashioned a sword, the like of which was never seen in the country before.

From that day the young man wrought constantly with his father, and became the inventor of a peculiarly fine and well-tempered weapon, the making of which kept the two smiths, father and son, in constant employment, spread their fame far and wide, and gave them the means in abundance, as they before had the disposition to live content with all the world and very happily with one another.

The walls of the house where this celebrated smith, the artificer of the "Claidheamh Ceann-Ileach," lived and wrought, are standing to this day, not far from the parish church of Kilchoman, Islay, in a place called Caonis gall.

Many of the incidents in this story are common in other collections; but I do not know any published story of the kind in which the hero is a smith. This smith was a famous character, and probably a real personage, to whom the story has attached itself.

The gentleman who has been kind enough to send me this tale, does not say from whom he got it, but I have heard of the

Islay smith, who could make wonderful swords, all my life, and of the "Swords of the Head of Islay." The Brewery of Egg-shells, and the Throwing of the Fairy Changeling into the Fire, are well-known popular tales in collections from Ireland, Scotland, Wales, and, I think, Brittany. The man carried into the hill and there remaining for a long time, is also an incident common to many races, including the Jews, and one which I have heard in the Highlands ever since I can remember, though I do not remember to have heard any of the peasantry tell it as a story.

The belief that "the hill" opened on a certain night, and that a light shone from the inside, where little people might be seen dancing, was too deeply grounded some years ago to be lightly spoken of; even now, on this subject, my kind friend Mrs. MacTavish writes—"You may perhaps remember an old servant we had at the manse who was much offended if any one doubted these stories—(*I remember her perfectly*). I used to ask her the reason why such wonders do not occur in our day, to which she replied, that religious knowledge having increased, people's faith was stronger than it was in the olden time. In the glebe of Kilbrandon in Lorn is a hill called Crocan Corr—the good or beautiful hill where the fairies even in my young days were often seen dancing around their fire. I sometimes went out with others to look, but never succeeded in seeing them at their gambols.

"Are you aware that ——'s mother was carried away by the fairies—(*I know —— well*). So convinced were many of this absurdity, which I remember perfectly well, that it was with difficulty they got a nurse for his brother ——, who being a delicate child, was believed to have been conveyed away along with his mother, and a fairy left instead of him during his father's absence * * * The child however throve when he got a good nurse, and grew up to be a man, which, I suppose, convinced them of their folly. Mr. —— minister of —— had some difficulty in convincing a man whose wife was removed in a similar manner (*she died in childbed*), that his son, a boy twelve years of age, must have been under some hallucination when he maintained that his mother had come to him, saying she was taken by fairies to a certain hill in Muckairn, known to be the residence of the fairies.

"If any one is so unfortunate as to go into one of these hills, which are open at night, they never get out unless some one goes in quest of them, who uses the precaution of leaving a GUN or

SWORD across the opening, which the fairies cannot remove. A certain young woman was decoyed into one of these openings, who was seen by an acquaintance dancing with the merry race. He resolved on trying to rescue her, and leaving his gun at the entrance, went forward, and seizing the young woman by the hand, dragged her out before they could prevent him. They pursued them, but having got her beyond the gun, they had no longer power to keep her. She told him she had nearly dropped down with fatigue, but she could not cease dancing, though she felt it would soon kill her. The young man restored her to her friends, to their great joy."

(*I remember exactly the same incident told of a hill called Ben-cnock in Islay, and one similar of another hill called Cnock-doun.*)

"When poor women are confined, it is unsafe to leave them alone till their children are baptised. If through any necessity they must be left alone, the Bible left beside them is sufficient protection.

"Many were the freaks fairies were guilty of. A family who lived in Gaolin Castle, Kerrera, near Oban, had, as they supposed, a delicate child; it was advancing in years but not growing a bit; at length a visitor from Ireland came to the castle, and recognized her as the fairy sweetheart of an Irish gentleman of his acquaintance. He addressed her in Gaelic or Irish, saying—'THA THUSA SIN A SHIRACH BHEAG LEANNAN BRIAN MACBRAODH.'—There thou art, little fairy sweetheart of Brian MacBroadh. So offended was the elf at being exposed, that she ran out of the castle and leaped into the sea from the point called RUTHADH NA SIRACH, the fairies' point, to this day.

"Fairies were very friendly to some people whom they favoured, but equally mischievous where they took a dislike. A hill in the farm of Dunvuilg in Craignish was one of their favourite haunts, and on a certain occasion they offered to assist an honest tenant's wife in the neighbourhood, for whom they had a kindness, to manufacture a quantity of wool she had for clothing for her family. She was very glad to have their services, and being always an active race, they set to work directly, repeating 'CIRADH, CARDADH, TLAMADH, CUIGEAL, BEARTIGHE GU LUATH BURN LUAIDH AIR TEINE CORR IONNDRAIDH MHOR MHAITH BEAN AN TIGHE FHIN.' Teazing, carding, mixing, distaff, weaving loom, water for waulking on the fire, the thrifty housewife herself is the best at sitting up late.

"In the heat of their operations an envious neighbour came to the door crying—'DUNBHUILG RA THEINE,' Dunvuilg on fire! Dunvuilg is on fire! Dunvuilg is on fire! was re-echoed by all the little company. 'M' UIRD IS' M' INNEAN! M' UIRD IS' M' INEANN! MO CHLANN BHEAG S' MO DHAOINE MORA! MO CHLANN BHEAG S' MO DHAOINE MORA!'—'Dunvuilg on fire; my hammers and my anvil—my hammers and my anvil; my little children and my grown men—my little children and my grown men!' and they all scampered off, but not till they had nearly finished the housewife's web.

"There is a field in the farm in which I was born, said to have been the scene of fairy operations. They were seen at work, and heard encouraging each other with 'CAOL ACHADH MHAIDH BUANADH GU TETH.' The corn in the field was found in stooks in the morning.

"It is quite common to remark, that the fairies are at some meal as the time of day may indicate when there is rain with sunshine, but I never heard the reason why.—(*In England it is the d——l beating his wife.*)

"The night following the 13th of May, or May-day, old style, is a particularly busy season with both fairies and witches. Then every herd and dairy-maid and cannie housewife uses various arts to ward off the many evils the enemy has the power of inflicting. One device which I have seen used was putting a little tar in the right ear of each cow beast in the byre; but all these charms or giosragan, as they are called, had always some reason. Tar has a disinfecting quality, as is well known, and used to be put on clothing under the arms when a person had to go into a house where there was any infectious disease."

The Dunbhulaig story is all over the Highlands, and there seem to be many places so called. Mr. John MacLean, Kilchamaig, Tarbert, Argyle, has sent me a version which varies but little from that told by Mrs. MacTavish. The scene is laid on the Largie side of Kintyre. The farmer's wife was idle, and called for the fairies, who wove a web for her and shouted for more work. She first set them to put each other out, and at last got rid of them by shouting "Dunbhulaig on fire!" The fairies' rhyme when working was—

"Is fad abhras 'n aon laimh air dheradh,
Ciradh cardadh tlamadh cuigel,

Feath a bhearst fithidh gu luath,
'S uisge luaidh air teine
Obair, obair, obair, obair,
Is fad abhras 'n aon laimh air dheradh.

Which Mr. MacLean translates freely—

" Work, work, for a single hand
Can but little work command,
Some to tease, and card, and spin ;
Some to oil and weave begin ;
Some the water for waulking heat,
That we may her web complete.
Work, work, for a single hand
Can but little work command."

The rhyme, when they depart in hot haste, is—

" Mo mhullachan caise m'ord a's m innean,
Mo bhean 's mo phaisde s' mo gogan ima,
Mo bho s' mo gobhair s' mo chiste beag mine,
Och, och, ochone gur truagh tha mise ! "

Freely translated thus by Mr. MacLean—

" My wife, my child, alas, with these,
My butter pail and little cheese,
My cow, my goat, my meal-chest gone,
My hammers too, och, och, ochone ! "

Or more closely thus—

" My mould of cheese, my hammer, and anvil,
My wife and my child, and my butter crock ;
My cow and my goat, and my little meal kist ;
Och, och, ochone, how wretched am I ! "

I heard another version of the same story in Lewis from a medical gentleman, who got it from an old woman, who told it as a fact, with some curious variations unfit for printing. And my landlady in Benbecula knew the story, and talked it over with me in September this year. The versions which I have of this story vary in the telling as much as is possible, and each is evidently the production of a different mind, but the incidents are nearly the same in all, and the rhyme varies only in a few points. Dunbhulaig is the same in Kintyre, Lorn, Lewis, and Benbecula. I am not aware that the story has ever before been reduced to writing.

The Man in the Hill is equally well known in Kirkcudbright, but the *hill*, has become a *mill*, and the fairies Brownies. The fairies of Kirkcudbright seem to have carried off children, like the Island Elves ; to have borrowed meal, like those of Sutherland, and to have behaved like their brethren elsewhere. The following four stories were got for me by the sisters of Miss Mary Lindsay, who has lived so long with us as to have become one of the family.

KIRKCUDBRIGHT.

Kirkcudbright, Tuesday, Feb. 1859.

MY DEAR MARY,—I went to Johnny Nicholson last night, and he told me the following fairy story. I must give it in his own words :—

1. "You have been often at the Gatehouse," said he, "well, you'll mind a flat piece of land near Enrick farm ; well, that was once a large loch ; a long way down from there is still the ruin of a mill, which at that time was fed from this loch. Well, one night about the Hallowe'en times, two young ploughmen went to a smiddy to get their socks (of their ploughs) and colters repaired, and in passing the said mill on their way home again they heard music and dancing, and fiddling, and singing, and laughing, and talking ; so one of the lads would be in to see what was going on ; the other waited outside for hours, but his companion never came out again, so he went home assured that the brownies had got hold of him. About the same time the following year, the same lad went again to the smiddy on the same errand, and

this time he took another lad with him, but had the precaution to put the Bible in his pocket. Well, in passing the mill the second time, he heard the same sounds of music and dancing. This time, having the Bible in his hand, he ventured to look in, when who should he see but his companion whom he had left standing there that day twelvemonths. He handed him the Bible, and the moment he did so, the music and dancing ceased, the lights went out, and all was darkness; but it is not said what his companion had seen, or had been doing all that time."

2. Another story he told me was about a boy of the name of Williamson, whose father, an Irish linen packman, was drowned on his way from Ireland, where he had gone to purchase linen; so the boy was brought up by his mother and grandfather, an old man of the name of Sproat, who lived in Borgue. The boy disappeared often for two and three, and often ten days at a time, and no one knew where he went, as he never told when he returned, though it was understood the fairies took him away. Upon one occasion the Laird of Barmagachan, was getting his peats cast, and all the neighbours round were assisting. At this time the boy had been away for ten days, and they were all wondering where he could be, when lo and behold, the boy is sitting in the midst of them. "Johnny," said one of the company, who were all seated in a ring, eating their dinner, "where did ye come from?" "I came with our folks," said the boy (meaning the fairies). "Your folks; who are they?" "Do you see yon barrow of peats a couping into yon hole? there's where I came from." An old man of the name of Brown, ancestor of the Browns of Langlands, who are still living in Borgue, advised the grandfather to send the boy to the Papist priest, and he

would give him something that would frighten away the fairies; so they accordingly sent the boy, and when he returned home he wore a cross hung round his neck by a bit of black ribbon. When the minister and kirk-session heard of it they excommunicated the old grandfather and old Brown for advising such a thing. They believed in fairies, but not in anything a Papist priest could do. However, the boy was never after taken away; and some of the oldest men now alive remember that boy as an old man. The whole affair is recorded in the books of the kirk-session of Borgue, and can be seen any day.

3. One day as a mother was sitting rocking her baby to sleep, she was surprised, on looking up, to see a lady of elegant and courtly demeanour, so unlike any one she had ever seen in that part of the country, standing in the middle of the room. She had not heard any one enter, therefore you may judge it was with no little surprise, not unmingled with curiosity, that she rose to welcome her strange visitor. She handed her a chair, but she very politely declined to be seated. She was very magnificently attired; her dress was of the richest green, embroidered round with spangles of gold, and on her head was a small coronet of pearls. The woman was still more surprised at her strange request. She asked, in a rich musical voice, if she would oblige her with a basin of oatmeal. A basinful to overflowing was immediately handed to her, for the woman's husband being both a farmer and miller, had plenty of meal at command. The lady promised to return it, and named the day she would do so. One of the children put out her hand to get hold of the grand lady's spangles, but told her mother afterwards that she felt nothing. The mother was afraid the child would lose the use of her hands, but no such calamity ensued. It would have

been very ungrateful in her fairy majesty if she had struck the child powerless for touching her dress, if indeed such power were hers. But to return to our story, the very day mentioned, the oatmeal was returned, not by the same lady, but by a curious little figure with a yelping voice; she was likewise dressed in green. After handing the meal she yelped out, "Braw meal, it's the top pickle of the sin corn." It was excellent; and what was very strange, all the family were advised to partake of it but one servant lad, who spurned the fairy's meal; and he dying shortly after, the miller and his wife firmly believed it was because he refused to eat of the meal. They also firmly believed their first visitor was no less a personage than the Queen of the Fairies, who having dismissed her court, had not one maid of honour in waiting to obey her commands. A few nights after this strange visit, as the miller was going to bed, a gentle tap was heard at the door, and on its being opened by him, with a light in his hand, there stood a little figure dressed in green, who, in a shrill voice, but very polite manner, requested him to let on the water and set the mill in order, for she was going to grind some corn. The miller did not dare to refuse, so did as she desired him. She told him to go to bed again, and he would find all as he had left it. He found everything in the morning as she said he would. So much for the honesty of fairies.

4. A tailor was going to work at a farm-house early one morning. He had just reached it, and was going to enter, when he heard a shrill voice call out, "Kep fast, will ye?" and on looking quickly round, he was just in time to receive in his arms a sweet, little, smiling baby of a month old, instead of a little lady in green, who was standing to receive the child. The tailor turned and ran home as fast

as he could, for tailors are generally nimble kind of folks, and giving the baby to his wife, ran off again to his work, leaving his better half in no pleasant mood with the little intruder, as she very politely termed the little innocent. Having reached the farm-house, the tailor found the inhabitants all thrown into confusion by the screaming, yelping, little pest, as they called their little nurseling, for the little woman in green had given in exchange this little hopeful for their own sweet little one, which was safe with the tailor's wife. They found out afterwards it was the nurse who had done it. The doctor was sent for, but all was in vain; day nor night rest they got none. At last one day, all being absent but the tailor, who was there following his trade, he commenced a discourse with the child in the cradle. "Will hae ye your pipes?" says the tailor. "They're below my head," says the tenant of the cradle. "Play me a spring," says the tailor. Like thought, the little man, jumping from the cradle, played round the room with great glee. A curious noise was heard meantime outside; and the tailor asked what it meant. The little elf called out, "It's my folk wanting me," and away he fled up the chimney, leaving the tailor more dead than alive. Their own child was brought home, the guilty nurse dismissed, and the tailor's wife amply rewarded for the care of the child. She was heard to say, "It was a glad sight the wee bit bairn."

5. The Macgowans of Grayscroft in Tongland, and latterly of Bogra, had the power of witchcraft to a considerable extent, and it descended from one generation to another. At the time we refer to, Abraham Macgowan and his daughter Jenny resided at Grayscroft. Jenny had an unlimited power from Old Nick to act as she pleased. The ploughmen at that time in their employ were Harry Dew and Davie Gordon, young men

about twenty-two years of age; they had been there for the last twelve months; and conversing one day together, the following took place:—

Harry—"Losh man, Davie, what makes ye sae drowsy, lazy, and sleepy-like the day, for I am verra sure ye work nae mair than I do; ye eat the same and sleep the same as I do, and yet ye are so thin and wearied and hungry-like, I dinna ken ava what ails ye; are ye weel eneugh, Davie?" "I'm weel eneugh, Harry, but it's a' ye ken about it; sleep a night or twa at the bedside, and maybe you'll no be sae apt to ask me sic questions again. Harry—"The bedside, Davie! what differ will that make? I hae nae mair objections to sleep there than at the wa'." This being agreed to, they exchanged places. Nothing occurred to disturb either of them till the third night, although Harry kept watch: their bed was on the stable loft, when, about midnight, the stable door was opened cautiously, and some one was heard (by Harry only) coming up the ladder and to the bedside, with a quiet step. A bridle was held above the one next the bedside, and the words, "Up horsey," whispered in his ear; in one moment Harry was transformed into a horse at the stable door. The saddle was got on with some kicking and plunging, but Jenny gets mounted, and off they set by the Elfcraigs, Auld Brig o' Tongland, the March Cleughs, and on till they reach the Auld Kirk of Buittle. Harry was tied to the gate along with others. Meg o' Glengap was there on her dairymaid, now a bonny mare, neat in all her proportions. "Tib" o' Criffle came on her auld ploughman, rather wind-broken. "Lizzy," frae the Bennan, came on her cot wife, limping with a swelled knee. "Moll o' the Wood" came on a herd callant frae the "How o' Siddick." When all the horses were mustered, there was some snorting and kicking and neighing amongst them. Fairies, witches, brownies, and all met in the kirk and had a blithe holiday, under the patronage of his Satanic majesty, which continued till the crowing of the cock. Wearied with his gallop, Harry, when the charmed bridle was taken off, found himself in his own bed and in his own shape. Harry is determined to be revenged; he finds the charmed bridle in a hole in the kitchen in a week after; he tries it on Jenny, using the same words, when Jenny is transformed into the auld brown mare of the farm; he takes her to the neighbouring smithy, and gets her, after much ado, shod all round, when he returns and leaves her, after securing the wonderful bridle.

Next morning Harry is ordered to go for a doctor, as his mistress is taken ill. He goes into the house to ask for her; pulls the bed clothes off her, and discovers there was a horse shoe on each hand and foot, when Harry says, "Jenny, my lass, that did ye." Jenny played many more similar tricks on her neighbour lads and lasses.

SUTHERLAND.

In Sutherland the fairy creed is much the same as elsewhere in Scotland, but there is a generic term for supernatural beings, which is rarely used in West Country Gaelic. Here are a few of a large and very good collection of Sutherland stories.

1. Duncan, surnamed More, a respectable farmer in Badenoch, states as follows:—"A matter of thirty summers ago, when I was cutting peats on the hill, my old mother that was, was keeping the house. It was

sowens she had in her hand for our supper, when a little woman walked in and begged a lippie of meal of her. My mother, not knowing her face, said, 'And where do you come from?' 'I come from my own place and am short of meal.' My mother, who had plenty by her in the house, spoke her civil, and bound her meal on her back, following her a few steps from the door. She noticed that a little kiln in the hill side was smoking. The wife saw this too, and said, 'Take back your meal, we shall soon have meal of our own.' My mother pressed ours on her; but she left the pock lying; and when she came to the running burn went out of sight; and my mother just judged it was a fairy."

2. Once upon a time there was a tailor and his wife, who owned a small croft or farm, and were well to do in the world; but had only one son, a child, that was more pain than pleasure to them, for it cried incessantly and was so cross that nothing could be done with it. One day the tailor and his helpmeet meant to go to a place some miles distant, and after giving the child its breakfast, they put it to bed in the kitchen, and bid their farm servant look to it from time to time; desiring him also to thrash out a small quantity of straw in the barn before their return. The lad was late of setting to work, but recollected before going off to the barn, that he must see if the child wanted for anything. "What are you going to do now?" said the bairn sharply to Donald, as he opened the kitchen door. "Thrash out a pickle of straw for your father; lie still and do not *girr*, like a good bairn." But the bairn got out of bed, and insisted then and there in being allowed to accompany the servant. "Go east, Donald," said the little master, authoritatively, "Go east, and when ye come to the big brae, chap ye (anglicè *rap*) three times; and when *they*

come, say ye are seeking Johnnie's flail." The astonished Donald did as he was bid, and by rapping three times, called up a fairy ("little man") who, giving him the flail, sent him off with it in an unenviable state of terror.

Johnny set to with a will, and in an hour's time, he and Donald had thrashed the whole of the straw in the barn; he then sent Donald back to the brae, where the flail was restored with the same ceremony, and went quietly back to bed. At dusk the parents returned; and the admiration of the tailor at the quantity and quality of the work done, was so great, that he questioned Donald as to which of the neighbours had helped him to thrash out so much straw. Donald, trembling, confessed the truth; and it became painfully evident to the tailor and his wife that the child was none of theirs. They agreed to dislodge it as soon as possible, and chose as the best and quickest way of doing so, to put it into a creel (open basket), and set it on the fire. No sooner said than done; but no sooner had the child felt the fire, than starting from the creel, it vanished up the chimney. A low crying noise at the door attracted their attention; they opened, and a bonny little bairn (which the mother recognised by its frock to be her own), stood shivering outside. It was welcomed with rapture from its sojourn among "the little people," and grew up to be a douse and wise-like *lad*, says my informant.

3. The burn of Invernauld, and the hill of Durchâ, on the estate of Rosehall, are still believed to be haunted by the fairies, who once chased a man into the sea, and destroyed a new mill, because the earth for the embankment of the mill-dam had been dug from the side of their hill. The hill of Durchâ is also the locality assigned for the following tale:—

4. A man, whose wife had just been delivered of her first-born, set off with a friend to the town of Lairg, to have the child's birth entered in the session-books, and to buy a cask of whisky for the christening fête. As they returned, weary with a day's walk, or as it is called in the Highlands "*travelling*," they sat down to rest at the foot of this hill, near a large hole, from which they were, ere long, astonished to hear a sound of piping and dancing. The father feeling very curious, entered the cavern, went a few steps in, and disappeared. The story of his fate sounded less improbable *then* than it would now; but his companion was severely animadverted on; and when a week elapsed, and the baptism was over, and still no signs of the lost one's return, he was accused of having murdered his friend. He denied it, and again and again repeated the tale of his friend's disappearance down the cavern's mouth. He begged a year and a day's law to vindicate himself, if possible; and used to repair at dusk to the fatal spot, and call and pray. The term allowed him had but one more day to run, and as usual, he sat in the gloaming by the cavern, when, what seemed his friend's *shadow*, passed within it. He went down, heard reel tunes and pipes, and suddenly descried the missing man tripping merrily with the fairies. He caught him by the sleeve, stopped him, and pulled him out. "Bless me! why could you not let me finish my reel, Sandy?" "Bless me!" rejoined Sandy, "have you not had enough of reeling this last twelvemonth?" "Last twelvemonth!" cried the other, in amazement; nor would he believe the truth concerning himself till he found his wife sitting by the door with a yearling child in her arms, so quickly does time pass in the company of THE "*good people.*"

5. Of the Drocht na Vougha or Fuoah—the bridge of

the fairies or kelpies, now called the Gissen Briggs, a bar across the mouth of the Dornoch Firth—it is said that the Voughas being tired of crossing the estuary in cockle shells, resolved to build a bridge across its mouth. It was a work of great magnificence, the piers and posts, and all the piles being headed and mounted with pure gold. Unfortunately, a passer by lifted up his hands and blessed the workmen and the work; the former vanished; the latter sank beneath the green waves, where the sand accumulating, formed the dangerous quicksands which are there to this day.

6. The Highlanders distinguish between the water and land or *dressed* fairies. I have given one story which shows that they are supposed to be "spirits in prison;" it is not the only legend of the kind. In a Ross-shire narrative, a beautiful green lady is represented as appearing to an old man reading the Bible, and seeking to know, if for such as her, Holy Scripture held out any hope of salvation. The old man spoke kindly to her; but said, that in these pages there was no mention of salvation for any but the sinful sons of Adam. She flung her arms over her head, screamed, and plunged into the sea. They will not steal a baptized child; and "Bless you!" said to an unbaptized one, is a charm against them. A woman out shearing had laid her baby down under a hedge, and went back from time to time to look at it. She was going once to give it suck, when it began to yell and cry in such a frightful way that she was quite alarmed. "Lay it down and leave it, as you value your child," said a man reaping near her; half an hour later she came back, and finding the child apparently in its right mind again, she gave it the breast. The man smiled, told her that he had seen her own infant carried off by the "good people," and a fairy

changeling left in its place. When the "folk" saw that their screaming little imp was not noticed, and got nothing, they thought it best to take it back and replace the little boy.

As fairies are represented as having always food, and riches, and power, and merriment at command, it cannot be *temporal* advantages that they seek for their children, probably some spiritual ones are hoped for by adoption or marriage with human beings, as in the romantic legend of Undine; and that this tempts them to foist their evil disposed little ones on us. They never maltreat those whom they carry away.

BADENOCH.

The Badenoch account of the fairies is much the same. I have received eight stories from a Highland minister, who has been kind enough to interest himself in the matter, at the request of the Countess of Seafield. These show, that according to popular belief, fairies commonly carried off men, women, and children, who seemed to die, but really lived underground. In short, that mortals were separated from fairies by a very narrow line.

1. A man sees fairies carding and spinning in a sheal ing where he is living at the time. Amongst them is Miss Emma MacPherson of Cluny, who had been dead about one hundred years.

2. A woman, benighted, gets into a fairy hill, where she promises to give her child, on condition that she is let out. She gives her child when it is born, and is allowed to visit it "till such time as the child, upon one

occasion, looked at her sternly in the face, and in a very displeased mood and tone upbraided her for the manner in which she had acted in giving her child over unto those amongst whom it was now doomed to dwell." The mother scolded, found herself standing on the hillock outside, and never got in again.

3. A lad recognizes his mother, who had been carried off by fairies, but who was believed to be dead. She was recovered from the fairies by a man who threw his bonnet to a passing party, and demanded an exchange. The rescuer gave up the wife, and she returned home. Of this story I have several versions in Gaelic and in English, and I believe it is in print somewhere.

4. An old woman meets her deceased landlord and landlady, who tell her that the fairies have just carried off a young man, who is supposed to be dead. They advise her not to be out so late.

5. The young Baron of Kincardine is entertained by fairies, who steal his father's snuff for him when he asks for a pinch.

6. The young baron meets a bogle with a red hand, tells, and is punished.

7. The baron's dairymaid, when at a shealing, has a visit from a company of fairies, who dance and steal milk.

8. "A man, once upon a time, coming up from Inverness late at night, coming through a solitary part called Slockmuic, was met by crowds of people, none of whom he could recognize, nor did they seem to take any notice of him. They engaged in close conversation, talked on subjects not a word of which he could pick up. At length accosting one individual of them, he asked who they were? 'None of the seed of Abram nor of Adam's race; but men of that party who lost favour at the

Court of Grace.'" He was advised not to practise late at night travelling in future.

Thomas MacDonald, gamekeeper at Dunrobin, also gives me a fairy tale, which is "*now commonly believed in Badenoch.*"

9. A man went from home, leaving his wife in child-bed. Her temper had never been ruffled. He found her a wicked scold. Thinking all was not right, he piled up a great fire, and threatened to throw in the occupant of the bed, unless she told him "where his own wife had been brought." She told him that his wife had been carried to Cnoc Fraing, a mountain on the borders of Badenoch and Strathdearn, and that she was appointed successor.

The man went to Cnoc Fraing. He was suspected before of having something supernatural about him; and he soon found the fairies, who told him his wife had been taken to Shiathan Mor, a neighbouring mountain. He went there and was sent to Tom na Shirich, near Inverness. There he went, and at the "Fairy Knoll" found his wife and brought her back. "*The person who related this story pretended to have seen people who knew distant descendants of the woman.*"

ROSS.

The Ross-shire account of fairies is again much the same. The people say very little about them, and those who have been kind enough to note stories picked up amongst their less instructed neighbours, have only sent fresh evidence to prove that the fairy creed is the same there as everywhere, and that it is not quite extinct.

1. I have a story, got through the kindness of Mr. Osgood Mackenzie, in which a Lowland minister speaks slightingly of the fairies. "He was riding home through a dark glen, and through an oak wood, where there was many a green tolman (mound). He was surrounded by a squad of little men, leaping before him and dancing behind him. They took him off the horse and carried him up through the skies, his head under him now, and his feet under again, the world running round; and at last they dropped him near his own house.

2. In another story, a lot of fairies borrow a weaver's loom at night, without his leave, and make a web of green cloth from stolen wool.

BEARNAIRIDH.

There was in Beàrnairidh in the Harris, a man coming past a knoll, and taking the road, and he heard churning in the hill. Thirst struck him. "I had rather," said he, "that my thirst was on the herdswoman." He had not gone but about twenty rods away when a woman met him, and she had a fine green petticoat on tied about her waist, and she had a vessel of warm milk between her two hands. She offered him a draught, and he would not take it.

"Thou one that sought my draught, and took not my draught, mayest thou not be long alive."

He went to the narrows, and he took a boat there over; and coming over the narrows he was drowned.

Bha aunn am Beàrnairidh aunns na h-Earadh, fear a' tighinn seachad air cnoc a' gabhail an rathaid agus chual e aunns a' chnoc maistreadh. Bhuail am pathadh e. "B' fheàrr leom," ars' esan, "gon robh mo phathadh air a' bhanachaig." Cha deach e ach mu thuaiream fichead slat air falbh, an uair a choinnich boireannach e, agus còta briagh, uain' urr' air a cheanghal mu 'miadhon, agus cuman blàthaich aic' eadar a da làimh. Thairg i da deoch, 's cha ghabhadh e i. "Fhir a dh' iarr mo dheoch, 's nach do ghabh mo dheoch, na mu fada 'bhios thu beò." Ghabh e 'ionnsuidh a chaolais, agus ghabh e bàt' a sin thairis, 's a' tighinn thairis air a' chaolas chaidh a bhàthadh.

From Malcolm MacLean, who learnt it from his grandfather, Hugh MacLean.
North Uist, August 11, 1859.

The Argyllshire stories, which I can well remember as a child, are of the same stamp. The fairies lived in hills, they came out now and then and carried people away; and they spent their time inside their dwellings in dancing to the pipes. They stole milk, and they were overcome by charms, which men sold to those who believed in them. They could not withstand a rowan-tree cross; nor could they follow over a running stream.

There is a small waterfall in a wood which I know, where it used to be said that the fairies might be seen on moonlight nights, fishing for a magic chain from boats of sedge leaves. They used to drag this chain through the meadows where the cattle fed, and the milk came all to them, till a lad, by the advice of a seer, seized one end of the chain and ran for his life, with the fairy troop in pursuit; he leaped the lin and dropped the chain; and the lin is called the chain lin still.

MAN.

The Manks fairy creed is again the same. Similar beings are supposed to exist, and are known by the name of FERISH, which a Manksman assured me was a genuine Manks word. If so, fairy may be old Celtic, and derived from the same root as Peri, instead of being derived from it.

The fairies in the Isle of Man are believed to be spirits. They are not supposed to throw arrows as they are said still to do in the Highlands. None of the old peasants seemed to take the least interest in "elf shots," the flint arrows, which generally lead to a story when shown elsewhere. One old man said, "The ferish have no body, no bones;" and scorned the arrow heads. It is stated in Train's history, that no flint-arrow heads have ever been found in the Isle of Man; but as there are numerous barrows, flint weapons may yet be discovered when some one looks for them.

Still these Manks fairies are much the same as their neighbours on the main land. They go into mills at night and grind stolen corn; they steal milk from the cattle; they live in green mounds; in short, they are like little mortals invested with supernatural power, thus: There was a man who lived not long ago near Port Erin, who had a LHIANNAN SHEE. "He was like other people, but he had a fairy sweetheart; but he noticed her, and they do not like being noticed, the fairies, and so he lost his mind. Well, he was quite quiet like other people, but at night he slept in the barn; and they used to hear him talking to his sweetheart, and scolding her sometimes; but if any one made a noise he would be quiet at once."

Now, the truth of this story is clear enough; the man went mad; but this madness took the form of the popular belief, and that again attributed his madness to the fairy mistress. I am convinced that this was believed to be a case of genuine fairy intercourse; and it shows that the fairy creed still survives in the Isle of Man.

DEVONSHIRE.

The same is true of Devonshire. In May 1860 I was told that many of the farmers "are so superstitious as to believe in PISKIES;" they are "never seen, but they are often heard laughing at people in the dark, and they lead them away." My informant said that when he was young he used to hear so many stories about piskies from the old women about the fireside, that he used to be frightened to go out at night.

"When the young colts are out running wild, their manes get rough and hang down on both sides, and get tangled with the wind like; not like manes of horses that are well kept (here the speaker pointed with his whip at the sleek pair which he was driving); and when the farmers find stirrups like in the hair of the mane, they say the piskies has been a ridin' of them."

In short, this notice of fairy belief might be extended to fill volumes; every green knoll, every well, every hill in the Highlands, has some fairy legend attached to it. In the west, amongst the unlearned, the legends are firmly believed. Peasants never talk about fairies, for they live amongst them and about them. In the east the belief is less strong, or the believers are more ashamed of their creed. In the Lowlands, and even in England, the stories survive, and the belief exists, though men have less time to think about it. In the south the fairy creed of the peasants has been altered, but it still exists, as is proved occasionally in courts of law. There is a ghost which walks under the North Bridge in Edinburgh; and even in the cultivated upper strata of society in this our country, in France, and elsewhere, fairy superstition has only gone down before other stronger beliefs, in which a table is made the sole partition between this world and the next, Whether we are separated from the other world by a deal board or a green mound, does not seem to make much difference; and yet that is the chief difference between the vagrant beliefs of the learned and unlearned.

An old highlander declared to me that he was once in a boat with a man who was struck by a fairy arrow. He had the arrow for a long time; it was slender like a straw for thickness. He himself drew it out of the temple of the other man, where it was stuck in the skin through the bonnet. They were then miles from the shore, fishing. A man, whom the fairies were in the habit of carrying about from island to island, told him that he had himself thrown the dart at the man in the boat by desire of *them;* "*they* made him do it."

My informant evidently believed he was speaking truth, as my more educated friends do when they tell me sgeulachd about Mr. Hume.

For my own part, I believe *all* my friends; but I cannot believe in fairies, or that my forbears have become slaves of a table to be summoned at the will of a quack. I believe that there is a stock of old credulity smouldering near a store of old legends, in some corner of every mind, and that the one acts on the other, and produces a fresh legend and a new belief whenever circumstances are favourable to the growth of such weeds. At all events, I am quite sure that the fairy creed of the peasantry, as I have learned it from them, is not a whit more unreasonable than the bodily appearance of the hand of Napoleon the First to Napoleon the Third in 1860, as it is described in print; and the grave books which are written on "Spiritual Manifestations" at home and abroad. What is to be said of the table which became so familiar with a young lady, that it followed her upstairs and jumped on to the sofa!

XXIX.

THE FINE.

THE Feen were once, and their hunting failed, and they did not know what they should do. They were going about strands and shores gathering limpets, and to try if they should fall in with a pigeon or a plover. They were holding counsel together how they should go to get game. They reached a hill, and sleep came on them. What should Fionn see but a dream. That it was at yon crag of rock that he would be, the longest night that came or will come; that he would be driven backwards till he should set his back to the crag of rock. He gave a spring out of his sleep. He struck his foot on Diarmid's mouth, and he drove out three of his teeth. Diarmid caught hold of the foot of Fionn, and he drove an ounce of blood from every nail he had. "Ud! what didst thou to me?"—"What didst thou thyself to me?"—"Be not angry, thou son of my sister. When I tell thee the reason, thou wilt not take it ill."—"What reason?"—"I saw a dream that at yonder crag I would pass the hardest night I ever passed; that I should be driven backwards till I should set my back to the crag, and there was no getting off from there." "What's our fear! Who should frighten us! Who will come!" "I fear, as we are in straits just now, that if this lasts we may become useless." They went and they cast lots who should go and who should stay.

The Feinn altogether wished to go. Fionn was not willing to go, for fear the place should be taken out before they should come (back). "I will not go," said Fionn. "Whether thou goest or stayest, we will go," said they.

The rest went, but Fionn did not go. They stopped, on the night when they went, at the root of a tree; they made a booth, and they began to play at cards. Said Fionn, when the rest were gone, "I put him from amongst heroes and warriors any man that will follow me out." They followed after Fionn. They saw a light before them, and they went forward where the light was. Who were here but the others playing at cards, and some asleep; and it was a fine frosty night. Fionn hailed them so stately and bravely. When they heard the speaking of Fionn, those who were laid down tried to rise, and the hair was stuck to the ground. They were pleased to see their master. Pleasant to have a stray hunting night. They went home. Going past a place where they used to house, they saw a house. They asked what house was that. They told them there was the house of a hunter. They reached the house, and there was but a woman within, the wife of the fine green kirtle. She said to them, "Fionn, son of Cumal, thou art welcome here." They went in. There were seven doors to the house. Fionn asked his gillies to sit in the seven doors. They did that. Fionn and his company sat on the one side of the house to breathe. The woman went out. When she came in, she said, "Fionn, son of Cumal, it is long since I was wishing thy welfare, but its little I can do for thee to-night. The son of the king of the people of Danan is coming here, with his eight hundred full heroes, this night." "Yonder side of the house be theirs, and this side ours, unless there come men of Eirinn." Then they came, and they sat within. "You will not let a man on our side," said Fionn, "unless there comes one that belongs to our own company." The woman came in again, saying, "The middle son of the king of the people of Danan is coming, and his five hundred brave heroes with him." They came, and more of them staid without on a knoll. She came in again, saying, "The youngest son of the king of the people of Danan is coming, and his five hundred swift heroes with him." She came in again, saying, "That Gallaidh was coming, and five hundred full heroes."—"This side of the house be ours, and that be theirs, unless there come of the men of Eirinn." The people of Danan made seven ranks of themselves, and the fourth part of them could not cram in. They were still without a word. There came a gillie home with a boar that had found death from leanness and without a good seeming, and he throws that in front of Fionn with an insult. One of Fionn's gillies caught hold of him, and he tied his four smalls, and threw him below the board, and they spat on him. "Loose me, and let me stand up; I was not in fault, though it was I that did it, and I will bring thee to a boar as good as thou ever ate."—"I will do that," said Fionn; "but though thou shouldst travel the five-fifths of Eirinn, unless thou comest before the day comes, I will catch thee." They loosed him; he went away, and gillies with him. They were not long when they got a good boar. They came with it, and they cooked it, and they were eating it. "A bad provider of flesh art thou," said Gallaidh to Fionn. "Thou shalt not have that any longer to say;" and the jawbone was in his hand. He raised the bone, and he killed seven men from every row of the people of Danan, and this made them stop. Then a gillie came home, and the black dog of the people of Danan with him, seeking a battle of dogs. Every one of them had a pack of dogs, and a dozen in every pack. The first one of them went and slipped the first dozen. The black dog killed the dozen; he killed them by the way of dozen and dozen, till there was left but Bran in loneliness. Said Fionn to Conan, "Let slip Bran, and, unless Bran makes it out, we are done." He loosed him. The two dogs began at each other. It was not long till Bran began to take driving; they took fear when they saw that; but what was on Bran but a venomous claw. There was a golden shoe on the claw of Venom, and they had not taken off the shoe. Bran was looking at Conan, and now Conan took off the shoe; and now he went to meet the black dog again; and at the third "spoch" he struck on him; he took his throat out. Then he took the heart and the liver out of his chest. The dog took out to the knoll; he knew that foes were there. He began at them. A message came in to Fionn that the dog was doing much harm to the people without. "Come," said Fionn to one of the gillies, "and check the dog." The gillie went out, and (was) together with the dog; a message came in that the gillie was working worse than the dog. From man to man they went out till Fionn was left within alone. The Feen killed the people of Danan altogether. The lads of the Feen went out altogether, and they did not remember that they had left Fionn within. When the children of the king saw that the rest were gone, they said that they would get the head of Fionn and his heart. They began at him, and they drove him backwards till he reached a crag of rock. At the end of the house he set his back to it, and he was keeping them off. Now he remembered the dream

He was tightly tried. Fionn had the "Ord Fianna," and when he was in extremity it would sound of itself, and it would be heard in the five-fifths of Eirinn. The gillies heard it; they gathered and returned. He was alive, and he was no more. They raised him on the point of their spears: he got better. They killed the sons of the king, and all that were alive of the people, and they got the chase as it ever was.

NA FEINNE.

BHA 'n Fhìnn uair agus cheileadh an t-seilg orra, 's cha robh fios aca dé dhianadh eud. Bha eud a' falbh feadh tragha as cladach a' cruinneachadh bhàirneach, 's feuch an aimscadh calman na feadag orra. Bha eud a' gabhail comhairle comhla airson gum falbhadh eud airson seilg fhaotainn. Ràinig eud cnoc 's thàinig cadal orra. Dé chunnaic Fionn ach bruadar, gur h' ann aig a' charragh chreig' ud shìos a bhiodh e 'n oidhche a b' fhaide leis a thig na 'thàinig. Gum biodh e 'ga iomain air ais gus an cuireadh e 'dhriom ris a' charragh chreige. Thug e leum as a chadal, 's bhuail e chas air bial Dhiarmaid, 's chuir e tri fiaclan as. Rug Diarmaid air cas Fhinn 's chuir e unnsa fala bhàr h' uile fìn' a bh' aige. "Ud dé rinn thu orm?" "De rinn thu fhin ormsa?" "Na gabh thusa mìothlachd a mhic mo pheathar; nur a dh' innseas mi duit an reusan cha gabh thu gu don' e." "De 'n reusan?" "Chunna mi bruadar gur h-ann aig a' charragh sin shìos a chuirinn seachad an oidhche bu doirbhe chuir mi riabh; gum bithinn air m' iomain air m' ais gus an cuirinn mo dhriom ris a' charragh, 's cha robh dol as an sin." "De 's eagal duinn? Co chuireadh eagal oirnn? Co thig?" arsa Diarmaid. "Tha eagal orm, a's sinn air anacothrom an drasd, ma leanas so gum fagar gun fheum sinn," arsa Fionn. Dh' fhalbh eud 's thilg eud croinn co dh' fhalbhadh 's co dh' fhanadh. Bha 'n Fhéinn uil' airson folbh. Cha robh Fionn deònach folbh, eagal gun d' thugt' amach an t-àite ma 'n d' thigeadh eud. "Cha n fholbh mi," ursa Fionn. "Còca dh' fholbhas na dh' fhanas thu falbhaidh sinne," ursa iadsan. Dh' fholbh càch, ach cha d' fholbh Fionn. Stad eud, an oidhche sin a dh' fholbh eud, aig bonn craoibhe. Rinn eud bùth agus thòisich eud air iomairt chairtean. Ursa Fionn nur dh' fholbh càch, "Tha mi 'ga chur a cuid laoich na gaisgich duine sam bith a leanas a mach mi. Dh' fholbh eud as déigh Fhinn. Chunnaic eud solusd rompa. Ghabh eud air an aghaidh far an robh 'n solusd. Co bha 'n so ach càch a' cluichd air chairtean, 's oidhche bhriagh reothaidh ann. Chuir Fionn fàilt orra go flathail, fialaidh. Nur a chual eud bruidhinn Fhinn thug an fheadhain a bha na'n laidhe làmh air éiridh, 's bha 'n gruag air leantail ris a' ghrunnd. Bha eud toilicht' am maighstir fhaicinn. Taitneach còrr oidhche seilg fhaotainn, chaidh eud thun a' bhaile. 'Dol seachad air àite 'b' àbhaist daibh a bhi tighich chunnaic eud tigh, dh' fheoraich eud dé 'n tigh a bha 'n siud. Thuirt eud riu gun robh tigh sealgair. Ràinig eud an tigh, 's cha robh stigh ach boireannach. Bean a chòta chaoil uaine. Urs' i riu, "Fhinn Mhic Cumhail 'se do bheatha an so." Chaidh eud a stigh. Bha seachd dorsan air an tigh. Dh' iarr Fionn air a ghillean suidhe ann an seachd dorsan an tighe. Rinn eud sin. Shuidh Fionn 'sa chuideachd san darna taobh de n tigh a ligeil an analach. Chaidh a' bhean a mach. Nur a thàinig i stigh thuirt i, "Fhinn Mhic Cumhail 's fhad' o'n a bha mi 'g altachadh le slàinte dhuit, ach 's beag is urra mi dheanadh riut a nochd; tha mac righ sluagh de Danainn a' tighinn an so a nochd agus ochd ciad làn ghaisgeach aige." "An taobh ud de 'n tigh acasan, 'san taobh so againne, mar an d' thig e dh' fhearaibh Eirinn." Thàinig eud an sin 's shuidh eud a stigh. "Cha lig sibh duin' air ar taobhne," ursa Fionn, "mar an d' thig duine 'bhoineas d'ar cuideachd fhìn. Thàinig a' bhean a stigh a rithisd ag ràdh. "Tha mac miadhonach righ Sluagh de Dana 'tighinn agus còig ciad treun ghaisgeach aige." Thàinig eud 's dh' fhan còrr dhiu mach air cnoc. Tháinig i stigh a rithisd ag ràdh, "Tha mac is òige righ Sluagh de Dana tighinn agus còig ciad lùgh-ghaisgeach leis." Thàinig i stigh a ris ag ràdh gun robh Gallaidh a' tighinn agus còig ciad làn ghaisgeach leis. "An taobh so' n tigh againne, 's an taobh sin acasan, mar an d' thig e dh' fhearaibh Eirinn," arsa Fionn. Rinn an Sluagh de Dana seachd streathan dhiu fhìn, 's cha do theachd an ceathramh cuid a stigh dhiu. Bha eud na 'n tàmh gun smid. Thàinig gille dachaidh le torc a fhuair bàs leis a' chaoile, gun sgath math, 's tilgear siud air bialthaobh Fhinn le tàmailt. Rug h-aon de ghillean Fhinn air agus cheanghail e cheithir chaoil; thilg e fo 'n bhòrd e 's bha eud a caitheadh smugaidean air. "Fuasgail mis' agus lig 'nam sheasamh mi, cha mhi bu choireach gad is mi rinn e, agus bheir mi go torc thu cho math 's a dh' ith thu riabh." "Ni mise sin," arsa Fionn, "ach gad a shiùbhla tu còig chòigeabh na h-Eireann, mar an d' thig thu man d' thig an latha, beiridh mis' ort." Dh' fhuasgail eud e. Dh' fhalbh e 's gillean leis. Cha b' fhada bha eud nur a fhuair eud deagh thorc. Thàinig eud leis, 's bhruich eud e, 's bha eud 'ga itheadh. "S dona 'm biataiche feòl' thu," ursa Gallaidh ri Fionn. "Cha bhi sin agadsa na 's fhaide r'a ràdh," arsa Fionn agus cnàimh a' chiobhuill aige 'na laimh. Chaith e 'n cnàimh, agus mharbh e seachd daoin' as gach streath de n t-Sluagh de Dana, agus chuir so eud 'nan stad. Thàinig gille an sin dachaidh, 's cù dugh Sluagh de Dana leis' aig iarraidh còmhrag chon. Bha lodhainn chon aig a' h-uile fear diusan, as dusan anns a' h-uile lodhainn, agus dh' fhalbh a' chiad fhear diu agus dh' fhuasgail e chiad dusan. Mharbh an cù dugh an dusan. Mharbh e eud a lìon dusan a's dusan, gus nach d' fhàgadh ach Bran 'na ònrachd. Ursa Fionn ri Conan, "Lig fuasgladh do Bhran, agus mar dian Bran deth e tha sin deth." Dh' fhuaisgail e e. Thòisich an da chù air a chéile. Cha b' fhada gos an do thòisich Bran air gabhail iomanach. Ghabh eud eagal nur a chunnaic eud sin; ach dé bha air Bran ach crudha nimhe. Bha bròg òir air a' crudha nimhe, 's cha d' thug eud deth a' bhròg. Bha Bran ag amharc air Conan; 's thug Conan deth a' nis a' bhròg. Chaidh e nis an dàil a' choin duigh a rìs, 's air an treas spoch a bhuail e air, thug e 'n sgòrnan as. Thug e 'n sin an cridhe 's an gruan a mach as an uchd aige. Ghabh an cù mach thun a' chnoic; dh' aithnich gur h-e naimhdean a bh' ann; thòisich e orra. Thàinig brath a stigh go Fionn, gon robh 'n cù dianadh mòran cron air an t-sluagh a muigh. "Thalla," ursa Fionn, ri fear de na gillean, "agus caisg an cù." Chaidh an gille mach comhla ris a' chù. Thàinig brath a stigh gon robh an gille 'g obair na bu mhiosa na 'n cù. O fhear go fear chaidh eud a mach gos an d' fhàgadh Fionn a stigh 'na ònrachd. Mharbh an Fhìnn an Sluagh de Danainn uile. Dh' fhalbh gillean na Fìnne mach uile, 's cha do chuimhnich eud gun d' fhàg eud Fionn a stigh. Nur a chunnaic clann an righ gon d' fhalbh càch air fad 'thuirt eud gom faigheadh eud ceann Fhìnn 'sa chridhe. Thòisich eud air, agus dh' iomain eud air ais e 'gos an d' ràinig e carragh creige aig ceaunn an tighe. Chuir e dhriom ris, 's bha e 'gan cumail deth. Chuimhnich e 'n so air a' bhruadar. Bha e air fheuchainn go teaunn. Bha aig

Fionn an t-òrd Fianna, 's nur a bhiodh e 'na éigin sheinneadh e leis fhìn, agus chluint' aunn an còig chòigeabh na h-Eireann e. Chual na gillean e; chruinnich eud 's thill eud. Bha e beò, 's cha robh tuillidh air. Thog eud e air bharraibh nan sleagh. Chaidh e 'na b' fheàrr. Mharbh eud mic an righ 's na bha beò d' an sluagh. Fhuair eud an t-seilg mur a bha i riabh.

This story is one of the kind usually called SEANACHAS NA FEINE,—that is, the tradition, conversation, or tale or old stories, or ancient history, history or biography (Macalpine) of the people, best known to English readers as the Fingalians. These are called by a collective name, and are spoken of as *the* Feen or Fain. They are generally represented as hunters and warriors in Eirinn, but their country is the Feen. Bran's battle and his venomous claw in a golden shoe, is more like the fight of a tiger or cheetah than an Irish deer-hound.

The people of Danan are called Tuatha de danan, in manuscripts and books, and are supposed to be Scandinavians. The name, by a slight change in pronunciation, might mean the daring Northerns, the tenants of Danan, or the people of Danan, as here. Fionn, in various inflections, is pronounced Feeun, Een, Eeun. ORD FIANNA would seem to mean hammer of the Feean; if so, Fin may have acquired some of his gear of Thor, or he may be the same personage. The "ord Fiannar" is generally supposed to be a whistle, which sounded of itself, and was heard over the five-fifths of Erin.

This tale, and No. 24, 25, 26, 27, and the two which follow, were told to Hector MacLean "by four individuals, ALEXANDER MACDONALD, tenant, Barra, BAILEBHUIRGH, who heard them from his grandmother, Mary Gillies, about forty years ago, when she was more than eighty; NEILL MACLEAN, tenant, ditto, who learnt them from Donald MacNeill, who died about five years ago, about eighty years of age; JOHN CAMERON, ditto, who heard them from many, but cannot name any in particular. They state that these tales were very common in their younger days. They are pretty common still. They can tell nothing respecting the tales beyond the persons from whom they learnt them; of those from whom they learnt them they know nothing."

There are numerous prose tales of the Fingalians in Gaelic manuscripts, now in the Advocates' Library in Edinburgh (according to an abstract lent by W. F. Skene, Esq.) One is probably the same as this tale; it is No. 4 of the manuscript numbered 4, called THE BOOTH OF EOCHAIDH DEARG—a tale of Fingal decoyed into a tent, and his combats with monsters, giants, armies, etc.

Of this manuscript the author of the abstract, Ewen MacLachlan, says (1812):—"This volume is evidently a transcript, perhaps not older than half a century. The language bespeaks high antiquity."

With the exception of a few words, the language in this Barra tale is the ordinary language of the people of the island. It seems then, that this is a remnant of an old tale, rapidly fading from memory and mixing with the manners of the day, but similar to tales in manuscripts about one hundred years old, and to tales now told in Ireland. See Poems of Ossin, Bard of Erin, 1857.

XXX.

THE TWO SHEPHERDS.

THERE were out between Lochaber and Baideanach two shepherds who were neighbours to each other, and the one would often be going to see the other. One was on the east side of a river, and another on the west. The one who was on the west side of the river came to the house of the one who was on the east of it on an evening visit. He staid till it was pretty late, and then he wished to go home. "It is time to go home," said he. "It is not that which thou shalt do, but thou shalt stay to-night," said the other, "since it is so long in the night." "I will not stay at all events; if I were over the river I don't care more." The houseman had a pretty strong son, and he said, "I will go with thee, and I will set thee over the river, but thou hadst better stay."—"I will not stay at all events."—"If thou wilt not stay I will go with thee." The son of the houseman called a dog which he had herding. The dog went with him. When he set the man on the other side of the river, the man said to him, "Be returning now, I am far in thy debt." The strong lad returned, and the dog with him. When he reached the river as he was returning back home, he was thinking whether he should take the stepping-stones, or put off his foot-clothes and take below. He put off his foot-clothes for fear of taking the stepping-stones, and when he was over there in the river, the dog that was with him leaped at the back of his head. He threw her off him; she leaped again; he did the same thing. When he was on the other side of the river, he put his hand on his head, and there was not a bit of a bonnet on it. He was saying, whether should he return to seek the bonnet, or should he go home without it. "It's disgusting for me to return home without my bonnet; I will return over yet to the place where I put my foot-clothes off me; I doubt it is there that I left it." So he returned to the other side of the river. He saw a right big man seated where he had been, and his own bonnet in his hand. He caught hold of the bonnet, and he took it from him. "What business hast thou there with that?—It is mine, and thou hadst no business to take it from me, though thou hast got it." Over the river then they went, without a word for each other, fiercely, hatingly. When they went over, then, on the river, the big man put his hand under the arm of the shepherd, and he began to drag the lad down to a loch that was there, against his will and against his strength. They stood front to front, bravely, firmly on either side. In spite of the strength of the shepherd's son, the big man was about to conquer. It was so that the shepherd's son thought of putting his hand about an oak tree that was in the place. The big man was striving to take him with him, and the tree was bending and twisting. At last the tree was loosening in the earth. She loosened all but one of her roots. At the time when the last root of the tree slipped, the cocks that were about the wood crowed. The shepherd's son understood that when he heard the cocks crowing that it was on the short side of day. When they heard between them the cocks crowing, the big man said, "Thou has stood well, and thou hadst need, or thy bonnet had been dear for thee." The big man left him, and they never more noticed a thing near the river.

AN DA CHIOBAIR.

BHA, mach eadar Lochabar agus Bàideanach, da chìobair a bha 'nan nàbaidhean aig a chéile, 's bhiodh an darna fear, gu bicheanta, dol a dh' amharc an fhir eile. Bha fear air taobh na h-aird an iar de 'n abhainn, 's fear eile air taobh na h-aird an ear. Thàinig am fear a bh' air taobh na h-aird an iar de 'n abhainn 'ionnsuidh tigh an fhir a bh' air taobh na h-aird an ear di, air cheilidh. "Dh' fhan e gos an robh e go math anmoch, 's bha e 'n sin deònach air dol dachaidh. "Tha 'n t-am dol dachaidh," urs' esan. "Cha 'ne sin a ni thu ach fanaidh tu nochd," urs' am fear eile, "on a tha e cho fada 's an oidhche." "Cha 'n fhan mi codhiu ; na 'm bithinn thar na h-abhann tha mi coma tuillidh." Bha mac go math làidir aig fear an tighe 's thuirt e, "Théid mise leat 's cuiridh mi thar na h-aibhne thu ; ach 's fheàrra duit fantail." "Cha 'n fhan mi codhiu." "Mar am fan falbhaidh mise leat." Dh' eubh mac fir an tighe air galla 'bh' aig' a' ciobaireachd. Dh' fhalbh a' ghalla leis. Nur a chuir e null an duin' air an taobh eile de 'n abhainn thuirt an duine ris. "Bi tilleadh a nis tha mi fad ann a'd' chomain." Thill an gille làidir agus a' ghalla comhla ris. Nur a ràinig e 'n abhainn, agus e tilleadh air ais dachaidh, bha e smaointeachadh còca a ghabhadh e na sìnteagan, na chuireadh e dheth a chaisbheart agus a ghabhadh e go h-ìseal. Chur e dheth a chaisbheart eagal na sìnteagan a ghabhail, 's nur a bha e null anns an abhainn, leum a' ghalla bha leis ann an cùl a chinn. Thilg e deth i. Leum i rithisd. Rinn e 'n ni cianda. Nur bha e 'n taobh thall de 'n abhainn, chuir e làmh air a cheann, 's cha robh spìdeag de 'n bhoinneid air. Bha e 's an ag a gradh còca thilleadh e dh' iarraidh no boinneid, na rachadh e dhachaidh as a h' ioghnais. "'S ceacharra domh fhìn gun till mi dachaidh gun mo bhoinneid ; tillidh mi null fhathasd gos an àite an do chuir mi dhiom mo chaisbheart ; 's ann ann a tha amharus agam a dh' fhàg mi i." Thill e 'n so go taobh thaull na h-aibhne. Chunnaic e fear ro mhòr 'na shuidhe far an robh e, 'sa bhoinneid fhìn 'na làimh. Rug e air a' bhoinneid 's thug e uaidh' i. "Dé do ghnothach sa ris a sin?" "Mo chuid fhìn a th' ann, 's nach robh gnothach agadsa toirt uam, gad a tha i agad." Null, an sin, thar an abhainn dh' fhalbh eud, 's gun facal aca r'a chéile, go fiachach fuachach. Nur a chaidh eud a null, an sin, air an abhainn chuir am fear mòr a làmh fo achlais a' chìobair, 's thòisich e air a' ghille a tharuinn a sìos gu loch a bha 'n sin, an aghaidh a thoil 's an aghaidh a neart. Sheas eud aghaidh ri aghaidh, go treun calm' air gach taobh. A dh' aindeoin cho làidir 's a bha mac a' chìobair bha 'm fear mòr a' brath buadhachadh. 'Se smaointich mac a' chìobair a nis a làmh a chur timchioll air craobh dharaich a bha 'san àite. Bha 'm fear mòr a' strìth ra thoirt leis, 's bha chraobh a' lùbadh 's a' fàsgadh. Fo dheireadh bha chraobh a' fuasgladh as an talamh. Dh' fhuasgail i ach aon fhreumhach di. 'San am an d' fhuasgail an fhreumhach ma dheireadh de 'n chraoibh, ghairm na coilich a bha feadh na coille. Thuig mac a' chìobair, nur a chual e na coilich a' gairm, gon robh e air an taobh ghoirid de 'n latha. Nur a chual eud eatorra na coilich a' gairm thuirt am fear mòr, "'S math a sheas thu, 's bha feum agad air, airneo, bhiodh do bhoinneid daor duit." Dhealaich am fear mòr ris, 's cha d' fhairich eud sgath riabh tuillidh a chòir na n-aibhne.

There is a bogle story in W. Grant Stewart's "Highland Superstitions" (published 1823 and 1851), in which a man is dragged towards a river by a supernatural being, whom he kills with his dirk.

2. I have another story like this, which was sent to me by a young gentleman, a member of the Ossianic Society of Glasgow. It has some likeness to No. 28, The Smith, and is a good illustration of this part of popular mythology. When the people of Kintyre, Muintir Chean tireadh were coming home from the northern airt from fighting against Prince Charles, under their chieftain, the man of Skipnish, they were going together, each band that was nearest as neighbours. So one little company staid behind the great band, in Cean loch gilp, Lochgilphead. The one who was hindmost of this company, who was called by the nickname of Ian Dubh Mor, Big Black John, heard an unearthly noise, when he was come in front of a fall that was at

A MHAOIL DUBH, on the northern side of TAIRBAIRT CHEANTIREADH, Tarbert (which may be rendered Land's-end drawboat.)

He went on, and in a burn below the fall, a terrible being met him; he drew his blade. Said the being to him, "Strike me." "I will not strike, thou monster," said John; but BRODAIDH MI THU, "I will prod thee."

"Prod me," the being would say. "I will not prod thee, monster, but I will strike thee," John would say.

They fought thus for a great time till the cock crew; and the being said to Ian, "Thou wilt now be going, but before thou goest, take thy choice of the two following things—EALAN GUN RATH NO, RATH GUN EALAIN, speechless art, or artless speech."

John chose speechless art, and so it happened. He was a blacksmith, as skilful as ever drew hammer on anvil; but he was not much better for that; there was no penny he earned that he would not spoil, and that would not go in some way that was not easily explained. As an instance of art, he could mend a saw, though thou hadst a bit in either hand, in such a way that it could not be seen where it was broken; and a gun in the same way. There would be a covering on the smithy windows when he would be mending such things.

Big Black John got great power over witchcraft, BUITSEACHAS, and evil eye.

There was a man in Skipnish who had made money by smuggling, but he began to lose his money, for his malt refused to yield its product, till at last he lost the whole of what he had made; and he was a poor man. He went at last to IONARAIR, Ayr, where John was dwelling at that time. John told him that it was enmity that was doing the ill. He did not learn who was spoiling him. He said to him, "Go home and thou wilt get back the produce of the malt;" and so he did. Each TOGAIL (mashing) he made began to give more than the other, till the produce he got frightened him. He followed on thus till the loss was made up, and after that he got but the usual product.

The following are stories of the same kind. The prevailing notions are, that supernatural beings exist which cannot withstand the power of iron, and that there are men and women who deal with them. These are from Mr. Hector Urquhart, written in English, and given in his own words.

3. One day last week, as I was walking up Glenfyne, I overtook an old man who was carting coals up to the Lodge. "Good

day to you, John." "Good day to yourself," says John. From good days to showery days, I asked John if there was any virtue in iron against witchcraft or fairy spells. "Indeed, and that's what there is," says John. So, when we came to the Lodge, I wrote the following story from his telling :—"On a certain year and me a young lad, all our cows lost the milk, one after one; we guessed what was wrong with them, and my big brother lost no time in going to Appin, to consult the man of the RED BOOK. He no sooner entered his house than the man told him what moved him from home. 'It's your own neighbour's wife,' says he, 'that spoilt your cows; she is this moment in your house, inquiring whether you went from home to-day, and where did you go to ; and to make it double sure to you, that it's her who spoilt your cows, she will meet you under the lintel of your door coming out as you are going in. Go you now home, and take a shoe of an entire horse, and nail it to your byre-door ; but let no living person know of it.'

"My brother came home, and as the man of the red book told him, this identical woman met him on the threshold as he was going in to the house. I do not know how he managed to get hold of the laird's stallion, but the shoe was nailed on our byre door before sunrise next morning, so our cows had plenty milk from that day forth."

4. "This must be a wonderful book, John," says I ; "do you know how this man came to have it?" "Well," says John, "I'll tell you that."

"Once upon a time, there lived a man at Appin, Argyllshire, and he took to his house an orphan boy. When the boy was grown up, he was sent to herd ; and upon a day of days, and him herding, there came a fine gentleman where he was, who asked him to become his servant, and that he would give him plenty to eat and drink, clothes, and great wages. The boy told him that he would like very much to get a good suit of clothes, but that he would not engage till he would see his master ; but the fine gentleman would have him engaged without any delay ; this the boy would not do upon any terms till he would see his master. 'Well,' says the gentleman, 'in the meantime write your name in this book.' Saying this, he put his hand into his oxter pocket, and pulling out a large red book, he told the boy to write his name in the book. This the boy would not do ; neither would he tell his name, till he would acquaint his master first.

'Now,' says the gentleman, 'since you will neither engage, or tell your name, till you see your present master, be sure to meet me about sunset to-morrow, at a certain place.' The boy promised that he would be sure to meet him at the place about sunsetting. When the boy came home he told his master what the gentleman said to him. 'Poor boy,' says he, 'a fine master he would make; lucky for you that you neither engaged nor wrote your name in his book; but since you promised to meet him, you must go; but as you value your life, do as I tell you.' His master gave him a sword, and at the same time he told him to be sure and be at the place mentioned a while before sunset, and to draw a circle round himself with the point of the sword in the name of the Trinity. 'When you do this, draw a cross in the centre of the circle, upon which you will stand yourself; and do not move out of that position till the rising of the sun next morning.' He also told him that he would wish him to come out of the circle to put his name in the book; but that upon no account he was to leave the circle; 'but ask the book till you would write your name yourself, and when once you get hold of the book keep it, he cannot touch a hair of you head, if you keep inside the circle.'

"So the boy was at the place long before the gentleman made his appearance; but sure enough he came after sunset; he tried all his arts to get the boy outside the circle, to sign his name in the red book, but the boy would not move one foot out of where he stood; but, at the long last, he handed the book to the boy, so as to write his name therein. The book was no sooner inside the circle than it fell out of the gentleman's hand inside the circle; the boy cautiously stretches out his hand for the book, and as soon as he got hold of it, he put it in his oxter. When the fine gentleman saw that he did not mean to give him back the book, he got furious; and at last he transformed himself into a great many likenesses, blowing fire and brimstone out of his mouth and nostrils; at times he would appear as a horse, other times a huge cat, and a fearful beast (uille bheast); he was going round the circle the length of the night; when day was beginning to break he let out one fearful screech; he put himself in the likeness of a large raven, and he was soon out of the boy's sight. The boy still remained where he was till he saw the sun in the morning, which no sooner he observed, than he took to his soles home as fast as he could. He gave the book to his master; and this is how the far-famed red book of Appin was got."

I have heard many old people say that they went from all parts to consult the red book of Appin, though this is the best story I heard about it. You ask if there were virtue in iron; you must know that iron was the principal safeguard against evil spirits, etc., etc.; which I shall show in my next letter on the fairies.

5. The next is from the telling of a dancing master, a north country Highlander, and written by my friend Mr. John Campbell of Kilberry, in Argyllshire. The supernatural being described as Bauchan, is probably BOCAN, a little buck, a hobgoblin, a ghost, a sprite, spectre (Armstrong and other Dic.); and he seems but a half-tamed specimen of the same genus as the terrible being before described.

COLUINN GUN CHEANN, The Headless Trunk. Coluinn gun Cheann was a very celebrated Bauchkan, who favoured the family of the Macdonals of Morar, for ages immemorial, and was frequently seen about their residence, Morar House; which is situated on the main land, opposite the point of Slaate, in the Island of Skye. Though a protector of the family, he was particularly hostile to the neighbourhood, and waged war, especially with all the strong men he could meet with; for this purpose he particularly haunted the "Mile Reith," or "Smooth Mile," one end of which was not above 200 yards from the Mansion (I know the place well); the other end of the Mile terminated at a large stream, called the River Morar, famed in history for salmon fishing; after sunset, people did wisely to avoid that part, for then the "COLUINN GUN CHEANN" was sure to keep his vigils; and any stray man who passed was sure to become a victim, the bodies being always found dead, and in the majority of instances mutilated also. As he took care never to appear, except to a solitary passenger, it was in vain to send a party against him. He was seldom, if ever, seen by women, and did no harm either to them or to children. Once it happened that a distant relative, but intimate friend *of Raasay's*, dared his fate, and remained a victim on the ground. This came to the ears of "IAN GARBH, MACGILLIE CHALLUM, RAASAY," "Big John, the son of M'Leod of Raasay;" he was celebrated for his prowess and strength, and never had been vanquished in any fight, though he had tried with the strongest. He told his step-mother of the news he had heard from the Mainland, and asked her advice, as he usually did, before he undertook any exploit of the kind. She advised him to go, and avenge the blood of his friend. After his preparations were made, and not without a blessing from the Oracle, he set out on his circuitous journey, and met the "COLUINN" after sunset, on the Mile Reith, and a battle did ensue, and I daresay it was a very stiff one. Before sunrise it was necessary for the Coluinn to be off, as he never could be seen in daylight. Whether finding he made no progress discouraged him or not, we can't say, but Ian got the victory. Being determined to get a sight of the Coluinn, and also to prove his victory to others, Ian tucked him under his arm, to carry him to the nearest light. The Coluinn had never been heard to speak; but being in this predicament, called out, "LEIG AS MI," "Let me go." "CHA LEIG MI AS THU," "I will not let thee go." Leig as mi, he repeated; but still the answer was Cha leig mi as thu. "Leig as mi, agus chan fheachear an so mi gu brath tuileadh." "Let me go, and I shall never be seen here any more." "Ma bhoidachais thu air a leobhar, air a chonail, agus air a stocaidh dhubh, bi falbh.' "If thou swear that on the book, on the candle, and on the black stocking, begone!" After making the Coluinn promise this on his knees, Ian liberated him. The Coluinn flew off, singing the following doleful words—"S fada uam fein bonn beinn Hederin, s fada uam fein bealach a bhorbhan," which we can only translate by—

"Far from me is the hill of Ben Hederin,
Far from me is the pass of murmuring."

This lament was repeated as long as Ian could hear, and these words are still sung by women in that country to their children, to the following notes, which tradition says was the very air:—

In the next, from the same source, the same being appears fully tamed; still supernatural, still possessed of extraordinary strength, but attached to a family, and a regular brownie.

6. In the neighbourhood of Loch Traig, in Lochaber, Callum Mor MacIntosh held a little farm. There were rumours of his having intercourse with a mysterious personage called a bauchan, but of his first acquaintance with him there are no authentic accounts. One thing, however, is certain, that on some occasions he was supernaturally aided by this bauchan, while at others, having in some way excited his displeasure, Callum was opposed in all his schemes, and on several occasions they came the length of fighting hand to hand, Callum never suffering much injury. On one occasion, as Callum was returning from Fort-William market, he met his friend the bauchan within a short distance of his own house, and one of these contests took place, during which Callum lost his pocket-handkerchief, which, having been blessed and presented to him by the priest, was possessed of a peculiar charm. The fight being ended, Callum hurried home; but, to his dismay, found that he had lost his charmed handkerchief, for which he and his wife in vain sought. Callum felt certain he had to thank the bauchan for this mishap, and hurried back to the scene of action. The first object that met his view was the bauchan, busily engaged in rubbing a flat stone with the identical handkerchief. On seeing Callum, he called out, "Ah! you are back; it is well for you, for if I had rubbed a hole into this before your return you were a dead man. No doctor on earth or power could save you; but you shall never have this handkerchief till you have won it in a fair fight." "*Done*," said Callum, and at it they went again, and Callum recovered his handkerchief. Peats were almost unknown at that time, and Callum, when the weather grew cold, took his axe, and felled a large birch tree in the neighbouring forest, the branches supplied wood for the fire for several days, and Callum did not trouble himself to lay in a store nearer hand—when, lo! a snow storm came on, and blocked up the country, so that he was cut off from his supply. There was no means of access to the tree; and careful as Callum's wife was, the last branch was almost consumed,

and the fire burnt low. Up started Callum with an exclamation, "Oh! wife, would that we had the tree I felled in the forest! it would keep us warm this night." Hardly had he spoken when the house was shaken and the door rattled; a heavy weight had fallen near the door. Callum rushed to see what the cause was, and there was the wished-for tree, with the Bauchan grinning at him—"S ma am Bauchan fathast, ged a sgain an Sagart"—(the Bauchan is still kind, though the Priest should burst)—said the wife. On another occasion it happened that Callum left the farm he was in and went to one adjoining which he had taken carrying with him his wife and all his furniture. In the night-time Callum turned to his wife and said, "Well, it is well we have all with us; only one thing have we forgotten, the hogshead in which the hides are being barked; *that* we have forgotten." "No matter for that," said the wife; "there is no one to occupy the place yet a while, and we have time to get it home safe enough;" and so the matter rested; but on going round the end of the house next morning, what did Callum see but his own identical hogshead, hides and all. It had been transported the distance of five miles of most rugged, rocky district. None but a goat could have crossed the place, and in the time it would have bothered one to do it, but the Bauchan managed it, and saved Callum a most troublesome journey. If you will go and take a look at it—the spot is there yet—and I would like to see how soon you would manage it, let alone the hogshead.

Poor Callum, however, was obliged, with many of his neighbours, to leave Lochaber; indeed, he was amongst the first embarking at Arisaig for New York. The passage was a tedious one, but it ended at last, and without any particular adventures; but on arriving they had to perform a quarantine of many days. On getting pratique, Callum was in the first boat which landed, and happened to have stowed himself in the bows of the boat, and when she grounded, was the first man to jump on shore. Directly his feet touched the ground, who should meet him in the shape of a goat but the Bauchan, "Ha, ha Callum, ha mi sho air thoseach orst." Ha, Malcolm, I am here before thee. Here ends our story; but rumour says that Callum was the better of the Bauchan's help in clearing the lands of his new settlement, and that, till he was fairly in the way of prosperity, the Bauchan abstained from teasing and provoking poor Callum.

The next makes the supernatural beings robbers, and is a further argument in favour of the theory that all these traditions are fictions founded on fact; recollections of wild savages living in mountain fastnesses, whose power, and strength, and cavern dwellings were enlarged and distorted into magic arts, gigantic stature, and the under-ground world. I translate the story from Gaelic, written by Hector MacLean from the telling of JOHANNA MACCRIMMON in Berneray, August 1859. This woman is a native of Skye, and descended from the celebrated pipers. Her father, grandfather, and uncles were pipers. She learned the story from her grand-uncle Angus MacCrimmon.

7. A gentleman had AIREACH, a herd's dwelling, and he was out in a far-off glen long in the year with his herd women and his calf herd. They had every man they needed, and they were there till the middle of summer was. Then the herd woman said that she must go to seek things that she wanted.

The herd woman went away, and she had a great distance to go before she should reach the farm.

She said to the herd, in spite of the length of the path, that she would try to be back that night. When the evening was coming, the herd was wearying that the herd woman was not coming. Then he put the cattle to rights AGUS BHLIGH E EUD, and he milked them, and there were wild showers of snow in the beginning of the night. He went home when the beginning of night was, and he set in order his own food, after he had taken a thought—DUIL A THOIRT DETH—that the herd woman would not come. He took his foods and he shut the door as well as he could, thinking that no man would come near him that night. He put NA BEAIRTEAN FRAOICHE (the bundles of heather) behind the CÒMHLA (door),* and then he sat to toast himself at the fire because the SIDE (weather) was so cold. He was taking his dinner there, when he heard a great TARTAR (noise) coming towards the door. Then he got up from the door with great fear, and he noticed a being striking the door again. He was thinking, and he did not know what to do, that if the door were struck a third time it would be in.

---

* It is quite common in Highland cottages to keep a large bundle of heather or brushwood to stuff into the doorway on the windward side; sometimes it is the sole door.

He got up, and the door was struck a third time. Then he crouched in a corner at the lower end of the shealing when he saw the door being driven in.

He did not know now whether he should stay as he was or hide himself. When he noticed the door being pushed in, there came in a beast, and she went up to the fire.

The heather took fire and he saw this nasty beast standing at the fire. And she had a great long hair, and that creature was—A CNAMH A CIR—chewing the cud, as though there were a sheep or a cow. The horns that were on her were up to the top of the shealing. The poor man that was within thought that it was time for him to take his legs along with him, and he went out through the night and the winnowing and snow in it.

He found one of the horses, and he reached his master's house before the day came. Here there he struck in the door of his master furiously, and his master awoke and he went where he was, and he told his master the UAMHAS—terrible wonder that had come upon him since the herd woman left him.

The master went, and the eldest son he had and himself, and they took a gun with them. They went as fast as they could to try to catch the beast to kill her. There was the worth of much money in the shealing, and they thought it a loss that they should want it. Then when they were coming near the shealing the gentleman put a charge in the gun, to be all ready—DEISEAL.—(This word is said to be derived from South—about the old practice being to make a turn sun-wise before doing anything of importance).

They reached the shealing, and they let off a shot in. Though he let off the shot he did not notice a thing, and fear would not let one of them search within. They were thus at the door and they perceived the beast showing herself out. It was hardly that she dragged herself out of the door of the shealing.

There out went they—the gentleman and his son! They went in such a great perturbation, that they did not remember the horses; but they stretched out on foot, fleeing before the beast that was there. What but that the beast followed after them till they reached the house, and they thought she would have finished them before they should arrive. When they reached the farm, one of the gentlemen's men met him, and the gentleman told him that he was almost dead at all events, that he had hopes of reaching the house, and that he should go to try to meet the beast, and keep her back a space.

The man went to meet the beast that was here, and she full of the snow; and he looked keenly at her. He returned to his master to tell him what sort of beast it was, and he said, "Come out here that you may come and see the beast."

When they went out to see the beast, what was here but the buck goat, full of the snow, and the master was shamed that he should have fled from the like of that beast.

The herd fled by the way of the banks of the shore; when he saw his master running away, and they had no tale of him. Three of the servants were sent about the glen to try if they could find him; and they were not finding him at all.

He was lost thus for three days and three nights, and they had no hope that they would find him for ever. On the third day he was going at the side of the shore, and water-horses and wild beasts coming on land on the shores. What should he fall in with but a dwelling-place there. He went in. There was no man there but a little russet man. The little russet man put welcome on him, and he asked him to come forward—that he was welcome. He asked of the little russet man what was the meaning of his staying in such a place, that there was no man with him.

"Oh," said the little russet man, "it is not allowed me to tell anything."

"I will tell thee," said the herd, "what sent me in here. It is that I fled from UAMHAS—a terrible wonder."

"This is the thing thou shalt do," said the little russet man. "Thou shalt stretch thyself on this bed up here, and thing or thing that thou seest in thy sleep, remember on thy death that thou dost not tell it."

Then when he went to stretch himself in the bed, what should meet him in the bed but the body of a man; and he took to trembling with fear, but he did not move. He thought he would stay as he was; that the dead man was not to touch him at all events. Then he heard great speaking coming towards the house; he was not long so till he noticed a great clatter coming, and what was this but—SEISEAR FEAR (collective singular noun of number, six man)—six men coming in and a cow with them. The master that was over the six, said to the little russet man, "Didst thou see or perceive a man coming this way since early earliness."

"I did not see," said he, "he might come the way unknown to me."

"Shut the door," said the big man, "and all without be they without, and all within within."

Then they put the cow on the fire in a great caldron after they had torn it asunder in quarters. When they had put this on the fire it was not long till they noticed the next clatter, and what was here but another band coming.

What should this band have but another cow flayed, and they had a pit within, and there they salted her. When the flesh that was in the kettle was cooked, they took their supper all together.

The poor man that was here in the bed did not know on earth what he should do for fear. Here when it was coming near on the mouth of the day, the little russet man went out to look what likeness was on the night.

When he came in, said they to him, "What seeming is on the night?" "There is a middling seeming," said he; but it is I who saw the terrible man DUINE FUATHASACH since I went out, as though he were listening to you. I think that it is FHUAMHAIR CHREIG DALLAIG the giant of crag dallag, who is there.

There out went every man of them, and the one that would not wait on his bow he would seize on his sword to kill him.

When the little russet man, who was within, thought that they had hurried well from the house, he said to the one who was in the bed, "Thou one that art up come down as fast as thou didst ever." Then he stretched to the poor man who was in the bed, as fast as ever he did, a stocking full of dollars, and he gave him bread aud cheese. "If thou ever didst it, do it now," said the little russet man to the herdsman. The herdsman went, and he reached the house of his master whole and healthy.

The moral of this tale seems to be, that he who runs away from fancied danger may fall into real peril; but what bears upon the theory of the origin of such stories is, that the *real* peril is from "water-horses" and "robbers," who have a little red (RUAGH) man who plays the part of the enchanted princess, and the friendly cat, and the woman who is the slave of the giants, and the robbers; the character which appears in all collections of popular tales to befriend the benighted stranger, or the wandering prince. And what is more, the *fancied* danger was from a creature under the form of a goat. Why a man should be frightened by a goat, appears from the last of following two stories, translated from the Gaelic of Hector Urquhart, and written from the telling of John Campbell in Strath-Gairloch, Ross-shire. He is now (1859) sixty-three.

8. At some time of the world the load of Gearloch TIGHEARNA GHEARLOCH had a CEATHEARNACH, who used to be slaying FUATHAN, bogles, and routing out the spoilers. The name of this stalwart man was UISTEAN MOR MAC GHILLE PHADRIG. Uistean was on a day hunting, and he saw a great wreath of mist above him, and heard the sweetest music he ever heard, but he was not seeing a thing but the mist itself. He cast a shot that was in his gun at the wreath of mist, and the very finest woman he ever saw fell down at his side. He took her with him to his own house, but there was not a word of speech in her; and she was thus for a year with him, and she never saw a thing that she could not do. And Uistean was thus in the mountain as usual slaying the bogles, FUATHAN, and on a day at the end of a year, and he in the mountain, the night come on him as he was coming home. There he saw a light in a hill; he reached where the light was, and he stood in the door, and NA SITHICHEAN, the fairies, were within making music and dancing, and the butler that they had going round about amongst them and giving them the drink. Uistean was looking at this: and the butler said, "It is a year from this night's night that we lost the daughter of Iarla Anndrum, the Earl of Antrim. She has the power of the draught on her that she does not speak a word, till she gets a drink from the cup that is in my hand. And the butler was going round about till he reached where Uistean was, and he gave the CORN (cup) to Uistean. No sooner got Uistean a hold of the cup in his hand than he took his soles out (of that), and they after him. They were here coming close to (shearing on) Uistean, and when they were come within sight of the town the cock crowed. One said, "It is as well for us to return;" but another said, "It is but BOGAG FOGHAIR, a Spring soft one." At the end of a while another cock crowed. "But it is time to return now; this is the black cock of March"—and they returned; but Uistean did not let go the cup till they reached his own house, and till he had given a draught to her from the cup, and as soon

as she had drunk a draught from the cup, she had speech as well as another. And Uistean went on the spot, back with the cup, and he left it on the hill; and when Uistean came back to his own house she told him that she was the daughter of the Earl of Antrim, and that the fairies had taken her from childbed. Uistean gave her two choices, whether would she rather stay by him, or be sent back to Eirinn; and she had rather go home. They went, and when they reached the house of the Earl of Antrim, she stayed in a little house that was near upon the castle for that night, and when they began to give them news, the housewife told them that the daughter of the Earl of Antrim was exceedingly ill, and that there was no leech in Eirinn that could do her good. Uistean said that he was the great doctor of the King of the Gaeldom, and that he would heal her, and that he would not ask payment till she should be healed.

The Earl was right well pleased his like to be come about, and it was told to the one who was on the bed, that a great Scottish doctor was come to her town that could cure her. But this did not please her at all, and she would not let him come near her. But Uistean said that he would go there though it was ill with her; and he went where she was, with his naked sword in his hand. She who was in the bed cast an eye on him, and she said, "If I had been to put my thumb on the apple of thy throat on the night that thou wert born, thou couldest not do this to me this day."

And when Uistean went to the bed, she went as a flame of fire out at the end of the house.

Then Uistean gave his own daughter by the hand to the Earl of Antrim, whole and healthy. The Earl of Antrim gave Uistean his two choices, that he should stay with him, or a bag of gold and go home. Uistean took the bag of gold, and he came home; and he began at killing Fuathan, as he was before.

This story joins Fairies and Fuathan, and has many relations in other languages, and the next joins the whole to the French Loup Garou, of which I heard from a peasant in France in November 1859, but the wolf is a goat in the Highlands.

9. Some time after this, word went to Uistean that there was a Fuath on TOMBUIDHE GHEARRLOCH on the yellow knoll of Gairloch, and this Fuath was killing much people, and sending others out of the husk (or the gates) of their hearts, A COCHAIL

AN CRIDHE, because no man could take the path after the night or darkness should come.

Uistean came, and on the way at the foot of the knoll Uistean went into the house of a yellow-footed weaver that was living there. Said the weaver to Uistean, "Thou hadst best stop the night."

"Well, I will do that," said Uistean; "I am going to kill the Fuath of Tombuidh to-night."

"Perhaps that is not so easy," said the weaver; "with what wilt thou kill Gabhair Mhoil-Bhui, the goat of Maol-buidh?"

"With the gun," said Uistean.

"What," said the weaver, "if the gun will not suit?"

"If it will not suit," said he, "I will try the sword on her."

"What," said the weaver, "if the sword will not come out of the sheath?"

"Well," said Uistean, "I will try my mother's sister on her."

And on every arm that Uistean named, the weaver laid ROSAD, a spell, but on the dirk which he called his mother's sister the weaver could not lay a spell. Then Uistean went up to the top of the knoll, and on the top of the knoll was a pit in which the goat used to dwell.

She let out a MEIGAID bleat, and Uistean said, "Dost thou want thy kid thou skulker?"

"If I do, I have got it now," said she. Then Uistean laid hands on his gun, but she would not give a spark. Then he laid hands on his sword, but it would not come out of the sheath. "Where now is thy mother's sister?" said the goat.

When Uistean heard this he sprang on the goat, and the first thrust he gave her with the BIODAG dirk, she let out a roar.

"It seems odd to me, poor beast, if I do not give thy kid milk now."

And he did not see the goat any more. Uistean turned back to the weaver's house, and when he kindled a light, he found the weaver under the loom pouring blood.

"If it was thou who madest so much loss on the yellow knoll, thou shalt not get off any farther," said Uistean.

Then he killed the weaver under the loom, and no man was slain on the yellow knoll since then, by the goat or bogle.

These two stories are certain enough. It was by my mother I heard them, and many a tale there is of Uistean, if I had mind of them.

JOHN CAMPBELL, Strath Gairloch, Ross-shire.

10. I have another version of this same tale written by a school-master, at the request of Mr. Osgood Mackenzie. It is in very good Gaelic, but to translate it would be repetition, for it is almost the identical. I do not mention the name of the writer, for it might be displeasing to him. The narrator is Alexander Macdonald, Inverasdale. The goat is called GABHAR MHOR RHIBEAGACH FHEUSAGACH, a great hairy-bearded goat; and the dirk is called CATRIONA PUITHAR MO SHEANA MHATHAIR, Catherine, my grandmother's sister. He finds the BREABADAIR weaver in bed, with a wound in his thigh, and gives him his death thrust there.

I have given these specimens of a particular class of tales which are common enough, as they came to me, because they seem to be fair illustrations of the popular creed as to spirits; and to show that the so-called spirits are generally very near mortal men. My belief is, that bocan, bodach, fuath, and all their tribe, were once savages, dressed in skins, and that gruagach was a half-tamed savage hanging about the houses, with his long hair and skin clothing; that these have gradually acquired the attributes of divinities, river gods, or forest nymphs, or that they have been condemned as pagan superstitions, and degraded into demons; and I know that they are now remembered, and still somewhat dreaded, in their last character. The tales told of them partake of the natural and supernatural, and bring fiction nearer to fact than any class of tales current in the Highlands, unless it be the fairy stories of which a few are given under number 28, etc.

XXXI.

OSEAN AFTER THE FEEN.

From Barra.

OISEAN was an old man after the (time of the) Feen, and he (was) dwelling in the house of his daughter. He was blind, deaf, and limping, and there were nine oaken skewers in his belly, and he ate the tribute that Padraig had over Eirinn. They were then writing the old histories that he was telling them.

They killed a right big stag; they stripped the shank, and brought him the bone. "Didst thou ever see a shank that was thicker than that in the Feen?" "I saw a bone of the black bird's chick in which it would go round about."—"In that there are but lies." When he heard this, he caught hold of the books with rage, and he set them in the fire. His daughter took them out and quenched them, and she kept them. Ossian asked, with wailing, that the worst lad and dog in the Feen should lay weight on his chest. He felt a weight on his chest. "What's this?"—"I MacRuaghadh" (son of the red, or auburn one). "What is that weight which I feel at my feet?"—"There is MacBuidheig" (the son of the little yellow). They stayed as they were till the day came. They arose. He asked the lad to take him to such a glen. The lad reached the glen with him. He took out a whistle from his pocket, and he played it. "Seest thou anything going past on yonder mountain?"—"I see deer on it."—"What sort dost thou see on it?"—"I see some slender and grey on it."—"Those are the seed of the Lon Luath, swift elk; let them pass."—"What kind seest thou now?"—"I see some gaunt and grizzled."—"Those are the seed of Dearg dasdanach, the red Fierce: let them pass."—"What kind seest thou now?"—"I see some heavy and sleek."—"Let the dog at them Vic Vuiaig!" MacBhuieig went. "Is he dragging down plenty?"—"He is."—"Now, when thou seest that he has a dozen thou shalt check him." When he thought he had them, he played the whistle, and he checked the dog. "Now if the pup is sated with chase, he will come quietly, gently; if not, he will come with his gape open." He was coming with his gape open, and his tongue out of his mouth. "Bad is the thing which thou hast done to check the pup unsated with chase."—"When he comes, catch my hand, and try to put it in his gape, or he will have us." He put the hand of Oisean in his gape, and he shook his throat out. "Come, gather the stags to that knoll of rushes." He went, and that is done; and it was nine stags that were there, and that was but enough for Oisean alone; the lad's share was lost. "Put my two hands about the rushy knoll that is here;" he did that, and the great caldron that the Feen used to have was in it. "Now, make ready, and put the stags in the caldron, and set fire under it." The lad did that. When they were here ready to take it, Oisean said to him, "Touch thou them not till I take my fill first." Oisean began upon them, and as he ate each one, he took one of the skewers out of his belly. When Oisean had six eaten, the lad had three taken from him. "Hast thou done this to me?" said Oisean. "I did it," said he; "I would need a few when thou thyself hadst so many of them."—"Try if thou wilt take me to such a rock." He went down there, and he brought out the chick of a blackbird out of the rock. "Let us come to be going home." The lad caught him under the arm, and they went away. When he thought that they were nearing the house, he said, "Are we very near the house?" "We are," said the lad. "Would the shout of a man reach the house where we are just now?" *—"It would reach it."—"Set my front straight on the house." The lad did thus. When he was coming on the house, he caught the lad, and he put his hand in his throat, and he killed him. "Now," said he, "neither thou nor another will tell tales of me." He went home with his hands on the wall, and he left the blackbird's chick within. They were asking him where he had been since the day came; he said he had been where he had often passed pleasant happy days. "How didst thou go there when thou art blind?"—"I got a chance to go there this day at all events. There is a little pet yonder that I brought home, and bring it in." They went out to look, and if they went, there did not go out so many as could bring it home. He himself arose, and he brought it in. He asked for a knife. He caught the shank, he stripped it, and then took the flesh off it. He broke the two ends of the bone. "Get now the shank of the dun deer that you said I never saw the like of in the Feen." They got this for him, and he threw it out through the marrow hole. Now he was made truthful. They began to ask more tales from him, but it beat them ever to make him begin at them any more.

---

* A Lapp measure of distance is "a dog's bark."

OISEAN AN DEIGH NA FEINNE.

Bha Oisean 'na shean duin' an déigh na Fìnne 's e fuireachd an tigh a nighinne. Bha e daull, bodhar, bacach, 's bha naoidh deilg daraich 'na bhroinn, 's e 'g itheadh na càin a bh' aig Pàdraig air Eirinn. Bha eud an sin a' sgrìobhadh na seann eachdraidh a bha e 'g innseadh dhaibh. Mharbh eud damh ro mhòr; rùisg eud an calpa, 's thug eud a 'ionnsuidh an cnàimh. "A nis am faca tu calpa riabh a bu ghairbhe na sin 'san Fhìnn." "Chunna mi cnàimh isein an lòn duigh, 's rachadh e ma 'n cuairt an taobh a stigh dheth." "Cha n 'eil an sin ach na briagan." Nur a chual e so rug e air na leabhraichean le corraich, agus chuir e 'san tein' eud. Thug a nighean as an tein' eud, 's chuir i as eud, 's ghléidh i eud.

Dh' iarr Oisean de dh' achanaich an gill' agus an cù bu mhiosa bha 'san Fhìnn a chur cudthrom air uchd. Dh' fhairich e cudthrom air uchd. "Dé so?" "Mise Mac na Ruaghadh." "De 'n cudthrom ud a tha mi faotainn aig mo chasan?" "Tha Mac-Buidheig." Dh' fhan eud mur a bha eud gos an d' thàinig a latha. Nur a thàinig an latha dh' éiridh eud. Dh' iarr e air a ghille 'thoirt go leithid so de ghleann. Ràinig an gille an gleann leis. Thug e mach fìdeag a a phòca 's sheinn e i. "Am faic thu dad sam bith a dol seachad air an aonadh ud shuas?" "Chi mi féidh ann." Dé 'n seòrsa a chi thu ann?" "Chi mi feadhain chaola ghlas ann." "Sin agad sìol na Luine luaithe; lig seachad eud." "Dé 'n seòrsa chi thu 'n dràsd?" "Ch mi feadhain sheanga riabhach." "Sinn agad sìol na Deirge dàsanaich; lig seachad eud." "Dé 'n fheadhain a chi thu 'n dràsd?" "Chi mi feadhain throma loma." "Lig an cù thuca Mhic Bhuidheig!" Dh' fhalbh Mac Bhuidheig. "A bheil e leagail na leoir?" "Tha." "Nur a chi thu nis aon dusan aige caisgidh thu e." Nur a shaoil e gun robh eud aige sheinn e 'n fhìdeag 's chaisg e 'n cù. "Nis ma tha 'n cuillean buidheach seilge thig e gu modhail, socair; mur 'eil thig e 's a chraos fosgailt." Bha e tighinn 'sa chraos fosgailte 'sa theanga mach air a bhial. "'S dona 'n rud a rinn thu an cuilean a chasg 's gun e buidheach seilg. Nur a thig e beir air mo làimhsa 's fiach an cuir thu stigh na chraos i, no bidh sinn aige." Chuir e stigh làmh Oisein 'na chraos 's chrath e 'n sgòrnan as. "Thalla, cruinnich na daimh 'ionnsuidh an tom luachrach." Dh' fhalbh e 's dianar siud, agus 'se naoidh daimh a bh' ann, agus cha b' uilear do dh' Oisean siud 'na onrachd, 's bha cuid a' ghill air chaull. "Cuir mo dha laimhsa ma 'n tom luachrach a tha 'n so." Rinn e siud 's bha 'n coire mòr a b' àbhaist a bhi aig an Fhìnn ann, "Dian anis deas 's cuir na daimh anns a' choire 's cuir gealbhan foidhe." Rinn an gille siud. Nur a bha eud an so deas airson an gabhail, urs' Oisean ris. "Na bean thusa dhaibh gos an gabh mise mo dhial an toiseach." Thòisich Oisean orra, 'sa h-uile fear a dh' itheadh e bheireadh e fear de na deilg as a bhroinn. Nur a bha sia aig Oisean air an itheadh bha tri aig a ghill' air an toirt uaidhe. "An d' rinn thu so orm ?" urs' Oisean. "Rinn," urs' esan, "dh' fheumainnsa beagan, nur a bha mòran agad fhìn diu." "Fiach an d' thoir thu mis' ionnsuidh a leithid so do chreag." Rinn e siud. Chaidh e sios an sin 's thug e mach isean lòn duigh as a' chreig. "Thugainn a bhi falbh dachaidh." Rug an gill' air achlais air 's dh' fhalbh eud. Nur a bha e smaointeachadh gon robh eud a' teannadh air an tigh thuirt e. "A bheil sinn a' teannadh goirid o'n tigh." "Tha," urs' an gille, "An ruigeadh eubh duin' air an tigh far a bheil sin an dràsd." "Ruigeadh." "Cuir m' aghaidhsa dìreach air an tigh." Rinn an gille siud. Nur a bha e tigh'n air an tigh rug e air a' ghille 's chuir e làmh 'na sgòrnan 's mharbh e e. "So," urs' esan, "cha bhi thusa na fear eile 'g innseadh eachdraidh a'm' dhéigh-sa." Chaidh e dachaidh 's a làmhan 's a' bhalla 's dh' fhàg e isean an lòn duigh a stigh. Bha eud a' feòraidh deth càit' an robh e o thàinig an latha. Thuirt e gon robh e far am minig an do chuir e làithean sòlasach, toilichte seachad. "Demur a chaidh thus' an sin 's thu daull?" "Fhuair mi cothrom air a dhol ann an diugh co dhiu. Tha PEATA beag an siud a thug mi dachaidh 's thugaibh a steach e." Dh' fhalbh eud a mach a choimhead, 's ma dh' fhalbh, cha deach a mach na bheireadh dachaidh e. Dh' eiridh e fhìn a mach 's thug e steach e. Dh' iarr e corc. Rug e air a chalpa, 's rùisg e e, 's thug e 'n fheòil deth. Bhris e da cheann a' chnàimh. "Faighibh a nis calp' an daimh odhair a bha sibh ag radh nach fhaca mise riabh a leithid 's an Fhinn." Fhuair eud so dha 's thilg e mach romh tholl an smior aig e. Bha e 'n so air a dhianadh fìrinneach. Thòisich eud air iarraidh tuillidh eachdraidh air, ach dh' fhairtlich orra riabh toirt air tòiseachadh orra tuillidh.

2. A version of this was told to me by an old tinker at Inverary,

but, according to him, the books were destroyed. I took it to be the popular account of the Ossian controversy. Ossian, MacPherson, Dr. Smith, and their party, fused into "Ossian," Dr. Johnson, and his followers, condensed into "Padraig." The famous Red Book of Clanrannald has also become mythical. Its true history will be found in the book by the Highland Society. I was told in Benbecula how a man had found a book, containing the history of the Feen, in a moss ; and how he had parted with it to a blind beggar, who had sold part to a clergyman, the rest was in America. "The book was not dug up ; it was *on* the moss. It seemed as if the ancestors had sent it."

3. This story of the Blackbird's bone is common. I heard it myself from several men in South Uist, with variations. According to one, the deer's bone was to turn round on end in the blackbird's shank. Another version has been sent to me from Sutherland. According to J. H. Simpson, a similar tale is now told by the peasantry of Mayo. (Poems of Ossin, Bard of Erin, from the Irish, 1857, page 191.) Mr. MacLean very ingeniously suggests that the word which now means Blackbird (Londubh) may originally have meant Black-Elk. Armstrong's Dictionary gives Lòn, a meadow ; Lòn, a diet, a dinner, a store, provision, food ; Lon, an ousel, a blackbird, an *Elk ;* Lon, greed, prattle, hunger ; also, a rope of raw hides used by the people of St. Kilda. The word, then, may mean almost anything that can be eaten by man or beast in general ; and an elk in particular.

There are plenty of elks still living in Scandinavia. Their gigantic fossil bones are found in Irish bogs, and in the Isle of Man ; a whole skeleton is to be seen in the British Museum ; and it is supposed that men and elks existed together in Ireland. (See Wilson's Pre-historic Annals of Scotland, page 22 : 1851.) The story probably rests on a foundation of fact—namely, the discovery of fossil bones—mixed up with the floating traditions about the Feen which pervade both Ireland and Scotland, and which have been woven into poems for centuries in both countries. These *may* date from the days when men hunted elks in Erin, as they now do in Scandinavia. "Padraig" probably slipped in when that curious dialogue was composed, of which several versions are still extant in old manuscripts.

4. The Sutherland version is as follows :—

The last of the giants lived among the Fearn Hills (Ross-shire, and within sight of the windows of Skibo); he had an only daughter, married not to a giant, but to a common man.

His son-in-law did not always treat him well, for he was sometimes very hungry, and had to wear a hunger-belt.

One day at dinner his son-in-law said to him, "Did you ever, amongst the giants, eat such good beef, or from so large an ox?"

"Amongst us," said the last of the giants, "the legs of the birds were heavier than the hind quarters of your ox."

They laughed him to scorn, and said, that it was because he was blind that he made such mistakes; so he called to a servant and bid him bring his bow and three arrows, and lead him by the hand to a corrie which he named in the Balnagowan forest.

"Now," said he, "do you see such and such a rock?"

"Yes," said the servant.

"And is there a step in the face of it?"

"Yes," said the servant.

"Are there rushes at the foot of it?"

"Yes," said the servant.

"Then, take me to the steps, and put me on the first of them."

The servant did so.

"Look now, and tell me what comes."

"I see birds," said the fellow.

"Are they bigger than common?"

"No bigger than in Fearn," said the servant.

A little after, "What do you see?"

"Birds still," said the servant.

"And are they no bigger than usual?"

"They are three times bigger than eagles."

A little later, "Do you see any more birds?" said the giant.

"Yes, birds that the air is black with them, and the biggest is three times as big as an ox."

"Then guide my hand to the bow," said the blind giant; and the boy guided him so well that the biggest bird fell at the foot of the rock amongst the rushes.

"Take home a hind quarter," said the giant, and they carried it home between them.

When they came to the house of his son-in-law, he walked in with it, and aimed a tremendous blow at the place where his son-in-law usually sat. Being blind he did not see that the chair was empty; it was broken to pieces; but the son-in-law lived to repent, and treat the blind giant better.

I have another version written in English by Mr. Hugh MacColl, gardener at Ardkinglass, from which it appears that the blind old giant was Ossian, and that his father-in-law was Paul na nooi clerach, Paul of the nine clerks (whom I strongly suspect to be St. Patrick). They questioned him about deer; and this shows how stories alter, for DAMH means *ox* and *stag*, and in Sutherland it has become ox.

5. They would not believe that Ossian's black birds were so large. He got a boy and went to a hill, and pulled a tuft of rushes; and here again is another change in the translation from Gaelic to English; for TOM means a *knoll* and a *bush*. Under the tuft they find a yellow dog, and under another, firelocks and spades; which is another curious change from the bow and arrows. Then they go to a *hill* covered with wood, which suits the country about Stirling; and the lad is made to dig a hole with the spade, and put his head into it. The old giant whistles, and nearly splits the boy's head; and he does this thrice. The first time the boy sees deer as big as peat-stacks; the second, as large as house; the third, as large as hills; and they slip "cue baie mac kill e buiach," the yellow dog after them.

Then they kindle a fire and roast the deer. Here the bettle has dropped out, and the boy eats some, and old giant is furious; for if he had eaten all he could have recovered his sight. Then he took the boy to a wood, and made him shoot a blackbird on its nest, and he took home a leg, which was so heavy that it broke the table.

Then they tried to get the old man to tell them more about the Faen, but he would not, because they would not believe him; and the next day they went with the boy to a well, and wrung his neck, to keep him silent also.

Here, as in all the versions which I have got, the black*bird* seems to be hauled in to account for the Gaelic word, which is but rarely used, and whose meaning is forgotten. LON DUBH means black*bird* or black *Elk;* and surely deer as big as hills might have done to prove the wonders of the olden time. These three versions of the same story show, as well as any which I have, how the same tale changes in various localities, and why.

In Stirling and in Sutherland Gaelic is fading rapidly. Elks have ceased to exist in Scotland; and the tradition has changed with the times, and shapes itself to suit the ideas of the narrators, and the country about them.

XXXII.

THE BARRA WIDOW'S SON.

From Alexander MacNeill, tenant and fisherman, then at Tangual, Barra.

THERE was a poor widow in Barra, and she had a babe of a son, and Iain was his name. She would be going to the strand to gather shell-fish to feed herself and her babe. When she was on the strand on a day, what did she see but a vessel on the west of Barra. Three of those who were on board put out a boat, and they were not long coming on shore.

She went to the shore and she emptied out the shell-fish beside her. The master of the vessel put a question to her, "What thing was that?" She said that it was strand shell-fish the food that she had. "What little fair lad is this?"—"A son of mine."—"Give him to me and I will give thee gold and silver, and he will get schooling and teaching, and he will be better off than to be here with thee."—"I had rather suffer death than give the child away."—"Thou art silly. The child and thyself will be well off if thou lettest him (go) with me." With the love of the money she said that she would give him the child. "Come hither, lads, go on board; here's for you the key. Open a press in the cabin, and you will bring me hither a box that you will find in it." They went away, they did that, and they came. He caught the box, he opened it, he emptied it with a gush (or into her skirt), and he did not count it all, and he took the child with him.

She staid as she was, and when she saw the child going on board she would have given all she ever saw that she had him. He sailed away, and he went to England. He gave schooling and teaching to the boy till he was eighteen years on the vessel. It was Iain Albanach the boy was called at first, he gave him the name of Iain Mac a Maighstir (John, master's son), because he himself was master of the vessel. The "*owner*" of the vessel had seven ships on sea, and seven shops* on shore—each one going to her own shop with her cargo. It happened to the seven ships to be at home together. The *owner* took with him the seven skippers to the house, "I am growing heavy and aged," said he; "you are there seven masters; I had none altogether that I would rather than thou. I am without a man of clan though I am married; I know not with whom I will leave my goods, and I have a great share; there was none I would rather give it to than thee, but that thou art without clan as I am myself." "I," said the skipper, "have a son eighteen years of age in the ship, who has never been let out of her at all."—"Is not that wonderful for me, and that I did not hear of it!"—"Many a thing might the like of me have, and not tell it to you."—"Go and bring him down hither to me that I may see him." He went and he brought him down, and he set him in order. "Is this thy son?"—"It is," said the skipper. "Whether wouldst thou rather stay with me, or go with thy father on the sea as thou wert before, and that I should make thee an heir for ever?"—"Well then, it was ever at sea that I

* Buthanan, Booths.

was raised, and I never got much on shore from my youth; so at sea I would rather be; but as you are determined to keep me, let me stay with yourself."

"I have seven shops on shore, and thou must take thy hand in the seven shops. There are clerks at every one of the shops," said he. "No one of them will hold bad opinion of himself that he is not as good as I. If you insist that I take them, I will take the seventh one of them."

He took the seventh one of the shops, and the first day of his going in he sent word through the town, the thing that was before a pound would be at fifteen shillings; so that everything in the shop was down, and the shop was empty before the ships came. He (the owner) went in, he counted his money, and he said that the shop was empty. "It is not wonderful though it were, when the thing that was before a pound is let down to fifteen shillings."—"And, my OIDE, are you taking that ill? Do you not see that I would put out all in the shop seven times before they could put it out once."—"With that thou must take the rest in hand, and let them out so." Then he took the rest in hand, and he was a master above the other clerks. When the ships came the shops altogether were empty. Then his master said, "Whether wouldst thou rather be master over the shops or go with one of the seven ships? Thou wilt get thy choice of the seven ships."—"It is at sea I was ever raised and I will take a ship." He got a ship. "Come, send hither here to me the seven skippers." The seven skippers came. "Now," said he to the six skippers that were going with Iain, "Iain is going with you, you will set three ships before and three behind, and he will be in the middle, and unless you bring him whole hither to me, there is but to seize you and hang you."—"Well, then, my adopted father," said Iain, "that is not right. The ships are going together, a storm may come and drive us from each other; let each do as best he may." The ships went, they sailed, and it was a cargo of coal that Iain put in his own. There came on them a great day of storm. They were driven from each other. Where did Iain sail but to Turkey. He took anchorage in Turkey at early day, and he thought to go on shore to take a walk. He was going before him walking; he saw two out of their shirts working, and as though they had two iron flails. What had they but a man's corpse! "What are you doing to the corpse?"—"It was a Christian; we had eight marks against him, and since he did not pay us while he was alive, we will take it out of his corpse with the flails."—"Well then, leave him with me and I will pay you the eight marks." He seized him, he took him from them, he paid them, and he put mould and earth on him. It was soon for him to return till he should see more of the land of the Turk. He went on a bit and what should he see there but a great crowd of men together. He took over where they were. What did he see but a gaping red fire of a great hot fire, and a woman stripped between the fire and them. "What," said he, "are you doing here?" "There are," said they, "two Christian women that the great Turk got; they were caught on the ocean; he has had them from the end of eight years. This one was promising him that she would marry him every year: when the time came to marry him she would not marry him a bit. He ordered herself and the woman that was with her to be burnt. One of them was burnt, and this one is as yet unburnt."

"I will give you a good lot of silver and gold if you will leave her with me, and you may say to him that you burnt her." They looked at each other. They said that he would get that. He went and he took her with him on board, and he clothed her in cloth and linen.

"Now," said she, "thou hast saved my life for me; thou must take care of thyself in this place. Thou shalt go up now to yonder change-house. The man of the inn will put a question to thee what cargo thou hast. Say thou a cargo of coal. He will say that would be well worth selling in the place where thou art. Say thou it is for selling it that thou art come; what offer will he make for it. He will say, to-morrow at six o'clock there would be a *waggon* of gold going down, and a waggon of coal coming up, so that the ship might be kept in the same *trim*,* till six o'clock on the next night. Say thou that thou wilt take that; but unless thou art watchful they will come in the night when every man is asleep, with muskets and pistols; they will set the ship on the ground; they will kill every man, and they will take the gold with them."

He went to the man of the inn, and agreed with him as she had taught him. They began on the morrow, in the morning, to put down the gold, and take up the coal. The skipper had a man standing looking out that the vessel should be in trim. When the coal was out, and the ship was as heavy with the gold as she was with the coal; and when he was on shore, she got an order for the sailors to take her advice till he should come. "Put up," said she, "the sails, and draw the

* Trump.

anchors. Put a rope on shore." They did that. He came on board; the ship sailed away through the night; they heard a shot, but they were out, and they never caught them more.

They sailed till they reached England. Three ships had returned, and the three skippers were in prison till Iain should come back. Iain went up and he reached his adopted father. The gold was taken on shore, and the old man had two thirds and Iain a third. He got chambers for the woman, where she should not be troubled.

"Art thou thinking that thou wilt go yet?" said the woman to him. "I am thinking that I have enough of the world with that same."—"Thou wentest before for thine own will, if thou wouldst be so good as to go now with my will."—"I will do that."—"Come to that shop without; take from it a coat, and a brigis, and a waistcoat; try if thou canst get a cargo of herring and thou shalt go with it to Spain. When the cargo is in, come where I am before thou goest."

When he got the cargo on board he went where she was. "Hast thou got the cargo on board?"—"I have got it."

"There is a dress here, and the first Sunday after thou hast reached the Spain thou wilt put it on, and thou wilt go to the church with it. Here is a whistle, and a ring, and a book. Let there be a horse and a servant with thee. Thou shalt put the ring on thy finger; let the book be in thine hand; thou wilt see in the church three seats, two twisted chairs of gold, and a chair of silver. Thou shalt take hold of the book and be reading it, and the first man that goes out of the church be thou out. Wait not for man alive, unless the King or the Queen meet thee."

He sailed till he reached the Spain; he took anchorage, and he went up to the change-house. He asked for a dinner to be set in order. The dinner was set on the board. They went about to seek him. A trencher was set on the board, and a cover on it, and the housewife said to him—"There is meat and drink enough on the board before you, take enough, but do not lift the cover that is on the top of the trencher." She drew the door with her. He began at his dinner. He thought to himself, though it were its fill of gold that were in the trencher, or a fill of "daoimean,"* nothing ever went on board that he might not pay. He lifted the cover of the trencher, and what was on the trencher but a couple of herring. "If this be the thing she was hiding from me she need not," and he ate one herring and the one side of the other. When the housewife saw that the herring was eaten,—"Mo chreach mhor! my great ruin" said she; "how it has fallen out! Was I never a day that I could not keep the people of the realm till to-day?"—"What has befallen thee?" —"It is, that I never was a day that I might not put a herring before them till to-day."—"What wouldst thou give for a barrel of herrings?"—"Twenty Saxon pounds."—"What wouldst thou give for a ship load?" —"That is a thing that I could not buy."—"Well, then, I will give thee two hundred herring for the two herring, and I wish the ship were away and the herrings sold."

On the first Sunday he got a horse with a bridle and saddle,† and a gillie. He went to the church; he saw the three chairs. The queen sat on the right hand of the king, and he himself sat on the left; he took the book out of his pocket, and he began reading.

---

* Diamonds. † All riders have not these luxuries.

It was not on the sermon that the king's looks were, nor the queen's, but raining tears. When the sermon skailed he went out. There were three nobles after him, shouting that the king had a matter for him. He would not return. He betook himself to the change-house that night. He staid as he was till the next Sunday, and he went to sermon; he would not stay for any one, and he returned to the change-house. The third Sunday he went to the church. In the middle of the sermon the king and queen came out; they stood at each side of the (bridle) rein. When the king saw him coming out he let go the rein; he took his hat off to the ground, and he made manners at him. "By your leave; you needn't make such manners at me. It is I that should make them to yourself."—"If it were your will that you should go with me to the palace to take dinner."—"Ud! Ud! it is a man below you with whom I would go to dinner." They reached the palace. Food was set in the place of eating, drink in the place of drinking, music in the place of hearing. They were plying the feast and the company with joy and gladness,* because they had hopes that they would get news of their daughter. "Oh, skipper of the ship," said the queen, hide not from me a thing that I am going to ask thee." Any thing that I have that I can tell I will not hide it from you." "And hide not from me that a woman's hand set that dress about your back, your coat, your brigis, and your waistcoat, and gave you the ring about your finger, and the book that was in your hand, and the whistle that you were playing." "I will not hide it.

* This passage is one common to many reciters, and spoiled by translation.

With a woman's right hand every whit of them was reached to me." "And where didst thou find her? 'Tis a daughter of mine that is there." "I know not to whom she is daughter. I found her in Turkey about to be burned in a great gaping fire." "Sawest thou a woman along with her?" "I did not see her; she was burned before I arrived. I bought her with gold and silver. I took her with me, and I have got her in a chamber in England." "The king had a great general," said the queen, "and what should he do but fall in love with her. Her father was asking her to marry him, and she would not marry him. She went away herself and the daughter of her father's brother with a vessel, to try if he would forget her. They went over to Turkey; the Turk caught them, and we had not hope to see her alive for ever."

"If it be your pleasure, and that you yourself are willing, I will set a ship with you to seek her; you will get herself to marry, half the realm so long as the king lives, and the whole realm when he is dead." "I scorn to do that; but send a ship and a skipper away, and I will take her home; and if that be her own will, perhaps I will not be against it."

A ship was made ready; what should the general do but pay a lad to have him taken on board unknown to the skipper; he got himself hidden in a barrel. They sailed far; short time they were in reaching England. They took her on board, and they sailed back for Spain. In the midst of the sea, on a fine day, he and she came up on deck, and what should he see but an island beyond him; it was pretty calm at the time. "Lads, take me to the island for a while to hunt, till there comes on us the likeness of a breeze." "We will." They set him on shore on the island; when they left him on the island the boat returned. When the general saw that he was on the island, he promised more wages to the skipper and to the crew, for that they should leave him there; and they left Iain on the island.

When she perceived that they had left Iain on the island, she went mad, and they were forced to bind her. They sailed to Spain. They sent word to the king that his daughter had grown silly, as it seemed, for the loss of the form of her husband and lover. The king betook himself to sorrow, to black melancholy, and to woe, and to heart-breaking, because of what had arisen; and (because) he had but her of son or daughter.

Iain was in the island, hair and beard grown over him; the hair of his head down between his two shoulders, his shoes worn to pulp, without a thread of clothes on that was not gone to rags; without a bite of flesh on him, his bones but sticking together.

On a night of nights, what should he hear but the rowing of a boat coming to the island. "Art thou there, Iain Albanich?" said the one in the boat. Though he was, he answered not. He would rather find death at the side of a hill than be killed.

"I know that thou hearest me, and answer; it is just as well for thee to answer me, as that I should go up and take thee down by force." He went, and he took himself down. "Art thou willing to go out of the island?" "Well, then, I am; it is I that am that, if I could get myself taken out of it." "What wouldst thou give to a man that would take thee out of this?" "There was a time when I might give something to a man that would take me out of this; but to day I have not a thing." "Wouldst thou give one half of thy wife to a man that would take thee out of this?" "I have not that." "I do not say if thou hadst, that thou wouldst give her away." "I would give her." "Wouldst thou give half thy children to a man that would take thee out of this." "I would give them." "Down hither; sit in the stern of the boat." He sat in the stern of the boat. "Whether wouldst thou rather go to England or Spain?" "To Spain." He went with him, and before the day came he was in Spain.

He went up to the change-house; the housewife knew him in a moment. "Is this Iain!" said she. "It is the sheath of all that there was of him that is here."

"Poorly has it befallen thee!" said she. She went and she sent a message to a barber's booth, and he was cleansed; and word to a tailor's booth, and clothes were got for him; she sent word to a shoemaker's booth, and shoes were got for him. On the morrow when he was properly cleansed and arrayed, he went to the palace of the king, and he played the whistle. When the king's daughter heard the whistle she gave a spring, and she broke the third part of the cord that bound her. They asked her to keep still, and they tied more cords on her. On the morrow he gave a blast on the whistle, and she broke two parts of all that were on her. On the third day when she heard his whistle, she broke three quarters; on the fourth day she broke what was on her altogether. She rose and she went out to meet him, and there never was a woman more sane than she. Word was sent up to the king of Spain, that there never was a girl more sane than she; and that the bodily presence of her husband and lover had come to her.

A "coach" was sent to fetch Iain; the king and his great gentles were with him; he was taken up on the deadly points.* Music was raised, and lament laid down; meat was set in the place of eating, drink in the place of drinking, music in the place for hearing; a cheery, hearty, jolly wedding was made. Iain got one half of the realm; after the king's death he got it altogether. The general was seized; he was torn amongst horses; he was burned amongst fires; and the ashes were let (fly) with the wind.

After the death of the king and queen, Iain was king over Spain. Three sons were born to him. On a night he heard a knocking in the door. "The asker is come," said he. Who was there but the very man that took him out of the island. "Art thou for keeping thy promise?" said the one who came, "I am," said Iain. "Thine own be thy realm, and thy children and my blessing! Dost thou remember when thou didst pay eight merks for the corpse of a man in Turkey; that was my body; health be thine; thou wilt see me no more.

MAC NA BANTRAICH BHARRACH.

BHA bantrach bhochd ann am Barra, agus bha leanabh mic aice, agus 's e Iain a b' ainm dha. Bhiodh i dol do 'n tràigh a chruinneachadh maoraich airson i fhìn 's an leanabh a bheathachadh. Nur a bha i 'san tràigh latha bha 'n sin dé chunnaic i ach soitheach air an aird an Iar de Bharra. Chuir triuir de na bha air bòrd a mach bàta 's cha b' fhada bha eud a' tigh'n air

---

* This I take to be a phrase wrongly used; an old phrase, meaning that the personage was raised on spears. The passage is common.

tìr. Chaidh ise gos a' chladach 's dhòirt i 'm maorach làmh riutha. Chuir Maighstir an t-soithich ceisd urra de 'n rud a bha 'n siud. Thuirt i go 'n robh maorach cladaich, am biadh a bh' aice. "Dè 'n gilie beag, bàn a tha 'n so?" "Mac domh." "Thoir dhomhs' e, agus bheir mi dhuit òr agus airgiod, agus gheibh e sgoil as ionnsachadh, 's bidh e na 's fheàrr 'na bhi agads' an so." "'S fheàrr leam bàs fhuileann na 'm pàisd' a thoirt seachad." "Tha thu gòrrach, bidh thu fhìn 's an leanabh go math ma ligeas tu leam e." Le gaol an airgid thuirt i gon d' thugadh i 'n leanabh da. "Thallaibh an so ghillean. Theirigibh air bòrd; so duibh iuchair; fosglaibh *press* anns a *chabin*, 's bheir sibh thugamsa bòsdan a gheibh sibh ann." Dh' fhalbh eud; rinn eud siud 's thàinig eud. Rug e air bosca' dh' fhosgail e e—dhoirt e 'na sguirt e 's cha do chunnd e idir e, 's thug e leis an leanabh. Dh' fhan ise mur a bha i, 's nur chunnaic i 'n leanabh a dol air bòrd, bheireadh i na chunnaic i riabh go 'n robh e aice. Sheòl esan air falbh agus ghabh e go ruige Sasunn. Thug e sgoil a's ionnsachadh do 'n bhalach gos an robh e ochd bliadhna diag, air an t-soitheach. 'Se Iain Albannach a bh' air a' bhalach an toiseach. Thug esan Iain Mac a Mhaighstir air, a thaobh gom be fhìn maighstir an t-soithich. Bha aig *owner* an t-soithich seachd soithichean air muir, agus seachd bùthannan air tir—a' h-uile té gabhail thun a bùth fhìn le a luchd. Thachair do na seachd loingeas a bhi aig an tigh comhla. Thug an sealbhadair suas leis na seachd sgiobairean thun an tighe. "Tha mi 'fas trom aosd'," urs' esan. "Tha sibh an sin seachd maighstirean—cha robh gin agam gu léir a bu docha leam na thusa—tha mi gon duine cloinne gad a tha mi pòsda. Cha 'n 'eil fhios'am co aig a dh' fhàgas mi mo chuid, agus cuid mhòr agam. Cha robh gin a bu docha leam a thoirt da na thusa, ach go 'bheil thu gon chlann mar mi fhìn." "Tha agams'," urs' an sgiobair, "mac ochd bliadhna diag a dh' aois anns an t-soitheach gon a liginn aisd' idir." "Nach neònach leamsa sin agad 's gon mise g'a chluinntinn riabh." "'S iomadh rud a dh' fhaodadh a bhi aig mo leithidsa nach bithinn aig innseadh dhuibhse." "Falbh 's thoir thugams' a nuas e 's gom faicinn e." Dh' fhalbh e 's thug e nuas e, 's chuir e 'n òrdugh e. "An e so do mhacsa?" "'S e," urs' an sgiobair. "Còca 's fheàrr leat fuireachd agamsa, na falbh le t' athair air a' mhuir mur a bha thu roimhid, 's gun dian mise dìleabach dìot go bràthach." "Mata 's ann air muir a fhuair mi mo thogail riabh, 's cha d' fhuair mi dad o m' òig air tìr; le sin

’s ann air muir a b’ fheàrr leam a bhi ; ach o ’n tha sibhs’ a’ cur roimhibh go ’n cum sibh mi ’gom fan mi agaibh fhìn.” “Tha seachd bùthannan agam air tìr, agus feumaidh tu làmh a ghabh-ail anns na seachd bùthannan.” “Tha cléireach aig a h-uile fear riabh de na bùthannan,” urs’ esan ; “cha gabh h-aon aca droch bharail orra fhìn, nach ’eil eud cho math riumsa ; ma tha sibh a cur mar fhiachaibh ormsa go ’n gàbh mi eud, gabhaidh mi ’n seachdamh fear diu.

Ghabh e ’n seachdamh fear de na bùthannan, ’sa chiad latha da dol ann ’chuir e fios feadh a’ bhaile, an rud a bha roimhid punnd gom biodh e air còig tasdain diag, air alt ’s gon d’ thàinig ’h-uile rud a bhà a’ bhùth nuas ’s gon robh ’m bùth falamh ma’ n d’ thàinig na soithichean. Chaidh e stigh, chunndais e chuid airgid, ’s thuirt e go ’n robh ’m bùth falamh. “Cha n’ ioghnadh gad a bhitheadh, san rud a bha roimhid air punnd thu g’a ligeil sìos go còig tasdain diag.” “Agus, oide, ’bheil sibhse ’ga ghab-hail sin go h-olc ; nach ’eil sibh a’ faicinn gon cuirinnsa mach na bh’ anns a bhùth seachd uairean ma ’n cuireadh eudsan a mach aon uair e.” “Leis an sin feumaidh tu làmh a ghabhail ri càch agus an ligeil a mach mur sin.” Ghabh e n sin làmh ri càch, agus bha e ’na mhaighstir as cionn nan cléireach eile. Nur a thàinig na soithichean bha na bùthannan go léir falamh.

Thuirt a mhaighstir ris a nis, “Còca ’s fheàrr leat a bhi ’d’ mhaighstir thar nam bùthannan, na falbh le h-aon de na seachd soithichean ; gheibh thu do roighinn de na seachd soithichean.” “’S ann air muir a thogadh riabh mi ’s gabhaidh mi soitheach.” Fhuair e soitheach. “Thallaibh, cuiribh thugamsa na seachd sgiobairean.” Thàinig na seachd sgiobairean a ’ionnsuidh. “Nis,” urs’ esan, ris na sia sgiobairean a bha dol le Iain. “Tha Iain a’ dol leibh—cuiridh sibh tri soithichean air thoiseach, ’s tri air deireadh, ’s bidh esan ’sa mhiadhon ; ’s mur an d’ thoir sibh thugamsa slàn e cha ’n ’eil ach breith oirbh ’s ’ur crochadh.” “Mata m’ oide,” urs’ Iain, “cha ’n ’eil sin freagarrach. Tha na soithichean a’ falbh comhla ; faodaibh stoirm tighinn agus ar fuadach o chéile. Dianadh h-uile h-aon mar is fheàrr a dh’ fhao-das e.”

Dh’ fhalbh na soithichean—sheòl eud—agus ’se luchd guail a chuir Iain a stigh na thé fhìn. Thàinig latha mòr stoirm orra. Dh’ fhuadaicheadh o chéil’ eud. C’ a ’n do sheòl Iain ach do ’n Tuirc. Ghabh e acair ’s an Tuirc trath latha. Smaoinich e dol air tìr a ghabhail sràid. Bha e gabhail roimhe ’coiseachd.

Chunnaic e dithisd as an léintean ag obair, 's mar gom biodh da shùisid iaruinn aca. Dé bh' ac' ach corp duine. "Dé tha sibh a dianadh ris a' chorp." "'Se Crìosdaidh a bh' ann. Bha ochd mairg againn air, 's o'n nach do phàigh e sinn nur a bha e beo bheir sinn a a chorp leis na sùisdean e." "Mata ligibh leams' e agus pàighidh mi dhuibh na h-ochd mairg." Rug e air—thug e uath' e—phaigh a eud agus chuir e ùir as talamh air.

Bha e luath leis tilleadh air ais gos am faiceadh e tuillidh de dh' fhearann na Tuirc. Ghabh e air aghaidh treis, agus dé chunnaic e 'n sin ach grunnan mòr dhaoine cruinn. Ghabh e null far an robh eud. Dé chunnaic e ach craoslach mòr teine, de theine mhor leathann, agus boireannach rùisgt' eadar an teine 's eud fhìn. "De," urs' esan "a tha sibh a dianadh an so." "Tha," urs' eudsan, "da bhana Chriosdaidh a fhuair an Turcach mòr. Rugadh orra air a' chuan. Tha eud o cheann ochd bliadhna aige. Bha 'n te so 'gealltainn da gom pòsadh i e h-uile bliadhna. Nur thàinig an t-am cha phòsadh i bad doth. Dh' òrdaich e i fhìn 's am boireannach a bha comhla rithe 'losgadh. Loisgeadh an darna té dhiu 's tha i so gon losgadh fhathasd." "Bheir mi fhìn duibh tiodhlac math airgid agus òir ma ligeas sibh leam i, agus faodaidh sibh a ràdh ris gon do loisg sibh i." Sheall eud air a chéile. Thuirt eud gom faigheadh e siud. Dh' fhalbh e 's thug e leis air bord i, agus sgeadaich e i 'n aodach 's an anart.

"Nis," urs' ise, "shabhail thu mo bheatha dhomh. Feumaidh tu 'n aire thoirt ort fhìn 's an àite so. Théid thu suas a nis do 'n tigh sheins' ud shuas. Cuiridh fear an tigh sheinse ceisd ort dé 'n luchd a th' agad. Abraidh tusa luchd guail. Abraidh esan gor math a mhiadh siud 'san àite a bheil thu airson a reic. Abraidh tusa gor ann airson a reic a thàinig thu ; dé 'n tairgse bheir e air. Their esan, "A màireach air sia uairean bidh *waggon* òir a' dol a sios 's *waggon* guail a' dol a suas, air alt 's gon cumar an soitheach anns an aon *trump* go sia uairean an ath oìdhch.'" Abair thusa gon gabh thu siud ; ach anns an oidhche' mur am bi thusa a'd-earalas thig eud 's an oidhche, nur a tha h-uile duine na 'n cadal, le musgannan 's le dagannan ; cuiridh eud an soitheach air a ghrund ; marbhaidh eud a h-uile duine, 's 'bheir eud leo an t-òr. Chaidh e far an robh fear an tigh sheise agus chòrd e ris mar a sheòl is' e. Thòisich eud an la'r na mhàireach 'sa mhadainn air cur sìos an òir 's air toirt suas a' ghuail. Bha fear aig an sgiobair 'na sheasamh ag amharc gom biodh an soitheach ann an trump. Nur a bha 'n gual a mach, 'sa bha 'n soitheach cho trom leis an òr 's a bha i leis a ghual, 's nur a bha esan air tìr, fhuair is' òrdan na seòladairean a ghabhail a comhairle gos an d' thigeadh esan. "Cuiribh suas," urs' ise, "na siuil, 's tàirnibh na h' acraichean. Cuiribh ròp' air tir." Rinn eud siud. Thàinig esan air bòrd. Sheòl an soitheach air falbh feadh na h-oidhche. Chual eud urchair; ach bha eudsan a mach 's cha d' rug eud orra tuillidh. Sheòl eud go ruige Sasunn. Bha tri soithichean àir tilleadh, 's bha na tri sgiobairean am prìosan gos an tilleadh Iain. Ghabh Iain suas 's ràinig e oide. Chaidh an t-òr a thoirt air tìr, 's bha da dhrian aig a bhodach, 's drian aig Iain. Fhuair e seombraichean do 'n bhoireannach far nach cuirte dragh urra.

"A bheil thu smaointeachadh go falbh thu fhathasd," urs' am boireannach ris. "Tha mi smaointeachadh go bheil na leoir dhe 'n t-saoghal agam siud fhìn." "Dh' fhalbh thu roimhid le t' thoil fhìn; na 'm biodh tu cho math 's gom falbhadh thu nis le 'm thoilsa." "Ni mi sin." "Thalla do 'n bhuth ud a muigh, thoir as còt', agus brigis, agus peitean. Feuch am faigh thu luchd sgadain, agus théid thu do 'n Spàin leis. Nur a bhios an luchd a stigh thig far a bheil mise ma 'm falbh thu."

Nur a fhuair e 'n luchd air bòrd chaidh e far an robh i. "An d' fhuair thu 'n luchd air bord?" "Fhuair." "Tha deise 'n so, 's a chiad Domhnach an déigh dhuit an Spàin a ruigheachd, cuiridh tu umad i, agus theid thu do 'n eaglais leatha. So fìdeag, agus fàinne, agus leobhar. Bidh each agus gille leat. Cuiridh tu 'm fàinne air do mhiar, bidh an leobhar a'd' làimh. Chi thu anns an eaglais tri cathraichean, da chathair amluidh òir, agus cathair airgid. Beiridh tu air an leabhar 's bidh thu 'ga leubhadh; 's a' chiad duin' a théid a mach as an eaglais bi thus' amach; na fan ri duine beo mur an coinnich an righ sa bhan-righ thu."

Sheòl e go ruig an Spàin, ghabh e acarsaid, 's ghabh e suas do 'n tigh sheinse. Dh' iarr e dinneir a chur air dòigh. Chuireadh an dinnear air a bhòrd. Dh' iadhaicheadh sìos 'ga iarraidh. Chuireadh a sìos *trinsear* air a' bhòrd, agus mias air a mhuinn, agus thuirt bean an tigh sheinse ris, "Tha biadh a's deoch na leoir air a bhòrd ma 'r coinneamh; gabhaibh 'ur leoir, ach na togaibh a mhias a th' air muinn an *trinseir*." Tharruinn i 'n doras leatha. Thòisich e air a dhinneir. Smaoinich e aige fhìn gad a b' e 'làn òir a bhiodh anns an trinseir, na 'làn daoimean, nach deachaidh sgath riabh air a' bhòrd nach fhaodadh e phàigheadh. Thog e mhias bhàr an trinseir, 's dé bh' air an trinsear ach da sgadan. "Ma 's e so rud a bha i falach orm cha ruigeadh i leas e." Dh' ith e aon sgadan 's na darna taobh do 'n fhear eile. Nur chunnaic bean an tighe gan robh 'n sgadan ithte, "Mo chreach mhòr," urs' ise, "mar a dh' éiridh domh; nach robh mi latha riabh nach fhaodainn muinntir na rioghachd a ghleidheadh gos an diugh. De dh' éiridh dhuit?" "Tha nach robh mi latha riabh nach faodainn sgadan a chur air am bial-thaobh gos an diugh." "Dé bheireadh thu air baraille sgadan?" "Fichead punnd Sasnach." "Dé bheireadh thu air luchd soithich?" "Sin rud nach b' urra mi 'cheannach." "Mata bheir mise duit da chiad sgadan airson an da sgadain. B' fhearr leam gon robh 'n soitheach air falbh 's na sgadain creicte."

A chiad Di Domhnaich fhuair e each le strian as dìollaid, agus gille. Dh' fhalbh e do 'n eaglais. Chunnaic e na tri cathraichean. Shuidh a bhanrigh air an làimh dheas de 'n righ 's shuidh e fhìn air an làimh thosgail. Thug e mach an leobhar a a phòca 's thòisich e air leubhadh. Cha b' ann air searmoin a bha àir' aig an rìgh na aig a bhanrigh, ach a' sileadh nan diar. Nur a sgaoil an t-searmoin ghabh e mach. Bha triuir stàtan as a dhéigh, aig eubhach ris gon robh gnothach aig an rìgh ris. Cha tilleadh e. Thug e 'n tigh seins' an oidhche sin air. Dh' fhan e mar a bha e gos an ath Dhomhnach. Chaidh e 'n t-searmoin, cha 'n fhanadh e ri duine, 's thill e do 'n thigh sheinse. An treas Domhnach chaidh e do 'n eaglais. Am miadhan na searmoin thàinig an righ 's a' bhanrigh a mach. Sheas eud aig gach taobh do 'n t-sréin. Nur chunnaic an righ esan a tigh 'n a mach, lig e as an t-srian, thug e ada dheth do làr, 's rinn e modh dha. "Le 'r cead cha ruig sibh a leas a leithid sin de mhodh a dhianadh dhomhsa, 's ann a bu chòir dhomhsa dhianadh dhuibh fhìn." "Na 'm b' e 'ur toil gon rachadh sibh leinn a ghabhail dinnear do 'n *phaileas.*" "Ud ud 's e duine sìos uaibhse rachainns 'ghabhail dinnearach leis!"

Ràinig eud am paileas. Chuireadh biadh an àite 'chaitheadh dhaibh, agus deoch an àite 'h-òl, 's ceòl an àit' éisdeachd. Bha eud a' caitheadh na cuirme 's na cuideachd le solas 's le toil-inntinn, ri linn dùil a bhi aca gom faigheadh eud naigheachd air an nighinn. "A sgiobair na luinge," urs' a bhanrigh, "na ceil orm dad a tha mi dol a dh' fhoighneachd dìot." "Dad sam bith a th' agams' is urrainn mi innseadh dhuibh cha cheil mi oirbh." "Na ceilibh orm nach làmh boireannaich a chuir a' chulaidh sin ma'r driom, bhur cota, bhur brigis, 's 'ur peitean; 's a thug dhuibh am fàinne bha mu'r miar, 's an leobhar a bha 'nur làimh, 's an fhìdeag a bha sibh a' seinn." "Cha cheil mi. Le làimh dheas boireannaich a shìneadh a h-uile sgath dhiu sin domhsa." "'S c'àit' an d' fhuair thu i? 's nighean leams' a tha 'n sin." "Cha 'n 'eil fios agamsa co da 'n nighean i. Fhuair mis' i anns an Tuirc a' dol g'a losgadh ann an craoslach mòr teine." "Am fac thu boireannach comhla rithe?" "Cha 'n fhac. Bha i 'n deigh a losgadh ma 'n d' ràinig mi. Cheannaich mi ise le h-òr 's le airgiod, thug mi leam i, 's tha i ann an seombar an Sasunn." "Bha Seanailear mòr aig an rìgh," ars' a' bhanrigh, "'s dé rinn e ach gaol a ghabhail urra. Bha h-athair aig iarraidh urra phòsadh 's cha phòsadh i e. Dh' fhalbh i fhìn 's nighean bhràthar a h-athar le soitheach, fiach an ligeadh e air diochuimhn' i. Chaidh eud thairis do 'n Tuirc. Ghlac an Turcach eud, 's cha robh dùil againn a faicinn beò go bràthach.

Ma 'se 'ur toils' e, 's go bheil sibh fhìn deònach, cuiridh mise long leibh a 'h iarraidh; gheibh sibh i fhìn a' pòsadh, leith na rioghachd fad 's is beò an righ, 's an rioghachd uile nur a bhios e marbh." "Cha 'n fhiach leam sin a dhianadh, ach cuiridh sibhse soitheach agus sgiobair air falbh, 's bheir mise dachaidh i, 's ma 's e sin a toil fhìn dh' fhaoidte nach bi mise 'na aghaidh." Chaidh soitheach a dhianadh deas. Dé rinn an Seanailear ach gille phàigheadh' airson a thoirt air bòrd gon fhios do 'n sgiobair. Fhuair e 'san am, e fhìn fhalach ann am baraille. Sheòl eud, fada goirid gon robh eud, go ruige Sasunn. Thug eud is' air bòrd 's shèol eud air an ais airson na Spàin. Am miadhon a' chuain, latha briagh, thàinig esan agus ise nìos air an *deck*. Dè chunnaic e ach eilean an taobh thall deth. Bha e go math fèitheil 'san am. "Ghillean," ars' esan, "thugaibh mis' air an eilean treis a shealg, gos an d' thig coslas soirbheis oirnn." "Bheir," ars' àdsan. Chuir eud air tìr air an eilean e. Nur a dh' fhàg eud air an eilean e thill am bàta. Nur chunnaic an Seanailear gon robh e air an eilean, gheall e tuillidh tuarasdail do 'n sgiobair agus don sgiobadh, 's eud a 'fhàgail an siud agus dh'fhàg eud Iain air an eilean. Nur a mhothaich ise gon d' fhàg eud air an eilean e, chaidh i air a choitheach, s b' eigin a ceangal. Sheòl eud do 'n Spàin.

Chuir eud fios 'ionnsuidh an rìgh gon robh a nighean an déigh fas gòrach, a réir coslais, airson call aobhar a fir 's a leannain. Chaidh an rìgh go mulad, 's go leann-dugh, 's go bròn, 's go bristeadh cridhe ; chionn mur a dh' éiridh dha, 's gon a bhi aig' ach i do mhac na 'nighean.

Bha Iain 'san eilean, fhionna 's fhiasag air dol thairis air, a ghruag sios eadar a dha shlinnean, na brògan air an cnàmh, 's gun snàthainn aodaich air nach robh air falbh na bhìdeagan, gon ghreim feòl air, ach na cnàmhan a' leantail ra cheile. Oidhche de na h-oidhchean dé chual e ach iomram bàta tìgh 'n thun an eilean. "A bheil thu 'n sin Iain Albannaich?" ars' am fear a bha 's a bhàta. Gad a bha cha do fhreagair. B' fheàrr leis bàs fhaotainn taobh cnoic na gom biodh e air a mharbhadh. "Tha fhios' am go bheil thu 'gam chluinntinn agus freagair, 's cearta cho math dhuit mise fhreagairt, 's mi dhol suas, 's gon d' thoir mi nuas gon taing thu." Dh' fhalbh e 's ghabh e sìos. "A bheil thu deònach falbh as an eilean?" "Mata tha, 's mi tha 'sin, na 'm faighinn mo thoirt as." "Dé bheireadh thu do dhuine bheireidh as an so thu?" "Bha uair 's dh' fhaodoinn rud a thoirt do dhuine bheireadh as an so mi ; ach an diugh cha 'n 'eil sgath agam." "An d' thoireadh thu dha leith do rioghachd?" "Cha bhi rioghachd am feasd agam, na 'm bitheadh bheireadh." "An d' thugadh thu 'n darna leith de d' mhnaoi do dhuine bheireadh as an so thu?" "Cha 'n 'eil sin agam." "Cha 'n 'eil mise 'g radh gad a bhitheadh gon d' thugadh thu seachad i." "Bheireadh." "An d' thugadh thu leith do chloinne do dhuine bheireadh as an so thu?" "Bheireadh." "Nuas, suidh an deireadh a' bhàta." Shuidh e 'n deireadh a bhàta. "Co dhiu 's fheàrr leat dol do Shasunn na do 'n Spàin?" "Do 'n Spàin." Dh' fhalbh e leis, 's ma 'n d' thàinig an latha bha e 'san Spàin.

Ghabh e suas do 'n tigh sheinse. Dh' aithnich bean an tigh sheinse 'sa mhionaid e. "An e so Iain?" ars' ise. "'Se 'n truaill de na bh' ann deth a th' ann," ars' esan. "'S bochd mur a dh' éiridh dhuit," ars' ise. Dh' fhalbh i 's chuir i fios go buth bearradair s ghlanadh e, chuir i fios go bùth tàilleir 's fhuàradh aodach da, chuir i fios go bùth griasaich 's fhuaradh brògan da.

An la 'r na mhàireach, nur a bha e air a ghlanadh, 's air a sgeadachadh go dòigheil, chaidh e thun pàileas an rìgh, 's sheinn e 'n fhìdeag. Nur chual nighean an rìgh an fhìdeag thug i leum aisde, 's bhris i 'n treas earrann de 'n t sreang a bha 'ga ceangal. Dh' iarr eud urra fuireachd socair 's cheangail eud tuillidh sreang urra. An la 'r na mhàireach thug esan sgàl air an fhideig 's bhris i da earrann de na bh' urra. An treas latha, nur a chual i 'n fhìdeag, bhris i tri earrannan. Air a' cheathramh latha bhris i na bh' urra go léir. Dh' éiridh i 's chaidh i mach 'na chomhdhail, 's cha robh boireannach riabh a bu stòldacha na i. Chuireadh brath suas thun rìgh na Spàin nach robh nighean riabh na bu stòldacha na bha i, 's gon d' thàinig aobhar a fir 'sa leannain a 'h ionnsuidh.

Chuireadh *coach* a dh' iarraidh Iain. Bha 'n rìgh 's a mhòr uaislean comhla ris. Thugadh suas air bhàrr bas e. Thogadh ceòl 's leagadh bròn. Chuireadh biadh an àit' a chaithidh, deoch an àit' a h-òl, 's ceòl an àit' éisdeachd. Rinneadh banais, shunndach, eibhinn, aighearach. Fhuair Iain an darna leith de 'n rioghachd. An déigh bàis an righ bha 'n rioghachd uile go léir aige. Rugadh air an t-Seanailear, riasladh eadar eachaibh e, loisgeadh eadar thinean e, 's ligeadh an luath leis a' ghaoith.

An déigh bàis an righ 's na banrigh bha Iain 'na rìgh air an Spàin. Rugadh triuir mac da. Oidhche bha 'n sin chual e bualadh 'san dorus. "Tha 'n t-iarrtaich air tighinn," urs' esan. Dé bh' ann ach a cheart duin' a thug as an eilean e. "A bheil thu airson do ghealladh a chumail?" ars' am fear a thàinig. "Tha," ars' Iain. "Biodh do rioghachd 's do chlann agad fhìn 's mo bheannachdsa. A bheil cuimhn' agad nur a phàigh thu na h-ochd mairg airson cuirp an duin' anns an Tuirc? B'e sin mo chorp-sa. Slàn leat' cha 'n fhaic thu mise tuillidh."

Got this tale from Alexander MacNeill, tenant and fisherman, then at Tangval, Barra. Heard his father, Roderick MacNeill, often recite it. Roderick MacNeill died about twenty years ago, about the age of eighty years. Heard it from many other old men in youth, and says it was pretty common then.

July, 1859. H. MacLean.

The landscape, and the ways of the poor of Barra, are painted from nature: the flat strand, the shell-fish, the ship in the offing, the boat at the edge of the sea. Then comes the popular romance, in which the poor man is to become a prince. The life of shops and ships, dimly seen, but evident enough. Turkey and Spain fairly lost in a distant haze. The commercial principle laid down, that small profits make quick returns; and that men should buy in the cheapest, and sell in the dearest market; and all this woven with a love story, and mixed up with an old tale which Grimm found in Germany, and which Hans Andersen has made the foundation of one of his best tales. Alas! why did not the King of Spain send for the Barra widow to make it complete.

XXXIII.

THE TALE OF THE QUEEN WHO SOUGHT A DRINK FROM A CERTAIN WELL.

From Mrs. MacTavish, Port Ellen, Islay.

THERE was before now, a queen who was sick, and she had three daughters. Said she to the one who was eldest, "Go to the well of true water, and bring to me a drink to heal me."

The daughter went, and she reached the well. A LOSGANN (frog or toad) came up to ask her if she would wed him, if she should get a drink for her mother. "I will not wed thee, hideous creature! on any account," said she. "Well then," said he, "thou shalt not get the water."

She went away home, and her mother sent away her sister that was nearest to her, to seek a drink of the water. She reached the well; and the toad came up and asked her "if she would marry him if she should get the water." "I wont marry thee, hideous creature!" said she. "Thou shalt not get the water, then," said he.

She went home, and her sister that was youngest went to seek the water. When she reached the well the toad came up as he used, and asked her "if she would marry him if she should get the water." "If I have no other way to get healing for my mother, I will marry thee," said she; and she got the water, and she healed her mother.

They had betaken themselves to rest in the night when the toad came to the door saying :—

" A chaomhag, a chaomhag,	" Gentle one, gentle one,
An cuimhneach leat	Rememberest thou
An gealladh beag	The little pledge
A thug thu aig	Thou gavest me
An tobar dhomh,	Beside the well,
A ghaoil, a ghaoil."	My love, my love."

When he was ceaselessly saying this, the girl rose and took him in, and put him behind the door, and she went to bed; but she was not long laid down, when he began again saying, everlastingly :—

" A hàovaig, a hàovaig,
An cuineach leat
An geallug beag
A hoog oo aig
An tobar gaw,
A géule, a géule."

Then she got up and she put him under a noggin; that kept him quiet a while; but she was not long laid down when he began again, saying :—

" A hàovaig, a hàovaig,
Au cuineach leat
An geallug beag
A hoog oo aig
An tobar gaw,
A géule, a géule."

She rose again, and she made him a little bed at the fireside; but he was not pleased, and he began again saying, " A chaoimheag, a chaoimheag, an cuimhneach leat an gealladh beag a thug thu aig an tobar dhomh, a ghaoil, a ghaoil." Then she got up and made him a bed beside her own bed; but he was without ceasing, saying,

"A chaoimheag, a chaoimheag, an cuimhneach leat an gealladh beag a thug a thug thu aig an tobar dhomh, a ghaoil, a ghaoil." But she took no notice of his complaining, till he said to her, "There is an old rusted glave behind thy bed, with which thou hadst better take off my head, than be holding me longer in torture."

She took the glave and cut the head off him. When the steel touched him, he grew a handsome youth; and he gave many thanks to the young wife, who had been the means of putting off him the spells, under which he had endured for a long time. Then he got his kingdom, for he was a king; and he married the princess, and they were long alive and merry together.

SGEULACHD BAN-RIGH A DH' IARR DEOCH A TOBAR ARAID.

Bha banrigh ann roimhe so a bha tinn, agus bha triùir nighean aice. Thubhairt i ris an té 'bu shine, "Falbh do 'n tobar fhìor-uisg', agus thabhair do m' ionnsuidh deoch gu m' leigheas." Dh' fhalbh an nighean agus ràinig i 'n tobar. Thàinig losgann a nìos a dh' fharraid di am pòsadh i e na 'm faigheadh i deoch d'a màthair. "Cha phòs mis' thu 'chreutair ghrànnda! air aon chor." "Mata," ars' esan, "cha 'n fhaigh thu 'n t-uisge." Dh' fhalbh i dhachaidh, agus chuir a màthair air falbh a piuthar a b' fhaisge dhi a dh' iarraidh deoch do 'n uisge. Ràinig i 'n tobar, agus thàinig an losgann a nìos, agus dh' fharraid e dhi am pòsadh i e, na 'm faigheadh i 'n t-uisge. "Cha phòs mis' thu 'chreutair ghrànnd," ars' ise. "Cha 'n fhaigh thu 'n t-uisge mata," urs' esan. Thill i dhachaidh, agus chaidh a piuthar a b' òige 'dh' iarraidh an uisge. An uair a ràinig i 'n tobar thàinig an lossgann à nìos mar a b' àbhaist, agus dh' fharraid e dhi am pòsadh i e na 'm faigheadh i 'n t-uisge. "Mar am bheil sèol eil' agam air leigheas fhaotainn do m' mhàthair pòsaidh mi thu," ars' ise, agus fhuair i 'n t-uisge, agus shlànaicheadh a màthair.

Bha iad an déigh gabhail mu thàmh 'san oidhche an uair a thàinig an losgann do 'n dorus aig ràdh, "A chaomhag, a chaomhag an cuimhneach leat an gealladh beag a thug thu aig an tobar dhomh? A ghaoil! a ghaoil!" An uair a bha e gun tàmh aig ràdh mar so, dh' éiridh an nighean agus thug i stigh e, agus chuir i cùl an doruis e, agus chaidh i 'laidhe; ach cha robh i fada 'na luidhe an uair a thòisich e rithis air a ràdh, a choidh, "A chaomhag, a chaomhag an cuimhneach leat an gealladh beag a thug thu aig an tobar dhomh? A ghaoil! a ghaoil!" Dh' éirich i 'n sin agus chuir i fo noigean e. Chum sin sàmhach e tacan; ach cha robh i fada 'na luidhe an uair a thòisich e rithis air a ràdh, "A chaomhag, a chaomhag an cuimhneach leat an gealladh beag a thug thu aig an tobar dhomh? A ghaoil! a ghaoil!" Dh' éirich i rithis agus rinn i leaba bheag dha taobh an teine; ach cha robh e toilichte. Co luath agus a bha i 'na leaba thòisich e rithis air a ràdh, "A chaoimheag, a chaoimheag nach cuimhneach leat an gealladh beag a thug thu aig an tobar dhomh? A ghaoil! a ghaoil!" Dh' éirich i 'n sin agus rinn i leaba dha làmh ri 'leaba féin; ach bha e gun tàmh aig ràdh, "A chaoimheag, a chaoimheag an cuimhneach leat an gealladh beag a thug thu aig an tobar dhomh? A ghaoil! a ghaoil!" Ach cha robh i 'tabhairt feairt air a ghearan gus an dubhairt e rithe, "Tha seana chlaidheamh meirgeach cùl do leapa leis an fheàrra dhuit an ceann a thabhairt dhìom, na 'bhith 'gam' chumail am péin ni 's faide." Ghabh i 'n claidheamh agus gheàrr i'n ceann deth. An uair a bhoin an stàilinn da dh' fhàs e 'na òganach dreachmhor, agus thug e iomadh buidheachas do 'n ògbhean a bha 'na meadhon an druidheachd, foidh an robh e ré uin' fhad' a' fulann, a chur dheth. Fhuair e 'n sin a rìoghachd, oir bu rìgh e, agus phòs e 'bhana phrionnsa, agus bha iad fada beò gu subhach còmhla.

The lady who has been so kind as to write down this, and other stories, is one of my oldest friends. She has brought up a large family, and her excellent memory now enables her to remember tales, which she had gathered during a long life passed in the West Highlands, where her husband was a respected minister. The story is evidently a Celtic version of the Wearie Well at the Warldis End, of which Chambers has published one Scotch version, to which Grimm refers in notes "Der Froschkônig," in his third volume. There are many versions still current in Scotland, told in broad Scots; and it can be traced back to 1548. According to Grimm, it belongs to the oldest in Germany. This version clearly belongs to the Gaelic language, for the speech of the frog is an imitation of the gurgling and quarking of spring frogs in a pond, which I have vainly endeavoured to convey to an English reader by English letters; but which is absurdly like, when repeated in Gaelic with this intention. The persevering, obstinate repetition of the same sounds is also exceedingly like the habit of frogs, when disturbed, but not much frightened. Let any one try the experiment of throwing a stone into the midst of a frog concert, and he will hear the songsters, after a moment of stillness, begin again. First a half-smothered GUARK GUARK; then another begins, half under water, with a gurgle, and then more and more join in till the pond is in full chorus once again. GUARK, GUARK, GOOILL~~~~ GOOARK GOOILL~~~~

Holy healing wells are common all over the Highlands; and people still leave offerings of pins and nails, and bits of rag, though few would confess it. There is a well in Islay where I myself have, after drinking, deposited copper caps amongst a hoard of pins and buttons, and similar gear, placed in chinks in the rocks and trees at the edge of the "Witches' Well." There is another well with similar offerings, freshly placed beside it in an island in Loch Maree, in Ross-shire; and similar wells are to be found in many other places in Scotland. For example, I learn from Sutherland, that "a well in the black Isle of Cromarty, near Rosehaugh, has miraculous healing powers. A country woman tells me, that about forty years ago, she remembers it being surrounded by a crowd of people every first Tuesday in June, who bathed or drank of it *before* sunrise. Each patient tied a string or rag to one of the trees that overhung it before leaving. It was sovereign for headaches. Mr. —— remembers to have seen a well here called Mary's Well, hung round with votive rags."

Well worship is mentioned by Martin. The custom in his day, in the Hebrides, was to walk south about round the well.

Sir William Betham in his Gael and Cymbiri (Dublin: W. Curry, jun., & Co., 1834), says at page 235, "The Celtæ were much addicted to the worship of fountains and rivers as divinities. They had a deity called Divona, or the river god."

Divona Celtarum lingua fons addite Divii (*Ausonius*).

He quotes from "The Book of Armagh, a MS. of the seventh century,"—"And he (St. Patrick) came to *Fina Malge*, which is called *Slane*, because it was intimated to him that the *Magi honoured this fountain*, and made donations to it as gifts to a god." *For they sacrificed gifts to the fountain, and worshipped it like a god.*

The learned author explains how wells are now venerated in Ireland, and traces their worship back to remote ages; and to the East, by way of Spain, Carthage, and Egypt, Tyre and Sidon, Arabia, Chaldea, and Persia, where men still hang bits of rag on trees near wells. Baal, according to some of the authorities quoted, is mixed up with the well worship of the Irish Sceligs. Divona, the river god, or Baal, may therefore have degenerated into a toad; and the princess who married him may once have been a Celtic divinity, whose story survives as a popular tale in Germany and in Scotland.

The following story bears on the same subject, and may explain why gifts were left when a drink was taken from a well. The story was told to me long ago, while seated under shelter of a big stone waiting for ducks on the shore. It was told in Gaelic, and the pun upon the name of the lake is lost in any other language. The meaning of the name might be the weasel lake, or the lake of the falls; or perhaps the lake of the island; but the legend gives a meaning, which the sound of the name will bear, and it ought to be right if it is not.

XXXIV.

THE ORIGIN OF LOCH NESS.

From Mr. Thomas MacDonald, now gamekeeper at Dunrobin.

WHERE Loch Ness now is, there was long ago a fine glen. A woman went one day to the well to fetch water, and she found the spring flowing so fast that she got frightened, and left her pitcher and ran for her life; she never stopped till she got to the top of a high hill; and when there, she turned about and saw the glen filled with water. Not a house or a field was to be seen! "Aha!" said she, "Tha Loch ann a nis." (Ha Loch an a neesh). There is a lake in it now; and so the lake was called Loch Ness (neesh).

XXXV.

CONALL.

From Alexander MacNeill, tenant and fisherman, Barra.

THERE was an old king before now in Erin,* and a sister of his, whose name was MAOBH, had three sons. The eldest of them was Ferghus, the middlemost Lagh an Laidh, and the youngest one Conall.

He thought he would make an heir of the eldest one, Ferghus. He gave him the schooling of the son of a king and a "ridere," and when he was satisfied with school and learning he brought him home to the palace. Now they were in the palace.

Said the king, "I have passed this year well; the end of the year is coming now, and trouble and care are coming on with it."

"What trouble or care is coming on thee?" said the young man. "The vassals of the country are coming to reckon with me to-day." "Thou hast no need to be in trouble. It is proclaimed that I am the young heir, and it is set down in papers and in letters in each end of the realm. I will build a fine castle in front of the palace for thee. I will get carpenters, and stonemasons, and smiths to build that castle."

---

*In this tale Erin is spelt instead of Eirinn and Eireann; Alba and Sassun, *Scotland* and *England*, express the sound of the Gaelic words.

"Is that thy thought, son of my sister?" said the king. Thou hadst neither claim nor right to the realm unless I myself had chosen to give it to thee with my own free will. Thou wilt not see thyself handling Erin till I go first under the mould."

"There will be a day of battle and combat before I let this go on," said the young man.

He went away, and he sailed to Alba. A message was sent up to the king of Alba that the young king of Erin was come to Alba to see him. He was taken up on the deadly points.* Meat was set in the place for eating; drink in the place for drinking; and music in the place for hearing; and they were plying the feast and the company.

"Oh! young king of Erin," said the king of Alba, "it was not without the beginning of some matter that thou art come to Alba."

"I should not wish to let out the knowledge of my matter till I should first know whether I may get it."

"Anything I have thou gettest it, for if I were seeking help, perhaps I would go to thee to get it."

"There came a word with trouble between me and my mother's brother. It was proclaimed out that I was king of Erin; and he said to me that I should have nothing to do with anything till a clod should first go on him. I wish to stand my right, and to get help from thee."

"I will give thee that," said the king; "three hundred swift heroes, three hundred brave heroes, three hundred full heroes; and that is not bad helping."

"I am without a chief over them, and I am as ill off as I was before; but I have another small request, and if I might get it, I would wish to let it out."

---

* Probably lifted on spears.

"Anything I have that I can part from, thou shalt get it," said the king; "but the thing I have not, I cannot give it to thee. Let out thy speech, and thou shalt have it."

"It is Boinne Breat, thy son, at their head."

"My torture to thee! had I not promised him to thee, thou hadst not got him. But there were not born in Alba, nor in Erin, nor in Sassun, nor in any one place (those) who would gain victory over my son if they keep to fair play. If my son does not come back as he went, the word of an Eriannach is never again to be taken, for it is by treachery he will be overcome."

They went away on the morrow, and they sailed to the king of Sassun. A message went up to the king of Sassun that the young king of Erin had come to the place. The king of Sassun took out to meet him. He was taken up on the deadly points; music was raised, and lament laid down in the palace of the king of Sassun; meat was set in the place for eating; drink in the place for drinking; music in the place of hearing; and they were plying the feast and the company with joy and pleasure of mind.

"Oh! young king of Erin," said the king of Sassun, "it is not without the end of a matter that thou art come here."

"I got the schooling of the son of a king and a ridere. My mother's brother took me home. He began to speak about the vassals of the country and the people of the realm; that care and trouble were on him; and that he had rather the end of the year had not come at all. Said I to him, 'I will build thee a palace, so that thou shalt have but to wash thy face, and stretch thy feet in thy shoes.' Said he, 'My sister's son, thou hadst no right to the realm, and thou gettest it not till a clod goes on me, in spite of everything.' Said I, 'There will be a day of battle and combat between thee and me, before the matter is so.' I went away; I took my ship; I took a skipper with me; and I sailed to Alba. I reached Alba, and I got three hundred swift heroes, three hundred brave heroes, and three hundred full heroes; now I am come to thee to see what help thou wilt give me."

"I will give thee as many more, and a hero at their head," said the king of Sassun.

They went away, and they sailed to Erin. They went on shore on a crag in Erin, and the name of Carrig Fhearghuis is on that rock still. He reached the king. "Brother of my mother, art thou now ready?"—"Well, then, Fhearghuis, though I said that, I thought thou wouldst not take anger; but I have not gathered my lot of people yet."—"That is no answer for me. Thou hast Erin under thy rule. I am here with my men, and I have neither place, nor meat, nor drink for them."

"Oo!" said the king, "the storehouses of Erin are open beneath thee, and I will go away and gather my people."

He went away. He went all round Erin. He came to a place which they called "An t' Iubhar" (Newry). There was but one man in Iubhar, who was called Goibhlean Gobha (Goivlan Smith). He thought to go in, for thirst was on him; and that he would quench his thirst, and breathe a while. He went in. There was within but the smith's daughter. She brought him a chair in which he might sit. He asked for a drink. The smith's daughter did not know what she should do, for the smith had but one cow, which was called the Glas Ghoibhlean (Grey Goivlan), with the vessel he had for the milk of the cow; three times in the day it would go beneath the cow; three times in the day thirst would be on him; and he would drink the vessel each time, and unless the daughter had the vessel full she was not to get off. She was afraid, when the king asked for a drink, that unless she had the vessel full her head would be taken off. It was so that she thought the vessel should be set before the king at all hazards. She brought down the vessel, and she set it before him. He drank a draught; he took out the fourth part, and he left three quarters in it. "I would rather you should take it out altogether than leave it. My father has made an oath that unless I have the vessel full, I have but to die."

"Well, then," said the king, "it is a spell of my spells to leave the vessel as full as it was before."

He set the vessel on the board, he struck his palm on it, and he struck off as much as was above the milk, and the vessel was full; and before he went away, the girl was his own.

"Now, thou art going, oh king of Erin, and I am shamed; what wilt thou leave with me?"

"I would give thee a thousand of each hue, a thousand of each kind, a thousand of each creature."

"What should I do with that, for I wilt not find salt in Erin to salt them?"

"I would give thee glens and high moors to feed them from year to year."

"What should I do with that? for if Fearghus should kill you, he will take it from me, unless I have it with writing, and a drop of blood to bind it."

"I am in haste this night, but go to-morrow to the camp to Croc Maol Nam Muc," said the king; and he left his blessing with her.

Her father came.

"Far from thee—far from thee be it, my daughter!

I think that a stranger has been to see thee here this day."

"How dost thou know that?"

"Thou hadst a maiden's slow eyelash when I went out; thou hast the brisk eyelash of a wife now."

"Whom wouldst thou rather had been here?"

"I never saw the man I would rather be here than the king of Erin."

"Well, it was he; he left me a thousand of each hue, a thousand of each kind, a thousand of each creature.

"'What,' said I, 'shall I do with them, as I cannot get in Erin as much salt as will salt them?'

"Said he, 'I would give thee glens and high moors to feed them from year to year.'

"'What shall I do if Fearghus should kill you? I will not get them.'

"He said, 'I should have writing and a drop of his own blood to bind it.'"

They slept that night as they were. If it was early that the day came, it was earlier that the smith arose. "Come, daughter, and let us be going." She went, herself and the smith, and they reached the king in his camp.

"Wert thou not in the Iubhar yesterday?" said the smith to the king, "I was; and hast thou mind of thy words to the girl?"

"I have; but the battle will not be till to-morrow. I will give thee, as I said, to the girl; but leave her."

The smith got that, and he went away.

That night, when she had slept a while, she awoke, for she had seen a dream. "Art thou waking?"

"I am; what wilt thou with me? I saw a dream there: a shoot of fir growing from the heart of the king, one from my own heart, and they were twining about each other." "That is our babe son." They slept, and it was not long till she saw the next dream.

"Art thou waking, king of Erin?" "I am; what wilt thou with me?" "I saw another dream. Fearghus coming down, and taking the head and the neck out of me."

"That is, Fearghus killing me, and taking out my head and neck."

She slept again, and she saw another dream.

"Art thou sleeping, king of Erin?"

"I am not; what wilt thou with me now?"

"I saw Erin, from side to side, and from end to end, covered with sheaves of barley and oats. There came a blast of wind from the east, from the west, from the north; every tree was swept away, and no more of them were seen."

"Fearghus will kill me, and he will take the head and neck out of me. As quickly as ever thou didst (anything), seize my set of arms, and keep them. A baby boy is begotten between thee and me. Thou shalt suckle and nurse him, and thou shalt set him in order. Keep the arms. When thou seest that he has speech, and can help himself, thou shalt send him away through the world a wandering, till he find out who he is. He will get to be king over Erin; his son will be king over Erin; his grandson will be king over Erin. His race will be kings over Erin till it reaches the ninth knee. A child will be born from that one. A farmer will come in with a fish; he will cook the fish; a bone will stick in his throat, and he will be choked."

Maobh, the king's sister, the mother of Fearghus, had two other sons, and the battle was to be on the morrow. Lagh an Laidh and Connal; and Lagh an Laidh was the eldest.

"Whether," said Lagh an Laidh, "shall we be with our mother's brother or with Fearghus?"

"I know not. If our mother's brother wins, and we are with Fearghus, it is a stone in our shoe for ever; but if Fearghus wins, he will turn his back to us, because we were on the other side."

"Well, then, it is not thus it shall be; but be thou with Fearghus, and I will be with our mother's brother."

"It shall not be so; we will leave it to our mother."

"Were I a man," said Maobh, "I would set the field with my own brother."

"Well, then, I will be with Fearghus," said Lagh an Laidh, "and be thou with Fearghus, oh Connal!"

Fearghus went to Fionn; he blessed him in calm, soft words. Fionn blessed him in better words; and if no better, they were no worse.

"I heard that there was a day of battle and combat between thyself and thy mother's brother," said he.

"That is to be, and I came to you for help."

"It is but bold for me to go against thy mother's brother, since it was on his land that I got my keep. If thy mother's brother should win, we shall get neither furrow nor clod of the land of Erin as long as we live. I will do thus. I will not strike a blow with thee, and I will not strike a blow against thee."

Fearghus went home on the morrow, and they set in order for the battle. The king's company was on one side, and the company of Fearghus on the other. Fearghus had no GAISGICH heroes but Boinne Breat and his company. The great Saxon hero and his company, and Lagh an Laidh. Boinne Breat drew out to the skirt of the company; he put on his harness of battle and hard combat. He set his silken netted coat above his surety* shirt; a booming shield on his left side; how many deaths were in his tanned sheath!

He strode out on the stern steps like a sudden blaze; each pace he put from him was less than a hill, and greater than a knoll on the mountain side. He turned on them, cloven and cringing. Three ranks would he drive of them, dashing them from their shields, to their blood and their flesh in the skies.† Would he not leave one to tell the tale, or report bad news; to put in a land of holes or a shelf of rock. There was one little one-eyed russet man, one-eyed, and on one knee and one handed. "Thou shalt not be to tell a tale of me;" he went and he took his head off. Then Boinne Breat shunned the fight, and he took his armour off.

"Go down, Fearghus, and take off the head of thy mother's brother, or I will take it off."

Fearghus went down, he caught hold of his mother's brother, and he took his head off. The smith's daughter went to the arms, and she took them with her.

Lagh an Laidh kept on his armour. When he saw Fearghus going to take off the head of his mother's brother, he took a frenzy. Lagh and Laidh went about the hill to try if he could see Boinne Breat, who was unarmed. Boinne Breat thought that man was drunk

---

* Corr, the epithet applied to a shirt, is a word which gives the meaning of greatness or excess; and in *corran*, means an iron weapon, or a sickle. "A shirt of armour."

† This passage is common; I am not certain that it is correctly rendered.

with battle. He thought that he would turn on the other side of the hill to try if he could come to his own place. Lagh an Laidh turned on the other side against him. He thought to turn again to try if the battle frenzy would abate. The third time he said he would not turn for all who were in Albuin, or Eirinn, or Sassun. "It is strange thou, man, that wert with me throughout the battle, to be against me?" I will not believe but that thou hast taken the drunkenness of battle," said Boinne Breat.

"I am quite beside myself."

"Well, then," said he, "though I am unarmed, and thou under arms, remember that thou art no more to me than what I can hold between these two fingers."

"I will not be a traiter to thee, there behind thee are three of the best heroes in Albuin, or Eirinn, or Sassun."

He gave a turn to see the three heroes, and when he turned Lagh an Laigh struck off his head.

"My torture," said Fearghus, "I had rather my own head were there. An Eireannach is not to be taken at his word as long as a man shall live. It is a stone in thy shoe every day for ever, and a pinch of the land of Eirinn thou shalt not have."

Lagh and Laidh went away and he went to the mountain. He made a castle for himself there, and he stayed in it.

The smith's daughter came on well till she bore a babe-son. She gave him the name of Conal Mac Righ Eirinn. She nourished him well, and right well. When speech came and he could walk well, she took him with her on a wet misty day to the mountain amongst high moors and forests. She left him there astray to make out a way for himself, and she went home.

He did not know in the world what he should do, as he did not know where to go, but he found a finger of a road. He followed the road. What should he see but a little hut at the evening of the day at the way-side. He went into the hut: there was no man within: he let himself down at the fire-side. There he was till a woman came at the end of the night, and she had six sheep. She saw a great slip of a man beside the fire, who seemed to be a fool. She took great wonder when she saw him, and she said that he had better go out of that, and go down to the king's house, and that he would get something amongst the servants in the kitchen. He said he would not go, but if she would give him something that he might eat, that he would go to herd the sheep for herself. What should be the name of the woman but CAOMHAG Gentle. "If I thought that, I would give thee meat and drink," said she. On the morrow he went away with the sheep. "I have not a bite of grass for them," said she, "but a road; and thou shalt keep them at the edge of the road, and thou shalt not let them off it."

At the time of night he came home with them; on the morrow he went away with the sheep. There were near to the place where he was with them three fields of wheat that belonged to three gentlemen. The sheep were wearing him out. He went and he levelled the dyke, and he let them in from one to the other till they had eaten the three fields. On a day of days, the three gentlemen gathered. When they came, he had let the fields be eaten by the sheep.

"Who art thou? Thou hast eaten the fields?"

"It was not I that ate them at all; it was the sheep that ate them."

"We will not be talking to him at all; he is but a

fool. We will reach Caomhag to see if the sheep are hers."

They reached Caomhag. They took her with them to the court. This was the first court that Fearghus had made after he got the crown.

The kings had a heritage at that time. When they did not know how to split justice properly, the judgment-seat would begin to kick, and the king's neck would take a twist when he did not do justice as he ought.

"I can make nothing of it," said the king, "but that they should have the tooth that did the damage."

The judgment-seat would begin to kick, and the king's neck took a turn. Come here one of you and loose me; try if you can do justice better than that." Though there were thousands within, none would go in the king's place. They would not give the king such bad respect, as that any one of them would go before him.

"Is there a man that will loose me?"

"There is not, unless the herd of Caomhag himself will loose thee."

Caomhag's herd was set down.

"Loose for me, my little hero, and do justice as it should (be done), and let me out of this."

"(Nor) right nor justice will I do before I get something that I may eat."

Then he got something which he ate.

"What justice didst thou do thyself?" said he.

"I did but (doom) the tooth that did the damage to be theirs."

"What was in the way that thou didst not give death to Caomhag? This is what I would do:—Caomhag has six sheep, and though the six sheep were taken from her, they would not pay the gentlemen. Caomhag will have six lambs, the gentlemen shall have the six lambs, and she herself shall have the sheep to keep."

The turn went out of the king's neck. He went away, and they did not ask who he was, and he got no skaith.

There was another gentleman, and he had a horse, and he sent him to a smithy to be shod. The smith had a young son and a nurse under the child. What should it be but a fine day, and it was without that the horse was being shod, and she never saw a horse shod before; and she went out to see the shoeing of the horse. She sat opposite to the horse, and he took the nail and the shoe, and he did not hit the hoof with the nail but he put it in the flesh, and the horse struck the child, and drove the cup of his head off. They had but to go to justice again to the king, and the justice the king made for them was, that the leg should be taken off the horse. The judgment-seat began to kick again, and the king's neck took a twist. The herd of Caomhag was there, and they asked him to loose the king. He said that he would not do a thing till he should first get something to eat.

He got that. He went where the king was.

"What law didst thou make?"

"The leg to be taken off the horse?"

"That will not pay the smith. Send hither to me the *groom* that broke the horse, and the gentleman to whom he belongs. Send over here the smith and the nurse."

The gentleman and the groom came.

"Well then, my gentleman, didst thou make this groom break this horse as he should?"

The groom said that he had done that as well as he knew (how to do it).

"No more could be asked of thee. Well, smith, didst thou give an order to the nurse to stay within without coming out of her chamber?"

"I did not give it," said the smith, "but (she might do) as she chose herself."

"My gentleman," said he, "since thou art best kept, I will put a third of the EIRIC of the smith's son on thee, and another third on the smith himself, because he did not measure the nail before he put it to use, and another third on the nurse and the groom because she did not stay within in her chamber, and in case he left some word or other untaught to the horse."

The gentleman went away and the smith; the judgment-seat stopped, and she hadn't a kick; the turn came out of the king's neck, and they let him go as usual.

Said the king—"If he has travelled over the universe and the world, there is a drop of king's blood in that lad; he could not split the law so well as that if it were not in him. Let the three best heroes I have go, and let them bring me his head."

They went after him. He gave a glance from him and what should he see coming but they. They came where he was. "Where are you going?"—"We are going to kill thyself. The king sent us to thee."

"Well, then, that was but a word that came into his mouth, and it is not worth your while to kill me."

"He is but a fool," said they.

"Since he sent you to kill me, why don't you kill me?"

"Wilt thou thyself kill thyself, my little hero?" said they.

"How shall I kill myself?"

"Here's for thee a sword and strike it on thee about the neck, and cast the head off thyself," said they.

He seized on the sword, and gave it a twirl in his fist. "Fall to killing thyself, my little hero."

"Begone," said he, "and return home, and do not hide from the king that you did not kill me."

"Well, then, give me the sword," said one of them.

"I will not give it; there are not in Erin as many as will take it from my fist," said he.

They went and they returned home. As he was going by himself, he said, "I was not born without a mother, and I was not begotten without a father. I have no mind (of) ever coming to Erin, and I know that it was in Erin I was born. I will not leave a house in which there is smoke or fire in Erin till I know who I (am)."

He went to the Iubhar. What was it but a fine warm day. Whom did he see but his mother washing. He was coming to a sort of understanding, so that he was thinking that it was his mother who was there. He went and he went behind her, and he put his hand on her breast. "Indeed," said he, "a foster son of thy right breast am I." She gave her head a toss. "Thy like of a *tarlaid* drudge, I never had as a son or a foster son."—"My left hand is behind thy head, and a sword in my right hand, and I will strike off thy head unless thou tell me who I am."—"Still be thy hand, Conall, son of the king of Erin."

"I knew myself I was that, and that there was a drop of the blood of a king's son in me; but who killed my father?"

"Fearghus killed him; and a loss as great as thy

father was slain on the same day—that was Boinne Breat, son of the king of Alba."

"Who slew Boinne Breat?"—"It is a brother of Fearghus, whom they call Lagh an Laidh."

"And where is that man dwelling?"

"He could not get a bit on the land of Erin when once he had slain Boinne Breat; he went to the hills, and he made him a 'còs'* in the forest, amongst '*uille biaste*,' monsters, and untamed creatures."

"Who kept my father's arms?"—"It is I."

"Go fetch them, and bring them hither to me." She brought them.

He went and put the arms on him, and they became him as well as though they had been made for himself.

"I eat not a bit, and I drink not a draught, and I make no stop but this night, until I reach where that man is, wheresoever he may be."

He passed that night where he was. In the morning, on the morrow he went away; he went on till there was black upon his soles and holes in his shoes. The white clouds of day were going, and the black clouds of night coming, and without his finding a place of staying or rest for him. There he saw a great wood. He made a "còs," in one of the trees above in which he might stay that night. In the morning, on the morrow he cast a glance from him. What should he see but the very *uile bheist*, whose like was never seen under the sun, stretched without clothing, without foot coverings, or head covering, hair and beard gone over him. He thought, though he should go down,

* Còs, a hollow or cave; here a kind of dwelling scooped out in the side of a hill.

that he could not do for him. He put an arrow in a "*crois*," and he "fired" at him. He struck him with it on the right fore-arm, and the one who was below gave a start. "Move not a sinew of thy sinews, nor a vein of thy veins, nor a bit of thy flesh, nor a hair of thy locks, till thou promise to see me a king over Erin, or I will send down of slender oaken darts enough to sew thee to the earth." The uile bheist did not give him yielding for that. He went and he fired again, and he struck him in the left fore-arm. "Did I not tell thee before, not to stir a vein of thy veins nor a bit of thy flesh, nor a hair of thy locks till thou shouldst promise to see me king over Erin."—"Come down then, and I will see thyself or myself that before this time to morrow night." He came down.

"If I had known that it was thy like of a drudge that should dictate thus to me, I would not do it for thee for anything; but since I promised thee I will do it, and we will be going."

They went to the palace of the king. They shouted Battle or Combat to be sent out, or else the head of Fearghus, or himself a captive.

Battle and combat they should get, and not his head at all, and they could not get himself a captive.

There were sent out four hundred swift heroes, four hundred full heroes, and four hundred strong heroes.

They began at them. The one could not put from the other's hand as they were killed.

They shouted battle or combat again, or else the head of Fearghus to be sent out, or himself a captive.

"It is battle and combat thou shalt have, and not at all my head, and no more shalt thou get myself a captive."

There were sent out twelve hundred swift heroes,

twelve hundred full heroes, and twelve hundred stout heroes.

The one could not put from the other's hand as they killed of them.

They shouted battle and combat, or else the head of Fearghus, or himself a captive.

Battle and combat they should have, and not the head of Fearghus at all, nor himself a captive.

There were sent out four hundred score to them. The one could not put from the other as they killed.

They shouted battle and combat.

"Those who are without," said Fearghus, "are so hard (to please) that they will take but my head, and unless they get (it) they will kill all there are in Erin and myself after them. Take one of you a head from one of those who were slain, and when Lagh an Laidh comes and asks my head, or myself a captive, give it to him, and he will think it is my head."

The head was given to Lagh an Laidh. He went where Conall was with it.

"What hast thou there?" said Conall.

"The head of Fearghus."

"That is not the head of Fearghus yet. I saw him a shorter (time) than thyself, but turn and bring hither to me the head of Fearghus."

Lagh an Laidh returned.

"Let another go to meet him in the king's stead, and say that it is his head he shall get, not himself a captive.

This one went to meet Lagh an Laidh. He seized him and took the head out of his neck.

He reached Conall. "What hast thou there?"—"The head of Fearghus."

"That is not the head of Fearghus yet; turn and bring to me the head of Fearghus."

Lagh an Laidh returned.

"The one who is without is so watchful, and the other is so blind, that there is no man in Erin but they will kill unless they get myself."

"Where art thou going, Lagh an Laidh?" said Fearghus.

"I am going to seek thy head, or thyself as a captive."

"It's my head thou shalt get, and not myself as a captive; but what kindness art thou giving thy brother?

"The kindness that thou gavest thyself to me, I will give it to thee."

He took the head out of his neck, and he took it with him. He came where Conall was.

"What hast thou there?"—"The head of Fearghus."—"It is not."—"Truly it is."—"Let me see it."

He gave it to him. He drew it, and he struck him with it, and he made two heads of the one. Then they began at each other.

They would make a bog on the rock, and a rock on the bog. In the place where the least they would sink, they would sink to the knees, in the place where the most they would sink, they would sink to the eyes.

Conall thought it would be ill for him to fall after he had got so near the matter.

He drew his sword, and he threw the head off Lagh an Laidh.

"Now I am king over Erin, as I myself had a right to be."

He took his mother and her father from the Iubhar, and took them to the palace; and his race were in it till the ninth knee. The last one was choked, as a babe, with a splinter of bone that went crosswise into his throat, and another tribe came in on EIRINN.

CONALL.

Bha sean righ roimhe so ann an Eirinn agus bha triùir mac aig piuthar dha. Be 'm fear a bu shine dhiu Fearghus, am fear a bu mhiadhonaiche Lagh an Làigh, 's am fear a b' òige Conall. Smaointich e gon dianadh e oighre do 'n fhear a bu shine Fearghus. Thug e sgoil mhic righ agus ridire dha, agus nur a bha e buidheach sgoil agus ionnsachaidh thug e dhachaidh e do 'n phàileas. Bha eud an so anns a' phaileas. Urs' an righ, "Chuir mi seachad a' bhliadhna so go math. Tha ceann na bliadhna nis a' tighinn 's tha trioblaid agus cùram a' tigh 'n orm leatha." "Dé 'n trioblaid na 'n cùram a tha tigh 'n ort?" urs' am fear òg. "Tha tuath na duthcha tigh 'n a chunndas rium an diugh." "Cha ruig thu leas cùram a bhi ort 'tha e air eubhach a mach gor mis' an t-oighr' òg 's air a chur sìos ann am paipeirean 's an litrichean anns gach ceàrn de 'n rioghachd. Togaidh mise caisteal bòidheach air bialthaobh a' phàileas duit. Gheibh mi saoir agus clachairean agus goibhnean gos a' chaisteal sin a thogail." "An e sin smaointinn a th' agad a mhic mo pheathar," ars' an Righ, "cha robh ceart na còir agad air an rioghachd fhaotainn mar an tograinn fhìn a toirt duit le m' thoil fhìn. Cha 'n fhaic thusa laimhseachadh Eirinn agad gos an d' théid mise an toiseach fo 'n ùir." "Bidh latha blàir agus batailt ann ma 'n lig mise sin air aghaidh," urs' am fear òg.

Dh' fhalbh e agus sheòl e go ruig Alba. Chuireadh brath a suas thun righ Alba gon robh rìgh òg Eirinn air tigh 'n go ruig Alba g'a choimhead. Thugadh suas air bharraibh bas e. Chuireadh biadh an àit' a chaithidh, deoch an ait a h-òl, agus ceòl an àit' éisdeachd. Bha eud a' caitheadh na cuirm agus na cuideachd.

"A rìgh òg Eirinn," ursa righ Àlba, "cha n' ann gon cheann gnothaich a thàinig thusa go ruig Alba." "Cha bu mhath leam fios mo gnothaich a ligeil a mach gos am biodh fhios'am am faighinn an toiseach e." "Dad 's am bith a th' agamsa gheibh thus' e, chionn na'm bithinn aig iarraidh cuideachaidh cha lughaide gon rachainn a t' ionnsuidh-s' airson fhaotainn." "Facal a thàinig ann an doilgheas eadar mis' agus brath 'r mo mhàthar." "Bha e air eubhach a mach go 'm bu mhi righ Eirinn; 's thuirt e rium nach biodh gnothach agam ri ni gos an rachadh plochd airsan an toiseach. Tha toil agam mo chòir a sheasamh agus cuideachadh fhaotainn uaitse." "Bheir mise sin duit," ars' an Righ, "tri chiad lùgh ghaisgeach, tri chiad treun-ghaisgeach, agus tri chiad làn-ghaisgeach, 's cha don' an cuideachadh sin." "Tha mise gon cheannard as an cionn, 's tha mi cho dona 's a bha mi roimhid; ach tha iarrtas beag eil' agam, agus na 'm faighinn e bhithinn deònach air a ligeil a mach." "Rud sam bith a th' agamsa," ars' an Righ, "'s is urra mi dealachadh ris gheibh thu e, ach rud nach 'eil agam cha n' urra mi 'thoirt duit; ach lig amach do chainnt 's gheibh thu e." "'Se sin Boinne Breat do mhac air an ceann." "Mo ghonadh dhuit, na 'm bithinn gon a ghealltainn duit cha n' fhaigheadh thu e; ach cha do rugadh an Albainn, na 'n Eirinn, na 'n Sasunn, na 'n aon àite na gheibheadh buaidh air mo mhacsa, ach fantainn aig ceartas; mar an d' thig mo mhacs' air ais mar a dh' fhalbh e cha 'n 'eil facal Eireannaich ri ghabhail tuillidh, chionn 's ann am foill a thigt' air."

Dh' fhalbh eud an la 'r na mhàireach 's sheòl eud 'ionnsuidh righ Shasuinn. Chaidh brath suas go righ Shasuinn gon robh righ òg Eirinn an déigh tigh 'n do 'n àite. Ghabh righ Shasuinn 'na chomhdhail 's thugadh suas air bharraibh bas e. Thogadh ceòl 's leagadh bron ann am pàileas righ Shasuinn. Chuireadh biadh an àit' a chaitheadh, deoch an àit' a h-òl, agus ceòl an àit' éisdeachd. Bha eud a' caitheadh na cuirm 's na cuideachd le aighear 's le toilinntinn.

"A righ òg Eirinn," ursa righ Shasuinn, "cha n' ann gon cheann gnothaich a thàinig thu 'n so." "Fhuair mise sgoil mhic righ agus ridire. Thug brath 'r mo mhàthar dachaidh mi. Thòisich e air bruidhinn mo thuath na duthcha 's mo mhuinntir na rioghachd, gon robh curam agus trioblaid air, 's gom b' fhearr leis nach d' thàinig ceann na bliadhn' idir. Ursa mise ris togaidh mise paileas duit, air alt 's nach bi agad ach t' aodann a nigheadh 's do chasan a shìneadh ann a'd' bhrògan. Urs' esan, "A mhic mo pheathar cha robh còir agad air an rioghachd, 's cha 'n fhaigh thu i, gos an d' theid plochd ormsa, aona chuid a dheoin na dh' aindeoin." Ursa mi ris, "Bidh latha blàir agus batailt eadar mis' agus thusa ma 'm bi chùis mur sin." Dh' fhalbh mi, ghabh mi go long, thug mi leam sgioba, agus sheòl mi go ruig Alba. Ràinig mi Alba, 's fhuair mi tri chiad lùgh-ghaisgeach, tri chiad treun-ghaisgeach, agus tri chiad làn-ghaisgeach. Nis thàinig mi 't' ionnsuidhsa fiach de 'n cuideachadh a bheir thu dhomh."

"Bheir mise dhuit urad eile agus gaisgeach air an ceann," ursa Righ Shassuinn.

Dh' fhalbh eud agus sheòl eud go Eirinn. Chaidh eud air tìr aig Carraig an Eirinn 's tha Carraig Fhearghuis mar ainm air a' charraig sin fhathasd. Ràinig e 'n righ. "A bhrath'r mo mhàthar, a' bheil thu nis deas." "Mata Fhearghuis gad a thuirt mise siud shaoil mi nach gabhadh thu corruich; ach tha mise gon mo chuid sluaigh a chruinneachadh fhathasd." "Cha fhreagair sin domhsa, tha Eirinn agadsa fo d' smachd, tha mise 'n so le m' dhaoine 's cha 'n eil àite, na biadh, na deoch agam dhaibh." "U!" urs' an righ, "Fhearghuis tha taighean taisg Eirinn fosgailte fodhad, agus falbhaidh mise 's cruinnichidh mi mo chuid sluaigh.

Dh' fhalbh an righ, chaidh e ma 'n cuairt Eirinn. Thàinig e go àite ris an canadh eud an t-Iubhar. Cha robh ach aon duine 'san Iubhar ris an canadh eud Goibhlean Gobha. Smaointich e gabhail a stigh 's am pathadh air, 's gon caisgeadh e phathadh 's gon ligeadh e treis analach. Ghabh e stigh. Cha robh stigh ach nighean a' ghobha. Thug i a 'ionnsuidh cathair air an suidheadh e. Dh' iarr e deoch. Cha robh fios aig nighean a' ghobha dé dhianadh i. Cha robh aig a' ghobh ach an aon mhart ris an abradh eud a' Ghlas Ghoibhlean. Leis a' chòrn a bh' aige ri bainne na bà, 's tri uairean 's an latha a rachte fo 'n mhart. Tri uairean 'san latha bhiodh pathadh airsan, 's dh' òladh e 'n còrn air a h-uile siubhal. Mar am biodh an còrn làn aig a nighinn cha robh ri dol as a chionn aice. Bha eagal urra, nur a dh' iarr an righ deoch, mur am biodh an còrn làn aice gom biodh an ceann air a thoirt dith. 'Se smaointich i gom bu chòir an còrn a chur air bialthaobh an righ codhiu. Thug i nuas an corn 's chuir i air a bhialthaobh e. Dh' òl e deoch, 's thug e 'n ceathramh cuid as, 's dh' fhàg e tri earrannan ann. "B' fhearr leam sibh a 'thoirt as go léir na fhàgail. Thug m' athair mionnan mar am bi 'n corn làn nach eil agam ri dol go chionn." "Mata," ars' an righ, "'s geas de m' gheasans' an còrn fhàgail cho làn 'sa bha e roimhid." Chuir e 'n corn air a' bhord, bhuail e bhas air, 's chuir e dheth na bha as cionn a' bhainne, 's bha 'n corn làn. Man d' fhalbh an righ fhuair e 'n nighean da fhìn. "Tha thu falbh a righ Eirinn 's mise an deigh mo mhaslachaidh; dè tha thu fàgail agam?" "Bheireamsa sin duit mìl' as gach dath, mìl' as gach seòrsa, mìl' as gach creutair." "Dé ni mise deth sin, 's nach fhaigh mi 'shalann an Eirinn na shailleas sin?" "Bheiream dhuit glinn a's monaidh a bheothaicheas eud o bhliadhna go bliadhna." "Dé ni mise dheth sin? ma mharbhas Fearghus sibhse 'màireach bheir e uam e, o 'n nach robh e agam le sgriobhadh agus boinne fala 'ga cheanghal." "Tha orms' a nochd cabhag, ach theirig am màireach do 'n champ go Cnoc maol nam Muc," ars' an righ, agus dh' fhàg e beannachd aice. Thàinig a h-athair. "Bhuais e, bhuais e nighean, cha 'n 'eil dùil' am fhìn nach robh arbhalach ga d' choimhead an so an diugh." "Cémur a tha thu 'g aithneachadh sin?" "Bha rasg maull maighdinn agad nur a chaidh mi mach; tha rasg brisg mnà agad an dràsd." "Co b' fhearr leat a bhi ann?" "Cha 'n fhaca mi duine riabh a b' fhearr leam a bhi ann na righ Eirinn." "Mata 's e bh' ann. Dh' fhàg e agam mìl as gach dath, mìl' as gach seòrsa, mìl' as gach creutair. De, ursa mise, ni mise dhiu, 's nach fhaigh mi de shalann an Eirinn na shailleas eud? Urs' esan, "Bheiream duit glinn agus monaidhean a bheathaicheas eud o bhliadhna go bliadhna." Dé ni mi ma mharbhas Fearghus sibhse, cha 'n fhaigh mi sin? Thuirt e rium gom faighinn sgrìobhadh 's boinne da fhuil fhìn 'ga cheanghal."

Chaidil eud an oidhche sin mar a bha eud. Ma bu mhoch a thainig an latha bu mhoiche na sìn a dh' éiridh an gobha. "Thalla 'nighean, bitheamaid a' falbh." Dh' fhalbh i fhìn 's an gobha 's ràinig eud an righ anns a' champ. "Nach robh thu anns an Iubhar an dé?" urs' an gobha ris an righ. "Bha." "Bheil cuimhn' agad air do bhriathran ris an nighinn so. "Tha, ach cha bhi 'm blar ann gos am màireach, bheir mi dhuit mar a thuirt mi ris an nighinn ach go fag thu ise." Fhuair an gobha siud agus dh' fhalbh e.

An oidhche sin, nur a bha ise treis na cadal, dhùisg i, 's i 'n déigh aislig fhaicinn. "A' bheil thu 'd' dhùsgadh?" "Tha, dé do ghnothach domh?" "Chunnaic mi aislig an siud, gathar giubhais a' fàs a cridh' an righ, fear a m' chridhe fhìn, 's eud a' snaomadh 'na chéile. "Sin leanabh mic an déigh a ghineach eadar thus' a's mis' a nochd." Chaidil eud an uair sin, 's cha b' fhada chaidil eud gos am fac i 'n ath aislig. "A bheil thu 'd' dhùsgadh a righ Eirinn?" "Tha, dé do ghnothach domh?" "Chunnaic mi aislig eile, Fearghus a' tigh 'n a nuas 'sa toirt a' chinn 's an amhuich agam fhìn asam." "Sin Fearghus gam mharbhadhsa 'sa toirt a' chinn 's an amhùich asam." Chaidil i rìs agus chunnaic i aislig eile. "A bheil thu 'd' chadal a righ Eirinn?" "Cha 'n 'eil, dé do ghnothach domh an drasd?"

" Chunnaic mi Eirinn, o thaobh go taobh agus o cheann go ceann, air a chomhdach le sguaban eòrn' agus coirce; thàinig oiteag shoirbheis o 'n ear, o 'n iar, a 'n tuath; sguabadh air falbh a h-uile craobh, 's cha 'n fhacas gin riabh tuillidh dhiu." " Marbhaidh Fearghus mise 's bheir e 'n ceann 's an amhach asam; co luath 's a rinn thusa riabh beir air mo chuid arm, agus gléidh eud. Tha leanabh mic air a ghineach eadar mis' a's thusa. Bheir thu cìoch a's altram da, 's cuiridh thu 'n òrdugh e. Gléidh na h-airm. Nur a chi thu gom bi cainnt as comhnadal aige cuiridh tu air falbh e, feadh an t-saoghail, air seachran, gos am faigh e mach co e fhìn. Gheibh esan 'na righ air Eirinn, bidh a mhac 'na righ air Eirinn, bidh otha 'na righ air Eirinn, bidh a shliochd na 'n righrean air Eirinn, gos an ruig an naoidheamh glùn. Bidh leanabh air a bhreith do 'n fhear sin, thig tuathanach a stigh le iasg, bruichidh e 'n t-iasg, 's théid cnàimh 'na amhuich, 's tachdar e."

Bha dithisd mac eil' aig Maobh (Piuthar an righ, màthair Fhearghuis) 's bha 'm blàr ri bhi ann a màireach, Lagh an làidh agus Conall, agus 'se Lagh an làidh a bu shine. "Co dhiu," ursa Lagh an làidh, "a bhios sinn le brath'r ar màthar na le Fearghus?" "Cha 'n 'eil fhios 'am; ma bhuidhneas Bràthair ar màthar agus gom bi sinn le Fearghus, 's clach 'nar bròig go bràth'ch e; ach ma bhuidhneas Fearghus cuiridh e cùl ruinn, o 'n a bha sinn air ann taobh eile." " Mata cha 'n ann mar sin a bhitheas, ach bi thusa le Fearghus, 's bidh mise le bràthair ar màthar." " Cha 'n ann mur sin a bhitheas, ligidh sinn g' ar màthair e." "Na 'm bithinnsa 'm fhirionnach," ursa Maobh, "bhithinn a' cur a bhlàir le m bhràthair fhin." "Mata bidh mis' aig Fearghus," ursa Lagh an làidh, "'s bi thus' aig Fearghus a Chonaill."

Dh' fhalbh Fearghus 'ionnsuidh Fhinn, 's bheannaich e dha ann am briathran ciuine, mìne. Bheannaich Fionn da ann am briathran a b' fheàrr; mur am b' eud a b' fheàrr cha b' eud a bu mhiosa. " Chuala mi gon robh latha blàir agus batailt eadar thu fhìn agus bràthair do mhàthar," ars' esan. "Tha sinn ri bhi ann 's thainig mi 'ur ionnsuidhsa airson cuideachaidh." "Cha 'n 'eil e ach dàna domhsa dol an aghaidh bhràthair do mhàthar, 's gur ann air fhearann a fhuair mi mo chumail; ma bhuidhneas bràthair do mhàthar cha 'n fhaigh sinn sgrìob na plochd de dh' fhearann Eirinn a neas 's is beò sinn. 'S e so a ni mi, cha bhuail mi buille leat, 's cha bhuail mi buille 't' aghaidh."

Chaidh Fearghus dachaidh an la 'r na mhàireach. Chuir eud an òrdugh airson a' bhlàir. Bha cuideachd an righ air an darna taobh 's cuideachd Fhearghuis air an taobh eile. Cha robh 'ghaisgich aig Fearghus ach Boinne Breat 'sa chuideachd, an gàisgeach mòr Sasunnach 's a chuideachd, agus Lagh an làidh.

Tharruinn Boinne Breat a mach an iomall na cuideachd. Chaidh e na chulaidh chath agus chruaidh-chomhrag. Chuir e 'chòtan sròl sìoda air uachdar a chòrr-léine, sgiath bhucaideach air a thaobh clì, gom bu lianar oideadhar 's an truaill chairtidh. Theann e mach air na ceumannan moiteil mur bhoillsgeadh. Gach ceum a chuireadh e uaidhe, bu lugh' e na beinn, 's bu mhoth' e na meall-chnoc sléibhe. Thionndàidh e riutha go gìogach, gagach ; tri dithean gon cuireadh e dhiu ; gan cailceadh o 'n sgiathan g'am fuil agus g'am feoil, anns ann iarmailt ; nach fhàgadh e fear innsidh sgeoil na chaitheadh tuairisgeil, a chur an talamh toll, na 'n sgeilpidh chreag. Bha aon fhear beag, càm, ruadh ann, air leith shùil 's air leith ghlùn 's air leith làimh. "Cha bhi thus' ann a dh' innseadh sgeoil ormsa." Dh' fhalbh e 's thug e 'n ceann deth. Dh' òb Boinne Breat 's chuir e dheth airm. "Falbh sios Fhearghuis 's thoir an ceann de bhràthair do mhàthar no bheir mise deth e." Chaidh Fearghus sìos, rug e air bràthair a mhàthar 's thug e 'n ceann deth. Thug nighean a' ghobha thun nan arm 's thug i leath' eud. Chum Lagh an làidh air a chuid armaibh, nur a chunnaic e Fearghus a' dol a thoirt a' chinn de bhràthair a mhàthar. Ghabh e feirg. Chaidh Lagh an làidh ma 'n cuairt a chnuic fiach am faiceadh e Boinne Breat 's e gon armaibh. Smaointich Boinne Breat gor misg chath a ghabh an duin' ud. Smaointich e gon tilleadh e air an taobh eile de 'n chnoc fiach an d' thigeadh e go àite fhìn. Thiondaidh Lagh an làidh air an taobh eile 'na aghaidh. Smaointich e tilleadh a rìs fiach an traoigheadh e 'mhire-'chatha. An treas uair thuirt e nach tilleadh e airson na bha 'n Albainn, na 'n Eirinn, na 'n Sasunn. "'S neònach, fhir a bha leam fad an lath', thu bhi 'm' aghaidh." Cha chreid mi nach misg chath a ghabh thu thugad !" "Direach as an aodann a tha mi." "Mata," urs' esan, "gad a tha mise gon armaibh, agus thusa fo armaibh, cuimhnich nach moth' orm thu agus na chumas mi eadar an da mhiar sin." "Cha 'n 'eil mi ri bhi 'm brath foille dhuit ; sin air do chùl an triuir ghaisgeach is fhearr an Albainn, na 'n Eirinn, na 'n Sasunn." Thug e tionndadh air a dh' fhaicinn nan triuir ghaisgeach, agus nur a thionndaidh e thug Lagh an làidh an ceann deth. "Mo ghonadh," ursa Fearghus, "b' fhearr leam mo cheann fhìn a bhi ann. Cha 'n 'eil Eireannach ri ghabhail air fhacal a neas is beò duine tuillidh. 'S clach a'd' bhròig e h-uile latha go bràthach, agus greim de dh' fhearann Eirinn cha 'n fhaigh thu."

Dh' fhalbh Lagh an làidh agus chaidh e 'n bheinn. Rinn e caisteal dà fhìn ann agus dh' fhan e ann. Bha nighean a' ghobha tigh'n air a h-aghaidh go math gos an d' rug i leanabh mic. Thug i Conall mac righ Eirinn mar ainm air. Bheathaich i go math 's go ro mhath e. Nur thàinig càinnt a's coiseachd go math dha thug i leath' e, latha bog, ceòthar, do 'n bheinn feadh monaidh agus coille. Dh' fhàg i 'n siud e air seachran, go bhi dianadh an rathaid dha fhìn, agus chaidh ise dachaidh.

Cha robh fios aig air an t-saoghal de dhianadh e, gon fhios aige c'a 'n rachadh e, ach fhuair e miar de rathad mòr, 's lean e 'n rathad. Dé chunnaic e ach bothan beag, feasgar de latha, taobh an rathaid mhòir. Ghabh e stigh do 'n bhothan. Cha robh duine stigh ann. Lig e e fhìn ri taobh an teine, sìos, gon bhiadh gon deoch. Bha e 'n sin gos an d' thàinig boireannach dachaidh an deireadh na h-oidhche agus sia caoraich aice. Chunnaic i stiall mhòr duine taobh an teine cosail ri bhi 'na amadan. Ghabh i iongantas mòr nur a chunnaic i e, 's thuirt i ris, gom b' fhearra dha falbh e siud agus dol sios go tigh an righ, 's gom faigheadh e rud a miosg nan gillean anns a' chidsinn. Thuirt e nach rachadh, ach na 'n tugadh i dha rud a dh' itheadh e, gom biodh e falbh a bhuachailleachd nan caorach air a son fhìn. Dé'n t-ainm a bh' air a bhoireannach ach Caomhag. "N' an saoilinn sin gheibheadh thu biadh a's deoch," ars' ise.

An la 'r na mhaireach dh' fhalbh e leis na caoraich. "Cha 'n 'eil greim feoir agamsa dhaibh," urs' ise, "ach rathad mòr, 's cumaidh tu eud air iomall an rathaid mhòir, 's cha lig thu dheth eud." An am na h-oidhche thàinig e dachaidh leo. An la 'r na mhàireach dh' fhalbh e leis na caoraich. Bha, dlùth air an àite 'n robh e leo, tri pàircean cruinneachd a bheanadh do thri daoin' uaisle. Bha na caoraich ga shàrachadh ; dh' fhalbh e 's leag e 'n gàrradh, 's lig e stìgh eud o thé go té, gos an d' ith eud na tri pàircean. Latha de na làithean chruinnich na tri daoin' uaisle. Nur a thàinig eud bha esan an déigh na pàircean a ligeil itheadh leis na caoraich. "Ciod thuige dh' ith thu na pàircean." "Cha mhis' a dh' ith eud idir 's ann a dh' ith na caoraich eud." "Cha bhi sinn a' bruidhinn ris idir, cha 'n 'eil ann ach amadan, ruige sinn Caomhag fiach an leathaise na caoraich." Rainig eud Caomhag. Thug eud leo 'ionnsuidh na cùirt i. B'i so a' chiad chuirt do Fhearghus a dhiànadh an déigh dha 'n crùn fhaotainn.

Bha fàgail aig na righrean 'san am ud. Nur nach b' aithne dhaibh an ceartas a sgoltadh dòigheil, thòiseachadh cathair a bhreathanais air breabadaich, 's rachadh car an amhuich an righ nur nach dianadh e ceartas mur bu chòir dha.

"Cha 'n urra mise dad a dhianadh," urs' an righ, "ach an fhiacaill a rinn an sgath i bhi aca." Thoisich cathair a' bhreathanais ri breabadaich, 's chaidh car an amhuich an righ. "Thigeadh fear agaibh an so agus fuasglaibh orm, fiach an dian sibh an ceartas na 's fhear na siud." Gad a bhiodh mìltean a stigh cha rachadh gin an àit' an righ; cha rachadh eud a thoirt do dhroch mhios air an righ gon rachadh gin diu air a bhialthaobh. "A bheil duin' a dh' fhuasglas orm?" "Cha n 'eil mar am fusgail buachaille Chaomhaig fhìn ort." Chuireadh sìos buachaille Chaomhaig. "Fuasgail orm a laochain, 's dian an ceartas mur is còir, 's lig a so mi." "Ceartas na còir cha dian mise gos am faigh mi 'n toiseach rud a dh' itheas mi." Fhuair e 'n sin rud a dh' ith e. "De 'n ceartas a rinn thu fhìn?" ars' esan. "Cha d' rinn mis' ach an fhiacaill a rinn an sgath a bhi aca." "Ciod thuige nach d' thug thu 'm bàs do Chaomhaig? So mur a dhianainnsa. Tha sia caoraich aig Caomhaig, 's gad a bheirte uaithe na sia caoraich cha phaigheadh eud na daoin' uaisle. Bidh sia uain aig Caomhaig, 's gheibh na daoin' uaisle na sia uain' 's bidh na caoraich aice fhìn a' cumail." Dh' fhalbh an car a amhuich an righ. Dh' fhalbh esan, 's cha d' fhoighneachd eud co e, 's cha d' fhuair e sgath.

Bha duin' uasal eil' ann, 's bha each aige, 's chuir e thun ceardach e gos a bhi air a chrùidheadh. Bha mac òg aig a' ghobha, 's banaltrum fo 'n leanabh. Dé bh' ann ach latha briagh, 's is ann a mach a bha 'n t-each 'ga chrùidheadh, 's cha 'n fhac is' each ga chrùidheadh riabh, 's chaidh i mach a dh' fhaicinn crùidheadh an eich. Shuidh i ma choinnimh an eich, 's thug esan an tairg 'sa chruidh, 's cha d' amais e 'n crodhan leis an tairg ach chuir e 'san fheoil i, agus bhuail an t-each an leanabh, 's chuir e copan a' chinn deth.

Cha robh ac' ach dol go ceartas a rithisd thun an righ. 'Se 'n ceartas a rinn an righ dhaibh a' chas a thoirt bhar an eich. Thòisich cathair a bhreathanais air breabadaich, 's chaidh car an amhuich an righ. Bha buachaille Chaomhaig a làthair. Dh' iarr eud air fuasgladh air an righ. Thuirt e nach dianadh e sgath gos am faigheadh e rud ri itheadh an toiseach. Fhuair e siud. Chaidh e far an robh 'n righ. "Dé 'n lagh a rinn thu?" "A chas a thoirt bhàr an eich." "Cha phàigh sin an gobha." "Cuiribh thugams' an *groom* a dh' ionnsaich an t-each, agus an duin' uasal da 'm bean e." Chuireadh a naull an so an gobha agus a' bhanaltrum. Thàinig an duin' uasal 's an *groom.* "Seadh, a dhuin' uasail, an d' thug thus' air a' *ghroom* an t-each so ionnsachadh mur a bu chòir dha?" Thuirt an groom gon d' rinn e siud cho math 's a b' aithne dha. "Cha b' urrainnear tuillidh iarraidh ort." Seadh a ghobha an d' thug thus' ordugh do d' bhanaltrum fantainn a stigh, gon tigh'n amach as a seombar?" "Cha d' thug," urs' an gobha, "ach mur a thogradh i fhìn." "A dhuin' uasail," ars' esan, "o 'n is tusa 's fhearr cumail, cuiridh mise trian ort de dh' éirig mhic a' ghobha, agus trian eil' air a' ghobha fhìn, o 'n nach do thomhais e 'n tairg ma 'n do chuir e go feum i; agus trian eil' air a bhanaltrum 's air a *ghroom;* o 'n nach d' fhan *is'* a stigh na seombar; 's gon fhios nach d' fhàg *esan* facal air choraigin gon ionnsachadh do 'n each." Dh' fhalbh an duin' uasal agus an gobha; agus stad cathair a' bhreathanais, 's cha robh car aice; thàinig an car e amhuich an righ; 's lig eud esan air falbh mur a b' àbhaist.

Urs' an righ, "ma shiubhail e 'n domhan agus an saoghal tha boinne dh' fhuil mhic righ anns a ghill' ud. Cha b' urrainn e 'n lagh a sgoltadh cho math an siud mar am biodh e ann; falbhadh na tri gaisgich is fhearr a th' agam agus thugadh eud a'm' ionnsuidh a cheann." Dh' fhalbh eud as a dhéigh. Thug e sùil uaidhe, 's dé chunnaic e a' tighinn ach eud. Thàinig eud far an robh e. "C'a' bheil sibh a dol?" "Tha sinn a' dol ad' mharbhadh fhìn; chuir an righ gad' ionnsuidh sinn." "Mata cha 'n 'eil an sin ach rud a thàinig 'na bhial, 's cha ruig sibh a leas mo mharbhadh." "Cha 'n 'eil ann ach amadan," ars' eudsan. "O 'n a chuir esan sibhse gum' mharbhadh, nach marbh sibh mi?" "Am marbh thu fhìn thu fhìn a laochain?" ars' iadsan. "Dé mur a mharbhas mi mi fhìn?" "So dhuit claidheamh agus buail mu 'n amhuich ort e, 's tilg an ceann dìot fhìn," ars' iadsan. Rug e air a' chlaidheamh; chuir e car deth 'na dhorn. "Siud a laochain air thu fhìn a mharbhadh." "Falbhaibh," ars' esan, "agus tillibh dachaidh, 's na ceilibh air an righ nach do mharbh sibh mise." "Mata thoir dhomh an claidheamh," ursa fear diu.

"Cha d' thoir. Cha 'n 'eil an Eirinn na bheir as mo dhorn e," ars' esan. Dh' fhalbh eud agus thill eud dachaidh.

Air dha bhi falbh leis fhin thuirt e, "Cha do rugadh mi gon mhàthair, 's cha do ghineadh mi gon athair. Cha chuimhne leam tigh'n do dh' Eirinn riabh, agus tha fios agam gur h-ann an Eirinn a rugadh mi ; cha 'n fhàg mi tigh 's a bheil smùid na tein' ann an Eirinn gos am bi fhios agam co mi."

Chaidh e dha 'n Iubhar. Dé bh' ann ach latha briagh blàth. Co chunnaic e ach a mhàthair a nigheadaireachd. Bha e tigh'n go seòrs' aithne, air alt 's gon robh e smaointeachadh gur i mhàthair a bh' ann. Dh' fhalbh e agus chaidh e air a cùl, 's chuir e 'làmh sìos 'na broilleach, 's thug e chìoch dheas a mach. "Dearbh," urs' esan, "'s dalta cìche deise dhuit mi." Thug i 'n togail sin air a ceann. "Do leithid de thàrlaid cha robh agamsa riabh, na mhac, na na dhalta!" "Tha mo làmh chlì ann an cùl do chinn, agus tha claidheamh ann a'm' laimh dheis, agus cuiridh mi 'n ceann dìot mar an innis thu domh co mi." "Fois air do laimh a Chonaill mhic righ Eireann." "Dh' aithnich mi fhìn sin, gom b'e sin mi, 's gon robh boinne dh' fhuil mhic righ annam ; ach co mharbh m' athair?" "Mharbh Fearghus ; agus diùbhail cho mòr ri t' athair mharbhadh a' cheart latha, b' e sìn Boinne Breat mac righ Alba." "Co mharbh Boinne Breat?" "Tha bràthair do Fhearghus ris an can eud Lagh an làidh." "'S c'àit' a bheil an duine sin a fuireachd?" "Cha 'n fhaigheadh e sgath air fearann Eirinn aon uair 's gon do mharbh e Boinne Breat. Chaidh e 'n bheinn, 's rinn e còs 'sa choille miosg h-uile biast a's creutair mi-ghnàthaichte." "Co ghléidh airm m' athar?" "Tha mise." "Theirig agus faigh eud 's thoir thugams' eud." Thug i a 'ionnsuidh eud, Dh' fhalbh esan agus chuir e na h-airm air, agus thigeadh eud dha cho math 's gad a dhèanta dha fhìn eud. "Cha 'n ith mi greim, 's cha 'n òl mi deoch, 's cha dian mi stad ach a nochd, gos an ruig mi far a bheil an duine sin, ge b'e àit' a bheil e." Chuir e 'n oidhche sin seachad far an robh e.

Anns a' mhadainn an la 'r na mhàireach dh' falbh e. Ghabh e air aghaidh, gos an robh dughadh air a bhonnaibh, agus tolladh air a bhrògaibh. Bha neoil gheal' an latha 'falbh 's neoil dhugha na h-oidhche 'tighinn, 's gon e faighinn àite stad na tàmh dha. Chunnaic e coille mhòr ann an sin. Dhian e còs ann an té de na craobhan go h-ard anns am fanadh e 'n oidhche sin. Anns a' mhadainn an la 'r na mhàireach thug e sùil uaidhe. Dé chunnaic e ach an aon uilebheist, nach fhacas riabh a leithid fo 'n ghréin, 'na shìneadh gon aodach, gon chaisbheart, gon cheann aodach; fhionn' agus fhiasag air dhol thairis air. Smaointich e gad a rachadh e sìos nach dianadh e feum air. Chuir e saighead ann an crois 's loisg e air. Bhuail e anns a ghairdean deas air i, 's thug am fear a bha shìos breab as. "Na gluais féithe de t' fhéithean, na cuisle de t' chuislean, na bìdeag de t' fheoil, na ròinean de d' ghruaig; gos an geall thu gom faic thu mise 'nam righ air Eirinn, no cuiridh mise sìos dheth shleaghan caola, daraich na dh' fhuaigheas ris an talamh thu." Cha d' thug an uilebheist géill dha siud. Dh' fhalbh e agus loisg e rithisd, agus bhuail e anns a ghairdean thoisgeil e. "Nach d' thuirt mi riut roimhid gon cuisle de d' chuislean a ghluasad, na bìdeag de t' fheoil, na ròinean de d' ghruaig, gos an gealladh thu gom faiceadh thu mise nam righ air Eirinn." "Thig a nuas mata, 's chi mi thu fhìn na mi fhìn ann fo 'n am so 'n ath-oidhch." Thàinig e 'nuas. "Nam biodh fhios'am gur e do leithid de thàrlach a chuireadh a leithid mar fhiachaibh orm, cha dianainn duit air chor sam bith e; ach o 'n gheall mi duit e ni mi e, 's bidh sinn a' falbh."

Ghabh eud 'ionnsuidh pàileas an righ. Dh' eubh eud cath na còmhrag a chur amach, air neo ceann Fhearghuis, na e fhìn mar phrìosanach. Cath a's còmhrag a gheibheadh eud, 's cha b'e cheann; 's idir cha 'n fhaigheadh eud e fhìn mar phrìosanach. Chuireadh a mach ceithir chiad lùgh-ghaisgeach, ceithir chiad làn-ghaisgeach, agus ceithir chiad treùn-ghaisgeach. Thòisich eud orra. Cha chuireadh an darna fear o laimh an fhir eile mur a mharbhadh eud. Dh' eubh eud cath as comhrag a rìs, air-neo ceann Fhearghuis a chur amach, na e fhìn mar phrìosanach. "'Se cath as còmhrag a gheibh thu; 's idir cha 'n fhaigh thu mo cheann, 's cha mhotha 'gheibh thu mi fhìn mar phrìosanach." Chuireadh a mach da chiad diag lùgh-ghaisgeach, da chiad diag làn-ghaisgeach, agus da chiad diag treùn-ghaisgeach. Cha chuireadh an darna fear a laimh an fhir eile mur a mharbhadh eud diu sin. Dh' eubh eud cath as còmhrag, air neo ceann Fhearghuis, na e fhìn mar phrìosanach. Cath as comhrag a gheibheadh eud, 's cha b' e ceann Fhearghuis; 's idir cha 'n fhaigheadh eud e fhìn 'na phrìosanach. Chuireadh a mach ceithir chiad fichead a 'n ionnsuidh. Cha chuireadh an darna fear o 'n fhear eile mur a mharbhadh eud. Dh' eubh eud cath na comhrag. "Tha 'n fheadhain a tha mach cho olc," ursa Fearghus, "'s nach gabh eud ach mo cheann, agus mur am faigh eud marbhaidh eud na bheil an Eirinn, 's mi fhìn as an déigh. Thugadh fear agaibh an ceann bhar aon de na chaidh a mharbhadh, agus nur a thig Lagh an làidh 's a dh' iarras e mo cheann na mi fhìn a'm' phrìosanach, thugaibh dha e, agus saoilidh e g'an e mo cheannsa bhios ann." Thugadh an ceann do Lagh an làidh. Chaidh e far an robh Conall leis. "Dé th' agad an sin?" ursa Conall. "Ceann Fhearghuis." "Cha 'n e sin ceann Fhearghuis fhathasd, 's mise 's giorra chunnaic e na thu fhìn; ach till 's thoir thugamsa ceann Fhearghuis." Thill Lagh an làidh. "Rachadh fear eile 'na choinneamh an àit' an righ, 's abradh e gur e cheann a gheibh e, 's nach e fhìn mar phrìosanach. Chaidh am fear so an coinneamh Lagh an làigh. Rug e air 's thug e 'n ceann as an amhuich aige. Ràinig e Conall. "Dé th' agad an sin?" "Ceann Fhearghuis." "Cha 'n e sin ceann Fhearghuis fhathasd. Till agus thoir am' ionnsuidh ceann Fhearghuis." Thill Lagh an làidh. "Tha 'm fear a tha muigh cho beachdail, 's am fear eile cho daull, 's nach 'eil duin' an Eirinn nach marbh eud mar am faigh eud mi fhìn." "C' a' bheil thu dol a Lagh an làidh?" ursa Fearghus. "Tha mi dol a dh' iarraidh do chinnsa na thu fhìn mar phrìosanach." "'Se mo cheann a gheibh thu, 's cha mhi fhìn mar phrìosanach; ach dé bhàigh a tha thu toirt do d' bhràthair?" "A bhàigh a thug thu fhin domhsa bheir mise duits' e." Thug e 'n ceann as an amhuich aige 's thug e leis e. Thàinig e far an robh Conall. "Dé th' agad an sin?" "Ceann Fhearghuis." "Cha 'n e." "Go dearbh 's e." "Lig fhaicinn e." Thug e dha e. Tharruinn e e agus bhuail e air, 's rinn e da cheann de 'n aon. Thòisich eud an so air a chéile. Dhianadh eud bogan air a chreagan agus creagan air a bhogan, 's an t-àite bu lugha rachadh eud fodha gan glùinean, 's an t-àite bu mhotha rachadh eud fodha rachadh eud fodha 'gan sùilean. Smaointich Conall go 'm bu dona dha tuiteam 's e 'n déis dol cho goirid do'n ghnothach. Tharruinn e chlaidheamh agus thilg e 'n ceann de Lagh an làidh. Tha mise nis a' m' righ air Eirinn mur bu chòir domh fhìn a bhi.

Thug e mhàthair 's a h' athair as an Iubhar, 's thug e go ruig am pàileas eud. 'S bha shliochd ann gos an naoidheamh glùn. Thacadh an t-aon ma dheireadh, 'na leanabh, le bìdeag de chnaimh a chaidh tarsuinn 'na amhuich, 's thainig treubh eile stigh air Eirinn.

ALEXANDER M'NEILL.

Heard it recited by his father and by several others in his youth.

This story is one of a number, all of which relate to a certain Conall, who was a natural son of a king of Eirinn, and came to be king himself.

There are generally two elder brothers born of the queen (instead of three uncles), who are less brave than the illegitimate brother. The mother is generally the daughter of an old man who has magical arts. The king stays in his house at first for a whole year, and fancies it one day; all sorts of adventures, and poetical ornaments, and descriptions of dress, and feats of skill are joined to this frame-work, and the stories are always told with a great deal of the measured prose which seems to belong to the particular class of which this is a specimen. They are always long. I think they are the remains of compositions similar to portions of the manuscripts in the Advocates' Library and elsewhere—which are a curious jumble of classical and native allusions woven into a story; which, for want of a better illustration, may be compared with the old romances of other tongues.

The story, translated into English, loses part of its merit, which consists of the rapid utterance of a succession of words which convey, by their sound and rhythm alone, the idea of the fight which they describe; the sounds—

"Dā chĕeăd djĕeăg Lān-gāsh-gāch
Dā chĕeăd djĕeăg Lōō-gāsh-gāch
Dā chĕeăd djĕeăg Trāin-gāsh-gāch

Gān cā'lchg-ăg ōn sgēē-ān
Gām fūil ăgŭs gām feō-īl
Ans ăn ēēàr-māilt.

By the constant repetition of the sounds *djee*, *gash*, *gach*, suggest the singing, creaking, clashing, and hacking of blades and armour, and the rhythm, which varies continually, and must be heard to be understood, does the same.

The narrator heard it from his father and other old men in his youth. I have heard similar passages frequently from others, since the beginning of this year, and I remember to have heard something of the kind as a child.

One of the names, or one like it, occurs in a MS., said to be of the twelfth century, in a tale called "The Story of Art MacCuinn, King of Ireland, and the Battle of Magh Muckruinne," which extends to forty-three pages. Art MacCon wins a battle and becomes king of Ireland. All I know of the story is from an abstract; it is said to be mixed with poetry. The tales about Conall are all over the Highlands, and those who repeat them are generally old men. I have several versions written which differ materially from this.

XXXVI.

MAGHACH COLGAR.

From Alexander MacNeill, Barra.

FIONN, the son of Cumal. FIONN MAC CUMHAIL was in Eirinn, and the king of Lochlann in Lochlann. The king of Lochlann sent MAGHACH COLGAR to Fionn to be taught. The king of the SEALG sent to him his own son, whom they called INNSRIDH MAC-RIGH NAN SEALG. They were of age, six years (and) ten. Then they were in Erin with Fionn, and Fionn taught Maghach, son of the king of Lochlann, every learning he had.

There came a message from the king of Lochlann, that he was in the sickness of death for leaving the world; and that the Maghach must go home to be ready for his crowning. Maghach went away, and the chase failed with the FEINN, and they did not know what they should do.

Maghach wrote a letter to Fionn from Lochlann to Eirinn: "I heard that the chase failed with you in Eirinn. I have burghs on sea, and I have burghs on shore: I have food for a day and a year in every burgh of these—the meat thou thinkest not of, and the drink thou thinkest not of; come thou hither thyself and thy set of FIANTACHAN. The keep of a day and a year is on thy head."

Fionn got the letter, and he opened it: "He is

pitiable who would not do a good thing in the beginning of youth ; he might get a good share of it again in the beginning of his age. Here is a letter came from my foster-son from Lochlann that he has burghs on sea and burghs on shore, food for a day and a year in every one of them—the drink that we can think of, and the drink that we do not think of ; the meat we can think of, and the meat that we do not think of—and it is best for us to be going."

"Whom shall we leave," said FIACHERE MACFHINN (the trier son of Fionn) his son, "to keep the darlings and little sons of Eireann."

"I will stay," said FIACHERE MACFHINN.

"I will stay," said DIARMID O'DUIBHNE, his sister's son.

"I will stay," said INNSRIDH MACRIGH NAN SEALG, his foster-son.

"I will stay," said CATH CONAN MAC MHIC CON.

"We will stay now," said they—the four.

"Thou art going, my father," said Fiachere, "and it is as well for thee to stay ; how then shall we get word how it befalls thee in Lochlainn ?"

"I will strike the ORD FIANNT (hammer of Fiant) in Lochlainn, and it will be known by the blow I strike in Lochlainn, or in Eirinn, how we shall be."

Fionn and his company went, they reached Lochlainn. Maghach Colgar, son of the king of Lochlainn, went before to meet them.

"Hail to thee, my foster father," said Maghach.

"Hail to thyself, my foster-son," said Fionn.

"There is the business I had with thee ; I heard that the chase had failed in Eirinn, and it was not well with me to let you die without meat. I have burghs on sea and burghs on shore, and food for a day and

"There is still a small delay on that."

Fiachaire began in the one end of the company, and Innsridh MacRigh nan Sealg in the other, till the two glaves clashed on each other. They returned to the burgh.

"Who is that?" said Fionn.

"I am Fiachaire, thy son, and Innsridh, son of the king of the Sealg, thy foster son,

With whom was the hideous fight
That was on the battle place (battle ford)
To-day.

It was with me and with three hundred score of Greeks."

"Mind the place of battle; there are four hundred score of the Greeks, and a great warrior at their head coming to seek my head to be theirs at their great meal to-morrow."

They went and they reached the place of battle.

"Where are you going?" said Fiachaire MacFhinn to the Greeks.

"Going to seek the head of Mhic Cumhail, to be ours at our great meal to-morrow."

"It's often that man's head might be sought, and be on my own breast at early morning."

"Close up from the way, and leave way for the people."

"There is a small delay on that yet."

He himself and Innsridh MacRigh nan Sealg began at them till they had killed every man of them, and till the two glaves clashed on each other. They returned home, and they reached the burgh.

"Who's that without?" said Fionn.

"I am Fiachaire, thy son, and Innsridh, son of the king of the Sealg, thy foster-son,

With whom was the hideous fight
That was at the battle place (ford)
To-day."

"It was with me and so many of the Greeks."

"How was my foster-son off there?"

"Man upon man, and if there had been no one besides, he had lacked none."

"Mind the place of battle. There are twice as many as came out, a good and heedless warrior at their head, coming to seek my head, to be theirs at their great meal to-morrow."

They reached the place of battle; and when they reached it, there came not a man of the people.

"I won't believe," said Fiachaire MacFhinn, "that there are not remnants of meat in a place whence such bands are coming. Hunger is on myself, and that we ate but a morsel since we ate it in Eirinn. And come thou, Innsridh, and reach the place where they were. They will not know man from another man, and try if thou canst get scraps of bread, and of cheese, and of flesh, that thou wilt bring to us; and I myself will stay to keep the people, in case that they should come unawares."

"Well, then, I know not the place. I know not the way," said Innsridh, son of the king of Sealg, "but go thyself and I will stay."

Fiachaire went, and Innsridh staid, and what should they do but come unawares.

"Where are ye going," said Innsridh?

"Going to seek the head of Mhic Cumhail, to be ours at our great meal to-morrow."

"It is often that man's head might be sought, and be on my own breast at early morning."

"Close up, and leave way for the people."

"There is a small delay on that yet." Innsridh began at them, and he left not one alone.

"What good did it do thee to slay the people, and that I will kill thee," said the great warrior at their head.

"If I had come out, from my meat and from my warmth, from my warmth and from my fire, thou shouldst not kill me." He and the warrior began at each other. They would make a bog of the crag, and a crag of the bog, in the place where the least they would sink they would sink to the knees, in the place that the most they would sink they would sink to the eyes. The great warrior gave a sweep with his glave, and he cut the head off Innsridh MacRigh nan Sealg.

Fiachaire came. The warrior met him, and with him was the head of Innsridh.

Said Fiachaire to the great warrior, "What thing hast thou there ?"

"I have here the head of Mhic Cumhail."

"Hand it to me."

He reached him the head. Fiachaire gave a kiss to the mouth, and a kiss to the back of the head.

"Dost thou know to whom thou gavest it ?" said Fiachaire to the warrior.

"I do not," said he. "It well became the body on which it was before."

He went and he drew back the head, and strikes it on the warrior's head while he was speaking, and makes one head of the two. He went and he reached (the place) where Fionn was again.

"Who is that without ?" said Fionn.

"I am Fiachaire, thy son,

With whom was the hideous fight
That was at the battle place
To-day."

"It was with Innsridh, thy foster-son, and with the Greeks."

"How is my foster-son from that?"

"He is dead without a soul. Thy foster-son killed the Greeks first, and the great Greek killed him afterwards, and then I killed the great Greek."

"Mind the place of combat. There is Maghach, son of the king of Lochlann, and every one that was in the Greek burgh with him."

He went and he reached the place of combat.

"Thou art there, Fiachaire?" said Maghach Colgar.

"I am."

"Let hither thy father's head, and I will give thee a free bridge in Lochlainn."

"My father gave thee school and teaching, and every kind of DRAOCHD (Magic) he had, and though he taught that, thou wouldst take the head off him now, and with that thou shalt not get my father's head, until thou gettest my own head first."

Fiachaire began at the people, and he killed every man of the people.

"Thou has killed the people," said Maghach, "and I will kill thee."

They began at each other.

They would make a bog of the crag, and a crag of the bog, in the place where the least they would sink, they would sink to the knees; in the place where the most they would sink, they would sink to the eyes. On a time of the times the spear of Mhaghach struck Fiachaire, and he gave a roar. What time should he give the roar but when Diarmid was turning step from the chase in Eirinn.

"If he has travelled the universe and the world,"

said Diarmid, "the spear of the Maghach is endured by Fiachaire."

"Wailing be on thee," said Conan. "Cast thy spear and hit thy foe."

"If I cast my spear, I know not but I may kill my own man."

"If it were a yellow-haired woman, well wouldst thou aim at her."

"Wailing be on thee now; urge me no longer."

He shook the spear, and struck under the shield (chromastaich).

"Who would come on me from behind in the evening, that would not come on me from the front in the morning?" said Maghach.

"'Tis I would come on thee," said Diarmid, "early and late, and at noon."

"What good is that to thee," said Maghach, "and that I will take the head off Fiachaire before thou comest."

"If thou takest the head off him," said Diarmid, "I will take off thy head when I reach thee."

Diarmid reached Lochlann. Maghach took the head off Fiachaire. Diarmid took the head off the Maghach. Diarmid reached Fionn.

"Who's that without?" said Fionn.

"It is I, Diarmid,

With whom was the hideous fight
That was on the battle place
To-day."

"It was with so many of the Greeks, and with the the Maghach, son of the king of Lochlann, and with Fiachaire, thy son; Fiachaire killed all the Greeks, Maghach killed Fiachaire, and then I killed Maghach."

"Though Maghach killed Fiachaire, why didst thon

kill Maghach, and not let him have his life? But mind the place of combat, and all that are in the burghs of the Greeks coming out together."

"Whether wouldst thou rather, Cath Conan, go with me or stay here?"

"I would rather go with thee."

They went, and when they reached the place of combat, no man met them. They reached where they were; they sat there, and what should Cath Conan do but fall asleep, they were so long coming out. It was not long after that till they began to come, and the doors to open. There was a door before every day in the year on every burgh, so that they burst forth all together about the head of Diarmid. Diarmid began at them, and with the sound of the glaves and return of the men, Cath Conan awoke, and he began thrusting his sword in the middle of the leg of Diarmid. Then Diarmid felt a tickling in the middle of his leg. He cast a glance from him, and what should he see but Cath Conan working with his own sword.

"Wailing be on thee, Cath Conan," said Diarmid; "pass by thy own man and hit thy foe, for it is as well for thee to thrust it into yonder bundle* as to be cramming it into my leg. Do not thou plague me now till I hit my foe!"

They killed every man of the people.

They thought of those who were in the burgh, and they without food; each one of them took with him the full of his napkin, and his breast, and his pouches.

"Who's that without?" said Fionn.

"I am Diarmid, thy sister's son."

---

* There is a pun here, which cannot be rendered; a *boot* or a *bundle*, as of hay, or a crowd of men.

"How are the Greeks?"

"Every man of them is dead, without a soul."

"Oh, come and bring hither to me a deliverance of food."

"Though I should give thee food, how shouldst thou eat it, and thou there and thee bound?"

He had no way of giving them food, but to make a hole in the burgh above them, and let the food down to them.

"What is there to loose thee from that?" said Diarmid.

"Well, that is hard to get," said Fionn; "and it is not every man that will get it; and it is not to be got at all."

"Tell thou me," said Diarmid, "and I will get it."

"I know that thou wilt subdue the world till thou gettest it; and my healing is not to be got, nor my loosing from this, but with the one thing."

"What thing is it that thou shouldst not tell it to me, and that I might get it?"

"The three daughters of a king, whom they call King Gil; the daughters are in a castle in the midst of an anchorage, without maid, without sgalag (servant), without a living man but themselves. To get them, and to wring every drop of blood that is in them out on plates and in cups; to take every drop of blood out of them, and to leave them as white as linen."

Diarmid went, and he was going till there were holes in his shoes and black on his soles, the white clouds of day going, and the black clouds of night coming, without finding a place to stay or rest in. He reached the anchorage, and he put the small end of his spear under his chest, and he cut a leap, and he was in the castle that night. On the morrow he returned, and he took with him two on the one shoulder and one on the other shoulder; he put the small end of his spear under his chest, and at the first spring he was on shore. He reached Fionn; he took the girls to him; he wrung every drop of blood that was in every one of them out at the finger ends of her feet and hands; he put a black cloth above them, and he began to spill the blood on those who were within, and every one as he spilt the blood on him, he would rise and go. The blood failed, and every one was loosed but one, whom they called Conan.

"Art thou about to leave me here, oh Diarmid."

"Wailing be on thee; the blood has failed.

"If I were a fine yellow-haired woman, its well thou wouldst aim at me?"

"If thy skin stick to thyself, or thy bones to thy flesh, I will take thee out."

He caught him by the hand and he got him loose, but that his skin stuck to the seat, and the skin of his soles to the earth. "It were well now," said they, "if the children of the good king were alive, but they should be buried under the earth." They went where they were, and they found them laughing and fondling each other, and alive. Diarmid went, and took them with him on the shower top of his shoulder, and he left them in the castle as they were before, and they all came home to EIRINN.

MAGHACH COLGAR.

BHA Fionn MacCumhail ann an Eirinn, agus righ Lochlann ann an Lochlann. Chuir righ Lochlann Maghach Colgar thun Fhinn a 'ionnsachadh. Chuir righ nan Sealg a 'ionnsuidh a mhac fhin ris an canadh eud Innsridh Mac righ nan Sealg. Bha iad aig aois sia bliadhna diag. Bha eud an sin ann an Eirinn aig Fionn. Dh' ionnsuich Fionn do Mhaghach mac righ Lochlann h-uile h-ionnsachadh a bh' aige. Thainig brath o righ Lochlann gon robh e 'n galar a bhàis airson an saoghal fhàgail, 's gom feumadh am Maghach dol dachaidh go bhi 'n làthair airson a chrùnadh. Dh' fhalbh Maghach dachaidh, agus cheileadh an t-seilg air an Fheinn, 's cha robh fios aca dé dhianadh eud.

Sgriobh Maghach litir go Fionn a Lochlainn do dh' Eirinn. "Chuala mi gon do cheileadh an t-seilg oirbh ann an Eirinn. Tha bruighean air muir agam 's tha bruighean air tìr agam, tha lòn la a's bliadhn' agam anns a h-uile brugh dhiu sin, am biadh nach smaointich thu 's an deoch nach smaointich thu. Thig thusa 'n so thu fhìn agus do chuid Fhiantachan. Tha lòn la agus bliadhn' air do chionn."

Fhuair Fionn an litir 's dh' fhosgail e i, "'S mairg nach dianadh rud math an tùs òige, gheibheadh e rud math an tùs a shine deth rithisd. Tha litir an so air tigh'n o 'm dhalt' a Lochlainn go 'bheil bruighean air muir agus bruighean air tìr aige, lòn la a's bliadhna 's a h-uile té dhiu, an deoch a smaointicheas sinn 's an deoch nach smaointich sinn, am biadh a smaointicheas sinn 's am biadh nach smaointich sinn, agus 's ann is fhearra dhuinn a bhi falbh."

"Co dh' fhàgas sibh," ursa Fiachaire MacFhinn a mhac, "a ghleidheadh mùirn agus màcan na h-Eireann." "Fanaidh mis'," ursa Fiachaire MacFhinn. "Fanaidh mis'," ursa Diarmaid O Duibhne mac a pheathar. "Fanaidh mis'," urs' Innsridh Mac righ nan Sealg a dhalta. "Fanaidh mis'," ursa Cath Conan Mac mhic Con. "Fanaidh sinn a nis," urs' àdsan an ceithrear so.

"Tha thu falbh, m' athair," ursa Fiachaire, "agus tha e cho math dhuit fantail." "Dé nis mur a dh' éireas duit ann an Lochlainn?" "Buailidh mis' an t-ord Fiannt' ann an Lochlainn, 's aithneachar air a bhuill' a bhuaileas mi ann an Lochlainn na 'n Eirinn démur a bhitheas sinn."

Dh' fhalbh Fionn 's a chuideachd. Ràinig eud Lochlainn. Chaidh Maghach Colgar mac righ Lochlainn 'nan coinneamh agus 'nan comhdhail. "Failt' ort m' oide," ursa Maghach. "Failt' ort fhin a dhalta," ursa Fionn. "Siud an gnothach a bh' agam riut, chuala mi gon do cheileadh an t-seilg an Eirinn, 's cha bu mhath leam 'ur ligeadh bàs gon bhiadh. Tha bruighean air muir agam, 's tha bruighean air tìr agam agus lòn la a's bliadhn' anns' a h-uile gin diu ; agus co-dhiu feadhain is roighniche leat ?" "'S ann air tìr a chleachd mi bhi riabh, 's cha 'n ann air muir, 's gabhaidh mi feadhain air tìr," ursa Fionn. Ghabh eud a stigh ann a h-aon diu. Bha dorus ma choinneamh h-uile latha sa' bliadhn' air an tigh ; h-uile seorsa bìdh a's dibhe stigh ann. Shuidh eud air cathraichean. Rug eud, a h-uile fear, air forc agus air sgithin. Thug eud sùil uatha, 's dé chunnaic eud air an àraich, ach gon toll fosgailte, ach snidhe reòta. Thug eud an togail sinn orra go éiridh. Lean na cathraichean ris an talamh, lean eud fhìn ris na cathraichean, lean na làmhan ris na sgeanan, 's cha robh comas air éiridh as an siud. 'Se latha ma seach a bhiodh Fiachaire MacFhinn agus Innsridh Mac Righ nan Sealg a' falbh a ghleidheadh na seilg, agus bha Diarmaid O Duibhne agus Conan a' falbh an lath eile. Air tilleadh dhaibh air an ais, dé chual eud ach buill' an uird aig Fionn 'ga bhualadh ann an Lochlainn. "Ma shiubhail e 'n domhan agus an saoghal tha m' oid' ann an geall a chuirp agus anama." Dh' fhalbh Fiachaire MacFhinn agus Innsridh Mac Righ nan Sealg a Eirinn agus ràinig eud Lochlainn. "Co siud a mach air a bhruighin ?" "Tha mis'," ursa Fiachaire MacFhinn, "agus Innsridh Mac Righ nan Sealg." "Co tha 'n siud air an àth chomhrag ?" "Siud da chiad fhichead de na Greugachaibh air tigh'n a mach, agus Iall mòr air an ceann, a tigh'n a dh' iarraidh mo chinnsa gos a bhi ac' air an diat mhòr a màireach." Dh' fhalbh Fiachaire MacFhinn agus Innsridh Mac Righ nan Sealg agus ràinig eud an t-àth chomhrag. "C' a' bheil sibh a dol ?" ursa Fiachaire MacFhinn. "Tha sinn a' dol a dh' iarraidh ceann Mhic Cumhail gos a bhi againn air ar diat mhòr a màireach." "'S minig a rachadh go 'iarraidh 's gor moch air mhadainn air mo mhinid fhìn e." "Teann," urs' Iall, "agus lig rathad dha 'n t-sluagh." "Tha fuireachd beag air an sin," ursa Fiachaire. Theann Fiachaire Mac-Fhinn a mach anns an darna ceann diu, thòisich Innsridh Mac Righ nan Sealg anns a' cheann eile, gos an do bhuail an da chlaidheamh ri chéile. Thill eud agus ràinig eud am brugh. "Co aig' a bha 'n càth grannd a bh' air an àth chomhrag an diugh ?" ursa Fionn. "Agams'," ursa Fiachaire, "'s aig Innsridh Mac Righ nan Sealg."

"Dèmur a bha mo dhalta dheth sinn ?" "Fear air an fhear," ursa Fiachaire, "'s mar an robh fear a bharrachd aige, cha robh gin 'na uireasbhuidh." "Thar an àr do 'm dhalt'," ursa Fionn, "'s gon a chnàimh ach maoth fhathasd ; ach cuimhnich an t-àth chomhrag. Siud tri chiad fichead de na Greugachaibh a' tigh 'n a mach a dh' iarraidh mo chinnsa go bhi ac' air an diat mhòr a màireach." Dh' fhalbh Fiachaire MacFhinn agus Innsridh Mac Righ nau Sealg agus ràinig eud an t-àth chomhrag. "C' ait' a bheil sibh a dol?" ursa Fiachaire MacFhinn. "Dol a dh' iarraidh ceann Mhic Cumhail gos a bhi againn air ar diat mhòr a màireach." "'S minig a rachadh a dh' iarraidh ceann an duine sinn fhìn 's gor moch air mhadainn air mo mhinid fhin e." "Teann agus lig rathad do 'n t-sluagh." "Tha fuireachd beag air an sin fhathasd." Thòisich Fiachair' anns an darna ceann de 'n chuideachd, 's Innsridh Mac Righ nan Sealg anns a cheann eile, gos an do bhuail an da chlaidheamh air a cheile.

Thill eud 'ionnsuidh na bruighne a rìs. "Co siud?" ursa Fionn. "Tha mise Fiachaire do mhac, agus Innsridh Mac nan Sealg do dhalta."

"Co aig a bha 'n cath grannd' a bh' air an àth 'n diugh?" "Bha agamsa 's aig tri chiad fichead de na Greugachaibh." "Cuimhnich an t- àth chombrag; siud ceithir chiad fichead de na Greugachaibh 's gaisgeach mòr air an ceann, a' tigh'n a dh' iarraidh mo chinnsa go bhi ac' air an diat mhòr a màireach." Dh' fhalbh eud 's ràinig eud an t- àth chomhrag. "C' àit' a' bheil sibh a dol?" ursa Fiachaire Mac-Fhinn ris na Greugachaibh. "Dol a dh' iarraidh ceann Mhic Cumhail gos a bhi againn air ar diat mhòr a màireach." "'S minig a rachadh a dh' iarraidh ceann an duine sin, 's gor moch air madainn air mo mhionaid fhìn e." "Teann as an rathad agus leig rathad dha 'n t-sluagh." "Tha fuireach beag air an sin fhathasd." Thòisich e fhéin agus Innsridh Mac Righ nan Sealg orra, gos an do mharbh eud a h-uile duine dhiùbh, 's an do bhuail an da chlaidheamh air a cheile. Thill eud dachaidh 's ràinig eud am brugh. "Co siud a muigh?" ursa Fionn. "Tha mise, Fiachaire do mhac, agus Innsridh Mac Righ nan Sealg do dhalta." "Co aig a bha 'n cath grannd' a bh' air an àth an diugh?" "Bha agamsa 's aig na h' uiread dheth na Greugachaibh." "Demur a bha mo dhalta dheth an sin?" "Fear air an fhear, 's mur robh fear a bharrachd, cha robh gin 'na uireasbhuidh." "Cuimhnich an t-àth chomhrag. Siud a dha uiread 's a thainig a mach an dé tighinn a mach an diugh, gaisgeach gon chiall air an ceann, a' tighinn a dh' iarraidh mo chinnsa go bhi ac' air an dìot mhòr a màireach."

Ràinig eud an t-àth chomhrag, 's nur a ràinig eud cha d' thàinig duine de 'n t-sluagh. "Cha chreid mi," ursa Fiachaire

MacFhinn, "a it' as a bheil a leithid siud de bhuidheann a' tighinn, nach bi fuighleach bìdh ann. Tha 'n t-acras orm fhìn, 's nach d' ith sinn mìr o'n a dh'ith sinn ann an Eirinn e, agus thalla thus' Innsridh, 's ruig an t-àit an robh eud, 's cha 'n aithnich eud duine seach duin' eile, agus fiach am faigh thu criomagan de dh' aran, agus de chàis', agus de dh' fheòil a bheir thu g'ar n' ionnsuidh, 's fanaidh mi fhìn a' gleidheadh an t-sluaigh, gon fhios nach d' thigeadh eud gon fhios domh." "Mata cha 'n 'eil mis' eòlach, cha 'n aithne dhomh an rathad," urs' Innsridh Mac Righ nan Sealg, "ach falbh fhéin, agus fanaidh mise."

Dh' fhalbh Fiachaire, agus dh' fhan Innsridh, agus dé rinn àdsan, ach tighinn gon fhios da. "C'a' bheil sibh a dol?" urs' Innsridh. "Dol a dh' iarraidh ceann Mhic Cumhail gos a bhi againn air ar dìot mhòr a màireach." "'S minig a dh' iarradh ceann an duine sin, 's gur moch air mhadainn air mo mhionaid fhìn e." "Teann agus lig rathad do 'n t-sluagh." "Tha fuireach beag air an sin fhathasd." Thòisich Innsridh orra 's cha d' fhàg e gin diubh na ònrachd. Dé 'm maith a rinn e duit an sluagh a mharbhadh 's go marbh mis' thus?" urs' an gaisgeach mòr a bh' air an ceann. "Na 'n d' thiginnsa mach o m' bhiadh, agus o m' bhlàthas, o m' bhlàthas, agus o m' theine, cha mharbhadh thusa mi." Thòisich e fhéin 's an gaisgeach air a chéile. Dhianadh eud bogan de 'n chreagan, agus creagan de 'n bhogan. An t-àite bu lugha 'rachadh eud fodha rachadh eud fodha go 'n glùinean, 's an t-àite bu mho 'rachadh eud fodha, rachadh eud fodha go 'n sùilean. Thug an gaisgeach mór tarruinn air a' chlaidheamh, 's thilg e 'n ceann bhar Innsridh Mac Righ nan Sealg.

Thàinig Fiachaire. Choinnich e 'n gaisgeach, 's ceann Innsridh aige. Ursa Fiachaire ris a' ghaisgeach mhòr, "Dé 'n rud a th' agad an sin?" "Tha agam an so ceann Mhic Cumhail." "Fiach dhomh e." Shìn e dha 'n ceann. Thug Fiachaire pòg dà bhial 's pòg do chùl a chinn. "Am bheil fhios agad co dha thug thu e?" ursa Fiachaire, ris a' ghaisgeach. "Cha n' eil," urs' esan. "Is maith a thigeadh e air a cholainn air an robh e roimhe." Dh' fholbh e, agus tharruing e 'n ceann is buailear air ceann a ghaisgich e, neas a bha e bruidhinn, is dianar aon cheann de 'n dhà. Dh' fhalbh e, is ràinig e far an robh Fionn a rìs.

"Co siud a muigh?" ursa Fionn. "Tha mise, Fiachaire do mhac." "Co aig a bha an cath grannd a bh' air an àth chomhràg an diugh?" "Bha aig Innsridh do dhalta, is aig na Greugachaibh."

"Demur a tha mo dhalta deth sin?" Tha e marbh gon anam. Mharbh do dhalta na Greugaich an toiseach, is mharbh an Greugach mòr esan a rithisd, is mharbh mis' an sin an Greugach mòr."

"Cuimhnich an t-àth chomhrag. Siud Maghach Mac Righ Lochlann, is a h-uile gin a bha 's a bhrugh Ghreugach leis." Dh' fhalbh e is ràinig e 'n t-àth chomhrag. "Tha thu 'an sin Fhiachaire," ursa Maghach Colgar. "Tha." "Leig thugam ceann d' athar, is bheir mi dhuit drochaid shaor ann an Lochlainn." "Thug m' athair duit sgoil as ionnsachadh, 's a h-uile seorsa draochd a bh' aige, 's gad a dh ionnsaich e sinn duitse, bheireadh tu an ceann deth rithisd; agus leis a sin cha 'n fhaigh thusa ceann m' atharsa, gos am faigh thu mo cheann fhìn an toiseach."

Thòisich Fiachaire air an t-sluagh, is mharbh e h-uile duine de 'n t-sluagh. "Mharbh thus' an sluagh," ursa Maghach, "'s marbhaidh mis' thusa." Thòisich eud air a cheile. Dhianadh eud bogan de 'n chreagan agus creagan de 'n bhogan. An t-àite bu lugha rachadh eud fodha, rachadh eud fodha g'an glùinean, 's an t-àite bu mho a rachadh eud fodha rachad eud fodha g'an sùilean. Uair de na h-uairean, bhuail sleagh Mhaghaich Fiachaire is thug e ràn as. Dé 'n t-am 's an d' thug e ràn as ach mar a bha Diarmaid a tionndadh ceum o'n t-seilg 'an Eirinn. "Ma shiubhail e 'n domhan agus an saoghal," ursa Diarmaid, "tha sleagh a Mhaghaich air giùlan Fhiachaire." "Amhradh ort," ursa Conan, "caith de shleagh, agus amais do namhaid." "Ma chaitheas mise mo shleagh, cha 'n 'eil fhios' a'm nach ann a mharbhainn mo dhuine fhin." "Nam bu bhean bhadanach bhuidhe bhiodh ann 's maith a dh' amaiseadh thu i." "Amhradh ort a nis, na h-athnuadhaich mi na 's fhaide." Chrath e 'n t-sleagh, 's bhuail e e fo 'n chromastaich. "Co 'thigeadh orm a thaobh mo chùil anns an anmoch, nach d' thigeadh orm a thaobh m' aghaidh anns a' mhadainn?" ursa Maghach. "Mise thigeadh ort," ursa Diarmaid, "moch a's anmoch 's air a mhiadhon latha." "Dé 'm maith a ni sin duitse?" ursa Maghach, "'s gon d' thoir mis' an ceann de dh' Fhiachaire mu 'n d' thig thu." "Ma bheir thus' an ceann deth," ursa Diarmaid, "bheir mise an ceann diotsa nur a ruigeas mi." Ràinig Diarmaid Lochlainn. Thug Maghach an ceann bhàrr Fhiachaire. Thug Diarmaid an ceann bhàrr Mhaghaich. Ràinig Diarmaid Fionn, "Co siud a muigh?" ursa Fionn. "Tha ann mise Diarmaid." "Co aig a bha 'n cath grannd a bh' air an àth chomhrag an diugh?" "Bha e aig no h-uiread de na Greugachaibh, 's aig a Mhaghach Mac Rìgh Lochlann, 's aig Fiachaire do mhac. Mharbh Fiachaire h-uile gin de na Greugachaibh, mharbh Maghach Fiachaire, 's mharbh mis' an sin Maghach." "Gad a mharbh Maghach Fiachaire carson a mharbh thusa Maghach, nach do leig thu leis beo? Ach cuimhnich an t-àth chomhrag, 's a h-uile h-aon am bruighean nan Greugach a tighinn a mach comhla." "Co dhiubh 's fhearr leats', a Chath Conan, falbh leamsa, na fantainn an so?" "Is fhearr leam falbh comhla riutsa." Dh' fhalbh eud, 's 'nur a ràinig eud an t-àth chomhrag cha do choinnich duine eud. Ràinig eud far an robh eud. Shuidh eud an sin is dé rinn Cath Conan ach tuiteam 'na chadal, leis cho fada 's bha eud gon tighinn a mach. Cha b' fhada 'na dheigh sin gos an do thòisich eud ri tighinn, agus na dorsan ri fosgladh. Bha dorns ma choinneamh a h-uile latha 's a bhliadhn' air gach brugh air alt 's gon do mhaom eud a mach uile ma cheann Dhiarmaid. Thòisich Diarmaid orra, agus le fuaim nan claidhean agus le tilleadh nan daoine dhùisg Cath Conan, 's thòisich e air dinneadh a' chlaidheamh ann am miadhon a chalp' aig' Diarmaid. Fhuair Diarmaid an so tachas ann am miadhon a chalp' aige. Thug e sùil uaithe, is de chunnaic e ach Cath Conan ag obair leis a chlaidheamh aige fhéin? "Amhradh ort, a Chath Conain," ursa Diarmaid, "seachainn do dhuine fhéin, agus amais do namhaid, 's gor co maith dhuit a bhi 'ga dhinneadh anns a bhota ud shuas, 's a bhi 'ga dhinneadh a'm' chalpasa. Na h-athnuadhaich thusa mis' anis, ach an amais mis' air mo namhaid." Mharbh eud a h-uile duine dhe 'n t-sluagh.

Smaointich eud air an fheadhain a bha 's an àraich 's eud gon bhiadh. Thug gach aon diubh leis làn neapaigin, 'sa bhrollaich, 's a phòcaidean. "Co siud a muigh?" ursa Fionn. "Tha mise Diarmaid mac do pheathar." "Démur a tha na Greugaich?" "Tha a h-uile duine dhiubh marbh gon anam." "O thalla, agus thoir thugam teanachdas de bhiadh." "Gad a bheirinnsa dhuit biadh demur a dh' itheadh thu e, 's thu ann an sin, 's thu ceangailte?"

Cha robh saod aig air biadh a thoirt daibh, ach a bhi 'tolladh a' bhrugh as an cionn, 's a' leigeil a bhìdh sìos a 'n ionnsuidh. "De tha go d' fhuasgladh as a sin?" ursa Diarmaid. "Mata is deacair sinn fhaotainn," ursa Fionn, "'s cha 'n e h-uile fear a gheibh e, 's cha 'n 'eil e ri fhaotainn idir." "Innis thusa dhomhs' e," ursa Diarmaid, "agus gheibh mi e." "Tha fhios' am gon cìosnaich thu 'n saoghal gos am faigh thu e, agus cha 'n 'eil mo leigheas-sa ri fhaotainn, na fuasgladh as an so, ach aon rud." "Dé 'n aon rud a th' ann, nach innis thu dhomhs' e, 's gom faighinn e?" "Triùir nigheanan righ ris an can eud Righ Gil." Tha na tri nigheanan ann an caisteal ann am miadhon acarsaid, gon searbhant, gon sgalag, gon duine beo ach eud fhìn. Eud sin fhaotainn, 'sa h-uile boinne fala th' annt' fhàsgadh asda, 's a cuir air trinsearan, 's ann an copain,—a h-uile diar fal' a th' annt a thoirt asda, 's am fàgail cho geal ris an anart."

Dh' fhalbh Diarmaid, 's bha e 'falbh gos an robh dubhadh air a bhonnaibh, agus tolladh air a bhrogan, is neoil gheal an latha 'falbh, 's neoil dhubha na h-oidhche tighinn, is gon e faighinn àite stad na tàmh dha. Ràinig e 'n acarsaid, 's chuir e ceann caol a shleagh fo 'uchd, 's ghearr e leum, s bha e 'sa chaisteal an oidhche sin. An la 'r na mhàireach thill e. Thug e leis dithisd air an darna guallainn 's a h-aon air a' ghualainn eile. Chuir e ceann caol a shleagh fo 'uchd, 's air a chiad leum bha e air tìr. Ràinig e Fionn. Thug e d'a ionnsuidh na nigheanan. Dh' fhàisg e h-uile diar fala bh' anns na h-uile té riabh a mach air miaraibh a cas agus a làmh. Chuir e brat dubh air an uachdar. Thòisich e air dortadh na fal' air an fheadhain a bha stigh, 's a h-uile fear a dhoirteadh e'n fhuil air, dh' eireadh e, is dh' fhalbhadh e. Theirig an fhuil, is bha h-uile fear air fhuasgladh ach h-aon ris an canadh eud Conan.

"An ann a brath mis' fhàgail an so a tha thu Dhiarmaid?" "Amhradh ort, theirig an fhuil." "Nam bu bean bhriagh, bhadanach, bhuidhe mise, 's maith a dh' amaiseadh tu mi." "Ma leanas do chraicionn riut fhéin, na do chnamhan ri d' fheoil, bheir mis' as thu." Dh' fhalbh, e, agus rug e air làimh air. Fhuair e ma sgaoil, ach gon do lean craicionn a mhàis ris an àite shuidhe, agus craicionn nam bonn ris an talamh. "Bu mhaith a nis," urs' eudsan, "na'm biodh clann an righ mhaith beò, ach 's còir an tiodhlacadh fo 'n talamh." Dh' fhalbh eud far an robh eud, 's fhuair eud eud a gàireachdaich 's a' beadradh r'a chéile, is eud beo. Dh' fhalbh Diarmaid, is thug e leis eud air fras mhullach a ghuaillean, 's dh' fhàg e eud 's a chaisteal mur a bha eud roimhe. Thàinig eud uile dhachaidh do dh' Eirinn.

Got this tale from Alexander MacNeill, fisherman, then Tangval, Barra; says he learnt it from his father, and that he heard it recited by him and others ever since he remembers; says it has been handed down orally from one person to another from time immemorial. MacNeill is about sixty years of age, and can neither read, write, nor speak English. His father died twenty years ago, aged eighty years.

Barra, July 1859.

I know nothing like this anywhere out of the Highlands, but I have heard similar wild rambling stories there all my life.

The heroes are the heroes of Ossian, with the characters always assigned to them in Gaelic story. Fionn, the head of the band, but not the most successful; Diarmaid, the brown-haired admirer of the fair sex; Conan, the wicked, mischievous character, who would be the clown in a pantomime, or Loki in Norse mythology. They are enchanted in a BRUGH, which I have translated burgh, on the authority of Armstrong; and they fight crowds of Greeks on a place, if it be A for AITE; or at a ford, if it be ATH, which is pronounced in the same way. Greeks, GREUGACHIBH, may possibly be GRUAGACH-ibh, the long-haired people mentioned in the first story, changed into Greeks in modern times; or "GRUAGACH" may be a corruption from "Greugach," and this story compounded by some old bard from all the knowledge he had gathered, including Greeks, just as the fore-word to the Edda is compounded of Tyrkland, and Troja, and Odin, and Thor, the Asia men and the Asa, and all that the writer knew. The story as told is extravagant. Men in Eirinn and in Lochlainn, Ireland, and Scandinavia, converse and throw spears at each other. The hammer of Fionn is heard in Ireland when struck in Lochlan. But one of the manuscripts in the Advocates' Library throws some light on this part of the tale. If the scene were an island in the Shannon, men might converse and fight in the ford well enough. The MS. is a quarto on paper, with no date, containing five tales in prose, a vocabulary, and poems, and is attributed to the twelfth century. "Keating considers the subject of Tale 2, which contains forty-two pages, as authentic history." One of the people mentioned is Aol or Æul, a son of Donald, king of Scotland, who is probably "Great Iall," unless Iall is Iarl, an Earl. Tale 3 sends Cuchullin first to Scotland to learn feats of agility from Doiream, daughter of King Donald, thence to Scythia, where a seminary is crowded with pupils from Asia,

Africa, and Europe. He beats them all, goes through wonderful adventures, goes to Greece, returns with certain Irish chiefs, arrives in Ireland, and is followed by his son, a half Scythian, whom he kills at a ford. No. 4, the story of the children of Lir, changed into swans, is very curious.

No. 5 is called the rebellion of MIODACH, son of COLGAR, against Fingal, and seems to resemble Maghach Colgar.

Colgar, king of Lochlin, proposes to assume the title of Sovereign of the Isles, and to subjugate Ireland. He is beaten by Fingal, who gives him a residence *in an island in the Shannon.* After eighteen years he comes to propose riddles to Fingal, and invites him to an entertainment. They, the Fingalians, go, and *are enchanted*, sing their own dirge, are overheard by a friend sent by Ossian. *Some Greek Earls* (Gaelic, Iarla) appear, and there is a great deal of fighting. Ossian dispatches DIARMAD O DUIBHNE and FATHACH CANNACH, who *guard a ford* and perform feats. Oscar, son of Ossian, performs prodigies of valour, and kills Sinnsir.

This abstract of an abstract, lent me by Mr. Skene, is sufficient to shew that this old manuscript tale still exists in fragments, as tradition, amongst the people of the Isles.

The transcriber who copied it into the Roman hand in 1813, considers the MS. to be written in very pure Gaelic. It is referred to the twelfth or thirteenth century, is characterized by exuberant diction, groups of poetical adjectives, each beginning with the same letter as the substantive. In short, Tale 5 seems to be a much longer, better, and older verson of the tale of Maghach Colgar. The transcriber makes a kind of apology for the want of truth in these tales at the end of his abstract. He was probably impressed with the idea that Ossian and his heroes sang and fought in Scotland, and that Uirsgeul meant a *new* tale or novel, unworthy of notice. My opinion is that the prose tales and the poems, and this especially, are alike old compositions, founded on old traditions common to all Celts, and perhaps to all Indo-European races, but altered and ornamented, and twisted into compositions by bards and reciters of all ages, and every branch of the race; altered to suit the time and place—adorned with any ornament that the bard or reciter had at his disposal; and now a mere remnant of the past.

It is a great pity that these MSS. in the Advocates' Library are still unpublished. They could not fail to throw light on the period when they were written.

It is remarkable that the so-called Greeks in this story seem to want the head of Fionn for dinner.

XXXVII.

THE BROLLACHAN.

From Widow M. Calder, a pauper, Sutherland.

IN the mill of the Glens, MUILION NA GLEANNAN, lived long ago a cripple of the name of Murray, better known as "Ally" na Muilinn. He was maintained by the charity of the miller and his neighbours, who, when they removed their meal, put each a handful into the lamiter's bag. The lad slept usually at the mill; and it came to pass that one night, who should enter but the BROLLACHAN,* son of the FUATH.

Now the Brollachan had eyes and a mouth, and can say two words only, MI-FHEIN, myself, and THU-FHEIN, thyself; besides that, he has no speech, and alas no shape. He lay all his lubber-length by the dying fire; and Murray threw a fresh peat on the embers, which made them fly about red hot, and Brollachan was severely burnt. So he screamed in an awful way, and soon comes the "Vough," very fierce, crying, "Och, my Brollachan, who then burnt you?" but all he could say was "mee!" and then he said "oo!" (me and thou, mi thu); and she replied, "Were it any other, would n't I be revenged."

Murray slipped the peck measure over himself, and

*** Brollachan is a Gaelic expression for any shapeless deformed creature.—COLLECTOR. I should translate it breastling, or bantling.—J. F. C.**

hid among the machinery, so as to look as like a sack as possible, ejaculating at times, "May the Lord preserve me," so he escaped unhurt; and the "Vough" and her Brollachan left the mill. That same night a woman going by the place, was chased by the still furious parent, and could have been saved had she not been nimble to reach her own door in time, to leave nothing for the "Vough" to catch but her heel; this heel was torn off, and the woman went lame all the rest of her days.

The word spelt Vough, is probably spelt from ear; but it is the Gaelic word Fuath, which is spelt Fouah in the map of the estate where the mill is. The story was told in Gaelic to D. M., gamekeeper, and written by him in English.

Of the same mill another story was got from the same source, called—

1. Moulion na Fuadh. One of John Bethune's forebears, who lived in Tubernan, laid a bet that he would seize the kelpie of Moulin na Fouah and bring her bound to the inn at Inveran. He procured a brown, right-sided, maned horse, and a brown black-muzzled dog; and, by the help of the latter, having secured the Vough, he tied her on the horse behind him, and galloped away. She was very fierce, but he kept her quiet by pinning her down with an awl and a needle. Crossing the burn at the further side of Loch Midgal, she became so restless that he stuck the shoemaker's and the tailor's weapons into her with great violence. She cried out, "Pierce me with the awl, but keep that slender hair-like slave (the needle) out of me. When he reached the clachan of Inveran, where his companions were anxiously waiting for him, he called to them to come out and see the Vough. Then they came out with lights, but as the light fell upon her she dropt off, and fell to earth like the remains of a fallen star—a small lump of jelly. (These jellies are often seen on the moors; dropt stars resembling the medusie on the shore —Collector. They are white, do not seem to be attached to the ground, and are always attributed to the stars. They are common on moors, and I do not know what they are.—J. F. C.)

The same creature, or one of her kind.

2. In Beann na Caltuinn, one day called to Donald MacRobb, "Will you eat any charcoal, Donald?" "No," he said; "my wife will give me supper when I go home."

3. And it is said, that a family of Munroes had, many generations ago, married with the Vougha of Beann na Caltuinn. Their descendants had manes and tails till within the last four generations.

4. Four or five miles from Skibo Castle is Loch Nigdal, with a great granite rock of the same name to the north of it; at one end is a burn which passes the mill where the Brollachan entered. It is haunted with a Banshee (that is, female fairy), which the miller's wife saw about three years ago. She was sitting on a stone, quiet, and beautifully dressed in a green silk dress, the sleeves of which were curiously puffed from the wrists to the shoulder. Her long hair was yellow, like ripe corn; but on nearer view she had no nose.

5. A very old, coarse, and dirty Banshee belongs to a small sheep-farm of Mr. Dempster's. A shepherd found her apparently crippled at the edge of the moss, and offered her a lift on his back. In going, he espied her feet, which were dangling down, and seeing that she was web-footed, he threw her off, flung away the plaid on which she had lain, and ran for his life.

From all these it appears that the Fuath in Sutherland is a water-spirit; that there are males and females; that they have web-feet, yellow hair, green dresses, tails, manes, and no noses; that they marry men, and are killed by light, and hurt with steel weapons; that in crossing a stream they become restless. From the following stories it appears that they are hairy, have bare skin on their faces, and have two large round eyes.

The Rev. Mr. Thomas Pattieson has sent me a story from Islay, which he has written in English, but which he picked up amongst the people. It is as follows; but I have ventured to shorten it a little :—

6. *The Water Horse.*—There is a small island off the Rhinns of Islay, where there is a light-house now, but which was formerly used for grazing cattle only. There is a fearful tide, and it is dangerous to cross the Sound in bad weather. A man and a woman had charge of a large herd of cattle there, and the woman was left alone one night, for the man had to go to the

mainland, and a storm coming on, he could not return. She sat at her peat fire in her cabin, when suddenly she heard a sound as of living creatures all about the hut. She knew her fellow-servant could not have returned, and, thinking it might be the cows, she glanced at the window which she had left open. She saw a pair of large round eyes fastened upon her malignantly, and heard a low whining laugh. The door opened, and an unearthly creature walked in. He was very tall and large, rough and hairy, with no skin upon his face but a dark livid covering. He advanced to the fire and asked the girl what her name was. She answered as confidently as she could, "MISE MI FHIN"—me myself. The creature seized the girl, and she threw a large ladle full of boiling water about him, and he, yelling, bounded out. A great noise ensued of wild unearthly tongues, questioning their yelling companion as to what was the matter with him, and who had hurt him. "Mise mi Fhin, Mise mi Fhin—me myself, me myself," shouted the savage; and thereupon arose a great shout of laughter. No sooner did that pass than the girl rushed out in terror, turned one of the cows that was lying outside from its resting-place, and having made a circle about her, lay there herself. The storm raged, and she heard the rushing of many footsteps, loud laughter, and sounds of strife. When morning dawned, she was safe, protected by the consecrated circle, but the cow she had disturbed was dead.

An Islay pilot told me this year that water-horses still haunt a glen near the island. Rattling chains are heard there. An account was published some years ago in newspapers of the appearance of a mermaid near the spot.

7. I myself heard the groundwork of this story long ago from John Piper; and I heard a similar story this year in Man. (See Introduction.) It is the same as the Brollachan. The creature was scalded by a woman (who had said her name was MI FHIN when he came in), because he wanted to eat her porridge; and when he told his friends Myself had burned him, they said, "Ma 's thu fhin a losg thu fhin bi gad' leigheas fhin thu fhin—If it was thyself burnt thyself, be thyself healing thyself."

8. I again heard a similar story this year from a gentleman whom I met in an inn at Gairloch. He had a large knowledge of Highland tales, and we spent several pleasant evenings together. He has every right to stories, for one of his ancestors

was a clever doctor in his day, and is now a magician in legends. Some of his MSS. are in the Advocates' Library.

Mr. Pattieson points out the resemblance which this bear to part of the story of Ulysses, and, for the sake of comparison, here it is from the ninth book of Pope's Odyssey :—

9. Ulysses goes into the cave of the Cyclop with some of his companions. The Cyclop was a one-eyed shepherd, and his cave is described as a dairy; his flocks were goats and sheep, which he milked when he came home :—

"Scarce twenty-four wheeled cars compact and strong.
The massy load could bear or roll along."

He was a giant, therefore, living under ground; and he ate two of the strangers raw. He spoke Greek, but claimed to be of a race superior to the Greek gods. He ate two more Greeks for breakfast, and two for supper. Then got drunk on wine given him by Ulysses, which was better than his own. Ulysses said, "No man is my name;" and the giant promised to eat him last, as a return for his gift of rosy wine, and went to sleep.

Then they heated a stake in the fire, and drilled his eye out. The Cyclops assembled at his "well-known roar," asked what was the matter, and were told—

"Friends, no man kills me, no man in the hour
Of sleep oppresses me with fraudful power.
If no man hurt thee, but the hand divine
Inflicts disease, it fits thee to resign.
To Jove or to thy father Neptune pray,
The brethren cried, and instant strode away."

It seems, then, that the Cyclop was a water-being as well as the Fuath and water-horse of Gaelic story, and the kelpie. There is no word in Gaelic that could be corrupted into Kelpie, but he is the same as Each uisge. The Gaelic tradition may have been taken from Homer; but if so, the plagiarist must have lived some time ago, for the story is now widely spread, and his edition must have had some other reading for *ουτις*, because the Gaelic word is "myself," in all versions I know.

10. The Cailleach Mhore of Clibrick was a very rich and wicked old woman (I have already shown that there is some reason to suppose she was a Lapp; and no Lapp ever offered me anything, often as I have been amongst them), who, though she

had plenty of the good things of this world, never gave anything away, and never asked a traveller to sit down in her house. A bold man once laid a wager that he would circumvent her. He accordingly walked into her kitchen, when she craved to know whence he came and what was his destination. "I come from the south and am going north," said he. "And what is your name?" said the hag of Greyside. "My name is WILLIAM DEAN SUIDHE." "WILLIAM dean Suidhe!" (sit down) she repeated; when he flung himself into a chair, and making her a bow, said, "That will I when the mistress bids me." She was very angry, and, taking out an enormous bannock as round as the moon, began to eat without taking any notice of him. "Your piece seems a dry one, mistress," said William. "The fat side is to me," said the witch. And indeed she had one side spread with butter about an inch thick. "The side that is to you shall be to me," he retorted; and caught at the cake. He called her a satanic old Cailleach, and left the hut carrying his piece away as a trophy. The old woman was left cursing, and praying that the cake might kill him; but he had too much sense to touch it, and his ill-wisher (the hag) foolishly finishing the remainder, died of its unhallowed effects, to the great relief of her neighbours.

Those who maintain popular stories are as old as the races who tell them, will probably consider the Brollachan, and the Water-horse, and the Greek story, as so many versions of an older original. In this case Homer has a strong claim; but he has an equal claim to several other stories in this collection, which Grimm and the Arabian Nights claim as popular lore. Sindbad, and Conal Crobhi, and Grimms' Robber, if plagiarists, are far more guilty than the Brollachan; and Murachadh Mac Brian, who follows, is quite as bad.

XXXVIII.

MURACHADH MAC BRIAN.

From Donald Shaw, old soldier, Ballygrant, Islay.

THERE were three men in the land of Ceann Coire, in Erin—that was Moorchug MacBreean, and Donachug MacBreean, and Breean Borr, their father. They got a call to go to dine in a place which they called MAGH O DORNA. They took with them threescore knives, threescore bridles, and threescore red-eared white horses. They sat at the feast, and no sooner sat they at the feast than they saw the maid of Knock Seanan, in Erin, passing by. Then out would go Moorchug, then out would go Donachug, and then out would go Brian Borr, their father, after them.

They were not long gone when they saw a great lad coming to meet them.

Brian Borr blessed him in the FISNICHE FAISNICHE—soft, flowing, peaceful words of wisdom.

He answered in better words, and if they were no better they were no worse.

"What man art thou?" said Brian Borr. "A good lad am I, seeking a master." "Almighty of the world against thee, beast! Dost thou wish to be hanged with a sea of blood about thine eyes! 'Tis long I would be ere I would hire thee at thy size." "I care not, may be Murachadh would hire me." He reached Murachadh. Murachadh blessed him in the

FISNICHE FAISNICHE—soft, flowing, peaceful words of wisdom. The lad answered him in better words, and if no better they were no worse.

"What man art thou?" says Muracadh. "A good lad am I, seeking a master," said he. "What wages will thou be asking?" "Two-thirds of thy counsel to be mine,* and thyself to have but one, till we come from chasing the maiden."

"If thou gett'st that," said Murachadh, "man got it not before, and no man will get it after thee, but sure if thou wouldst not honour it, thou wouldst not ask it."

When they had agreed he took a race after the maiden, and he was not long gone when he came back. "Almighty of the world against thee," said Brian Borr. "Dost thou wish to be hanged with a sea of blood about thine eyes? I knew he was without a gillie in the first of the day the man that hired thee, and had he taken my counsel he had not hired thee."

"I will not do a good turn to-day till the buttons come off my bigcoat." Then they got a tailor, and the tailor had not as much skill as would take the buttons off the greatcoat. Then he took shears out of the rim of his little hat, and he took the buttons off his greatcoat in a trice.

Then he took another race after the maiden, and he was not long away when he came back. "Almighty of the great world against thee," said Brian Borr. "Dost thou wish to be hanged with a sea of blood about thine eyes? I knew that he was without a gillie in the first of the day the man that hired thee, and had he taken my counsel he had not hired thee."

* "Da dhrian de d' comhairle." I am not sure of this translation.

"I wont do a good turn to-day till the buttons go on the bigcoat again, for the women will chase me." They got a tailor, and the shears would not cut a grain, and the needle would not sew a stitch. Then he got shears and a needle himself out of the rim of his little hat, and he sewed the buttons on the bigcoat again. He took another little race after the maiden, and he was not long gone when he came back. "Almighty, &c. . . . ," said Brian Borr.

"I will not do a good turn to-day till the thorn in my foot comes out." Then they got a leech, but the leech had not skill enough to take the thorn out of the foot. Then he himself took out a little iron that he had in the rim of his little hat, and he took the thorn out of his foot, and the thorn was a foot longer than the shank."

"Oov! oov!" said Brian Borr, "that is a wondrous matter, the thorn to be longer than the shank." "Many a thing," said he, "is more wondrous than that; there is good stretching at the end of the joints and bones." Then he took a little race away, and he was not long gone when he came back, and he had a wild duck roasted on the fire, not a bit burned or raw in her, and she was enough for every one within. "This is the best turn thou hast done yet," said Brian Borr.

"I will not do a good turn to-day till I get a little wink of sleep." They went to the back of Knock Seanan, in Erin, behind the wind and before the sun, where they could see each man, and man could not see them. He slept there; and when he awoke, what but the maid of Knock Seanan was on the top of the hill! He rose, he struck her a blow of his palm on the ear, and he set her head back foremost. "Almighty, &c. . . . ," said Brian Borr.

"Set the head right on the maiden."—"If my master asks me that, I will do it, and if he does not ask, I will not do it to-day for thee."

"There she is," said Murachadh, "and do to her as thou wilt." Then struck he a fist on her, and he knocked her brains out. They were not long there when they saw a deer and a dog chasing it. Out after it went they, and the sparks that the hound sent from his toes were hitting Murachadh's gillie right in the face. The sparks that Murachadh's gillie sent from his toes were striking Murachadh right in the face, and the sparks that Murachadh sent from his toes were hitting Donachadh right in the face, and the sparks that Donachadh sent from his toes were hitting Brian Borr right in the face. In the time of lateness Murachadh lost his set of men; nor father, nor brother, nor gillie, nor deer, nor dog, was to be seen, and he did not know to what side he should go to seek them. Mist came on them.

He thought he would go into the wood to gather nuts till the mist should go. He heard the stroke of an axe in the wood, and he thought that it was the man of the little cap and the big bonnet. He went down and it was the man of the little cap who was there. Murachadh blessed him; in the fisniche foisniche, soft flowing peaceful words of wisdom; and the youth blessed him in better words; and if no better they were no worse. "I am thinking, then," said the lad, "that it is of the company of Murachadh Mac Brian thou art." "It is," said he. "Well! I would give thee a night's share for the sake of that man, though there should be a man's head at thy belt." Murachadh feared that he would ask him to put the faggot on his back, and he was right feared that he would ask him to carry the axe home for its size. "Good lad," said he, "I am sure thou art tired enough thyself after thy trouble and wandering. It is much for me to ask thee to lift the faggot on my back; and it is too much to ask thee to take the axe home."

He went and he lifted the faggot of fuel on his own back, he took the axe with him in his hand; they went the two to the house of that man; and that was the grand house! Then the wife of that man brought up a chair of gold, and she gave it to her own man; and she brought up a chair of silver, and she gave it to Murachadh; she brought up a stoup of wine, and she gave it to Murachadh, and he took a drink out of it; he stretched it to the other, and after he had drunk what was in it he broke it against the wall. They were chatting together, and Murachadh was always looking at the housewife. "I am thinking myself," said the man of the house, that thou art Murachadh Mac Brian's self."—"Well, I am."—"I have done thee two discourtesies since thou camest to the house, and thou hast done one, to me. I sat myself in the chair of gold, and I set thee in the silver chair; I broke the drinking cup; I failed in that I drank a draught from a half-empty vessel. Thou didst me another discourtesy: thou art gazing at my wife there since thou camest into the house, and if thou didst but know the trouble I had about her, thou wouldst not wonder though I should not like another man to be looking at her." "What," said Murachadh, "is the trouble that thou hast had about her that man had not before, and that another man will not have again after thee?"—"Sleep to-night and I will tell thee that to-morrow."—"Not a cloud of sleep shall go on mine eye this night till thou tellest me the trouble that thou hast had."

"I was here seven years with no man with me but

myself. The seanagal (soothsayer) came the way one day, and he said to me, if I would go so far as the white Sibearta, that I would get knowledge in it. I went there one fine summer's day, and who was there but the Gruagach of the island and the Gruagach of the dog setting a combat. The Gruagach of the island said to me, if I would go in before her to help her, that she would give me her daughter to marry when we should go home. I went in on her side, I struck a fist on the Gruagach of the dog, and I knocked her brains out. Myself and the Gruagach of the island went home, and a wedding and a marriage was made between myself and her daughter that very night; but, with the hero's fatigue, and the reek of the bowl, I never got to her chamber door. If the day came early on the morrow, 'twas earlier still that my father-in-law arose shouting to me to go to the hunting hill to hunt badgers, and vermin, and foxes. At the time of lifting the game and laying it down, I thought that I had left my own wife without a watchman to look on her. I went home a hero, stout and seemly, and I found my mother-in-law weeping; and I said to her, 'What ails thee?' 'Much ails me, that three monks have just taken away the woman thou didst marry thyself.'

"Then took I the good and ill of that on myself, and I took the track of the duck on the ninth morn. I fell in with my ship, and she was drawn her own seven lengths on dried dry land, where no wind could stain, or sun could burn, or the scholars of the big town could mock or launch her. I set my back to her, and she was too heavy; but I thought it was death before or behind me if I did not get my wife, and I set my pith to her, and I put her out. I gave her prow to the sea, and her stern to the land; helm in her stern, sails in her prow, tackle to her ropes, each rope fast and loose, that could make port and anchorage of the sea isle that was there. I anchored my ship, and I went up, and what was there but the three monks casting lots for my wife. I swept their three heads off, I took my wife me and I set her in the stern of the ship; I hoisted the three speckled flapping sails against the tall tough splintery masts. My music was the plunging of eels and the screaming of gulls; the biggest beast eating the beast that was least, and the beast that was least doing as she might. The bent brown buckie that was in the bottom of ocean would play haig on its mouth, while she would cut a slender corn straw before her prow, with the excellence of the steering. There was no stop or rest for me, while I drove her on till I reached the big town of my mother and father-in-law. Music was raised and lament laid down. There were smooth drunken drinks, and coarse drinks drunken. Music in fiddle-strings to the ever-healing of each disease, would set men under evil eye, and women in travail, fast asleep in the great town that night. With the hero's fatigue and the reek of the bowl, I slept far from the wife's chamber.

"If it was early that the day came on the morrow, 'twas still earlier that my father-in-law arose shouting to me to go to the hunting hill to hunt badgers, and vermin, and foxes. At the time of lifting the game and laying it down, I thought that I had left my own wife without a watchman to look on her. I went home a hero, stout and seemly, and I found my mother-in-law weeping. 'What ails thee to-night?' 'Much ails me, that the wet-cloaked warrior has just taken away the bride thou didst marry thyself.'

"Then took I the good and ill of that on myself, and I took the track of the duck on the ninth morn. I fell in with my ship; I set my back to her, and she was too heavy: and I set my pith to her and I put her out. I gave her prow to the sea, and her stern to the land; helm in her stern, sails in her prow, tackle to her ropes, each rope fast and loose, that could make a choice port and anchorage of the big town of the wet-cloaked warrior. I drew my ship her own seven lengths on dried dry land, where wind could not stain, or sun burn her; and where the scholars of the big town could not play pranks or launch her. I left my harness and my spears under the side of the ship; I went up, and a herd fell in with me. 'What's thy news to-day, herd?' said I to him. 'Almighty, etc.,' said the herd, 'if my news is not good, a wedding and a marriage between the wet-cloaked warrior and the daughter of the Island Gruagach: and that there is neither glad nor sorry in the realm that is not asked to the wedding.' 'If thou wouldst give me the patched cloak on thee, I would give thee this good coat that I have on, and good day besides for that.' 'Almighty, etc. . . . . .' 'That is not the joy and wonder that I have to take in it before the sun rises to sky to-morrow." I struck him a blow of my fist in the midst of his face, and I drove the brains in fiery slivers through the back of his head, I put on the patched cloak, and up I went, and the men had just assembled to the wedding. I thought it was lucky to find them gathered. I went amongst them as falcon through flock, or as goat up rock, or as a great dog on a cold spring day going through a drove of sheep. So I would make little bands of large bands, hardy* castles which might be heard in the four airts of heaven,

* I cannot make sense of this phrase.

slashing of blades, shearing heroic shields, till I left not one would tell a tale or withhold bad news; how one would be one-legged, and one one-handed; and though there were ten tongues in their heads, it is telling their own ills and the ills of others that they would be. I took with me my wife, and I set her in the stern of the boat. I gave her prow to sea and her stern to land; I would make sail before, and set helm behind. I hoisted the three speckled flapping sails against the tall tough splintery masts. My music was the plunging of eels and the screaming of gulls; the beast that was biggest eating the beast that was least, and the beast that was least doing as she might; the bent brown buckie that was at the bottom of the sea would play HAIG! on her great mouth, as she would split a slender oat stubble straw with the excellence of the steering.

"We returned to the big town of my father-in-law. Music was raised, and lament laid down. There were smooth drunken drinks and coarse drinks drunken. Music on strings for ever healing each kind of ill, would set wounded men and women in travail asleep in the big town that night. With the hero's fatigue and the reek of the bowl, I never got to my bride's chamber that night.

"If it was early that the day came on the morrow, earlier than that my father-in-law arose shouting to me to go to the hunting hill, to go to hunt brocks, and vermin, and foxes. At the time of lifting the game, and of laying it down, I thought that I had left my own bride without a watchman to watch over her. I went home a hero, stout and seemly, and I found my mother-in-law weeping. 'What ails thee?' said I. 'Much ails me,' said she, 'that the great hero, son of the King of SORCHA (light), has just taken the bride that thou didst wed, away; and he was the worst of them all for me.' Let it be taken well and ill, that was for me. I took the track of the duck on the ninth morn. I fell in with my ship; I set my back to her, and she was too heavy for me; I set my back to her again and I set her out. I gave prow to sea, and stern to land; I'd set helm in her stern, and sails in her prow, and tackles in her middle against each rope that was in her loose and fast, to make choice port and anchorage of the big town of the great hero king of Sorcha. I drew my ship her own seven lengths from ebb, on dry land, where wind would not stain, and sun would not burn, the scholars of the big town could make neither plaything or mocking, or launching of her.

"I went up and a beggar fell in with me. 'What's thy tale to day, oh beggar?' 'Mighty of the world be against thee! dost wish to be hanged with a sea of blood about thine eyes; great and good is my tale; a wedding and a marrying between the great hero, son of the king of Sorcha, and the daughter of the island Gruagach; and that there is neither glad nor sorry in the land that is not called to the wedding.' 'If thou wouldst give me thy cloak, I would give thee good pay and this good coat that I have on for it.' 'Mighty of the world, thou beast, dost wish to be hanged with a sea of blood about thine eyes?' 'That is not the wonder and joy that I am to get from it, before the sun rises in heaven to-morrow.' I struck him a blow of my fist in the midst of his face, and I drove the brain in flinders of flame through the back of his head. The bride knew somehow that I would be there, and she asked that the beggars should first be served. I sat myself amidst the beggars; and each that tried to take bit from me, I gave him a bruise 'twixt my hand and my side; and I'd leave him there, and I'd catch the meat with the one of my hands, and the drink with the other hand. Then some one said that the big beggar was not letting a bit to the heads of the other beggars. The bride said, to be good to the beggars, and they themselves would be finished at last. When all the beggars had enough they went away, but I lay myself where I was. Some one said that the big beggar had laid down drunk. The man of the wedding said, to throw the beast out at the back of a hill, or in the shelter of a dyke, till what was in his maw should ebb. Five men and ten came down, and they set their hand to lifting me. On thy two hands, oh Murachadh; but it was easier for them to set Cairn a Choinnich in Erin from its base, than to raise me from the earth. Then came down one of the men that was wiser than the rest; I had a beauty spot, and there never was man that saw me once but he would know me again. He raised the cap and he knew who it was, That fortune should help you here to-night! 'Here is the upright of Glen feite, the savage * Macallain, pitiless, merciless, fearless of God or man, unless he would fear Murachadh Mac Brian.' When I myself heard that, I rose to put on my tackling for battling and combat; I put on my charmed praying shirt of satin, and smooth yellow silk stretched to my skin, my cloudy coat above the golden shirt, my kindly coat of cotton above the kindly cloak, my boss-covered hindering sharp-pointed shield on my left side, my hero's hard slasher in my right hand, my spawn of narrow knives in my

---

* FEAMANACH,—Feaman means a tail, but whether this means the man with the tail or not, I do not know.

belt, my helm of hardness about my head to cover my comely crown, to go in the front of strife, and the strife to go after it; I put on my hindering, dart-hindering resounding mail, without a flaw, or without outlet, blue-grey, bright blue, "LEUDAR LEOTHAR." Lochliner, the long-light and high-minded; and I left not a man to tell a tale or withhold bad news. If there was not one on one foot, and one one-handed, and though there were ten tongues in their heads, it is telling their own ills, and the ills of the rest that they would be. I took my bride with me, I set her in the ship, I hoisted the three speckled flapping sails against the tall tough splintery trees. My music was the plunging of eels and screaming of gulls; the beast that was biggest eating the beast that was least, and the beast that was least doing as it might; the bent brown buckie that was in the bottom of the sea she would play Haig on her mouth as she would split a slender oat stubble before her prow, with the excellence of the steering. 'Twas no stop or stay for me, as I drove her on till I reached the big town of my father-in-law."

"That was my first rest, Murachadh, and is it wondrous that I dislike any man to be gazing at her?" "Indeed, it is not wonderful,' said Murachadh. Murachadh lay down that night, and he found himself on the morrow in the tower of CHINNECOIRE in Erin, where were his father and his grandfather; and the deer and the dog, and his father and his brother, were in before him.

MURCHADH MAC BRIAN.

BHA triùir dhaoine ann an duthaich Chinn a Choire ann an Eirinn; b' e sin Murchadh Mac Brian, agus Donnachadh Mac

Brian, agus Brian Bòrr an athair. Fhuair iad cuireadh a dhol gu dinneir gu h-àite ris an abradh iad Magh O Dòrna. Thug iad leotha tri fichead sgian, agus tri fichead srian, agus tri fichead each cluas-dearg, geal. Shuidh iad aig a' chuirm, 's cha luaith shuidh iad aig a' chuirm, na chunnaic iad gruagach Chnoc Seanain an Eirinn a' dol seachad. Siod a mach gabhaidh Murchadh; siod a mach gabhaidh Donnachadh; agus siod a mach gabhaidh Brian Bòrr, an athair 'nan déigh. Cha b' fhada 'bha iad air folbh nur a chunnaic iad òlach mòr a' tighinn 'nan coinneamh. Bheannaich Brian Bòrr e ann am briathran fisniche, foisniche, fìle, mìle, ciùin an seanachas. Fhreagair esan ann am briathran a b' fheàrr, 's mar am b' iad a b' fheàrr cha b' iad a bu mheasa. "De 'n duine thusa?" ursa Brian Bòrr. "Is gille math mi ag iarraidh maighstir." "Uile chumhachdan an t-saoghail a' t' aghaidh a bhiasd; am math leat do chrochadh is sian fala ma t' shùilean; 's fhada bhithinn fhéin mam fasdainn thu aig do mheud." "Is coma leam cò-aca; dh' fhaoidte gum fasdadh Murchadh mi." Ràinig e Murchadh, 's bheannaich Murchadh e ann am briathran fisniche foisniche, fìle, mìle, ciùin an seanachas. Fhreagair an t-òlach e ann am briathran a b' fheàrr, 's mar am b' iad a b' fhearr cha b' iad a bu mheasa. "De 'n duine thusa?" ursa Murchadh. "'S gille math mi 'g iarraidh maighstir," urs' esan. "De 'n turasgal a bhios thu 'g iarruidh?" "*Da dhrian de d' chomhairle* gus an d' thig sin o ruith na gruagaich, 's gun a bhi agad féin ach an t-aon." "Ma gheobh thusa sin," ursa Murchadh, "cha d' fhuair fear romhad e, 's cha 'n fhaigh fear a' d' dheigh e; ach 's cinnteach mar am b' airidh thu air nach iarradh thu e."

Nur a chòrd iad thug e roid an déigh na gruagaich, 's cha b' fhada 'bha e air folbh nur a thill e. "Uile chumhachdan an t-saoghail a' t' aghaidh," ursa Brian Bòrr, "am math leat do chrochadh is sian fala ma t' shùilean? dh' aithnich mi gun robh e gun ghillle, toiseach an latha, am fear a dh' fhasdaidh thu, 's nan gabhadh e mo chomhairlesa cha 'n fhasdadh e thu." "Cha dèan mi turn math an diugh gus an d' thig na géineagan bhàr a' chòta mhòir." Fhuair iad an siod tàilleir, 's cha robh de dh' innleachd aig an tàillear na 'bheireadh na géineagan bhàr a' chòta mhòir. Thug e 'n sin siosar a mach a bile na h-ata bige, 's thug e na géineagan bhar a chòta mhòir ann am mionaid. Thug e roid an sin an déigh na gruagaich a rithisd, 's cha b' fhada bha e air folbh nur a thill e. "Uile chumhachdan an t-saoghail a' t' aghaidh," ursa Brian Bòrr, "am math leat do chrochadh is sian fala ma t' shùilean; dh' aithnich mi gun robh e gun ghille toiseach an latha am fear a dh' fhasdaidh thu, 's na 'n gabhadh e mo chomhairlesa cha d' fhasdaidh e thu." "Cha déan mi turn math an diugh gus an d' théid na géineagan air a chòta mhòr a rithisd; no ma chi mnathan a' bhaile mi bidh a h-uile te dhiu as mo dhéigh." Fhuair iad tàillear, 's cha ghearradh a shiosar gréim, 's cha 'n fhuaigheadh a shnàthad beum. Thug e fhein an sin siosar is snàthad a bile na h-ata bige, 's chuir e na géineagan air a' chòta mhòr a rithisd. Thug e roid bheag eile an déigh na gruagaich, 's cha b' fhada 'bha e air folbh nur a thill e. "Uile chumhachdan an t-saoghail a' t' aghaidh," ursa Brian Bòrr; "dh' aithnich mi gun robh e gun ghille toiseach an latha am fear a dh' fhasdaidh thu, 's na'n gabhadh e mo chomhairlesa cha d' fhasdaidh e thu." "Cha dèan mi turn math an diugh gus an d' thig am bior a th' ann a'm' chois aisde." Fhuair iad an siod léigh, 's cha robh do dh' innleachd aig an léigh na bheireadh am bior as a chois. Thug e féin iarunn beag a bh' aige am bile na h-ata bige a mach, 's thug e 'm bior as a chios, 's bha 'm bior troigh na b' fhaide na 'n lurga. "Ubh! ubh!" ursa Brian Bòrr, "'s iongantach an gnothach sin, am bior a bhi na b' fhaide na 'n lurga!" "'S iomadh," urs' esan, "rud is iongantaiche na sin; tha sìneadh math an ceann nan alt 's nan cnàmh." Thug e roid bheag air folbh an sin, 's cha b' fhada 'bha e air folbh nur a thill e, 's lach aig air a ròsdadh air an teine, 's gun bhall loisgte na amh innte, 's bha sàith a h-uile duine stigh innte. "'S e so turn is fhearr a a rinn thu fhathsd," ursa Brian Bòrr.

"Cha dean mi turn math an diugh gus am faigh mi luchdan beag cadail." Dh' fholbh iad air chùl Chnoc Seanain an Eirinn, air chùl gaotha, 's air aghaidh gréine far am faiceadh iad gach duine 's nach faiceadh duine iad. Chaidil e 'n sin, 's nur a dhùisg dé 'bha ach gruagach Chnoc Seanain air mullach a' chnoic. Dh' èiridh e, 's bhuail e buille d'a bhois urra 'sa chluais, 's chuir e 'n ceann cùl air bheul-thaobh. "Uile chumhachdan an t-saoghail a' t' aghaidh," ursa Brian Bòrr, "am math leat do chrochadh is sian fala ma t' shùilean. Cuir an ceann gu ceart air a' ghruagaich." "Ma dh' iarras mo mhaighstir sin orm ni mi e, 's mar an iarr cha dèan mi 'n diugh air do shons' e." "Sin agad i," ursa Murchadh, "'s dean do roghainn rithe." Bhuail e 'n sin a dhòrn urra, 's chuir e 'n t-ionachuinn aisde.

Cha b' fhada 'bha iad an sin nur a chunnaic iad fiadh, agus

gadhar 'ga 'ruith. Mach as a dhéigh gabhaidh iad; 's na spreadan a bha 'n gadhar a' cur as a ladharan, bha iad a bualadh gille Mhurchaidh an clàr an aodainn; na spreadan a bha gille Mhurchaidh a' cur as a ladharan, bha iad a' bualadh Mhurchaidh an clàr an aodainn; 's na spreadan a bha Murchadh a' cur as a ladharan, bha iad a bualadh Dhonnachaidh an clàr an aodainn; 's na spreadan a bha Donnachadh a' cur as a ladharan, bha iad a bualadh Bhrian Bòrr an clàr an aodainn. An am an anamoich chaill Murchadh a chuid daoine. Cha robh 'athair, na bhrathair, na 'ghille, na 'm fiadh, na 'n gadhar r'a fhaicinn; 's cha robh fios aige dé 'n taobh a rachadh e a 'n iarraidh. Thàinig ceò orra.

Smaointich e gun rachadh e stigh do 'n choille 'chruinneachadh chnuthan gus am folbhadh an ceò. Chual e buille tuaigh anns a' choille, is smaointich e gum b'e fear na h-ata bige 's na boinneide mòire bh' ann. Ghabh e sìos, 's is e fear atan bhig a bh' ann. Bheannaich Murchadh e ann am briathran fisniche, foisniche, fìle, mìle, ciùin an seanachas; 's fhreagair an t-òlach e ann am briathran a b' fheàrr, 's mar am b-iad a b' fheàrr cha b' iad a bu mheasa. "Tha dùil am féin," urs' an t-òlach sin, "gur h-ann do chuideachd Mhurchaidh Mhic Brian thu." "'S ann," urs' esan. "Mata bheirinnsa cuid na h-oidhche dhuit airson an duine sin, ged a bhiodh ceann duine air do chrios." Bha eagal air Murchadh gun iarradh e air a' chual a chur air a' mhuinn, 's bha ra eagal air gun iarradh e air an tuagh a ghiùlan dachaidh aig a meud. "Ghille mhath," urs' esan, "tha mi cinnteach gu' bheil thu féin glé sgìth an déigh t' allabain is t' ànraidh. Tha e mòr leam iarraidh ort a' chual a thogail air mo mhuinn, 's tha e ra mhòr leam iarruidh ort an tuagh a thoirt dachaidh."

Dh' fholbh e 's thog e chual chonnaidh air a mhuinn fein; thug e leis an tuagh 'na làimh; dh' fholbh iad 'nan dithisd gu tigh an duine sin, 's b' e sin an tigh ciatach. Thug, an sin, bean an duine sin a nìos cathair òir, 's thug i d'a fear féin i; 's thug i nìos cathair airgid, 's thug i do Mhurchadh i. Thug i nìos stòpan fìon, 's thug i do Mhurchadh e, 's thug e deoch as. Shìn e do 'n fhear eile e, 's an déigh dhàsan na bh' ann òl bhrìsd e ris a bhall' e.

Bha iad a' seanachas còmhla, 's bha Murchadh daonnan ag amharc air bean an tighe. "Tha dùil' am féin," ursa fear an tighe, "gur tu Murchadh Mac Brian fein." "Mata 's mi." "Rinn mise da mhìomhodh ortsa o'n a thàinig thu thun an tighe, 's rinn thusa h-aon ormsa. Shuidh mi féin anns a' chathair òir, 's chuir mi thusa anns a chathair airgid. Bhrisd mi 'n còrn dibhe ; bha de dh' easbhuidh orm gun deoch òl a soitheach leith fhalamh. Rinn thusa mìomhodh eile ormsa ; tha thu 'g amharc air a' mhnaoi sin agam, o'n a thainig thu thun an tighe, 's na 'm biodh fhios agad na fhuair mi 'dhragh rithe, cha bhiodh iongantas ort ged nach bu mhath leam duine eile 'bhi 'g amharc urra." "Dé," ursa Murchadh, "an dragh a fhuair thusa rithe, nach d' fhuair fear romhad, 's nach fhaigh fear eile a'd' dheigh?" "Cäidil a nochd 's innsidh mi sin duit a màireach." "Cha d' théid neul cadail air mo shùil a nochd, gus an innis thu dhomh dé 'n dragh a fhuair thu rithe."

"Bha mi 'n so seachd bliadhna gun duine leam ach mi fein. Thàinig an seanaghal latha an rathad, 's thuirt e rium na 'n rachainn gus an ruig an sibearta geal gum faighinn fiosrachadh ann. Dh' fholbh mi 'n sin latha bòidheach samhraidh, 's co' bh' ann ach gruagach an eilean, 's gruagach a ghadhair a' cur blàir. Thuirt gruagach an eilean rium na 'n rachainn a stigh air a h-aghaidh a chuideachadh leatha gun d' thugadh i dhomh a nighean r'a pòsadh nur a rachamaid dhachaidh. Chaidh mi stigh air a beulthaobh. Bhuail mi dòrn air gruagach a ghadhair 's chuir mi 'n t-ionachuinn aisde. Chaidh mi féin agus gruagach an eilean dhachaidh, 's rinneadh banais agus pòsadh eadar mi féin agus a nighean an oidhche sin fein ; ach le sgìos a' ghaisgich, 's athar na pòit, cha d'fhuair mise dol a laidhe leatha an oidhche sin. Ma 's moch a thàinig an latha an la 'r na mhàireach, bu mhoiche na sin a dh' éiridh m' athair céile, a ghlaodhach rium, a dhol do 'n bheinn sheilg a dhol a shealg bhrochd, uilc, agus shionnach. An am togail na sithinn agus a leagalach smaointich mi gun d' fhàg mi mo bhean féin gun fear faire na coimhid urra. Chaidh mi dhachaidh mar churaidh ro chalma, 's fhuair mi mo mhàthair cheile 'caoineadh, 's thuirt mi rithe, "Dé th' ort?" "'S mòr a th' orm ; an triùir mhanach an déigh a' bhean ud a phòs thu féin a thoirt air folbh."

Ghabh mi olc 's a mhath siod orm féin, 's ghabh mi lorg na lach air an naoidheamr tràth. Thachair mo long orm, 's bha i air a tarruinn a seachd fad féin, air fearann tioram, tràighte, far nach dubhadh gaoith, agus nach loisgeadh grian, 's nach dèanadh sgoilearan baile mhoir magadh na fochaid urra. Chuir mi mo dhrìom rithe, 's bha i ra throm ; ach smaointich mi gum bu bhàs romham agus na 'm dhéighinn e mar am faighinn mo bhean, 's chuir mi mo spionnadh rithe, 's chuir mi mach i. Thug mi 'toiseach do mhuir 's a' deireadh do thir; stiùir 'na deireadh; siuil 'na toiseach; 's beairt na buill; aghaidh gach buill ceangailt, agus fuasgailt'; a' deanadh cala agus acarsaid do dh' eilean mara 'bha sin.

Dh' acraich mi mo long, 's ghabh mi suas; 's dé 'bha 'sin ach an triùir mhanach a' cur crann feuch co leis aca bhiodh i 'san oidhche. Sgrìob mi na tri cinn diu; thug mi leam mo bhean; 's chuir mi ann an deireadh na luing i. Thog mi na tri siùil bhreaca, bhaidealach an aodann nan crann fada, fulannach, fiùighidh. 'Se bu cheòl dhomh plubarsaich easgann, 's béicear-daich fhaoileann; a' bhéisd a bu mhotha 'g itheadh na béisd a bu lugha, 's a' bhéisd a bu lugha dèanadh mar a dh' fhaodadh i. An fhaochag chrom, chiar a bha 'n grunnd an aigean, bheireadh i *ñaig* air a beul mòr. Ghearradh i cuinnlean coirce romh a toiseach le feobhas an stiùraidh. Cha bu stad 's cha b' fhois dhomh, 's mi 'ga 'caitheadh, gus an d' ràinig mi baile-mòr mo mhàthair cheile agus m' athair céile. Thogadh an ceòl, 's leagadh am bròn. Bha deochanna mine, misgeach, 's deochanna garbha 'gan gabhail: ceòl ann an teudan fiodhlach, a' sìor leigheas gach galair, a chuireadh fir ghointe agus mnathan siùbhla 'nan cadal air a mhòr-bhaile an oidhche sin. Le athar na pòit, 's le sgios a' ghaisgich, cha do laigh mise leis a' bhean an oidhche sin.

Ma bu mhoch a thàinig an latha an la 'r na mhàireach, bu mhoiche na sin a dh' éiridh m' athair ceile a ghlaodhach rium fein a dhol do 'n bheinn sheilg, a dhol a shealg bhrochd, is uilc, is shionnach. An am togail na sithinn is a leagalach, smaointich mi féin gun d' fhàg mi mo bhean gun fear faire na feur choimhead urra. Ghabh mi dhachaidh a'm' churaidh ro chalma, 's fhuair mi mo mhàthair chéile 'caoineadh. "Dé th' ort a nochd?" Is mòr a th' orm, Macan na Falluinne fluiche an déigh a' bhean ud a phòs thu féin a thoirt air folbh."

Ghabh 'mi a mhath is olc siod orm fein. Ghabh mi lorg an lach air an naoidheamh tràth. Thachair mo long orm. Chuir mi mo dhrìom rithe, 's bha i ra throm leam. Chuir mi mo dhriom rithe a rithisd, 's chuir mi mach i. Thug mi 'toiseach do mhuir, 's a deìreadh do thìr. Dheanainn stiuir 'na deireadh, siuil 'na toiseach; 's beairt 'na buill; aghaidh gach buill a bh' innte ceangailt' agus fuasgailt'; a' deànadh rogha cala agus acarsaid do Bhaile-mòr Macan na Falluinne fliuiche. Tharruinn mi mo long a seachd fad féin air fearann tioram, tràighte, far nach dubhadh gaoith, 's nach loisgeadh grian, 's nach deanadh sgoilearan baile-mhòir culaidh mhagaidh na fhochaid di. Dh' fhàg mi mo luirg 's mo shleaghan fo thaobh na luinge. Chaidh mi suas, 's thachair buachaill' orm. Dé do naigheachd an diugh a bhuachaille? thuirt mi ris. "Uile chumhachdan an t-saoghail a' t' aghaidh a bhiasd, am math leat do chrochadh is sian fala ma t' shùilean ; 's mòr 's is math mo naigheachd ; banais agus pòsadh eadar Macan na Falluinne fliuiche 's nighean gruagach an eilean, 's nach 'eil mùirne na maird 'san rìoghachd nach 'eil cuireadh aca thun na bainnse." Nan d' thugadh thu domh an lùireach sin ort, bheirinn duit an còta math so 'th' orm féin, 's pàigheadh math a thuillidh air an sin." "Uile chumhachdan an t-saoghail a' t' aghaidh a bhiasd, am math leat do chrochadh is sian fala ma t' shùilean ; cha 'n e sin aighear agus *ioghnadh* a th' agam féin r'a ghabhail aisde ma 'n éirich grian air athar am màireach." Bhuail 'mi buill de m' dhorn air an clàr an aodainn 's chuir mi 'n t-ionachainn 'na chùibeanan teine trìd chùl a chinn.

Chuir mi orm an lùireach, 's ghabh mi suas, 's bha na daoine an déigh cruinneachadh thun na bainnse. Smaointich mi gun robh e fortanach dhomh am faotainn cruinn. Ghabh mi na 'm measg mar sheobhaig romh ealt, na mar ghobhair ri creig, na mar chù mòr ann an latha fuar Earraich a' dol romh threud chaorach. Sin mar a dheanainn buidhnichean beaga do bhuidhnichean mòra; caisteil chròdha 'chluinnt 'an ceithir àirdean an athair ; slachdarsaich lann a' gearradh nan sgiath sonnalach ; gus nach d' fhàg mi fear innsidh *sgeoil* na chumadh tuairisgeul ; mar am biodh fear air leith-chois 's fear air leith-làimh, 's ged a bhiodh deich teangannan 'nan ceann 's ann aig innseadh an uilc féin is uilc chàich a bhitheadh iad. Thug mi leam mo bhean féin, 's chuir mi ann an deireadh na luing i. Thug mi 'toiseach do mhuir 's a deireadh do thìr. Dheanainn siùil 'na toiseach, stiuir 'na deireadh. Thog mi na tri siùil bhreaca, bhaidealach an aodann nan crann fada, fulannach, fiughaidh. 'S e bu cheòl dhomh plubarsaich easgann, s béiceardaich fhaoileann ; a' bhéisd a bu mhotha 'g itheadh na béisd a bu lugha, 's a' bhéisd a bu lugha 'deanadh mar a dh' fhaodadh i. An fhaochag chrom, chiar a bha 'n grunnd an aigean bheireadh i *haig* air a beul mòr. Ghearradh i cuinnlean caol coirce le feobhas an stiùraidh. Thill sinn gu baile mòr m' athair céile. Thogadh an ceòl 's leagadh am bròn. Bha deochanna mine, misgeach, s deochanna garbha 'gan gabhail ; ceòl air teudan, a' sìor leigheas gach seorsa galair, a chuireadh fir ghointe agus mnathan siubhla 'nan cadal air a' mhòr-bhaile an oidhche sin. Le sgìos a ghaisgich, agus le athar na pòit, cha do laidh mise le m' mhnaoi an oidhche sin.

Ma bu mhoch a thàinig an latha an la 'r na mhàireach, bu mhoiche na sin a dh' éiridh m' athair céile a ghlaodhach rium a dhol do 'n bheinn sheilg, a dhol a shealg bhrochd, is uilc is shionnach. An am togail na sithinn is a leagalach, smaointich mi gun d' fhàg mi mo bhean féin gun fhear faire na fuar choimhead urra. Dh' fholbh mi dhachaidh mar churaidh ro chalma, 's fhuair mi mo mhàthair chéile 'caoineadh. Dé th' ort? "'S mòr sin, Macan mòr mac rìgh na Sorcha an déigh a' bhean ud a phòs thu féin a thoirt air folbh." Is e bu mheasa leam aca. Ghabhtar a mhath is olc siod orm fein. Ghabh mi lorg an lach air an naoidheamh tràth. Thachair mo long orm. Chuir mi mo dhrìom rithe, 's bha i ra throm leam. Chuir mi mo dhrìom rithe a rithisd, 's chuir mi mach i. Thug mi 'toiseach do mhuir 's a deireadh do thir. Dhéanainn stiuir 'na deireadh ; siùil 'na toiseach ; 's beairt na buillsgean ; aghaidh gach buill a bh' innte fuasgailt' agus ceangailte ; a' dèanadh rogha cala agus acarsaid do bhaile-mòr Macan mòr rìgh na Sorcha. Tharruin mi mo long a seachd fad féin o thràigh air fearann tioram, far nach dubhadh gaoith, 's nach loisgeadh grian, 's nach dèanadh sgoilearan baile-mhòir culaidh bhùird, na mhagaidh, na fhochaid di.

Ghabh mi suas 's thachair bleidire orm. "Dé do naigheachd an diugh a bhleidire?" "Cumhachdan an t-saoghail a' t' aghaidh ; am math leat do chrochadh is sian fala ma t' shùilean? 's mor agus is math mo naigheachd ; banais agus pòsadh eadar Macan mòr rìgh na Sorcha agus nighean gruagach an eilean ; 's nach 'eil mùirne na mairde 'san tìr nach 'eil air an cuireadh thun na bainnse." "Na'n d' thugadh thu féin dhomh do lùireach, bheirinn dhuit paigheadh math, agus an cota math so th' orm air a son?" "Cumhachdan an t-saoghail a' t' aghaidh a bhiasd ; am math leat do chrochadh agus sian fala ma t' shùilean ; cha 'n e sin aighear agus ioghnadh a th' agam féin r'a ghabhail aisde ma 'n éirich grian air athar am màireach." Bhuail mi buille do m' dhòrn air an clàr an aodainn, 's chuir mi 'n t-ionachainn 'na chùibeanan teine trìd chùl a chinn. Bha fhios aig bean na bainns' air altaigin gum bithinn ann, 's dh' iarr i na bleidirean a riarachadh an toiseach. Shuidh mi féin am meadhon nam bleidirean, 's a h-uile fear a theannadh ri mìr a thoirt uam bheirinn bruthadh dha eadar mo làmh 's mo thaobh, 's dh' fhàgainn an siod e, 's cheapainn am biadh leis an darna làmh, 's an deoch leis an làimh eile. Thuirt cuideigin nach robh am bleidire mòr a leigeil mìr an ceann nam bleidirean eile. Thuirt bean na bainnse iadsan a bhi math do na bleidirean, 's gum biodh iad féin réidh air a' cheann ma dheireadh. Nur a fhuair na bleidirean air fad an leòir dh' fholbh iad, ach laidh mi féin far an robh mi. Thuirt cuideigin gun robh am bleidire mòr an déigh laidhe air an daoraich, 's thuirt fear na bainnse a' bhiasd a thilgeil a mach air cùl cnoic na 'n sgàth gàrraidh, gus an traoghadh e na bha 'na bhrainn. Thàinig còig deug de na daoine 'nuas, 's thug iad làmh air mi féin a thogail. Air do dha làimh a Mhurchaidh gum b' fhasa dhaibh Càrn a Choilnnich an Eirinn a chura a bhonn na mise 'thogail o 'n talamh. Thàinig h-aon de na daoine 'bu ghlice na chéile nuas, bha ball seirc orm, 's cha robh duine chunnaic riamh mi nach aithneachadh a rithisd mi, 's thog e 'n currachd, 's dh' aithnich e co 'bh'ann. "Gun cuideachadh am fortan leibh an so a nochd. Tha 'n so Dìreach Ghleann féite Macallain, am feamanach gun iochd, gun trocair, gun eagal Ni Math, na duine; mar an dèanadh e do Mhurchadh Mac Brian e."

Nur a chuala mi féin siod dh' éiridh mi dhol ann a'm' threallaichean cath agus comhraig. Chuir mi orm mo léine sheuntaidh, sheumh de 'n t-sròl 's de 'n t-sìoda shleamhuinn bhuidhe, sìnte ri m' chraicionn; mo chòta caomh *cotain* air uachdar a chaomh bhroitinn; mo sgiath bhucaideach, bhacaideach, bharra-chaol air mo thaobh cli; mo shlachdanta cruaidh curaidh ann a'm' làimh dheis; m' iuchair sginnichdinn chaol air mo chrios; mo chlogada cruadhach ma m' cheann a dhìon mo mhaise mhullaich, a dhol an toiseach na h-iorguill 's an iorghuil a' dol 'na deireadh. Chuir mi orm mo lùireach thorantach, shìth thorantach, chorraghleusda, gun fhòtas, na gun os, ghormghlas, ghormghlan, leudar, leòthar, Lochlannach, fhada, aotrom, inntinneach; 's cha d' fhàg mi fear innsidh sgeoil na chumadh tuairisgeul; mar am biodh fear air leith-chos ann, 's fear air leith-làimh, 's ged a bhiodh deich teangannan 'nan ceann, 's ann aig innseadh an uilc fein is uilc chàich a bhithead iad.

Thug mi leam mo bhean 's chuir mi 'san luing i. Thog mi na tri siùil bhreaca, bhaidealach an aodann nan cranna fada, fulannach, fiùghaidh. 'S e bu cheòl dhomh plubarsaich easgann, 's béiceardaich fhaoileann; a bhéisd a bu mhotha aig itheadh na béisd a bu lugha, 's a bheisd a bu lugha a' dèanadh mar a dh' fhaodadh i. An fhaochag chrom, chiar a bha 'n grunnd an aigean bheireadh i haig air a beul mòr. Ghearradh i cuinlean coirce romh a toiseach le feobhas an stiùraidh. Cha bu stad 's cha b' fhois dhòmh, 's mi 'ga caitheadh, gus an d' ràinig mi baile-mòr m' athair céile. Sin agad a' chiad oidhche a fhuair mise le m' bhean a Mhurchaidh, 's am b' iongantach ged nach bu mhath leam duine sam bith a bhith 'g amharc urra. "Gu dearbh cha b' iongantach," ursa Murchadh. Chaidh Murchadh an oidhche sin a laidhe, 's fhuair e e féin an là'r na mhàireach ann an tùr Chinn a Choire ann an Eirinn, far an robh athair agus a sheanair; 's am fiadh, 's an gadhar, is athair, 's a' bhràthair a stigh air thoiseach tir.

This tale was taken down in May 1859, from the recitation of Donald Shaw, then aged sixty-eight, a pauper, living at Ballygrant in Islay, who was in the 42nd Highlanders at Waterloo. He served in the army about three years. He said that he had learned it from one Duncan MacMillan, a Colonsay man, well advanced in years, about fifty years ago. On the 6th of July, Hector MacLean wrote :—"Shaw died a few days ago, and so far as I can ascertain, there is none in Islay, Jura, or Colonsay, that can recite the same tale now."

I have only met with one man who knew it by this name; MacPhie, at the Sound of Benbecula, a very old man, who gave me the outline of it. Some of the language is exceedingly difficult; some words none of us can make out; and MacPhie's version, and most of his stories, were full of such language.

The tale then is found in Islay and South Uist, and traced to Colonsay, and is certainly about fifty years old. I have several other tales which resemble it in some degree.

The little hat with everything in it, and the great coat and buttons, are Irish. There is much communication between Ireland and the Isles at this day. The language spoken on the opposite coasts is all but identical, and this is probably common to Ireland and the Isles.

There is something like it in Mr. Simpson's book; and some of his words resemble words in this story, and seem to have puzzled the Irish translators as much as they have puzzled me. The phrase, "As a falcon through a flock of birds," is in Mr. Simpson's work. The man with the bundle of wood is something like the giant in Grimm's Valiant Tailor. The servant who drew a thorn longer than his leg out of his foot, may be some supernatural personage. The measured prose descriptions of sailing, arming, and fighting, are common all over the West Highlands amongst the eldest and poorest men, and similar passages occur in manuscripts.

For descriptions of costume and for language, the tale is very curious, and worth the labour bestowed on it, which is considerable. I have endeavoured to translate closely, and at the same time to imitate this tale ; but it is a very weak attempt, I well know.

The manners described are partly those of the day. The politeness and discourtesy in the house of the man with the little hat, are purely Highland. The breaking of the tumbler is a mark of great respect ; no meaner lip should touch the glass drained to an honoured guest ; but the glass must be first filled and emptied —no half cups are allowed. The best seat should be the guest's. The telling of the story in the evening is the real amusement of the poorer classes now, and used to be much more common.

The description of the sailing of a boat amongst the fish and birds is true to nature ; so is the expression *the track of the duck ;* none but a man familiar with the habits of birds on a sea-coast could think of such a phrase. Ducks feed on shore, and return to the sea at daylight.

The experience of the old soldier probably makes the drink wine, not whisky ; and *Sibearta* is probably white Siberia, derived from the same source ; if not, I can make nothing of it.

The dress described may be the old dress of the Isles, as depicted on tombstones, with a cotton coat slipped in. In an account of the Danes and Norwegians in England and Ireland, by J. J. A. Worsaae, London, 1852, it is stated that Magnus Barfod sat himself at the helm while his ship was drawn over the Peninsula of Tarbet (draw-boat) ; acquired the sovereignty of the Western Isles ; and adopted the dress generally worn there. "They went about the streets (in Norway) with bare legs, and wore short coats and cloaks, whence Magnus was called by his men, Barfod or Barbeen (barefoot or barelegs," says the Icelandic historian, Snorro Sturleson, who, as well known, lived in the first half of the thirteenth century. It is remarkable enough that this is the oldest account extant of the well-known Scotch Highland dress, whose antiquity is thus proved."

The tale might be taken partly from the Odyssey. The man disguised as a beggar, going to a wedding where his own wife was the bride, and where he knocks out the brains of a beggar with a single blow, and makes a general slaughter afterwards, is very like Ulysses, Penelope, Irus, and the Suitors, but similar incidents are common in popular tales. There is a story in the Decameron which somewhat resembles the incident of the wife carried away. On the whole, I think this story is a remnant of an old bardic composition, of which very little remains.

The word GRUAGACH is here used both for a maiden and for a woman with a daughter; it usually means *a maiden*, rarely a chief; sometimes it seems to mean a conjuror, or philosopher, or instructor; often the being called Brownie. It probably means any one with long hair; from GRUAG, the hair of the head.

GLOSSARY.

ALLABAN ANRADH, painful, wandering.

ATHAR NA POIT, the evil effect of drinking.

BEART NA BUIL, tackle in her ropes.

BEUCARSAICH, screaming.

BROCHD AGUS OLC, badgers and evil creatures, vermin.

BUCAIDACH, pimply, *boss* covered, or perhaps hollow.

CALA AGUS ACARSAID, port and anchorage.

CNOCK SEANAN, (?) Hill of Jewels, from sean or seun, a jewel.

CRANNA FADA FULANNACH, trees or masts, long-enduring.

FILE, MILE, soft, fluent.

FISNICHE FAISNICHE, words whose meaning is lost in the islands; probably Irish; perhaps knowing, delaying, that is wise, eloquent.

LEUDAR LEOTHAR LOCHLANNACH, (?) perhaps a description of the man; the epithet Lochlannach is the only one of the three which is comprehensible, and this line probably belongs to something else.

LORG NA LACH, the track of the duck; path, towards the sea.

LURACH, a coat of mail, also a patched cloak.

MAGH O DORNA, (?) plain of pebbles, from dornag, a stone, that can be held in dorn, the fist.

NEAM-A-LACH, (?) not to be found in dictionaries.

PLUBARSAICH, an expressive word for plunging about.

XXXIX.

THE THREE WIDOWS.

From Hector Boyd, Fisherman, Barra.

THERE were three widows, and every one of them had a son apiece. Dòmhnull was the name of the son of one of them.*

Dòmhnull had four stots, and the rest had but two each. They were always scolding, saying that he had more grass than they had themselves. On a night of the nights they went to the fold, and they seized on the stots of Dòmhnull and they killed them. When Dòmhnull rose and went out in the morning to see the stots, he found them dead.

He flayed the stots, and he salted them, and he took one of the hides with him to the big town to sell. The way was so long that the night came on him before he reached the big town. He went into a wood and he put the hide about his head. There came a heap of birds, and they lighted on the hide; he put out his hand and he seized on one of them. About the brightening of day he went away; he betook himself to the house of a gentleman.

The gentleman came to the door, and he asked what he had there in his oxter. He said that he had a soothsayer. "What divination will he be doing?"

---

* (*Lit.*) It was Domhnull that was on the son of one of them.

"He will be doing every sort of divination," said Dòmhnull. "Make him do divination," said the gentleman.

He went and he wrung him, and the bird gave a RAN.* "What is he saying?" said the gentleman. "He says that thou hast a wish to buy him, and that thou wilt give two hundred pounds Saxon for him," said Dòmhnull. "Well, surely!—it is true, doubtless; and if I were thinking that he would do divination, I would give that for him," said the gentleman.

So now the gentleman bought the bird from Dòmhnull, and he gave him two hundred pounds Saxon for him.

"Try that thou do not sell him to any man, and that there is no knowing that I might not come myself to seek him yet. I would not give him to thee for three thousand pounds Saxon were it not that I am in extremity."

Dòmhnull went home, and the bird did not do a pinch of divination ever after.

When he took his meat he began at counting the money. Who were looking at him but those who killed the stots. They came in.

"Ah, Dòmhnull," said they, "How didst thou get all the money that is there?"

"I got it as you may get it too. It's I that am pleased that you killed the stots for me," said he. "Kill you your own stots and flay them, and take with you the hides to the big town, and be shouting, 'Who will buy a stot's hide,' and you will get plenty of money."

They killed the stots, and they flayed them. They

* There seems to be a pun here. RAN is a roar, a hoarse noise. RANN is a rhyme, a verse, a stanza.

took with them the hides to the big town, and they began at shouting, "Who will buy a stot's hide." They were at that work the length of the day; and when the people of the big town were tired making sport of them, they returned home.

Now they did not know what they should do. They were vexed because of the stots that were killed. They saw the mother of Dòmhnull going to the well, and they seized on her and they choked her.

When Dòmhnull was taking sorrow, so long was his mother coming, he looked out to try if he could see her. He reached the well, and he found her dead there.

He did not know what he should do. Then he took her with him home.

On the morrow he arrayed her in the best clothes she had, and he took her to the big town. He walked up to the king's house with her on the top of him. When he came to the king's house he met with a large well.

He went and he stuck the stick into the bank of the well, and he set her standing with her chest on the stick. He reached the door and he struck at it, and the maidservant came down.*

"Say to the king," said he, "that there is a respectable woman yonder, and that she has business with him."

The maidservant told that to the king.

"Say to him to say to her to come over," said the king.

"The king is asking thee to say to her to come over," said the maidservant to Dòmhnull.

"I won't go there; go there thyself; I am tired enough."

---

* The manners and customs of kings, according to west country fishermen, were primitive.

The maid went up, and she told the king that not a bit of the man would go there.

"Go there thyself," said the king.

"If she will not answer thee," said Dòmhnull to the maidservant, "thou shalt push her; she is deaf."

The maidservant reached where she was.

"Good woman," said the maidservant to her, "the king is asking yourself to come over."

She took no notice. She pushed her and she said not a word. Dòmhnull was seeing how it was without.

"Draw the stick from her chest," said Dòmhnull; "it's asleep she is."

She drew the stick from her chest, and there she went head foremost into the well.

Then he shouted out, "Oh my cattle! my cattle! my mother drowned in the well! What shall I do this day?" Then he struck his two palms against each other, and there was no howl he gave that could not be heard at three miles' distance.

The king came out. "Oh, my lad, never give it voice for ever, and I will pay for thy mother. How much wilt thou be asking for thy mother?"

"Five hundred pounds Saxon," said Dòmhnull.

"Thou shalt get that within the minute," said the king.

Dòmhnull got the five hundred Saxon pounds. He went where his mother was; he took the clothes off that were on her, and he threw her into the well.

He came home, and he was counting the money. They came—the two—where he was, to see if he should be lamenting his mother. They put a question to him—"Where had he got all the money that was there?"

"I got it," said he, "where you may get it if you yourselves should choose."

"How shall we get it?"

"Kill you your mothers, and take them with you on top of you, and take them about the big town, and be shouting, 'Who will buy old dead carlins?' and you get your fortunes."

When they heard that they went home, and each one of them began upon his mother with a stone in a stocking till he killed her.

They went on the morrow to the big town. They began at shouting, "Who will buy old carlins dead?" And there was no man who would buy *that*.

When the people of the big town were tired making sport of them, they set the dogs at them home.

When they came home that night they laid down and they slept. On the morrow, when they rose, they went where Dòmhnull was, and they seized on him and they put him into a barrel. They went with it to reel it down from a peak of rock. They were thus, and they had time about carrying it. The one said to the other, "Since the way was so long, and the day so hot, that they should go in to take a dram." They went in, and they left him in the barrel on the great road without. He heard a "TRISTRICH"* coming, and who was there but the shepherd, and a hundred sheep with him. He came down, and he began to play a "trump" (Jew's harp) which he had in the barrel. The shepherd struck a stroke of his stick on a barrel. "Who's in here?" said he. "It's me," said Dòmhnull. "What art thou doing in it?" said the shepherd. "I am making a fortune in it," said Dòmhnull, "and no man ever saw such a place with gold and silver. I have just filled a

* TRISTRICH: a word which exactly describes the tripping sound of a lot of sheep on hard ground.

thousand purses here, and the fortune is nearly made."

"It's a pity," said the shepherd, "that thou shouldest not let myself in a while."

"I won't let thee. It is much that would make me."

"And wilt thou let me in? Mightest thou not let me in for one minute, and mightest thou not have enough thyself nevertheless?"

"By the books, poor man, since thou art needful, I will not let thee in. (Do) thou thyself drive the head out of the barrel and come here; but thou shalt not get (leave) to be long in it," said Dòmhnull.

The shepherd took the head out of the barrel, and he came out; he seized on the shepherd by the two shanks, and he set him head foremost in the barrel.

"There is neither silver nor gold here," said the shepherd.

"Thou wilt not see a thing till the head goes on the barrel," said Dòmhnull.

"Oh, I don't see a shadow in here," said he.

"If thou seest not, so be it with thee," said Dòmhnull.

Dòmhnull went and he put on the plaid that the shepherd had, and when he put on the plaid the dog followed him. Then they came out and they seized the barrel, and they raised it on their shoulders. They went away with it.

The shepherd would say at the end of every minute, "It's me that's in it—it's me that's in it." "Oh, it's thou, roguey! belike it's thou?"

They reached the peak of the rock, and they let down the barrel with the rock and shepherd in its inside.

When they returned, whom did they see but Dòmhnull, with his plaid and his dog, and his hundred of sheep with him in a park.

They went over to him.

"Oh, Dòmhnull," said they, "how gottest thou to come hither?"

"I got as you might get if you would try it. After that I had reached the world over yonder, they said to me that I had plenty of time for going over there, and they set me over here, and a hundred sheep with me to make money for myself."

"And would they give the like of that to us if we should go there?" said they.

"They would give (that.) It's they that would give," said Dòmhnull.

"(By) what means shall we get going there?" said they.

"Exactly the very means by which you yourselves sent me there," said he.

They went and they took with them two barrels to set themselves into up above.

When they reached the place one of them went into one of the barrels, and the other sent him down with the rock. That one gave a roar below, and his brains just after going out with the blow he got.

The other one asked Dòmhnull what he was saying?

"He is shouting. 'Cattle and sheep, wealth and profit,'" said Dòmhnull.

"Down with me, down with me!" said the other one.

He did not stay to go into the barrel. He cut a caper down, and the brains went out of him.

Dòmhnull went home, and he had the land to himself.

NA TRI BANTRAICHEAN.

Bha tri bantraichean aunn, agus bha mac an t-aon aig a h-uile té dhiu. 'Se Dòmhnull a bh' air mac h-aon diu. Bha ceithir daimh aig Dòmhnull, 's cha robh ach dà dhamh an t-aon aig càch. Bhiodh eud a' trod daonnan, ag ràdh go 'n robh barrachd feòir aige-san 's a bh' aca fhìn. Oidhche dha na oidhchean chaidh eud do 'n chùith, agus rug eud air na daimh aig Dòmhnull, agus mharbh eud eud. Nur a dh' eiridh Dòmhnull 's a chaidh e 'mach 'sa mhadainn a sheaultainn air na daimh, fhuair e marbh eud. Dh' fheaunn e na daimh 's shaill e eud, 's thug e leis té dha na seicheachan dha 'n bhaile mhòr a 'creic. Bha 'n t-astar cho fada 's gon d' thàinig an oidhch' air mu 'n d' ràinig e 'm baile mòr. Chaidh e 'stigh do choille 's chuir e 'n t-seiche mu cheaunn. Thàinig grunnan ian 's laidh eud air an t-seiche. Chuir e 'làmh a mach 's rug e air fear dhiu. Mu shoillseachadh an latha dh' fhalbh e. Ghabh e go tigh duin' uasail. Thàinig an duin' uasal gos an dorusd 's dh' fhoighnichd e dé bh' aige 'na achlais an siud. Thuirt e go 'n robh fiosaiche. "De 'n fhiosachd a bhios e 'dianadh?" "Bidh a h-uile seòrsa fiosachd," ursa Dòmhnull. "Bheir air fiosachd a dhianadh," urs' an duin' uasal. Dh' fhalbh e agus dh' fhàisg e e 's thug an t-ian ràn as. "De 'tha e 'g ràdh?" urs' an duin' uasal. "Tha e 'g ràdh gom bheil toil agadsa 'cheannach, 's gon d' thoir thu dà chiad punnd Sasnach air," ursa Dòmhnull. "Mata, go cinnteach! tha e fiar gon teagamh, 's na 'm bithinn a smaointeachadh gon dianadh e fiosachd bheirinn sin air," urs' an duin' uasal. Cheannaich an duin' uasal, an so, an t-ian o Dhomhnull, 's thug e dà chiad punnd Sasnach dha air. "Fiach nach creic thu ri duine 'sam bith e, 's gon fhios nach d' thiginn fhìn a 'iarraidh fhathasd. Cha d' thugainn duit air tri mile punnd Sasnach e mur a' bhithe' gom bheil mi aunn a'm' éiginn." Dh' fholbh Dòmhnull dachaidh, 's cha d' rinn an t-ian greim fiosachd riabh tuillidh.

"Nur a ghabh e bhiadh thòisich e air cunntas an airgid. Co 'bha 'ga choimhead ach an fheadhainn a mharbh na daimh. Thàinig eud a stigh. "A Dhòmhnuill," urs' àdsan, "démur a fhuair thusa na 'bheil an sin de dh' airgiod?" "Fhuair mur a gheibh sibhs' e cuideachd. 'S mi 'bha toilichte go 'n do mharbh sibh na daimh orm," urs' esan. "Marbhadh sibhse na daimh agaibh fhìn, agus feannaibh eud, agus thugaibh leibh na seicheachan do 'n bhaile mhòr, 's bithibh ag eubhach co cheannachas seiche daimh, agus gheibh sibh na leòir de dh' airgiod." Mharbh eud na daimh 's dh' fheaunn eud eud. Thug eud leò na seicheachan do 'n bhaile mhòr, 's thòisich eud air eubhach co cheannachas seiche daimh. Bha eud ris an obair sin fad an latha ; 's nur a bha muinntir a' bhaile mhòir sgìth 'gabhail spòrs orra, thill eud dachaidh. Cha robh fios aca an so de 'dhianadh eud ; bha aireachas orra chionn na daimh a mharbhadh. Chunnaic eud màthair Dhòmhnuill a' dol do 'n tobar, 's rug eud urra 's thachd eud i. Nur a bha Dòmhnull a' gabhail mulaid fad 's a bha mhàthair gon tighinn, sheaull e 'mach fiach am faiceadh e i. Ràinig e 'n tobar 's fhuair e marbh an sin i. Cha robh fios aige de 'dhianadh e. Thug e leis dhachaidh an sin i. An la 'r na mhàireach 'sgeadaich e i aunns an aodach a b' fhearr a bh' aice 's thug e dha 'n bhaile mhòr i. Choisich e 'suas go tigh an rìgh 's i aig' air a mhuin. Nur a thàinig e go tigh an rìgh thachair tobar mòr ris. Dh' fhalbh e 's stob e 'm bata 'm bruach an tobair, 's chuir e 'na seasamh i 'sa h-uchd air a' bhata. Ràinig e 'n dorusd 's bhuail e aige, 's thàinig an searbhanta 'nuas. "Abair ris an rìgh," urs' esan, "gom bheil boireannach còir thallad, 's gom bheil gnothach aice ris." "Dh' innis an searbhanta siud dha 'n rìgh. "Abair ris a ràdh rithe tigh'n a naull," urs' an rìgh. "Tha 'n righ 'g iarraidh ort a ràdh rithe tigh'n a naull," urs' an searbhanta ri Dòmhnull. "Cha d' théid mis' aunn ; theirig fhìn aunn ; tha mise sgìth go leòir." Chaidh an searbhanta 'suas 's thuirt i ris an an rìgh nach rachadh bad dha 'n duin' aunn." "Falbh fhìn aunn," urs' an rìgh. "Mur am freagair i thu," ursa Dòmhnull ris an t-searbhanta, "putaidh tu i ; tha i bodhar." Ràinig an searbhanta far an robh i. "A bhoireannaich chòir," urs' an searbhanta rithe, "tha 'n rìgh 'g iarraidh oirbh fhìn tigh'n a naull." Cha d' thug ise feairt. Phut i i 's cha d' thuirt i facal. Bha Dòmhnull a' faicinn mur a bha 'muigh. "Tarruinn am bat' o a h-uchd," ursa Dòmhnull, "'s aunn 'na cadal a tha i." Tharruinn i 'm bat' o a h-uchd, agus siud an coinneamh a cinn a ghabh i aunns an tobar. Dh' eubh esan an so a muigh, "O m' fheudail ! m' fheudail ! mo mhathair air a bàthadh aunns an tobar ! De 'ni mis' an diugh !" Bhuail e 'n so a dha bhois ri chéile, 's cha 'n 'eil ràn a bheireadh e as nach cluinnte tri mìl' air astar. Thàinig an rìgh 'mach. "O ghille, na d' thoir guth go bràch air, 's pàighidh mise do mhàthair." "De 'bhios thu 'g iarraidh air do mhàthair ?" "Còig ciad punnd Sasnach," ursa

Dòmhnull. "Gheibh thu sin 'sa mhionaid," urs' an rìgh. Fhuair Dòmhnull na còig ciad punnd Sasnach. Chaidh e far an robh 'mhàthair, 's thug e dhi an t-aodach a bh' urra, 's thilg e 's an tobar i.

Thàinig e dhachaidh 's bha e 'cunntas an airgid. Thàinig àdsan 'nan dithisd far an robh e fiach am biodh e 'caoineadh a mhàthar. Chuir eud ceist air ca' 'n d' fhuair e na robh 'n siud de dh' airgiod. "Fhuair," urs' esan, "far am faigheadh sibhs' e na 'n toilicheadh sibh fhìn." "Démur a gheibh sin e?" "Marbhadh sibhs' 'ur màthraichean, 's thugaibh leibh air 'ur muin eud, 's theirigibh feadh a bhaile mhòir, 's bithibh ag eubhachd co a cheannachas seana chailleach mharbh, 's gheibh sibh 'ur fortan."

Nur a chual eud so chaidh eud dachaidh. Shiùd gach fear ac' air a mhàthair le clach am mogan gos an do mharbh e i. Dh' fhalbh eud an la 'r na mhàireach do 'n bhaile mhòr. Thòisich eud air eubhach, "Co cheannachas seana chailleach mharbh," 's cha robh duine 'cheannachadh siud. Nur a bha muinntir a 'bhaile mhòir sgìth 'gabhail spòrs orra, lig eud na coin aunnta dhachaidh.

Nur a thàinig eud dachaidh an oidhche sin chaidh eud a laidhe 's chaidil eud. An la 'r na mhàireach, nur a dh' éiridh eud, thàinig eud far an robh Dòmhnull, 's rug eud air, 's chuir eud aunn am barailt e. Dh' fhalbh eud leis gos a rìleadh a sìos le bàrr creige. Bha eud an so 's treis mu seach aca 'ga 'ghiulan air falbh. Thuirt an darna fear ris an fhear eile, o 'n a bha 'n t-astar cho fada 's an latha cho teith, go 'm bo chòir dhaibh dol a stigh a ghabhail drama. Chaidh eud a stigh, 's dh' fhàg eud esan aunns a bharailt air an rathad mhòr a muigh. Chual e tristrich a' tighinn, 's co 'bha 'n sin ach cìbear agus ciad caora leis. Ghabh e 'nuas; agus thòisich esan air seinn tromp a bh' aig' aunns a' bharailt. Bhuail an cìbear buille dha 'n bhat' air a' bharailt. "Co 'tha 'n so?" urs' esan. "Tha mis'," ursa Dòmhnull. "De 'tha thu 'dianadh aunn?" urs' an cibear. "Tha mi 'dianadh an fhortain aunn," ursa Dòmhnull; "'s cha 'n fhaca duine riabh a' leithid so de dh' àite le òr a's airgiod. Tha mis' an déigh mìle spòran a lianadh an so, 's tha m' fhortan thun a bhith dèante." "'S truagh," urs' an cibear, "nach ligeadh tu mi fhìn a stigh treis." "Cha lig; 's mòr a bheireadh orm e." "'S nach lig thu aunn mi, nach faodadh tu mo ligeil aunn aona mhionaid, 's nach faod thu na leòir a bhith agad fhìn co-dhiù." "An leòbhra 'dhuine bhochd, o 'n a tha thu feòmach ligidh mi aunn thu.

Cuir fhìn an ceaunn as a bharailt 's thig an so, ach cha n' fhad' a gheibh thu 'bhith aunn," ursa Domhnull. Thug an cìbear an ceann as a bharailt 's thàinig esan a mach. Rug e air dhà chois air a' chìbear 's chuir e 'n coinneamh a chinn 's a bharailt e. "Cha 'n 'eil airgiod na òr an so," urs' an cìbear. "Cha 'n fhaic thu dad gos an d' théid an ceaunn 'sa bharailt," ursa Dòmhnull. "O! cha 'n fhaic mise sgath an so," urs' esan. "Mur am faic biodh agad," ursa Dòmhnull.

Dh' fhalbh Dòmhnull 's chuir e air am breacan a bh' aig a' chìbear, 's lean an cù e nur a chuir e air am breacan. Thàinig àdsan, an so, a' mach 's rug eud air a' bharailt 's thog eud air an guaillean e. Dh' fhalbh eud leis. Theireadh an cìbear an ceaunn h-uile mionaid, "Mis' a th' aunn, mis' a th' aunn." "O 's tu bhraidean! 's dògh gor tu!" Ràinig eud bàrr na creige, 's lig eud sìos am barailt leis a' chreig 's an cìbear 'na bhroinn.

Nur a thill eud co chunnaic eud ach Dòmhnull le bhreacan 's le chù, 's ciad caor' aig' aunn am pàirc. Ghabh eud a null g'a ionnsuidh. "O Dhòmnuill," urs' àdsan, "démur a fhuair thusa tighinn an so?" "Fhuair mur gheibheadh sibhse na 'm fiachadh sibh ris. An deigh dòmhsa an saoghal thaull a ruighinn, thuirt eud rium gon robh ùine na leòir agam go dol a null, 's chuir eud a naull mi agus ciad caora leam go airgiod a dhianadh dhomh fhìn." "Agus an d' thugadh eud a' leithid sinn duinne na 'n rachamaid fhìn aunn?" urs' àdsan." "Bheireadh, 's eud a bheireadh," ursa Dòmhnull. "De 'n dòigh air am faigh sinn dol aunn," urs' àdsan. "Dìreach air an aon dòigh air an do chuir sibh fhìn mis' aunn," urs' esan.

Dh' fhalbh eud 's thug eud leotha da bharailt go eud fhin a chur unnta go h-àrd. Nur a ràinig eud an t-àite chaidh fear diu aunn a h-aon de na barailtean, 's chuir am fear eile sìos leis a' chreig e. Thug am fear sin ràn as shìos, 's an t-ionachainn an déigh dol as leis a' bhuill' a fhuair e. Dh' fhoighneachd am fear eile de Dhòmnull de 'bha e 'g ràdh. "Tha e 'g eubhach, Crodh a's caoraich, maoin a 's mathas," ursa Dòmhnull. "Sìos mi! sìos mi!" urs' am fear eile, 's cha d' fhan e ri dol aunns a bharailt. Gheàrr e leum sìos 's chaidh an t-ionachainn as. Thill Domhnull dachaidh 's bha 'm fearann aige da fhìn.

This story is marvellously like Big Peter and Little Peter (Norse Tales, p. 387), published in 1859. That, again, is equally like Grimm's "Little Farmer," p. 179 of the English translation,

1857 ; and that, again, resembles an Italian tale printed in 1567.

The incident of the man in the cupboard is common to German and Norse, it is not in the Gaelic tale, but it is the whole subject of the "Monk and the Miller's Wife" by Allan Ramsay, p. 520, vol. ii. of the edition published in 1800 ; and that has a much older relative in "the Friars of Berwick," published in "Scottish Ballads" by John Gilchrist, 1815, p. 327. That tale is said to be from Sibbald's Chronicle of Scottish Poetry, and Pinkerton's Scottish Poets, collated with the Bannatyne MS. That poem, of rather questionable propriety, contains none of the incidents in this Gaelic tale ; and it is clearly not derived from any of these modern books. The version translated was written down in Barra by Hector MacLean, in July, from the mouth of a fisherman.

In December, the following version was written down by the Rev. Mr. MacLauchlan of Edinburgh, a very highly respected gentleman, well known as one of the best Gaelic scholars of his day ; while he is also a zealous and active minister. He has interested himself in the collection of the popular lore of his country ; and he has been kind enough to write down several tales for me from the dictation of one of his parishioners. He gives the following pedigree, with his translation of the Gaelic, which he was good enough to send, and which was returned to him :—

2d. From Donald MacLean, born in Ardnamurchan, brought up from the age of 3 years in Mull (Jarvisfield), 69 years of age. Heard this from an old man in Ardnamurchan, Angus MacPhie, who died forty-five years ago. Reads a little English ; has never seen any of these stories in a book ; cannot write ; reads no Gaelic ; lives in the Grassmarket ; came to Edinburgh thirty-five years ago.

Ribin, Robin, and Levi the Dun (Levi-our).

Once in a time there lived three men in the same place, whose names were Ribin, Robin, and Levi-our. The men were not on friendly terms together, as the other two disliked Levi-our. On one occasion Levi-our was from home, when the other two, out of revenge, killed one of his cows. On his return, he flayed the cow, and dried the hide. He made two pockets, which he sewed to the hide, and put in there several pieces of money of different value. He went with the hide to the market town. He was trying at his leisure whether he could find any one to buy it. He saw a man, who had the appearance of being rich, come to the place in which he stood, and he made an offer for the hide; but Levi-our thought the price too small. Levi-our said that they had better go into the inn and have a dram. The gentleman assented, and they entered the inn. Levi-our called for such a dram as was suitable in the circumstances, and they got it. When they were about to pay for the dram Levi-our struck a stroke of his stick on the hide, and said, "Pay this, hide." The coin of money that was necessary to pay the dram leaped out on the floor. The gentleman asked him whether the hide would always pay in that way. He said it would. "Whatever a man drinks in an inn the hide will pay it." "Do you think," said the gentleman, "it will do that for me if I buy it?" "Oh, yes, the very same," said the other. "If it will, I'll give you a hundred merks for it," said he. "It is yours," said Levi-our, "if you give me that sum for it." The other paid the money and got the hide. The gentleman called for another dram which they drank together. Levi-our bade him strike the hide as he had done, and he would see that the hide would pay as it did for him. The other struck the hide and it did pay the money. Levi-our went away and left it there, and so pleased was the other with his purchase that he called for more drink in the inn. He struck the hide, and bade it pay for the drink, but nothing would come out of it; it would pay no more. Levi-our went home, and next morning he saw Ribin and Robin, his neighbours, coming to the house. He was engaged counting the money he got for the hide when the men came into his house. "Oh, Levi-our," said they, "where did you get all that money?" "One of my cows died," said he, "I flayed her, and carried the hide to the market town; I sold the hide and got all this money for it. There is a great price," said he, "to be had for raw hides." They went away home, and killed each of them a cow; they took the hides off them, and dried them. They went with them to the market town, and were then walking backwards and forwards asking who would buy raw hides. Several people came their way, and were offering, some half-a-crown, and some a crown for each hide. They were resolved not to sell them, unless they got the same price for them that Levi-our got for his. They saw that they could not succeed in that, so they were just obliged at last to return home with the hides. They went to Levi-our's house. Levi-our left, and went out of their way. There was nobody to be found within but an old woman, his mother. It was this they did—they killed Levi-our's mother out of revenge towards himself. When he returned home, he found his mother dead. He took the body, and instead of dressing it in grave-clothes, he put on his mother's usual dress, and went away with it to the market town. When he reached the market town, he looked about for a well, and he saw a great deep well there. He took two sticks, and propped the body of his mother, with the two sticks, at the side of the well. He saw a number of fine looking scholars flocking out from a school in the neighbourhood. He asked a boy, who seemed to be the son of a great influential and distinguished man, if he would be so good as go and tell the old woman who was standing near the well, that he was wishful to leave, and to ask her to come to him. The boy agreed, and went to the old woman. She took no notice of him. He returned to Levi-our, and said that she did not answer him. "Ud," said Levi-our, "go again and speak loud and resolutely to her, and tell her it is her own son wants her." The boy returned, and went up close to her, and as he thought she was deaf, he spoke loud to her. As she made no reply, he gave her a push, when down she tumbled into the well. Levi-our called out for the town-guard, and told them to seize the boy that had drowned his mother. The officers came immediately, arrested the boy, and put him in prison. Notice was given through the town, with the ringing of a bell, that such a young man had been imprisoned for drowning an old woman in a well. Who did the boy happen to be but the son of the provost of the town. The provost came to Levi-our and asked what he would take on condition of letting his son off, and as an equivalent for the life of his mother. Levi-our said it was not an easy matter to say, seeing he had so great a regard for his mother. "Oh," said the provost, "I will see your mother decently buried, and will give you besides five hundred merks in consideration of her having been drowned as happened." "Very well," said Levi-our, "as you are a respectable gentleman, I will accept that." Levi-our returned home. Next day he saw his two neighbours coming towards his house. He commenced counting the money he had got for his mother. "Oh," said they, "where did you get all that money?" "My mother died," said he, "and I went with her to the market town and sold her. There is a high price given for dead old women, to make powder of their bones." "Then," said they, "we, ourselves, will try the same thing." He who had no mother had a mother-in-law; so they killed an old woman each. Off they go next day to the market town, with the old women on their shoulders. They walked backwards and forwards through the streets, crying out who would buy dead old women. All the loose fellows and dogs in the town soon gathered around them. As they carried the dead women they had their feet around their necks, and their bodies hanging down along their backs. When they saw the number of people likely to gather round them, they began to get out of the way as fast as possible. Before they got to the other end of the town, there was nothing remaining of the old women but the feet, which hung around their necks. They threw these at last to the people, and made off as fast as they could. Levi-our, when he thought that they were likely to do him an injury, resolved that, by the time of their return home, he and his wife would have a great feast for them. He did so. He spread a splendid table, covered with meat and drink for them. He filled a portion af a sheep's gut with blood, and tied it round his wife's neck. "Now," said he, "when they come, I will call to you to place more upon the table, and when you don't lay down enough, I will rise and take my knife, and stick it into the piece of gut that is around your neck, and I will let you fall gently to the ground. Afterwards I will sound a horn. You will then rise and wash yourself, and be as you were—living and well." Ribin and Robin came to the house. "Come away, neighbours," said he, "you will be hungry after being in the market town." There was as much meat and drink before them as would serve a dozen of men. He was always bidding his wife to put down more and more. On one of these occasions Levi-our rose and put his pointed knife into the piece of gut that was round his wife's neck. "Oh Levi-our, senseless man as thou ever wert, what made you kill your wife?" "Get you on with your dinner," said he, "I'll bring her alive whenever I choose." They took such alarm, and became so much afraid that they couldn't eat their food. Levi-our rose, seized the horn, and sounded it. His wife rose and shook herself. "Now," said he, "see to it that you behave well hereafter, and that you don't refuse anything I require of you." Ribin and Robin went away. When they saw the strange things he could do, they could not remain any longer in his company. "Our own wives might very well provide us with such a feast as we had from Levi-our," said they, "and if they do not we will treat them just as Levi-our did." So soon as they returned home, they told their wives that they must prepare them a feast, and a better one than Levi-our gave them. Their wives did so, but they were not satisfied ; they were always asking for more. "Oh," said the women, "Levi-our has sent you home drunk, and you don't know what you are saying." Both of the men rose and cut the throats of their wives at once. They fell down and were shedding their blood. The men then rose and sounded a horn to raise them again. Though they should sound the horn to this very hour, the wives wouldn't rise. When they saw that the wives would not rise, they resolved to pursue Levi-our. When he saw them coming, he took to his heels and ran away. They looked at nothing else ; but after him they ran, determined to have his life. He hadn't run far on his way when he met in with a man having a flock of sheep. He said to the man, "Put off your plaid, and put on what I am wearing, there are two men coming who are resolved to have your life. Run as fast as you can, or you will be a dead man immediately." The man ran away as he was bidden, and they ran hard after him. They didn't halt until they had pushed him into the deep black pool of Ty-an-leòban. The man fell in, and he was never seen afterwards. They returned home. Next day, what did they see on looking out but Levi-our herding a fine flock of sheep. They came to the place where he was. "Levi-our," said they, "tho whole world won't satisfy you, didn't we think that we had pitched you last night into the pool of Ty-an-leòban." "Don't you see the sheep I found there?" said he. "Would we find the same if we went in?" said they. "Yes, if I were to put you in," said he. Off Ribin and Robin set, and off Levi-our set after them. They reached, and when they got to the hole they stood still. Levi-our came behind them, and pushed them both into the pool. "Fish for sheep there," he said, "if you choose." Levi-our came home, and got everything in the place for himself. I left them there.

I have a third version of this written by Hector MacLean, from the telling of Margaret MacKinnon in Berneray, in the Sound of Harris. It is called

3. Brian Briagach—Bragging Brian.—What should happen

but that a great merchant should come to the house of Lying Brian, and what should he have but a great grey mare, and he pretended that she made gold and silver; and what should the merchant do but covet this mare because she made gold and silver. Brian gave the mare money amongst her food, and the merchant found it when he looked for it, and he gave thousands for the mare, and when he got her she was coining money.

He took her with him, and he had her for a week, but a penny of money she did not coin. He let her alone till the end of a month, but money nor money she did not make.

Then he went at the end of the month, where Brian was, to talk to him (A CHAINEADH) for the lie, and to send the mare back again.

Brian killed a cow and filled the entrails with blood, and wrapped them about his wife under her clothes; and when the merchant came, he and his wife began to scold, and the merchant struck her, and she fell over for dead, and the blood ran about the floor.

Then Brian went and he catches two horns that were in the top of the bed, BARR NA LEAPA, and he blew into his wife's throat till he brought her alive again.

The merchant got the horns, and promised to say no more about the mare, and went home and killed his wife, and his sister, and his mother, and he began to blow into their throats with the horns, but though he were blowing for ever he had not brought them alive. Then he went where Lying Brian was to kill him. He got him into a sack, and was to beat him to death with flails, but Brian asked a little delay, and got out (it is not said how), and put in two big dogs. The men threw the sack out into the sea when they were tired of beating it.

What was more wonderful for the merchant at the end of a fortnight, than to see Brian and a lot of cattle with him.

"O CHIAL," "oh, my reason," said the merchant, "hast thou come back, O Brian!"

"I came," said Brian. "It was you that did the good to me; when you put me out on the sea I saw thy mother, and thy wife, and thy sister, since I went away; and they asked thee to go out on the sea in the place where thou didst put me out, and that thou thyself shouldst get a lot of cattle like this."

The merchant went and cuts a caper out AIR A BHAD on the

spot where he had put out Brian. He was drowned, and Brian got his house for himself.

I have a fourth version written by John Dewar, collected somewhere in Argyleshire, and sent May 1860.

4. EOBHAN IURRACH.—The hero and two others were working a town-land, BAILE FEARAINN, together. The one staid at home, and the others drowned his cow. He took off the hide, and hung it on the rafters, and when it was dry, he put a piece of money into each knee and hoof, and took it to the town, and he would cry out "CO A CHANICHEAS SEICH NA'M BUINN AIRGIOD"—"who will buy the hide of the pieces of money?" and he would strike a blow on the hide, and the money would fall on the street, and each piece as it fell he picked up and put it into his pocket.

He sold it, of course; and when the bargain was made, he knocked out all the money, to prove that it was no cheat, and put the money into his pocket, and went home.

The others killed their cattle, and when they could not sell the hides, they decided on killing Hugh, but he was outside listening to all they said.

They pulled down his house, but he was in the barn, and his mother-in-law alone was killed; for he had offered his own bed to his mother-in-law, and she had said,—

"Oh, my little hero, thou usest always to be kind to me."

Hugh took his mother-in-law's body to a place that was far from his own house, and there was a well-spring near the hostel, TIGH OSD, and there he propped up his mother-in-law with a stick under her chin, to keep her standing.

Then he went in and began to buy a drove from a drover, and sent out the drover to ask his deaf mother in to have a drink of beer, because she was very hard and would scold him for spending money if *he* asked her, but she would take it kindly if the drover did. The drover went, and after a while pushed the carlin, and she fell into the well. He got, CIAD MARG, a hundred marks from the drover by threatening him with the gallows.

He went home, told his friends that there was MIADH MÒR AIR CAILLEACHAN MARBH, great value on dead carlins; and they killed their mothers-in-law, and were like to be put in prison for trying to sell them. So they determined to serve out their tricky neighbour, and asked him and his wife to a dance at an inn. But Hugh tied a pudding full of blood about his wife's neck, and covered it up with a NEAPAIGIN, and when he and his wife got up to dance a reel he put the SKIAN DUBH, black knife, into the pudding, and the wife fell as dead.

Then Eobhan got a horn which hunters, MUINTER SEILGE, had at same time for the wood, and he put it to his wife, and he blew into the horn, and the horn gave a NUADHLAN, lamentable groan; and the wife of Hugh got up again, and she began to dance.

The neighbours bought the horn and tried FEARTAN NA H-ADHARC, the trick of the horn, on their own wives. They killed them, and blew, but though they were blowing still, their wives would not get up.

Then they caught Hugh and put him in a sack, to throw him over a fall. They went into an inn to drink beer. A drover came past, and Hugh in the sack began,—"I am going to the good place, I am going to the good place," etc. "Where art thou going?" said the drover. "It is," said Hugh, "they are going to put me where I will feel neither cold, nor weariness, nor hunger more. I shall not feel them, nor thirst." "Wilt thou let me there?" said the drover. And so the man was enticed into the sack, and thrown over the fall, and they heard him saying, "O CHOCH! O CHOCH! 'S O MO CHEANN MO CHEANN! alas, alas! and oh, my head! my head!"

When the neighbours came home and found Hugh counting money, and heard that he had got it at the bottom of the fall, they got sacks, and the one threw the other over the fall till there was but one left, and he tied the sack to his sides and threw himself over, and every one of them was killed; and Eobhan Iurach got the farms to himself, and the cattle that his neighbours had, and he took the possession of both artfully, AGUS GABH E SEILBH ANNDA GU SEOLDA.

The incident of getting riches by accusing people of killing a dead body is common to one of the African tales. Appendix to Norse tales—"The Ear of Corn and the Twelve Men."

The selling of something valueless, as a source of riches, is common to a story which I used to hear as a child, from John Piper my guardian, and which I lately found in another shape, in an English translation of Master Owlglass.

The story, as I remember it, was this:—A sailor who had got his money, and who knew that he would spend it all, went to visit his friends. On his way he paid double, and generously, for his board and lodging, and bargained that he should take off a certain old hat as payment on his way back.

A Jew accompanied him on his return, and seeing the effect of the hat, begged for it, offered for it, and finally bought it for a large sum. Then he tried it, got cudgelled by the innkeepers, and cursed the clever tar who had outwitted him.

Here, then, is a story known in tho Highlands for many years, with incidents common to Gaelic, Norse, English, German, and some African tongue, and with a peculiar character of its own which distinguishes it from all the others. I am indebted to the author of Norse Tales for a loan of the rare book mentioned in the following reference, which may throw some light on the story and its history :—

In Le Piacevole Notte di Straparola, 1567, the story is told of a priest and three rogues who outwit him and whom he outwits in return.

First, they persuade him that a mule which he has bought is an ass, and get it ; which incident is in another Gaelic story in another shape. Then he sells them a bargain in the shape of a goat, which is good for nothing.

Then he pretends to kill his house-keeper by sticking a knife into a bladder filled with blood, and brings her alive again with something which he sells to them for two hundred florins of gold, and they kill their three wives in earnest.

They are enraged, catch the priest, and put him into a sack, intending to drown him in a river. They set him down, and a shepherd comes, who hears a lamentable voice in a sack saying, "Me la vogliono pur dare, and io non la voglio"—They wish to give her to me, and I don't want her. The priest explains that the Lord of that city wants to marry him to his daughter, and by that bait (not the bait of riches) entices the shepherd into the sack. The shepherd is drowned. The priest takes the sheep, and the rogues, when they find the priest with the sheep, beg to be put into three sacks. They get in, are carried to the river by three "facconi," and disposed of ; and pre-Scarpacifico, rich in money and flocks, returned home and lived pleasantly, etc.

By what process this story got from Italian into Gaelic, or who *first* invented it, seems worth inquiry. One thing is clear ; the Italian version and the four Gaelic versions now given resemble each other very closely.

It seems possible that the amusements of the Court of Mary

Queen of Scots, or of the foreigners whose morals so enraged John Knox, may have descended to the Grassmarket and to the fishermen of the Western Isles. David Rizzio, a Turinese, has the credit of many Scotch airs. He was killed in 1567, and the edition of Straparola which I have before me, printed in Venice, 1567, if it be the first, may have found its way to Scotland through some of the countrymen of Rizzio. If that explanation be considered reasonable, it has still to be shewn how the story got to Germany and Norway : where the man in the cupboard went in : and whence came the soothsaying bird in the grey hide and the unsaleable dead carlins, for they are not in the Italian version.

Having carried the three widows' sons from Barra to the Grassmarket, where they are named Ribin, and Robin, and Levi-our ; thence to Norway, where they appear as Big and Little Peter ; thence to Germany, where they have no name ; and thence to the city of Postema in Italy in 1567,—as the narrator says, "There I left them."

XL.

THE SON OF THE SCOTTISH YEOMAN WHO STOLE THE BISHOP'S HORSE AND DAUGHTER, AND THE BISHOP HIMSELF.

From Donald MacLean, Grassmarket, Edinburgh. Written in Gaelic, and translated by the Rev. Mr. MacLauchlan.

THERE was once a Scottish yeoman who had three sons. When the youngest of them came to be of age to fellow a profession, he set apart three hundred marks for each of them. The youngest son asked that his portion might be given to himself, as he was going away to seek his fortune. He went to the great city of London. He was for a time there, and what was he doing but learning to be a gentleman's servant? He at last set about finding a master. He heard that the chief magistrate (provost*) of London wanted a servant. He applied to him, they agreed, and he entered his service. The chief magistrate was in the habit of going every day in the week to meet the Archbishop of London in a particular place. The servant attended his master, for he always went out along with him. When they had broken up their meeting on one occasion, they returned homewards, and the servant said to his master by the way,—

---

* The Gaelic "Probhaisd" is an adaptation of the English "Provost," as the latter is of the Latin "Propositus."

"That is a good brown horse of the bishop's," said he, "with your leave, master."

"Yes, my man," said the master, "he has the best horse in London."

"What think you," said the servant, "would he take for the horse, if he were to sell it?"

"Oh! you fool," said his master, "I thought you were a sensible fellow; many a man has tried to buy that horse, and it has defied them as yet."

"I'll return and try," said he.

His master returned along with him to see what would happen. This was on a Thursday. The young man asked the bishop, would he sell the horse? The bishop became amazed and angry, and said he did not expect that he could buy it.

"But what beast could you, or any man have," said the young man, "that might not be bought?"

"Senseless fellow," said the bishop; "how foolish you are! go away home, you shan't buy my horse."

"What will you wager," said the young man, "that I won't have the horse by this time to-morrow?"

"Is it my horse you mean?" said the bishop.

"Yes, your horse," said the young man. "What will you wager that I don't steal it?"

"I'll wager five hundred merks," said the bishop, "that you don't."

"Then," said the young man, "I have only one pound, but I'll wager that, and my head besides, that I do."

"Agreed," said the bishop.

"Observe," said the young man, "that I have wagered my head and the pound with you, and if I steal the horse he will be my own property."

"That he will, assuredly," said the chief magistrate.

"I agree to that," said the bishop.

They returned home that night.

"Poor fellow," said the chief magistrate to his servant by the way, "I am very well satisfied with you since I got you. I am not willing to lose you now. You are foolish. The bishop will take care that neither you nor any other man will steal the horse. He'll have him watched."

When night came, the young man started, and set to work; he went to the bishop's house. What did he find out there, but that they had the horse in a room, and men along with it, who were busy eating and drinking. He looked about him, and soon saw that he would require another clever fellow along with him. In looking about, who does he find but one of the loose fellows about the town.

"If you go along with me for a little time," said he, I will give you something for your pains."

"I'll do that," said the other.

He set off, and at the first start both he and his man reached the hangman of the city.

"Can you tell me," said he to the hangman, "where I can get a dead man?"

"Yes," said the hangman, "there was a man hanged this very day, after midday."

"If you go and get him for me," said the young man, "I'll give you something for your pains."

The hangman agreed, and went away with him to where the body was.

"Do you know now," said the young man, "where I can get a long stout rope?"

"Yes," said the hangman, "the rope that hanged the man is here quite convenient; you'll get it."

They set off with the body, both himself and his man.

They reached the bishop's house. He said to his man when they had reached—

"Stay you here and take charge of this, until I get up on the top of the house."

He put both his mouth and his ear to the chimney in order to discover where the men were, as they were now speaking loud from having drunk so much. He discovered where they were.

"Place the end of the rope," said he to his man, "round the dead man's neck, and throw the other end up to me."

He dragged the dead man up to the top of the chimney. The men in the room began to hear the rubbish in the chimney falling down. He let the body down by degrees, until at last he saw the bright light of the watchmen falling on the dead man's feet.

"See," said they, "what is this? Oh, the Scottish thief, what a shift! He preferred dying in this way to losing his head. He has destroyed himself."

Down from the chimney came the young man in haste. In he went into the very middle of the men, and as the horse was led out by the door, his hand was the first to seize the bridle. He went with the horse to the stable, and said to them that they might now go and sleep, that they were safe enough.

"Now," said he to the other man, "I believe you to be a clever fellow; be at hand here to-morrow evening, and I will see you again."

He paid him at the same time, and the man was much pleased. He, himself, returned to his master's stable with the bishop's brown horse. He went to rest, and though the daylight came early, earlier than that did his master come to his door.

"I wouldn't grudge my pains," said he, "if my poor Scotsman were here before me to-day."

"I am here, good master," said he, "and the bishop's brown horse beside me."

"Well done, my man," said his master, "you're a clever fellow. I had a high opinion of you before; I think much more of you now."

They prepared this day, too, to go and visit the bishop. It was Friday.

"Now," said the servant, "I left home without a horse, yesterday, but I won't leave in the same way to-day."

"Well, my man," said his master, "as you have got the horse, I'll give you a saddle."

So they set off this day again to meet the bishop, his master and himself riding their horses. They saw the bishop coming to meet them, apparently mad. When they came close together they observed that the bishop rode another horse, by no means so good as his own. The bishop and chief magistrate met with salutations. The bishop turned to the chief magistrate's servant,—

"Scroundel," said he, "and thorough thief!"

"You can't call me worse," said the other. "I don't know that you can call me that justly; for, you know, I told you what I was to do. Without more words, pay me my five hundred merks."

This had to be done, though not very willingly.

"What would you now say," says the lad, "if I were to steal your daughter to-night?"

"My daughter, you worthless fellow," said the bishop; "you shan't steal my daughter."

"I'll wager five hundred merks and the brown horse," said the lad, "that I'll steal her."

"I'll wager ten hundred merks that you don't," said the bishop.

The wager was laid. The lad and his master went home. "Young man," said his master, "I thought well of you at one time, but you have done a foolish thing now, just when you had made yourself all right."

"Never mind, good master," said he, "I'll make the attempt at any rate."

When night came, the chief magistrate's servant set off for the bishop's house. When he reached, he saw a gentleman coming out at the door.

"Oh," said he to the gentleman, "what is this going on at the bishop's house to-night?"

"A great and important matter," said the gentleman; "a rascally Scotsman who is threatening to steal the bishop's daughter, but I can tell you neither he nor any other man will steal her; she is well guarded."

"Oh, I'm sure of that," said the lad, and turned away. "There is a man in England, however," said he to himself, "who must try it."

He set off, and reached the king's tailors. He asked them whether they had any dresses ready for great people?

"No," said the tailor, "but a dress I have for the king's daughter and one for her maid of honour."

"What," said the chief magistrate's servant, "will you take for the use of these, for a couple of hours?"

"Oh," said the tailor, "I fear I dare not give them to you."

"Don't be in the least afraid," said the lad, "I'll pay you, and I'll return the two dresses without any injury or loss. You'll get a hundred merks," said he.

The tailor coveted so large a sum, and so he gave them to him. He returned, and found his man of the former night. They went to a private place, and got themselves fitted out in the dresses got from the tailor. When this was done as well as they could, they came to the bishop's door. Before he arrived at the door he found out that when any of the royal family came to the bishop's house they didn't knock, but rubbed the bottom of the door with the point of the foot. He came to the door, and rubbed. There was a doorkeeper at the door that night, and he ran and told the bishop.

"There is some one of the royal family at the door," said he.

"No," said the bishop, "there is not. "It's the thief of a Scotsman that is there."

The doorkeeper looked through the key-hole, and saw the appearance of two ladies who stood there. He went to his master and told him so. His master went to the door that he might see for himself. He who was outside would give another and another rub to the door, at the same time abusing the bishop for his folly. The bishop looked, and recognized the voice of the king's daughter at the door. The door is quickly opened, and the bishop bows low to the lady. The king's daughter began immediately to chide the bishop for laying any wager respecting his daughter, saying that he was much blamed for what he had done.

"It was very wrong of you," said she, "to have done it without my knowledge, and you would not have required to have made such a stir or been so foolish as all this."

"You will excuse me," said the bishop.

"I can't excuse you," she said.

In to the chamber he led the king's daughter, in which his own daughter was, and persons watching her.

She was in the middle of the chamber, sitting on a chair, and the others sitting all around.

Said the king's daughter to her, "My dear, your father is a very foolish man to place you in such great danger; for if he had given me notice, and placed you under my care, any man who might venture to approach you would assuredly not only be hanged, but burned alive. Go," said she to the bishop, "to bed, and dismiss this large company, lest men laugh at you."

He told the company that they might now go to rest, that the queen's daughter and her maid of honour would take charge of his daughter. When the queen's daughter had seen them all away, she said to the daughter of the bishop,—

"Come along with me, my dear, to the king's palace." He led her out, and then he had the brown horse all ready, and as soon as the Scotsman got her to where the horse stood, he threw off the dress he wore, in a dark place. He put a different dress above his own, and mounted the horse. The other man is sent home with the dresses to the tailor. He paid the man, and told him to meet him there next night. He leaped on the brown horse at the bishop's house, and off he rode to the house of his master. Early as daylight came, earlier came his master to the stable. He had the bishop's daughter in his bed. He wakened when he heard his master.

"I wouldn't grudge my pains," said the latter, "if my poor Scotsman were here before me to-day."

"Eh, and so I am," said the lad, "and the bishop's daughter along with me here."

"Oh," said he, "I always thought well of you, but now I think more of you than ever."

This was Saturday. He and his master had to go

and meet the bishop this day also. The bishop and chief magistrate met as usual. If the bishop looked angry the former day, he looked much angrier this day. The chief magistrate's servant rode on his horse and saddle behind his master. When he came near the bishop he could only call him "thief" and "scoundrel."

"You may shut your mouth," said he; "you cannot say that to me with justice. Send across here my five hundred merks. He paid the money. He was abusing the other.

"Oh man," said he, "give up your abuse; I'll lay you the ten hundred merks that I'll steal yourself to-night."

"That you steal me, you worthless fellow," said the bishop. "You shan't be allowed."

He wagered the ten hundred merks.

"I'll get these ten hundred merks back again," said the bishop, "but I'll lay you fifteen hundred merks that you don't steal me."

The chief magistrate fixed the bargain for them. The lad and his master went home.

"My man," said the master, "I have always thought well of you till now; you will now lose the money you gained, and you can't steal the man."

"I have no fear of that," said the servant.

When night came he set off, and got to the house of the bishop. Then he thought he would go where he could find the fishermen of the city, in order to see what might be seen with them. When he reached the fishermen he asked them whether they had any fresh-killed salmon? They said they had. He said to them—

"If you skin so many of them for me I will give you

such and such a sum of money, or as much as will be just and right."

The fishermen said they would do as he wished, and they did so. They gave him as many fish skins as he thought would make him a cloak of the length and breadth he wished. He then went to the tailors. He said to the tailors, would they make him a dress of the fish skins by twelve o'clock at night, and that they should be paid for it. They told him what sum they would take. They took the young man's measure and began the dress. The dress was ready by twelve o'clock. They could not work any longer as the Sunday was coming in. He left with the dress, and when he found himself a short way from the bishop's church he put it on. He had got a key to open the church and he went in. He at once went to the pulpit. The doorkeeper casting an eye in on an occasion, while a great watch was kept over the bishop, he went and said there was a light in the church.

"A light," said his master, "go and see what light it is." It was past twelve o'clock by this time.

"Oh," said the doorkeeper, coming back, "there is a man preaching in it."

The bishop drew out his time-piece, and he saw that it was the beginning of the Sunday. He went running to the church. When he saw the brightness that was in the church, and all the movements of the man that was preaching, he was seized with fear. He opened the door a little and put in his head that he might see what he was like. There was not a language under the stars that the man in the pulpit was not taking a while of. When he came to the languages which the bishop understood, he began to denounce the bishop as a man who had lost his senses. In the bishop ran, and down he is on his knees before the pulpit. There he began to pray, and when he saw the brightness that was about the pulpit, he took to heart the things that were said to him. At length he said to him, if he would promise sincere repentance, and go along with him, he would grant him forgiveness. The bishop promised him that he would.

"Come with me till I have a little time of you," said he.

"I will," said the bishop, "though thou shouldst ask me to leave the world."

He went along with him, and the young man walked before him. They reached the stable of the chief magistrate. He got a seat for the bishop, and he kept him sitting. He sat down himself. They required no light, for the servant's clothes were shining bright where they were. He was then expounding to the bishop in some languages which he could understand, and in others which he could not. He went on in that way untill it was time for his master to come in the morning. When the time drew near, he threw off the dress, bent down and hid it, for it was near daylight. The bishop was now silent, and the chief magistrate came.

"I wouldn't grudge my pains," said he, "if I had my poor Scotsman here before me to-day."

"Eh, so I am here," said he, "and the bishop along with me."

"Hey, my man," says his master, "you have done well."

"Oh, you infamous scoundrel," said the bishop, is it thus you have got the better of me?"

"I'll tell you what it is," said the chief magistrate, "you had better be civil to him. Don't abuse him. He has got your daughter, your horse, and your money, and as for yourself, you know that he cannot support you, so it is best for you to support him. Take himself and your daughter along with you and make them a respectable wedding." The young man left and went home with the bishop, and he and the bishop's daughter were lawfully married, and the father shewed him kindness. I left them there.

MAC AN TUATHANAICH ALBANAICH, A GHOID EACH, AGUS NIGHEAN AN EASBUIG, AGUS AN T-EASBUIG FHEIN.

Bha triùir mhac aig tuathanach Albanach uair de na bhann. An uair a thainig am fear a b' òige dhiubh gu aoise 'dhol ri ceàird, chuir e tri cheud marg mu choinnimh gach aon dhiubh. Dh' iarr am fear a b' òige a chuid d'a fhéin, gun robh e 'falbh a dheanamh an fhortain. Thug e baile mòr Lunnuin air. Bha e greis ann an sin, 'us ciod e bha e ag ionnsachadh ach a bhi 'n a ghille duine uasail! Chuir e forthas mu dheireadh c' àite am faigheadh e maighistir. Chuala e gun robh gille a dhìth air Probhaist Lunnuin. Ràinig e e, chord iad, 'us rinn e muinntireas aige. Bha am Probhaist a dol na h-uile la 's an t-seachduin a choinneachadh Ardeaspuig Lunnuin ann an àité sònruichte. Dh' fhalbh an gille le a mhaighistir, oir bhitheadh e mach leis daonnan. 'N uair a sgaoil iad a choinneamh a bh' aca aon la thill iad, 'us thubhairt an gille r'a mhaighistir air an rathad, "Is maith," ars' esa, "an t-each donn ud a th' aig an Easbuig, le 'ur cead, a mhaighistir." "Seadh, a laochain," ars' a mhaighistir, "tha an t-each is fhearr 'an Lunnuin aige." "Saoil mi," ars' an gille, "ciod e ghabhadh e air an each nan reiceadh e e." "Uh, amadain," ars' a mhaighistir, "shaoil leam gur balach ceart a bh' annad, is iomadh fear a dh' fheuch ris an each ud a cheannach 'us dh' fhairtlich orra fhathasd." "Tillidh mise 'us feuchaidh mi ris," ars' esan. Thill a mhaighistir comhluadh ris a dh' fhaicinn. Is ann air Diardaoine a thachair so. Thubhairt an gille ris an Easbuig, an reiccadh e an t-each. Ghabh an t-Easbuig ardan 'us miothlachd, 'us cha robh fiuthar aig gun ceannaicheadh esan e. "Mata ciod e am beathach bhitheadh agadsa no aig duine eile nach fhaodar a cheannach," ars' an gille? "Bhuraidh gun tùr," ars' an t-Easbuig, "tha thu amaideach, rach dhathigh, cha cheannaich thu m' eachsa." "Ciod e an geall a chuireas tu," ars' an gille, "nach bi e agamsa an dàr-sa màireach?" "'N e m' eachsa bhitheas agad," ars' an t-Easbuig. "Is e d' eachsa bhitheas agam," ars' esan, "ciod e an geall a chuireas tu rium nach goid mi e?" "Cuiridh mi coig ceud marg riut," ars' an t-Easbuig, "nach dean thu sin." "Mata," ars' an gille, "cha-n 'eil agamsa ach aon phunnd, ach cuiridh mi sin, 'us mo cheann riut gun goid mi e." "Is bargan e," ars' an t-Easbuig. "Thoir an aire," ars' esan, tha mi cur mo chinn agus am punnd riut, agus mu ghoideas mise e, is e mo chuid féin a bhitheas ann." "Bithidh e mar sin cinnteach," ars' am Probhaist. "Tha mi ag aontachadh ri sin," ars' an t-Easbuig. Chaidh iad dathigh an oidhche sin. "Ghille bhochd," ars' a mhaighistir ris air an rathad, "bha thu cordadh gu maith rium o fhuair mi thu. Tha mi duilich do chall a nis. Tha thu amaideach. Bheir an t-Easbuig an aire nach goid thusa no fear eile an t-each; cumaidh e faire air." Dh' fhalbh an gille 'n uair thainig an oidhche 'us ghabh e air; chaidh e gu tigh an Easbuig. Ciod e fhuair e mach ach gun robh an t-each stigh ann an seòmar aige, agus daoine ann an sin a gabhail da ag ith 'us ag òl. Sheall gille a Probhaist timchioll air 'us smuanaich e gum feumadh e fear tapaidh eile fhaighinn comhluadh ris. Suil d' an d' thug e uaith, ciod e chunnaic e ach fear a bhitheadh ri cron daonnan feadh a bhaile. "Ma theid thu comhluadh riumsa," ars' esa', "beagan ùine bheir mi rud eigin duit airson do shaothrach." "Ni mi sin," ars' am fear eile. Dh' fhalbh esan 'us air a cheud dol a mach "rainig e fhéin 'us an gille a fhuair e an crochadair a bha 's a bhaile, "An urrainn thu innseadh dhomhsa," ars' esan, "c' àite am faigh mi duine marbh?" "Is urrainn," ars' an crochadair, "chaidh duine a chrochadh an diugh fhéin an deigh mheadhoin latha." "Ma theid thu 'us gum faigh mise e," ars' esa, "bheir mi rud eigin duit." Dh' fhalbh e leis 'us ràinig iad an corp. "An aithne dhuit a nis," ars' esan, "c' àite am faigh mi ball mòr fad, làidir?" "Is aithne dhomh sin," ars' an crochadair, "tha am ball a chroch an duine an so goireasach dhuit 'us gheibh thu e." Dh' fhalbh e leis, e fhéin 'us an gille eile a fhuair e, 'us thug iad leo e. Chaidh iad gu tigh an Easbuig. Thubhairt e ris a ghille 'n uair a rainig e, "fuirich thusa an sin 'us thoir an aire dha so, ach an d' theid mise suas air mullach an tighe." Dh' fhuirich an gille, 'us chaidh esan suas air mullach an tighe. Chuir e a bheul 'us a chluais ris an t-siomalair ach am faigheadh e mach c' àite an robh na daoine, agus bruidheann labhar aca leis an òl. Fhuair e mach far an robh iad. "Cuir am ball," ars' esan, "timchioll air amhaich an duine mhairbh, 'us tilg an ceann eile aig ormsa." Shlaod e an duine marbh leis gu mullach an t-siomalair. Bha na daoine bha 's an t-seòmar a faireachduinn na bha de shalachar 's an t-siomalair a tuiteam. Bha esan a leigeadh leis 's a leigeadh leis an duine mhairbh, gus am faca e mu dheireadh an solus breagh bha aig luchd na faire' tighinn air cosaibh an duine mhairbh. "Faicibh," ars' iadsan, "ciod e tha so." "Oh! am meirleach Albanach," ars' iadsan, "nach e thug an oidheirp? B' fhearr leis a bheatha chall mar so no a cheann bhi aig an Easbuig, an ionnsuidh thug e air fhéin!" Leis an t-siomalair thainig an gille le cabhaig. Am meadhon nan daoine bha e a stigh 'us mar thainig an t-each mach air an dorus b'e a cheud làmh bha 'an srian an eich esan. Dh' fhalbh e leis an each an stabull 'us thubhairt e riu gum feudadh iad nis dhol a chodal, gun robh iad sabhailt gu leòr. "Tha mi creidsinn," ars' esan ris a ghille eile, "gu bheil thu 'n ad ghille tapaidh, bi aig laimh an ath oidhche 'us chi mi rìs thu." Phaigh e an gille, 'us an gille ro thoilichte. Dh' fhalbh esan dhathigh gu stabull a mhaighistir le each donn an Easbuig. Ghabh e mu thàmh 'us ge bu mhoch a thainig an la bu mhoich a thainig a mhaighistir gu dorus an stabuill. "Cha bu ghearain leam mo shaothair nam bitheadh m' Albanach bochd romham an so an diugh." "Tha mi ann a so, a' mhaighistir mhaith," ars' esan, "agus each donn an Easbuig agam." "Ud, a laochain, a ghille thapaidh," ars' a mhaighistir, "bha meas agam ort roimhe, ach tha meas mòr nis agam ort." Rinn iad reidh an la so rìs dhol a choinneachadh an Easbuig 'us b' e so Dehaoine. "Nis," ars' an gille, "dh' fhalbh mi gun each an dé, ach cha-n fhalbh mi mar sin an diugh." "Mata, a laochain, o 'n a fhuair thu fhéin an t-each, bheir mise diollaid duit." Dh' fhalbh iad an la so rìs 'an coinnimh an Easbuigh, a mhaighistir 'us esan air muin dà each. Chunnaic iad an t-Easbuig a tighinn 'n an coinnimh 'us coltas a chuthaich air. 'N uair a thainig iad an lathair a chéile, chunnaic iad gun robh an t-Easbuig air muin eich eile nach robh cho maith r'a each fhéin. Chaidh an t-Easbuig 's am Probhaisd an coinnimh a chéile le fàilte. Thionndaidh an t-Easbuig ri gille a Probhaisd, "Shlaoitir," ars' esan, "'us a dhearbh mheirlich." "Cha-n urrainn thu tuilleadh a ràdh rium," ars' gille a Probhaisd, "cha-n 'eil fhios agam an urrainn thu sin fhéin a radh rium le ceartas, thaobh, dh' innis mi dhuit gun robh mi dol g'a dheanamh ; gun tuilleadh de do sheanachas cuir an so mo chuig ceud marg am ionnsuidhse." B' éigin d'a sin a dheanamh ged nach robh e toileach. "Ciod e a their thu," ars' an gille, "ma ghoideas mi do nighean an nochd?" 'S e aon nighean a bh' aig 'us cha robh bu bhreagha na i 'an Lunnuin. "Mo nigheansa, a bhiasd," ars' an t-Easbuig, "cha ghoid thu mo nigheansa." "Cuiridh mi," ars' an gille, "an cuig ceud marg a thug thu dhomh 'us an t-each donn gun goid mi i." "Cuiridh mise deich ceud marg," ars' an t-Easbuig, "nach goid." Rinn iad cordadh. Dh' fhalbh esan 'us a mhaighistir dhathigh. "Laochain," ars' a mhaighistir, "bha mi a saoilsinn gu maith dhiot uaireigin, ach rinn thu tùirn amaideach a nis, 'n uair a fhuair thu thu fhéin ceart." "Coma leibhse, a mhaighistir mhaith," ars' esan, "bheir mi an ionnsuidh co dhiùbh." 'N uair thainig an oidhche, thog gille a Probhaist air, 'us chaidh e air falbh gu tigh an Easbuig. 'N uair a rainig e tigh an Easbuig, chunnaic e duine uasal 'tighinn a mach air an dorus. "Oh," ars' esan ris an duine uasal, "ciod e so aig tigh an Easbuig an nochd?" "Tha gnothuch mòr sònraichte," ars' an duine uasal, "Albanach musach tha an sud, agus e maoidheadh a nighean a ghoid. Gu dearbh cha-n 'eil gin an Albainn a ghoideas i leis an fhaire a th' oirre." "Uh, tha mi cinnteach nach 'eil," ars' an gille, agus thionndadh e uaith. "Tha fear an Sasunn an tràthsa," ars' esa, "a dh' fheumas feuchainn ris co dhiùbh." Dh' fhalbh e, agus thug e taillearan an teaghlaich rioghail air. Dh' fharraid e dhiubh an robh dad de dheiseachan deas aca do uaislibh mòra. "Cha-n 'eil," ars' an taillear, "ach deise a th' againn do nighean an righ, agus té d'a maighdean choimheadachd." "Ciod e," ars' gille a Probhaisd, "dh' iarras tu air iad sin fhéin car dà uair a dh' ùine?" "Oh," ars' an taillear, "tha eagal orm nach fhaod mi an toirt duit." "Na bitheadh eagal air bhith ort," ars' gille a Probhaisd, "paighidh mi thu agus bheir mi an da dheise gun bheud, gun mhillidh air an ais. Gheibh thu ceud marg," ars' esan. Shanntaich an taillear an t-airgiod mòr ud 'us thug e dha iad. Dh' fhalbh e 'us fhuair e an gille bh' aig an oidhche roimhe. Chaidh iad dh' aite sònruichte 's fhuair iad iad fhéin a chur 'an uidheam 's an da dheise. Dh' fhalbh iad 'n uair a fhuair iad iad fhéin cho maith 'us bu mhaith leo gu dorus an Easbuig. Fhuair e mach mun d'rainig e an dorus, 'n uair a thigeadh aon air bith do 'n teaghlach rioghal gu tigh an Easbuig, nach e an dorus a bhualadh a dheanadh iad, ach sgriob a thabhairt le barr an coise aig bonn an doruis. Thainig esan a dh' ionnsuidh an doruis agus rinn e sgrioba. Bha dorsair aig an dorus an oidhche sin, 'us dh' fhalbh e 'na ruith dh' ionnsuidh an Easbuig. "Tha aon de 'n teaghlach rioghail aig an dorus," ars' esan. "Cha-n 'eil," ars' an t-Easbuig, "is e th' ann am meirleach Albannach." Sheall an gille troimh tholl na h-iuchrach 'us chunnaic e gur e coslas da bhean uasail a bh' ann. Dh' fhalbh e dh' ionnsuidh a mhaighistir 'us dh' innis e dha. Chaidh a mhaighistir dh' ionnsuidh an doruis 'us sheall e fhéin. Bheireadh an gille a bha mach sgriob an tràthsa 's a rìs, 'us e a cath-throid ris an Easbuig, 'us e ri amaideachd. Sheall an t-Easbuig 'us dh' aithnich e gur e guth nighinn an rìgh bha 's an dorus. Fosgailear gu grad an dorus, 'us deanar a chromaidh gu làr rithe. Bhuail nighean an rìgh ris air son a nighean chur ann an geall 's am bith, gun robh feadhain a gabhail brath air airson a leithid a dheanamh. "Cha mhòr a b' fhiach thu a dheanadh a leithid gun fhios domhsa, 'us cha ruigeadh tu leas a leithid a dh' othail 'us a dh' amaideachd a dheanamh." "Gabhaibh sibh mo leithsgeul," ars' esan. "Cha-n urrainn mi do leithsgeul a ghabhail," ars' ise. Stigh thug e nighean an rìgh do 'n t-seòmar 's an robh a nighean 'us an fheadhain a bha 'g a faireadh. Bha ise 'am meadhon an t-seòmair air caithir 'n a suidhe 'us càch ceithir thimchioll oirre. Ars' nighean an rìgh rithe, "Mo ghaoil, 's e d' athair an duine gun tùr a chuir 's a chunnart thu, 'us nan d' thug e fios domhsa 'us do chuir far an robh mise, aon s 'am bith thigeadh a d' chòir, rachadh an crochach 'us a bharrachd air sin, an losgadh. Falbh," ars' ise ris an Easbuig, "a 'd chodal, 'us cuiribh fa sgaoil a chuideachd mhòr so mus bi iad a magadh oirbh." Thubhairt an t-Easbuig ris a chuideachd gum faodadh iad gabhail mu thàmh, gun d' thugadh nighean an rìgh, 's a maighdean choimheadachd an aire dh' a nigheansa. 'N uair a fhuair nighean an rìgh uile gu leir air falbh iad. "Thig thusa, a nighinn mo ghaoil, cuid a riumsa gu tigh rìgh na rioghachd." Mach a thug nighean an rìgh; bha an t-each donn goireasach aice, agus cho luath 's a fhuair an t-Albannach mach i far an robh an t-each donn, tilgear dheth ann an àite dorch an deise. Chuir e uidheam eile air as ceann 'eudaich fhéin 'us air muin an eich chuir e i. Cuirear dhathigh an gille leis na deiseachan dh' ionnsuidh an tàilleir. Phaigh e an gille 'us thubhairt e ris a choinneachadh an sud an ath oidhche. Leum esan suas air an each dhonn aig tigh an Easbuig, 'us air a thug e gu tigh a mhaighistir. Ge bu mhoch a thainig an la, bu mhoiche na sin a thainig a mhaigistir a dh' ionnsuidh an stàbuill. "Bha esan 'us nighean an Easbuig 'n an luidhe 'n a leabaidhse, 'us dhùisg e 'n uair dh' fhairich e a mhaighistir." "Cha bu chall leam mo shaothair," ars' esan, "nam bitheadh m' Albannach bochd romham an so an diugh." "Eh, gu bheil mi," ars' esan, "agus nighean an Easbuig agam ann a so." "Oh," ars' esan, "bha meas agam ort roimhe, ach a nis tha meas mòr agam ort." Be sin De-sathuirn. Bha aige-san agus aig a mhaighistir gu dhol a choinneachadh an Easbuig an la sin cuideachd. Chaidh an t-Easbuig agus am Probhaist an coinnimh a chéile mar a b' àbhaisd. Nam b' olc an coltas bh' air an Easbuig an la roimhe, bha e na bu mhios' uile an la sin. Bha gille a Phrobhaisd 'n a each 'us 'n a dhiollaid an deigh a mhaigh-istir. 'N uair a thainig e far an robh an t-Easbuig cha robh aig ris ach "a mheirlich 'us a shlaoitir?" "Faodaidh tu do bheul a dhùnadh," ars' an gille, "cha 'n urrainn thu sin fhéin a radh rium le ceartas. Cuir a null mo dheich ceud marg an so." Phàigh e an t-airgiod. Bha e'g a chàineadh. "Od dhuine," ars' esan, "leig dhiot do chaineadh, cuiridh mi an deich ceud marg riut gun goid mi thu fhéin an nochd." "Gun goid thu mise, a bhiasd," ars' esa, "cha n-fhaigh thu a chead." Chuir e an deich ceud marg ris. "Gheibh mi an deich ceud marg ud air ais," ars' an t-Easbuig, "ach cuiridh mise cuig ceud deug marg riut nach goid thu mise." "Ni mi cordadh riut," ars' an gille. Cheangail am Probhaist am bargan eadorra. Dh' fhalbh an gille 'us a mhaighistir dhathigh. "Laochain," ars' a mhaigh-istir, "bha meas mòr agam ort gus an diugh, caillidh tu na fhuair thu dh' airgiod agus cha-n urrainn thu an duine ghoid." "Cha-n 'eil eagal sam bith orm á sin," ars' an gille. 'N uair thainig an oidhche dh' fhalbh esan, 'us thug e timchioll tigh an Easbuig air. "An sin smuainich e gun rachadh e far an robh iasgairean a bhaile, dh' fheuchainn ciod e chitheadh e acasan. 'N uair a thainig e far an robh na h-iasgairean dh' fharraid e dhiubh, an robh dad de bhradanan aca air an ùr-mharbhadh. Thubhairt iad ris gun robh. "Ma dh' fheannas sibh," ars' esan, "na h-uiread so a dh' iasg, bheir mi dhuibh na h-uiread so dh' airgiod, no airgiod sam bith a 's còir dha bhi." Thubhairt na h-iasgairean gun deanadh, 'us rinn iad e. Thug iad dha de chroicinnean éisg na shaoil leis a dheanadh cleòchd, am faide 'us an leud a shir e. Dh' fhalbh e an sin dh' ionnsuidh nan tàillearan. Thubhairt e ris na taillearan, an deanadh iad deise dha de chroicinnean an éisg, a chionn dà uair dheug a st-oidhche, 'us gum faigheadh iad pàigheadh air a shon. Dh' innis iad dha ciod e an t-suim a ghabhadh iad. Ghabh iad tomhas a ghille 'us thòisich iad air an deise. Bha an deise ullamh chionn an da uair dheug. Cha-n fhaodadh iad 'bhi na b' fhaide; bha an Dòmhnach 'tighinn a stigh. Dh' fhalbh e leis an deise, 'us 'n uair a fhuair e e fhéin goirid o eaglais an Easbuig chuir e uime an deise. Fhuair e iuchar a dh' fhosgladh an eaglais 'us chaidh e stigh. Chaidh e do 'n chrannaig air ball. Sùil de 'n tug an dorsair uaith 'us faire mhòr air an Easbuig, dh' fhalbh e, 'us thubhairt e gun robh solus 's an eaglais. "Solus," ars' a mhaighistir, "rach thusa null 'us faic ciod e an solus a th' ann." Bha e an déigh an da uair dheug an so. "O," ars' an dorsair 'us e tighinn, "tha duine a' searmonachadh ann." Tharruing an t-Easbuig 'uaireadair 'us chunnaic e gun robh toiseach an Dòmhnaich a tighinn a stigh. Dh' fhalbh e 'n a ruith dh' ionnsuidh na h-eaglaise. 'N' uair a chunnaic e an soillse bha 's an eaglais 'us na h-uile car chuir an duine bha 'searmonachadh dheth, ghabh e eagal. Dh' fhosgail e beagan an dorus 'us chuir e a cheann stigh dh' fhaicinn ciod e an coltas a bh' air. Am fear bha 's a chrannaig cha robh cànain bha fo na rionnagan nach robh e toirt treis air. 'N uair a thigeadh e dh' ionnsuidh na h-uile cànain a thuigeadh an t-Easbuig is ann 'cur iomchar air an Easbuig a bha e gun robh e air call a chéill. Sud stigh an t-Easbuig agus theirigear air a ghlùnan aig bonn na crannaig. Thoisich esan air asluchadh ann an sin, 'us 'n uair chunnaic e an dearsadh bha 's a chrannaig ghabh e gu cùram leis na bha e ag radh ris. Mu dheireadh thubhairt e' ris, nan gealladh e dhasan gun deanadh e aithreachas glan 'us gum falbhadh e leis-san gun d' thugadh e maitheanas dha. Ghealladh an t-Easbuig sin da. "Falbh leamsa," ars' esan, "gus am faigh mi beagan ùine ort." "Falbhaidh," ars' an t-Easbuig, "ged a b' ann as an t-saoghal dh' iarradh tu orm falbh." Dh' fhalbh e leis, 'us dh' fhalbh an gille roimhe. Rainig iad stabull a Probhaisd. Fhuair e àite suidh do 'n Easbuig 'us chuir e 'n a shuidhe e. Shuidh e fhéin; cha ruigeadh iad a leas solus, oir bha eudach a ghille 'deanamh soluis far an robh iad. Bha e 'mìneachadh do 'n Easbuig an sin ann an canainean a thuigeadh, agus ann an cuid nach tuigeadh e. Bha e mar sin ach an robh an t-àm d'a mhaighistir tighinn 's a mhaduinn. 'N uair bha an t-am teann air laimh, thilg e dheth an deise, lùb e 'us chuir e am folach i, oir bha e ris an t-soillearachd. Bha an t-Easbuig samhach an so, 'us thainig am Probhaisd. "Cha bu ghearain leam mo shaothair nam bitheadh m' Albannach bochd romham an so an diugh." "Eh, gu bheil mi," ars' esan, "an so 'us an t- Easbuig agam." "Ud, a laochain," ars' a mhaighistir, "is maith a gheibhear thu." "Oh, a dhaoir-shlaoitir," ars' an t-Easbuig, "'n ann mar so a rinn thu an gnothuch orm?" "Innsidh mise dhuit mar a tha," ars' am Probhaisd, "is fhearr dhuit deanamh gu maith air, no bhi 'g a chàineadh; tha do nighean aig, agus tha d'each aig, agus d'airgiod, agus air do shon fhéin, cha ghleidh esa thusa, ach is fhearr dhuitse esan a ghleidheadh. Thoir e fhéin 'us do nighean leat 'us dean banais dhoibh le h-eireachdeas. Dh' fhalbh e 'us chaidh e dhathigh leis an Easbuig, 'us fhuair e e fhéin 'us a nighean a phòsadh gu ceart 'us rinn e gu maith ris. Dh' fhàg mise an sin iad.

I had the above tale from Donald M'Lean, now resident in the Grassmarket, Edinburgh. It is one of seven I took down from his recitation about the same time. M'Lean is a native of Ardnamurchan, but crossed at an early age to Glenforsa in Mull, where he spent several years. He heard this tale recited by an old man, Angus M'Phie, from Ardnamurchan, who died about fifty years ago, and he had received it also from tradition. M'Lean recites his tales without the slightest hesitation, although in some cases their recitation occupies a couple of hours. It will be manifest, too, from reading the original tale here given, that very little variation could be allowed in the words used, and that the very forms of expression and words must therefore be retained unchanged. M'Lean's is a remarkable instance of the power of memory in the uneducated, shewing that it is quite possible to retain and recite, with perfect accuracy, compositions which would form a volume. He obtained his tales from different parties, and says they were recited in the winter evenings at the firesides of the old Highlanders as their chief amusements. Some of them he heard before he was fourteen years of age, and never heard since, and yet he retains them accurately.

It will be observed in the tale now given that some of the terms used are modern, as, for instance, "Probhaisd" (Provost), and not known in our older Gaelic. It is remarkable, also, that the bishop of London is the party fixed upon to have his effects stolen. This would seem to indicate that the tale originated at a time when the Highlanders were acquainted with bishops, and would carry it back to a period previous to the Reformation, the inhabitants, both of Ardnamurchan and Mull, having been Presbyterians since that period; unless, indeed, the story has been imported into the Highlands from some other quarter. Its resemblance to the "Master Thief" in Mr. Dasent's "Tales from the Norse," cannot fail to strike any one acquainted with these interesting stories. The "Tuathanach" is translated "Yeoman," not that that term expresses with perfect accuracy the meaning of the Gaelic word, but it is the English term which comes nearest to it. The "Tuathanach" among the Celts is a "farmer," or one who holds his lands from another, but the word implies a certain amount of consequence and dignity, which would indicate that he must hold land of considerable extent. The term is manifestly either the radix, or a relative of the Latin "tenoe," whence the English "tenant," and it would seem also to be the real source of the word "Thane," or one who held as tenant the lands of the Crown. The tenants and their subholders were distinguished as "Tuath 'us Ceatharn," from which last is the Saxon "Kern."

T. M'L.

EDINBURGH, *May*, 1860.

2. Another version of this was told to me by Donald MacCraw, drover, September 1859, as we walked along the road in North Uist. It was given in return for a bit of another story, which also treats of clever thieves, part of which I learned from my piper guardian long ago. This was the fly which raised the fish.

Two thieves once came to a gallows, and the one said to the other,

"We have often heard about this thing, now let us try how it feels. I will put the rope about my neck, and do thou hang me, and when I have had enough, I will grin and then thou shalt let me down."

So the first thief was hanged, and when the rope tightened he grinned horribly, and was let down by his comrade as they had agreed.

"Well," said he, "What was it like?"

"Not so bad as I expected," said the other. "Now I will hang thee, and when thou hast enough, whistle."

So the second agreed, and he was strung up in his turn, and he grinned too; but because he would not whistle, his friend let him hang, and when he was tired of waiting, he emptied his pockets and left him there.

"Have you any more of that story?" said I.

"No; but I have one about a smith's servant," said MacCraw.

There was once, long ago, a smith in Eirinn, and he had a servant who was very clever at stealing; he could steal anything. His master was working with an UACHDARAN, gentleman, and the gentleman came to the smithy to have his "powney" shod, (the English word powney is commonly used in Island Gaelic), and he and the smith were well with each other, and they began to talk, and the smith to boast of his apprentice, and how well he could steal. At last he offered to bet that the lad could steal the gentleman's horse, and the gentleman wagered five notes that he would not. The smith laid down the money and the bet was made, and they told this to the lad.

Well, the gentleman went home, and he sent his gillies to watch the powney, and the lad went and he bought himself three bottles of whisky, and when the night came he went to the "square" (this word has also crept into Gaelic, and is applied to a set of farm buildings) of the gentleman, and he laid himself down amongst the litter, and he began to snore and snort and pretend to be drunk. So out came one of the watchmen to see what was the matter, and he began to handle the drunken man, and presently he felt a bottle in his pocket; then he drew it out, and he told the others, and they drank it all up. Then they said,

"Let us see if there is not another bottle in the other pocket."

So they went and they rolled over the drunken man, who kept on snoring and snorting, and they found a second bottle, and then they went into the stable again. At the end of a little while the lad heard them getting very "wordy" within, and soon they came out again a third time, and they rolled him about, and found the third bottle, and that finished them off and they fell fast asleep. Then the lad got up and stole the powney, and went to the smithy and then he went to sleep himself.

In the morning the gentleman came to the smithy, and he had to pay the bet, for the powney was there before him.

"Well," said the lad, "that is but a small matter, I will wager you now twenty notes that I will steal your daughter."

"I will take the wager," said the gentleman.

And the lad said, "Now master, lay down the twenty notes for me." So the smith laid them down, and the gentleman laid down his, and the wager was made.

(The word "note" is almost always used in Gaelic, because very filthy one pound notes are common in Scotland. The value of the note is expressed by "pound saxon." It seems to be necessary to produce the money, and to deposit it when a wager is laid.)

Now no time was fixed for stealing the daughter, so the gentleman went home and he set a watch on his daughter's room, who were to go in and out all night long. The lad went about the country and he travelled till he came to BAILLE PUIRT, a seaport town on the other side, for it was in Eirinn; and there he remained till he made friends with a ship captain, and after much talk (which was given by the narrator) the captain agreed to help him. So the lad dressed himself up as a woman, and the captain said, "Now I will say that I have a sister on board, and if we are asked to the house of the gentleman when the ship arrives, do thou as best thou canst."

So the ship sailed, and she sailed round Eirinn till she came to the gentleman's house, and then the captain went up and told how he had been a long voyage to the Indies.

Then the gentleman asked if he had any one else on board, and he said that he had a sister, and that she was very unwell.

"Oh!" said the gentleman, "ask her to come up and she shall sleep in my daughter's room."

So the captain's sister came up and they had a pleasant evening, and they all went to bed.

But the captain's sister could not sleep, and she said to the gentleman's daughter, "What are these men that are always walking about the room, and up and down before the windows?"

And the girl said, "There is a bad man who has laid a wager that he will steal me, and my father is afraid that he may come any night, and these are the watchmen who are guarding me. It is not for the money, but my father is so angry, because that bad man beat him once already."

"Oh," said the captain's sister, "I am so nervous after the

sea. I have a sort of nerves (the narrator used the English word) that I shall never sleep all night. I shall never get a wink of sleep! I would be so much obliged to you if you would have the goodness to send them away."

And so at last the men were sent away, but the captain's sister could not sleep a bit better, and she said,

"When I was in the Indies I used to be so troubled with the heat, that I got a habit of walking out at night, perhaps I could sleep if I were to take a little walk now. Will you be so very kind as to come out for a little walk with me.

So the gentleman's daughter got up, and out they went for a walk, but when they had walked a little way, the lad carried her off bodily to the smithy.

In the morning the gentleman came and he paid the bet, and it is told that the lad married the daughter.

"And is that all he ever stole?" said I.

"That's all I ever heard about it at all events," said MacCraw.

3. In the Sutherland collection is this reference. "The Master Thief (see Dasent's Tales, and Thorpe's Tales). This was some twenty or thirty years ago a common schoolboy's tale. I have tried in vain to get it written down in Gaelic, but they tell it with all that is in the Norwegian version, and more besides, such as the theft of some rabbits (how performed I cannot hear), and that of a lot of calves. The Master Thief stole these for the robbers, by imitating in the woods and upland pastures the cry of the cows." C.D.

4. Another bit of the Master Thief, as given in the Norse Tales, forms part of a story which is referred to in No. 48. It is the incident of the man who is persuaded to put his finger into what he believes to be a cask full of liquor, while the clever rogue rides off on his horse, on pretence of catching himself.

5. I have heard another of the incidents, as a theft, accomplished by tempting a man to run after broken-legged rabbits.

This story, then, is now widely spread in the Highlands, however it got there. The Rev. Mr. MacLauchlan, one of the best-known and most respected men in Edinburgh, gets one version from an old man in the Grassmarket, who gives it a pedigree of some fifty years; I got another myself from a drover in Uist; a very able collector in Sutherland says it was common there some twenty or thirty years ago, and is told still; and a scrap of the Norwegian version comes from Islay. They resemble other versions in other languages, but they resemble each other more than they do any published version which I know; and there seems to be but one explanation of the facts, namely, that this is some very old tradition, common to many races and languages, and derived from some original of unknown antiquity.

The incidents in the German of Grimm are shortly these:—

A poor old man is visited by a gentleman in a grand carriage, who turns out to be his son who had run away and become a master thief. They go to the Count, who sets him three tasks to try his skill: to steal his favourite horse; to take away from his wife and from him the counterpane of their bed, and the ring off the lady's finger; and, thirdly, to steal the parson and clerk out of the church, on pain of his neck.

He makes the watch drunk, and steals the horse. He makes the Count shoot at a dead body, and while the Count is gone to bury the supposed thief, he appears as the Count, and gets the ring and bed-cover from the Countess.

And he entices the parson and clerk into a sack by pretending to be St. Peter.

The Norse story has many more incidents, but amongst them are five tasks set by a great man to try the skill of the Master Thief:—

(1.) To steal the roast from the spit on Sunday, which he does by enticing the servants to run after three hares which he lets out of a bag.

(2.) To steal father Laurence, the priest, which he does by pretending to be an angel, and so enticing him into a sack.

(3.) To steal twelve horses from the stable, which he does by appearing as an old woman, and making twelve grooms drunk with a sleepy drink in brandy.

(4.) To steal the horse from under the squire, which he does nearly in the same way as the clever weaver in the Islay story.

(5.) To steal the sheet of the gentleman's bed, and the shift off his wife's back, which he does in nearly the same way as it is done in the German version.

And though the daughter is not stolen in the Norse tale, it is to gain the daughter that all these tasks are performed.

Now all these are clearly the same as the second "Favola"

in the first book of Straparola, printed in Venice, 1567. In this Italian story the scene is Perugia, the clever thief, a certain Çassandrino, and the man who tries his skill "Il Pretore," the Priest.

Cassandrino first steals the Priest's bed from under him, by breaking through the roof and throwing down the dead body of a recently buried doctor which he had dug up and dressed in his clothes. The Priest thinks that he has fallen down and killed himself, goes to bury him, and finds his bed gone when he returns.

Next he steals the horse from the stable. The watchman sleeps in the saddle; he props him up on sticks, and steals away the horse.

Lastly, he steals a country clergyman, whom he tempts into a sack by dressing as an angel and standing on an altar after matins, exclaiming, "Chi vuol andar in gloria entri nel sacco." He gets a hundred florins of gold each time, and is threatened with terrible punishment in case of failure. The disguise is a white robe, painted paper wings, and a shining diadem.

The Italian story again resembles, though in a less degree, the Egyptian story of Rhampsinitus, told in Herodotus. (Rawlinson's Herod., vol. ii., p. 191.)

The king had a treasure chamber built of hewn stone, but the builder contrived a turning-stone in the wall, and told the secret to his sons when he was about to die.

The sons plundered the treasury, and the king set a trap which caught one of them. The other cut his head off to prevent discovery, and went home with the head, leaving the body in the trap. The king, much puzzled, exposed the headless body, with guards beside it, to watch if any one should be seen weeping near it. The mother sent her son to get back the body, and he did very much as the clever thief in the modern stories, who stole the horses; he disguised himself, and enticed the guards into drinking till they fell asleep; then he shaved half their beards off, and took away the body.

Then the king sent his daughter to find out; and the clever thief went to her, and told her all about it; but when she tried to seize him, he gave her the hand of a dead man, which he had cut off and brought with him; and so he made his escape, leaving the hand.

Then the king proclaimed a free pardon for the clever thief who had outwitted him three times, and when he came he gave him his daughter in marriage.

Other references are given in Grimm's third volume (see page 260), from which it appears that this story is very widely spread in Europe. Now the Gaelic agrees with Herodotus, Straparola, and Grimm, in that there are three tasks accomplished by a clever thief; and the number three is almost universally used in Gaelic tales.

One of the Gaelic incidents, that of the drunken guards, agrees with the story in Herodotus, and is common to all those quoted.

The Gaelic agrees with the Italian, German, and Norse, in the theft of the horse and the clergyman.

The Gaelic alone has the theft of the daughter. The Norwegian version mentions the daughter, and so does the story of Rhampsinitus, and there seems to be fair ground for arguing that all this must have come from some original which it is vain to search for in any modern work or in any modern age. Such at least is my own opinion, and I have endeavoured to give others the means of judging for themselves so far as I am able, by giving all I get unaltered, and by naming all my authorities.

Another Gaelic story, the "Gillie Carrach," of which I lately (June 1860) received a long version from John Dewar, contains three incidents very like those in Herodotus; mixed with others which are new to me, and others which I have in Gaelic from other sources, one of which has a parallel in Italian and in Sanscrit.

It is curious to remark, that the very same ideas seem to have occurred to Herodotus, while on his travels, which now arise in the minds of worthy pedagogues in the Highlands. They object to old stories told by peasants, because they are "fictions," and not historically true. I have repeatedly met men who look on the telling of these tales as something almost wicked.

Thus wrote Herodotus, and those who object to traditionary fictions might take example by the father of history, and while they disbelieve the stories, write them down.

"Such as think the tales told by the Egyptians credible, are free to accept them for history. For my own part, I propose to myself, throughout my whole work, faithfully to record the traditions of the several nations."

Surely if Herodotus did not think it beneath him to record such frivolous things, and if men of the highest acquirements now make them a study, they are not wholly unworthy of notice.

XLI.

THE WIDOW AND HER DAUGHTERS.

From Mrs. MacGeachy, Farmer's Wife, Islay.

THERE was formerly a poor widow, and she had three daughters, and all she had to feed them was a kailyard. There was a great gray horse who was coming every day to the yard to eat the kail. Said the eldest of the daughters to her mother, "I will go to the yard to-day, and I will take the spinning-wheel with me, and I will keep the horse out of the kail." "Do," said her mother. She went out. The horse came; she took the distaff from the wheel and she struck him. The distaff stuck to the horse, and her hand stuck to the distaff. Away went the horse till they reached a green hill, and he called out, "Open, open, oh green hill, and let in the king's son; open, open, oh green hill, and let in the widow's daughter." The hill opened, and they went in. He warmed water for her feet, and made a soft bed for her limbs, and she lay down that night. Early on the morrow, when he rose, he was going to hunt. He gave her the keys of the whole house, and he said to her that she might open every chamber inside but the one. "By all she ever saw not to open that one." That she should have his dinner ready when he should come back, and that if she would be a good woman that he would marry her. When he went away she began to open the chambers.

Every one, as she opened it, was getting finer and finer, till she came to the one that was forbidden. It seemed to her, "What might be in it that she might not open it too." She opened it, and it was full of dead gentlewomen, and she went down to the knee in blood. Then she came out, and she was cleansing her foot; and though she were cleaning it, still she could not take a bit of the blood off it. A tiny cat came where she was, and she said to her, "If she would give a little drop of milk that she would clean her foot as well as it was before. "Thou! ugly beast! be off before thee. Dost thou suppose that I won't clean them better than thou?" "Yes, yes, take thine own away. Thou wilt see what will happen to thee when himself comes home." He came home, and she set the dinner on the board, and they sat down at it. Before they ate a bit he said to her, "Wert thou a good woman to-day?" "I was," said she. "Let me see thy foot, and I will tell thee whether thou wert or wert not." She let him see the one that was clean. "Let me see the other one," said he. When he saw the blood, "Oh! ho!" said he. He rose and took the axe and took her head off, and he threw her into the chamber with the other dead people. He laid down that night, and early on the morrow he went to the widow's yard again. Said the second one of the widow's daughters to her mother—"I will go out to-day, and I will keep the gray horse out of the yard." She went out sewing. She struck the thing she was sewing on the horse. The cloth stuck to the horse, and her hand stuck to the cloth. They reached the hill. He called as usual to the hill; the hill opened, and they went in. He warmed water for her feet, and made a soft bed for her limbs, and they lay down that night. Early in the morning he was going to hunt, and he said to her that she should open every chamber inside but one, and "by all she ever saw" not to open that one. She opened every chamber till she came to the little one, and because she thought "What might be in that one more than the rest that she might not open it?" She opened it, and it was full of dead gentlewomen, and her own sister amongst them. She went down to the knee in blood. She came out, and as she was cleaning herself, and the little cat came round about, and she said to her, "If thou wilt give me a tiny drop of milk I will clean thy foot as well as it ever was." "Thou! ugly beast! begone. Dost thou think that I will not clean it myself better than thou?" "Thou wilt see," said the cat, "what will happen to thee when himself comes home." When he came she set down the dinner, and they sat at it. Said he—"Wert thou a good woman to-day?" "I was," said she. "Let me see thy foot, and I will tell thee whether thou wert or wert not." She let him see the foot that was clean. "Let me see the other one," said he. She let him see it. "Oh! ho!" said he, and he took the axe and took her head off. He lay down that night. Early on the morrow, said the youngest one to her mother, as she wove a stocking—"I will go out with my stocking to-day, and I will watch the gray horse. I will see what happened to my two sisters, and I will return to tell you." "Do," said her mother, "and see thou dost not stay away. She went out, and the horse came. She struck the stocking on the horse. The stocking stuck to the horse, and the hand stuck to the stocking. They went away, and they reached the green hill. He called out as usual, and they got in. He warmed water for her feet, and made a soft bed for her limbs, and they lay down that night. On the morrow he was going to hunt, and he said to her—"If she would behave herself as a good woman till he returned, that they would be married in a few days." He gave her the keys, and he said to her that she might open every chamber that was within but that little one, "but see that she should not open that one." She opened every one, and when she came to this one, because she thought "what might be in it that she might not open it more than the rest?" she opened it, and she saw her two sisters there dead, and she went down to the two knees in blood. She came out, and she was cleaning her feet, and she could not take a bit of the blood off them. The tiny cat came where she was, and she said to her—"Give me a tiny drop of milk, and I will clean thy feet as well as they were before." "I will give it thou creature; I will give thee thy desire of milk if thou will clean my feet." The cat licked her feet as well as they were before. Then the king came home, and they set down his dinner, and they sat at it. Before they ate a bit, he said to her, "Wert *thou* a good woman to-day?" "I was middlin," said she; I have no boasting to make of myself. "Let me see thy feet," said he. She let him see her feet. "Thou wert a good woman," said he; "and if thou holdest on thus till the end of a few days, thyself and I will be married." On the morrow he went away to hunt. When he went away the little cat came where she was. "Now, I will tell thee in what way thou wilt be quickest married to him," said the cat. "There are," said she, "a lot of old chests within. Thou shalt take out three of them; thou shalt clean them. Thou shalt say to him next night, that he must leave these three chests, one about of them, in thy mother's house, as they are of no use here; that there are plenty here without them; thou shalt say to him that he must not open any of them on the road, or else, if he opens, that thou wilt leave him; that thou wilt go up into a tree top, and that thou wilt be looking, and that if he opens any of them that thou wilt see. Then when he goes hunting, thou shalt open the chamber, thou shalt bring out thy two sisters; thou shalt draw on them the magic club, and they will be as lively and whole as they were before; thou shalt clean them then, and thou shalt put one in each chest of them, and thou shalt go thyself into the third one. Thou shalt put of silver and of gold, as much in the chests as will keep thy mother and thy sisters right for their lives. When he leaves the chests in thy mother's house, and when he returns he will fly in a wild rage: he will then go to thy mother's house in this fury, and he will break in the door; be thou behind the door, and take off his head with the bar; and then he will be a king's son, as precious as he was before, and he will marry thee. Say to thy sisters, if he attempts the chests to open them by the way, to call out, 'I see thee, I see thee,' and that he wilt think that thou wilt be calling out in the tree." When he came home he went away with the chests, one after one, till he left them in her mother's house. When he came to a glen, where he thought she in the tree could not see him, he began to let the chest down to see what was in it; she that was in the chest called out, "I see thee, I see thee!"

"Good luck be on thy pretty little head," said he, "if thou canst not see a long way!"

This was the way with him each journey, till he left the chests altogether in her mother's house.

When he returned home on the last journey, and saw that she was not before him, he flew in a wild rage; he went back to the widow's house, and when he reached the door he drove it in before him. She was standing behind the door, and she took his head off with the bar. Then he grew a king's son, as precious as ever came; there he was within and they were in great gladness, She and himself married, and they left with her mother and sisters, of gold and silver, as much as left them well for life.

A BHAINTREACH.

Bha baintreach ann roimhe, 's bha tri nigheanan aice, 's is e na bha aice airson am beathachadh gàrradh càil. Bha each mòr glas a' h-uile latha 'tighinn do 'n ghàrradh a dh'itheadh a 'chàil. "Thuirt an té bu shine de na nigheanan r'a mathair theid mise d'an ghàrradh an diugh 's bheir mi leam a chuibheal, 's cumaidh mi 'n t-each as a' chàl." "Dean," urs' a mathair. Dh' fholbh i mach. Thainig an t-each. Thug i 'chuigeal as a' chuibheil 's bhuail i e. Lean a' chuigeal ris an each, 's lean a làmhsa ris a' chuigeil. Air folbh a bha'n t-each, gus an d' rainig e cnoc uaine, 's ghlaoidh e, "Fosgail, fosgail a chnuic uaine 's leig mac an righ stigh. Fosgail, fosgail a chnoic uaine 's leig nighean na baintrich a stigh." Dh' fhosgail an cnoc, 's chaidh iad a stigh. Rinn e uisge blàth d'a casan 's leaba bhog d'a leasan, 's chaidh i laidhe an oidhche sin. Mochthrath an la'r na mhaireach nur a dh' eiridh esan, bha e 'dol a shealgaireachd. Thug e dh'ise iuchraichean an tighe air fad, 's thuirt e rithe gum faodadh i h-uile seombar a stigh fhosgladh ach an t-aon; air na chunnaic i riamh gun am fear sin fhosgladh; a dhinneir-san a bhi aice reidh nur a thilleadh e; 's n' am biodh i 'na bean mhath gum pòsadh e i. Nur a dh' fholbh esan thòisich ise air fosglaidh nan seombraichean. A' h-uile fear mar a dh' fhosgladh i bha e' dol na bu bhreagha 's na bu bhréagha, gus an d' thàinig i gus an fhear a bh' air a bhacail. Their leatha dé 'dh fhaodadh a bhith ann nach fhaodadh i fhosgladh cuideachd. Dh' fhosgail i e, 's bha e làn do mnathan uaisle marbh, 's chaidh i sìos gus a' ghlùn ann am fuil. Thàinig i mach an sin, 's bha i 'glanadh a coise, 's ged a bhiodh i ga glanadh fathast cha b' urrainn i mìr de 'n fhuil a thoirt di. Thàinig cat crìon far an robh i, 's thuirt i rithe, na'd d' thugadh i dh' ise deur beag bainne, gun glanadh i 'cas cho math 's a bha i riamh. "Thusa 'bheathaich ghrànnda ! bi 'folbh romhad ; am bheil dùil agad nach glan mi féin iad na 's fheàrr na thusa ?" "Seadh, seadh ! leig dhuit ! Chi thu dé dh' éireas duit nur a thig e féin dachaidh !" Thàinig esan dachaidh, 's chuir ise an dinneir air a' bhòrd, 's shuidh iad sìos aice. Ma'n d' ith iad mìr thuirt esan rithe. "An robh thu a'd' bhean mhath an diugh ?" "Bha," urs' ise. "Leig fhaicinn dòmhsa do chas, 's innsidh mi dhuit cò-aca 'bha na nach robh." Leig i fhaicinn da an té 'bha glan. "Leig fhaicinn domh, an te eile," urs' esan. Nur a chunnaic e' 'n fhuil, "O ! ho !" urs' e, 's dh' éiridh e, 's ghabh e 'n tuagh, s. thug e' 'n ceann di, 's thilg e 'stigh do 'n t-seombar i leis an fheadhain mharbh, eile.

Chaidh e laidhe an oidhche sin, 's mochthrath an la 'r na mhàireach dh' fholbh e gu gàrradh na baintrich a rithisd. Thuirt an darna té do nigheanan na baintrich r'a màthair. "Théid mi mach an diugh, 's cumaidh mi 'n t-each glas as a' ghàrradh." Chaidh i 'mach a' fuaghal. Bhuail i 'rud a bha aice 'ga 'fhuaghal air an each ; lean an t-aodach ris an each ; 's lean a làmh ris an aodach. Ràinig iad an cnoc. Ghlaoidh e, mur a bh' àbhaist dha ris a' chnoc. Dh' fhosgail an cnoc, 's chaidh iad a stigh. Rinn e uisge blàth d'a easan, 's leaba bhog d'a leasan, 's chaidh iad a laidhe an oidhche sin. Mochthrath an la'r na mhàireach bha esan a' folbh a shealgaireachd, 's thuirt e rithe h-uile seombar a stigh fhosgladh, ach an aon fhear, 's air na chunnaic i riamh gun am fear sin fhosgladh. Dh' fhosgail i h-uile seombar gus an d' thàinig i gus an fhear bheag, 's air leahta dé dh' fhaodadh a bhith anns an fhear sin na 's motha na càch nach fhaodadh i 'fhosgladh. Dh' fhosgail i e, 's bha e làn de mhnathan uaisle marbha, 's a piuthar féin 'nam measg. Chaidh i sìos 'ga glùn ann am fuil. Thàinig i 'mach, 's bha i 'ga glanadh féin, 's thàinig an cat beag ma'n cuairt, 's thuirt i rithe, "Ma bheir thu dhòmhsa deur crìon bainne glanaidh mi do chas cho math 's a bha i riamh ?" "Thus' a bheathaich ghrannda ! Gabh romhad ! Am bheil dùil agad nach glan mi féin i na 's fheàrr na thusa ?" "Chi thu," urs' an cat, "dé dh' éireas duit nur a thig e fein dachaidh." Nur a thàinig e dhachaidh chuir ise sìos an dinneir, 's shuidh iad aice. Thuirt esan rithe. "An robh thu a'd' bhean mhath an diugh ?" "Bha," urs' ise. "Leig fhaicinn domh do chas, 's innsidh mi dhuit cò-aca 'bha na nach robh." Leig i fhaicinn da 'chas a bha glan. "Leig fhaicinn domh an te eile," urs' esan. Leig i fhaicinn i. "O ho!" urs' esan, 's ghabh e 'n tuagh, 's thug e 'n ceann di.

Chaidh e 'laidhe an oidhche sin. Mochthrath an la 'r na mhàireach, urs' an te b' òige r'a màthair, 's i figheadh stocaidh, "Théid mise 'mach le m' stocaidh an diugh, 's fairidh mi 'n t-each glas; chi mi dé thachair do m' dha phiuthair; 's tillidh mi dh' innseadh dhuibhse." "Dèan," urs' a màthair, 's feuch nach fan thu air folbh." Chaidh i' mach, 's thàinig an t-each. Bhuail i 'n stocaidh air an each. Lean an stocaidh ris an each, 's lean an làmh ris an stocaidh. Dh' fholbh iad, 's ràinig iad an cnoc uaine. Ghlaoidh e mar a b' àbhaist da, 's fhuair iad a stigh. Rinn e uisge blàth d'a casan 's leaba bhog d'a leasan, 's chaidh iad a laidhe an oidhche sin. An la 'r na mhàireach bha e 'folbh a shealgaireachd, 's thuirt e rithise na'n dèanadh i bean mhath gus an tilleadh e, ann am beagan làithean gum biodh iad pòsda. Thug e dhi na h-iuchraichean, 's thuirt e rithe gum faodadh i h-uile seombar a bha stigh fhosgladh ach am fear beag ud,—ach feuch nach fosgladh i 'm fear ud. Dh' fhosgail i h-uile gin; 's nur a thàinig i gus an fhear so, air leatha dé 'bhiodh ann nach fhaodadh i 'fhosgladh, na 's motha na càch, Dh' fhosgail i e, 's chunnaic i 'da phiuthar marbh an sin, 's chaidh i sìos g'a da ghlùn ann am fuil. Thàinig i mach, 's bha i 'glanadh a cas, 's cha b' urrainn i mìr de 'n fhuil a thoirt diu. Thàinig an cat crìon far an robh i, 's thuirt i rithe, "Thoir dhòmhsa deur crìon bainne, 's glanaidh mi do chasan cho math 's a bha iad riamh." "Bheir a chreutair—bheir mise dhuit do dhìol bainne ma ghlanas thu mo chasan." Dh' imlich an cat a casan cho math 's a bha iad riamh. Thàinig an rìgh an sin dachaidh, 's chuir iad a sìos a dhinneir, 's shuidh iad aice. Ma'n d' ith iad mìr thuirt esan rithe, "An robh thusa a'd' bhean mhath an diugh?" "Bha mi meadhonach," urs' ise, "cha 'n 'eil uaill sam bith agam r'a dhèanadh asam féin." "Leig fhaicinn domh do chasan," urs' esan. "Leig i fhaicinn da 'casan. Bha thusa a'd' bhean mhath," urs' esan, "'s ma leanas thu mur sin gu ceann beagan làithean bidh thu fhéin agus mise posda." An là'r na mhàireach dh' fholbh esan a shealgaireachd. Nur a dh' fholbh esan thàinig an cat beag far an robh ise. "Nis innsidh mise dhuit dé 'n dòigh air an luaithe am bi thu pòsd' air," urs' an cat. "Tha," urs' ise, "dorlach de sheana chisdeachan a stigh; bheir thu mach tri dhiu; glanaidh thu iad; their thu ris an ath oidhche gum feum e na tri chisdeachan sin, te ma seach dhiu, fhàgail ann an tigh do mhàthar, chionn nach 'eil feum an so orra, gu 'bheil na leòir ann as an ioghnais ; their thu ris nach fhaod e gin dhiu fhosgladh air an rathad, air no ma dh' fhosglas gum fàg thu e ; gun d' théid thu ann am bàrr craoibhe, 's gum bi thu 'g amharc, 's ma dh' fhosglas e gin dhiu gum faic thu. An sin nur a théid esan a shealgaireachd fosglaidh thu 'n seombar ; bheir thu 'mach do dha phiuthar ; tairnidh thu 'n slachdan draoidheachd orra ; 's bidh iad cho beò, shlàn 's a bha iad riamh. Glanaidh thu iad an sin, 's cuiridh thu té anns gach cisde dhiu, agus theìd thu féin 's an treas té. Cuiridh thu de dh' airgiod agus de dh' òr anns na cisdeachan na chumas do mhàthair agus do pheathraichean ceart r'am beò. Nur a dh' fhàgas e na cisdeachan ann an tigh do mhathar, 's a thilleas e, theid e ann am feirg choimheach. Folbhaidh e' n sin gu tigh do mhàthar anns an fheirg so, 's brisdidh e stigh an dorus. Bi thusa cùl an doruis, 's thoir dheth an ceann leis an t-sàbh, 's bidh e'n sin 'na mhac rìgh cho àluinn 's a bha e riamh, 's pòsaidh e thu. Abair ri d' pheathraichean, ma bheir e làmh air na cisdeachan fhosgladh air an rathad iad a ghlaodhach, "Chi mi thu," chi mi thu, "air alt, 's gun saoil' e gur tusa a bhios a glaodhach 's a' chraoibh."

Nur a thill esan dachaidh, dh' fholbh e leis na cisdeachan, te an deigh te, gus an d' fhàg e 'n tigh a màthar iad. Nur a thàinig e gu gleann far an robh e smaointeachadh nach fhaiceadh ise 's a' chraoibh e, thug e làmh air a' chisde leigeil sìos airson faicinn dé 'bh' innte. Ghlaoidh an te 'bha 's a' chisde, "Chi mi thu—Chi mi thu." "Piseach air do ceann beag, bòidheach," urs' esan, "man am fad' a chi thu." B'e so a bu dual dha air gach siubhal gus an d' fhàg e na cisdeachan air fad an tigh a mathar. Nur a thill e dhachaidh air an t-siubhal ma dheireadh, 's a chunnaic e nach robh ise roimhe, chaidh e ann am feirg choimheach. Dh' fholbh e air ais gu tigh na baintrich, 's nur a ràinig e 'n dorus chuir e roimhe e. Bha ise 'na seasamh air cùl an doruis, 's thug i 'n ceann deth leis an t-sàbh. Dh' fhàs e 'n sin 'na mhac rìgh cho àluinn 'sa thàinig riamh. Chaidh e stigh an sin, 's bha iad ann an 's bha iad ann an toil-inntinn mhòr. Phòs e fhéin agus ise, 's rinn iad banais aighearach shunndach. Chaidh iad dachaidh do 'n chaisteal, 's bha iad gu math comhla, 's fhuair a màthair 's a peathreuchean na 'chum gu math r'am beo iad.

From Catherine Milloy, Kilmeny, Islay, March 1859.

An old woman of the name of *Hutton*, in Cowal, told this to *Catherine Milloy*, a Cowal woman, married to a farmer at Kilmeny, *Angus MacGeachy*, a Campbelltown man. Written down from her dictation by *Hector MacLean*, Islay, May 1859.

This story is something like The Hoodie and The Daughter of the King of the Skies ; it has a bit like The Mermaid.

I have another version, told by Hugh Mac-in-deor, an old man at Bowmore, in Islay, who can recite a great many more stories ; he borders upon eighty, is very poor, and has had but little education. He tells MacLean that he learnt his stories long ago from one Angus Brown, who was known by the soubriquet of Aonghas Gruama frowning Angus, of whom very queer anecdotes are told. Mac-in-deor was able to play the pipes in his day. His father was considered an excellent piper ; and his son Dugald is allowed to be one of the best pipers in the island.

2d. A poor woman had three daughters and a kail-yard, and a horse used to come every day to eat the kail. The daughters went, one after the other, to drive him away with the distaff, and the distaff stuck to the horse and to their hands, and he dragged them in turn to a castle. *(It is not said that the horse became a man.)* The first was the eldest who slept in the castle ; on the morrow she got a key, and was told to look at all the rooms but one ; and to milk the "Three Red-brown Hornless Cows." She looked into the room of course, and sank to her knee in blood ; and "a grey great cat" came about and asked for a drop milk, and was refused.

When the "giant" came home he asked to see her foot, and it was red with blood ; and he smote her with the "White Glave of Light," and killed her.

The very same thing happened to the second. The youngest milked the three Red-brown Hornless Cows ; but peeped, and sank to her knee in blood, and saw her two dead sisters. The great grey cat asked for milk, and got it and drank it, and became a splendid woman, and told her that she was a king's daughter under spells ; and she told her to take some of the milk and to clean her foot with it, and that it would not leave a speck of the blood on her ; and so she did.

"Now," said the king's daughter, "when he comes in and sees that thy foot is clean, he will marry thee ; but thou wilt not be long alive if thou art with him. When he goes to the hunting hill, thou shalt take with thee AM BALLAN IOC, vessel of balsam (*ballan is a teat*), and rub it against the mouth of thy big sister; and thou shalt put her into a sack, and gold and silver with her, and thou shalt stuff the sack with hay; and when he comes home tell him that there is a whisp for the cow, and to leave it with thy mother; and the next day do the same with thy second sister; and on the third day, I will put thyself and the white glave of light into the sack. When he knows that thou art not with him, he will go after thee; and when he is coming in at the door, "SGAP" the head off him with the sword, and hold the sword on the SMIOR CHAILLEACH (spinal marrow) till it cools, before the head goes on again."

The girl did as she was told; and he took the three sisters alive, and his gold and his sword, in the sacks with the hay on his back to the mother, and said each time, "SO A CHAILLEACH SIN AGUD SOP DO'N BHO," "Here carlin, there thou hast a whisp for the cow."

On the third day he went home, and when he lay down and found that she was not there, he went to the poor woman's house, and the youngest daughter chopped his head off as he went in at the door; and then she went back to the castle and stayed in it with the king's daughter.

3d. This is manifestly the same story as "The history of Mr. Greenwood," in Mr. Peter Buchan's unpublished MS. The scene of that story is laid in the Western Isles; it is brought down to a much later period than the Gaelic story; and the language is not that of peasants.

It is the same as the Old Dame and her Hen, Norse Tales, No. III., published 1859, and it resembles bits of other tales in the same collection. It is the same as Fitcher's Vogel, Grimm, No. 46; and Old Rink Rank, 196. It is in French as Barbe Bleu; in English as Bluebeard; and according to the notes in Grimm's third volume, it is very old and very widely spread. Of all these the Norse and Gaelic resemble each other most.

The same idea pervades a number of other Gaelic stories, namely, that of a people living underground, who assumed the shape of various creatures, and lived by hunting; possessed gold and silver, and swords; carried off women and children; ate some, murdered others, and kept a larder of dead gentlewomen, whom it appears that they carried off, married, and murdered.

XLII.

THE TALE OF THE SOLDIER.

From John MacDonald, travelling tinker.

THERE was an old soldier once, and he left the army. He went to the top of a hill that was at the upper end of the town land, and he said—

"Well, may it be that the mischief may come and take me with him on his back, the next time that I come again in sight of this town."

Then he was walking till he came to the house of a gentleman that was there, John asked the gentleman if he would get leave to stay in his house that night. "Well. then," said the gentleman, "since thou art an old soldier, and hast the look of a man of courage, without dread or fear in thy face, there is a castle at the side of yonder wood, and thou mayest stay in it till day. Thou shalt have a pipe and baccy, a cogie full of whisky, and a bible to read."

When John got his supper, he took himself to the castle: he set on a great fire, and when a while of the night had come, there came two tawny women in, and a dead man's kist between them. They threw it at the fireside, and they sprang out. John arose, and with the heel of his foot he drove out its end, and he dragged out an old hoary bodach, and he set him sitting in the great chair; he gave him a pipe and baccy, and a cogie of whisky, but the bodach let them fall on the floor. "Poor man," said John, "the cold is on thee." John laid himself stretched in the bed, and he left the bodach to toast himself at the fireside; but about the crowing of the cock he went away.

The gentleman came well early in the morning.

"What rest didst thou find John?"

"Good rest," said John "thy father was not the man that would frighten me."

"Right, good John, thou shalt have two hundred '*pund*,' and lie to-night in the castle."

"I am the man that will do that," said John; and that night it was the very like. There came three tawny women, and a dead man's kist with them amongst them. They threw it up to the side of the fireplace, and they took their soles out (of that).

John arose, and with the heel of his foot he broke the head of the kist, and he dragged out of it the old hoary man; and as he did the night before he set him sitting in the big chair, and gave him pipe and baccy, and he let them fall. "Oh! poor man," said John, "cold is on thee." Then he gave him a cogie of drink, and he let that fall also. "Oh! poor man, thou art cold."

The bodach went as he did the night before; "but," said John to himself, "if I stay here this night, and that thou shouldst come, thou shalt pay my pipe and baccy, and my cogie of drink."

The gentleman came early enough in the morning, and he asked, "What rest didst thou find last night, John?" "Good rest," said John, "it was not the hoary bodach, thy father, that would put fear on me."

"Och!" said the gentleman, "if thou stayest to-night thou shalt have three hundred '*pund*.'"

"It's a bargain," said John.

When it was a while of the night there came four

tawny women, and a dead man's kist with them amongst them; and they let that down at the side of John.

John arose, and he drew his foot and he drove the head out of the kist, and he dragged out the old hoary man and he set him in the big chair. He reached him the pipe and the baccy, the cup and the drink, but the old man let them fall, and they were broken.

"Och," said John, before thou goest this night thou shalt pay me all thou hast broken;" but word there came not from the head of the bodach. Then John took the belt of his "abersgaic,"* and he tied the bodach to his side, and he took him with him to bed. When the heath-cock crowed, the bodach asked him to let him go.

"Pay what thou hast broken first," said John. "I will tell thee, then," said the old man, "there is a cellar of drink under, below me, in which there is plenty of drink, tobacco, and pipes; there is another little chamber beside the cellar, in which there is a caldron full of gold; and under the threshold of the big door there is a crocky full of silver. Thou sawest the women that came with me to-night?"

"I saw," said John.

"Well, there thou hast four women from whom I took the cows, and they in extremity; they are going with me every night thus, punishing me; but go thou and tell my son how I am being wearied out. Let him go and pay the cows, and let him not be heavy on the poor. Thou thyself and he may divide the gold and silver between you, and marry thyself my old girl; but mind, give plenty of gold of what is left to the poor, on

---

* Haversack.

whom I was too hard, and I will find rest in the world of worlds."

The gentleman came, and John told him as I have told thee, but John would not marry the old girl of the hoary bodach.

At the end of a day or two John would not stay longer; he filled his pockets full of the gold, and he asked the gentleman to give plenty of gold to the poor. He reached the house (went home), but he was wearying at home, and he had rather be back with the regiment. He took himself off on a day of days, and he reached the hill above the town from which he went away; but who should come to him but the Mischief.

"Hoth! hoth! John, thou hast come back?"

"Hoth! on thyself," quoth John, "I came; who art thou?"

"I am the Mischief; the man to whom thou gavest thyself when thou was here last."

"Ai! ai!" said John, "it's long since I heard tell of thee, but I never saw thee before. There is glamour on my eyes, I will not believe that it is thou at all; but make a snake of thyself, and I will believe thee."

The Mischief did this.

"Make now a lion of roaring."

The Mischief did this.

"Spit fire now seven miles behind thee, and seven miles before thee."

The Mischief did this.

"Well," said John, "since I am to be a servant with thee, come into my 'abersgaic,' and I will carry thee; but thou must not come out till I ask thee, or else the bargain's broke."

The Mischief promised, and he did this.

"Now," said John, "I am going to see a brother of mine that is in the regiment, but keep thou quiet."

So now, John went into the town; and one yonder and one here, would cry, "There is John the 'desairtair.'"

There was gripping of John, and a court held on him; and so it was that he was to be hanged about mid-day on the morrow, and John asked no favour but to be floored with a bullet.

The "Coirneal" said, "Since he was an old soldier, and in the army so long, that he should have his asking."

On the morrow when John was to be shot, and the soldiers foursome round all about him,

"What is that they are saying?" said the Mischief. "Let me amongst them and I wont be long scattering them."

"Cuist! cuist!" said John.

"What's that speaking to thee?" said the Coirneal.

"Oh! it's but a white mouse," said John.

"Black or white," said the Coirneal, "don't thou let her out of the 'abersgaic' and thou shalt have a letter of loosing, and let's see thee no more."

John went away, and in the mouth of night he went into a barn where there were twelve men threshing.

"Oh! lads," said John, "here's for you my old abersgaic, and take a while threshing it, it is so hard that it is taking the skin off my back."

They took as much as two hours of the watch at the abersgaic with the twelve flails; and at last every blow they gave it, it would leap to the top of the barn, and it was casting one of the threshers now and again on his back. When they saw that, they asked him to be out of that, himself and his agersgaic; they would not believe but that the Mischief was in it.

Then he went on his journey, and he went into a smithy where there were twelve smiths striking their great hammers.

"Here's for you, lads, an old abersgaic, and I will give you half-a-crown, and take a while at it with the twelve great hammers; it is so hard that it is taking the skin off my back."

But that was fun for the smiths; it was good sport for them the abersgaic of the soldier; but every "sgailc" it got, it was bounding to the top of the smithy. "Go out of this, thyself and it," said they; "we will not believe but that the 'Bramman'* is in it."

So then John went on and the Mischief on his back, and he reached a great furnace that was there.

"Where art thou going now, John?" said the Mischief.

"Patience a little, and thou'lt see that," said John.

"Let me out," said the Mischief," and I will never put trouble on thee in this world."

"Nor in the next?" said John.

"That's it," said the Mischief.

"Stop then," said John, "till thou get a smoke;" and so saying, John cast the abersgaic and the Donas into the midddle of the furnace, and himself and the furnace went as a green flame of fire to the skies.

AN SAIGHDEAR.

BHA seann saighdear ann, aon uair, agus threig e 'n t-arm. Chaidh e gu mullach cnoc 'bha 'm braigh 'bhaile, agus thubhairt

* This word I have never met before.

e, "Gu ma th' ann a thig an Donas, agus mise a thoirt leis air a dhruim, an ath uair a thig mise an sealladh a bhaile so a rithist." Bha e so a coiseachd, gus an d' thainig e gu tigh duin' uasail a bha 'n sin. Dh' fheoraich Iain do 'n duin' uasal, "Am feudadh e fantainn na thigh air an oidhche sin?" "Mata," ars' an duin' uasal, "bho 'n is seann saighdear thu, agus coslas duine calma gun fhiamh na eagal na d' ghnuis, tha caisteal ri taobh na coille sin thall, agus feuda tu fantainn ann gu latha ; gheibh thu piob 's tombaca, cuach làn uisge agus Biobull gu leubhadh." Dur a fhuair Iain a shuipeir, thug e 'n Caisteal air. Chuir e teine mòr air, agus dar a thainig tacan do 'n oidhche thainig dithis mhnathan ruadh a steach, 's ciste duine mhairbh eatorra ! Thilg iad i ri taobh na teallaich, 's leum iad a mach. Dh' eirich Iain, 's le sàil a choise, chuir e 'n ceann aiste. Tharruinn e mach seann bhodach liath, agus chuir e 'na shuidhe anns a' chathair mhòir e: thug e piob 's tombaca dha, agus cuach uisge, ach leig am bodach leo tuiteam air an urlar. "A dhuine bhochd," ars' Iain, "tha 'm fuachd ort." Chaidh Iain 'na shìneadh 'san leabaidh, 's dh' fhàg e 'm bodach ga gharadh ri taobh a' ghealbhain ; ach mu ghairm choileach dh' fhalbh e. Thainig an duin' uasal gu math moch 's a' mhaduinn. "De 'n tàmh a fhuair thu, Iain?" "Tàmh maith, ars' Iain, "cha b'e t' athair am fear a chuireadh eagal ormsa." "Ro mhaith, Iain ; gheibh thu dà cheud pund, agus luidh a nochd 's a' chaisteal." "'S mise an duin' a ni sin," thuirt Iain: agus air an oidhche so, b'e 'leithid cheudna. Thainig triur mhnathan ruadh, 's ciste duine mhairbh aca eadar iad. Thilg iad suas i ri taobh na teallaich, 's thug iad na bùinn asda. Dh' eirich Iain 's le sàil a choise, bhrist e ceann na ciste, 's shlaod e aiste an seann duine liath, agus mar a rinn e an oidhche roimhe, chuir e 's a' chathair mhòir e. Thug e dha piob 's tombaca, 's leig e leo tuiteam. "A dhuine bhochd," ars' Iain, "tha fuachd ort." Thug e 'n so cuach làn dibhe dha 's leig e le so tuiteam cuideachd. "O ! a dhuine bhochd, tha fuachd ort." Dh' fhalbh am bodach, mar a rinn e 'n oidhche roimhe. "Ach," ars' Iain ris fhein, "ma dh' fhanas mis' an so a nochd, agus gun d' thig thusa, paidhidh tusa mo phiob, 's mo thombaca, 's mo chuach dhibhe. Thainig an duin' uasal gle mhoch 's a mhaduinn, 's dh' fhoighneachd e, "De 'n tàmh a fhuair thu 'n raoir, Iain?" "Tàmh math," ars' Iain, "cha b'e 'm bodach liath t' athair a chuireadh eagal ormsa." "Ach," ars' an duin' uasal, "ma dh' fhanas tu 'nochd, gheibh thu tri chèud pund." "'S bargain e," ars' Iain. 'Nuair a bha e tacain do 'n oidhche, thainig ceathrar do mhnathan ruadha, 's ciste duine mhairbh aca eadar iad, 's leig iad sud sios ri taobh Iain. Dh' eirich Iain, 's tharruinn e 'chas, 's chuir e 'n ceann as a chiste, 's tharruinn e mach an seann duine liath, 's chuir e 's a' chathair mhoir e. Shìn e dha piob 's tombaca, an corn 's an deoch, ach leig an seann duine leo tuiteam, 's bhristeadh iad. Ach thubhairt Iain, "Ma'm falbh thusa 'nochd, paidhidh tu dhomhsa na bhrist thu," ach facal cha d' thainig a ceann a' bhodaich. Ghabh Iain an so crios abarsgaic, agus cheangail e 'm bodach ri chliathaich, 's thug e leis a luidhe e. Dar a ghoir an coileach fraoich dh' iarr am bodach air a leigeil as. "Paidh na bhrist thu 'n toiseach," ars' Iain. "Innse mise dhuit mata," ars' an seann duine, tha seilear dibhe shios fotham, anns am bheil pailteas dibhe, tombaca 's pioban : tha seomar beag eile laimh ris an t-seilear, anns am bheil coire làn òir, agus fo starsnaich an doruis mhoir, tha crogan làn airgiod. Chunnaic thu na mnathan ud a thainig leamsa 'nochd." "Chunnaic," ars' Iain. "*Well*, sin agad ceathrar mhnathan bho 'n d' thug mise na mairt, agus iad 'na n èigin ; tha iad a falbh leamsa na h-uil' oidhche mar so ga m' phianadh ; ach falbh thusa, agus innis do m' mhac, mar tha mis' air mo shàrachadh ; falbhadh esan agus paidheadh e na mairt, agus na biodh e trom air a bhochd. Feuda tu fhein agus esan an t-òr 's an t-airgiod a roinn eadaruibh, agus pòs fhein mo sheann nighean, ach cuimhnich thoir pailteas òir do na tha 'lathair do na bochdan, air an robh mise ro chruaidh, agus gheibh mise fois gu saoghal nan saoghal." Thainig an duin' uasal, agus dh' innis Iain dha mar a dh' innis mise dhuitse, ach cha phosadh Iain seann nighean a' bhodaich liath. An ceann latha no dhà, cha 'n fhanadh Iain ni b' fhaide. Lion e phòcaidean làn do 'n òr, 's dh' iarr e air an duin' uasal pailteas òir a thoirt do na bochdan. Rainig e 'n tigh, ach bha e 'gabhail fadail aig an tigh, agus b' fhearr leis bhi air ais 'san Reisimeid. Thog e air latha do na laithean, 's rainig e 'n cnoc a bha os ceann a bhaile, bho 'n d' fhalbh e. Ach co thainig g'a ionnsaidh ach an Donas ! "Hoth ! hoth ! Iain, phill thu." "Hoth ! ort fhein," ars' Iain, "phill : co thusa." "'S mis' an Donas, am fear do 'n d' thug thusa thu fhein, dar a bha thu 'n so ma dheireadh." "Ai ! ai !" ars' Iain, "'s fada bho na chuala mi iomradh ort, ach cha n' fhaca mi 'riamh roimhe thu : 's ann a tha spleùmas air mo shuilean ; cha chreid mi gur tu th' ann idir ; ach dean nathair dhiot fhein, agus creididh mi thu." Rinn an Donas so. "Dean a nis leomhan beuchdach." Rinn an Donas so! "Cuir a nis smugaidean teine seachd mile as do dheigh agus seachd mile romhad." Rinn an Donas so!! "Well," ars' Iain bho na tha mi gu bhi na m' ghill' agad, thig a steach na m' abarsgaic, agus giulanidh mis' thu; ach cha 'n fheud thu tighinn a mach gus an iarr mise, air neo tha 'm bargain briste." Gheall an Donas, 's rinn e' so. "Nis," ars' Iain, "tha mise dol a dh' fhaicinn brathair dhomh a tha 'san Reisimeid, ach fan thusa sàmhach." Chaidh Iain an so a stigh do 'n bhaile, agus ghlaodh fear thall 's fear a bhos, "So Iain an desairtair." Chaidh beireachd air Iain 's mòd a chuir air, agus 'se bh' ann gu 'n robh e gu bhi air a chrochadh mu mheadhon-latha 'màireach: agus cha do dh' iarr Iain do dh' fhabhor, ach e bhi air a thilgeil le peileir. Thubhairt an Còirneal, "bho 'n is e seann saighdear a bh' ann, agus e anns an arm cho fada, gu 'faigheadh e 'iarrtas." An la'ir na mhàireach, dar a bha Iain gu bhi air a thilgeil 's na saighdearan ceithir chuairt thimchioll air, "De sud a tha iad ag radh," ars' an donas, "leig mise 'nam measg 's cha 'n fhada a bhios mi 'gan sgapadh." "Cuist! cuist!" ars' Iain. "Dé sin a tha bruidhinn riut?" ars' an Còirneal. "O! cha 'n 'eil ach luch bhàn," ars' Iain. "Bàn na dubh i," ars' an Còirneal, "na leig thus' as an abarsgaic i, 's gheibh thu litir fhuasglaidh, 's na faiceam tuillidh thu." Dh' fhalbh Iain, agus am beul na h-oidhche chaidh e stigh do shabhall far an robh dà fhear dheug a bualadh. "O! 'illean," ars' Iain, "so dhuibh mo sheann abarsgaic, 's thugaibh greis bhualaidh oirre; bha i cho cruaidh, 's gu bheil i toirt a chraicinn dheth mo dhruim." Thug iad cho maith ri dà uair an uaireadair air an abarsgaic, leis an dà shuisd dheug, gus ma dheireadh na h-uile buille a bheireadh iad dhi, leumadh i gu mullach an t-sabhaill, 's bha i tilgeil fear air a dhruim an dràsta 's a rithist dheth na bualadairan. 'Nuair a chunnaic iad so dh' iarr iad air a bhi muigh a sud, e fhein 's abarsgaic; cha chreideadh iad fhein nach robh an Donas innte. Dh' fhalbh e 'n sin air a thurus, 's chaidh e steach do cheardaich, far an robh da gobha dhèug a bualadh nan òrd mòra, "So dhuibh, 'illean seann abarsgaic, 's bheir mi dhuibh leth-chrùn, 's thugaibh greis oirre leis an dà òrd mhòr dheug; tha i cho cruaidh, 's gu 'bheil i toirt a chraicinn dheth mo dhruim." Ach ge bha aoibh-inn, b' e na gobhainnan; bu mhaith an spors dhoibh abarsgaic an t-saighdeair, ach na h-uile sgailc a bha i faotainn, bha i leùm gu mullach na ceardaich. "Gabh mach a' so thu fhein 's ise," ars' iadsan, "bho 'n cha chreid sinn fhein nach eil am Bramman innte." Dh' fhalbh Iain air aghaidh mar so, 's an Donas air a dhruim !! 's rainig e fuirneis mhòr a bha 'sin. "Càit a nis am bheil thu dol, Iain," ars' an Donas. "Foighidinn beag, 's chi thu sin," ars' Iain. "Leig as mi," ars' an Donas, "'s cha chuir mi dragh ort 's an t-saoghal so." "No 'san ath fhear?" ars' Iain—"Seadh," ars' an Donas. "Stad mata," ars' Iain, "gus am faigh thu smoc," 's le so a radh, thilg Iain an abarsgaic 's an Donas an teis meadhoin na fuirneis, 's chaidh e fhein 's an fhuirneis 'na lasair uaine anns na spèuran !

This was written by Hector Urquhart, from the dictation of John MacDonald, and sent January 1860.

It is clearly the same story as that of the man who travelled to learn what shivering meant (Grimm), though it has only a very few of the incidents which are in the German version.

Another version of the same story was told me in English by a man whom I met in London, and have never been able to find again. (See Introduction.)

It is a story very widely spread in Europe ; and I believe this to be a genuine tradition, though I have but one Gaelic version of it.

John MacDonald, travelling tinker, has but a small stock of lore ; and the tinker whom I met in London could not read the card which I gave him, with a promise of payment if he would come and repeat his stock of stories. His female companion, indeed, could both read the card and speak French. The whole lot seemed to suspect some evil design on my part ; and I have never seen the one who told the story, or the woman since, though I met their comrade afterwards.

For the pedigree of Grimm's version, see vol. iii., p. 15, edition 1856.

XLIII.

THE SHARP GREY SHEEP.

From John Dewar, labourer, Glendaruail, Cowal.

THERE was a king and a queen, and they had a daughter, and the queen found death, and the king married another. And the last queen was bad to the daughter of the first queen, and she used to beat her and put her out of the door. She sent her to herd the sheep, and was not giving her what should suffice her. And there was a sharp (horned) grey sheep in the flock that was coming with meat to her.

The queen was taking wonder that she was keeping alive and that she was not getting meat enough from herself, and she told it to the henwife. The henwife thought that she would send her own daughter to watch how she was getting meat, and Ni Mhaol Charach,* the henwife's daughter, went to herd the sheep with the queen's daughter. The sheep would not come to her so long as Ni Mhaol Charach was there, and Ni Mhaol Charach was staying all the day with her. The queen's daughter was longing for her meat, and she said—"Set thy head on my knee and I will dress thy hair."† And Ni Mhaol Charach set her head on the knee of the queen's daughter, and she slept.

---

* Bald scabby thing.

† Fasgabhaidh.

The sheep came with meat to the queen's daughter, but the eye that was in the back of the head of the bald black-skinned girl, the henwife's daughter, was open, and she saw all that went on, and when she awoke she went home and told it to her mother, and the henwife told it to the queen, and when the queen understood how the girl was getting meat, nothing at all would serve her but that the sheep should be killed.

The sheep came to the queen's daughter and said to her—

"They are going to kill me, but steal thou my skin and gather my bones and roll them in my skin, and I will come alive again, and I will come to thee again."

The sheep was killed, and the queen's daughter stole her skin, and she gathered her bones and her hoofs and she rolled them in the skin; but she forgot the little hoofs. The sheep came alive again, but she was lame. She came to the king's daughter with a halting step, and she said, "Thou didst as I desired thee, but thou hast forgotten the little hoofs."

And she was keeping her in meat after that.

There was a young prince who was hunting and coming often past her, and he saw how pretty she was, and he asked, "Who's she?" And they told him, and he took love for her, and he was often coming the way; but the bald black-skinned girl, the henwife's daughter, took notice of him, and she told it to her mother, and the henwife told it to the queen.

The queen was wishful to get knowledge what man it was, and the henwife sought till she found out who he (was), and she told the queen. When the queen heard who it was she was wishful to send her own daughter in his way, and she brought in the first queen's daughter, and she sent her own daughter to herd in her place, and she was making the daughter of the first queen do the cooking and every service about the house.

The first queen's daughter was out a turn, and the prince met her, and he gave her a pair of golden shoes. And he was wishful to see her at the sermon, but her muime would not let her go there.

But when the rest would go she would make ready, and she would go after them, and she would sit where he might see her, but she would rise and go before the people would scatter, and she would be at the house and everything in order before her muime would come. But the third time she was there the prince was wishful to go with her, and he sat near to the door, and when she went he was keeping an eye on her, and he rose and went after her. She was running home, and she lost one of her shoes in the mud; and he got the shoe, and because he could not see her he said that the one who had the foot that would fit the shoe was the wife that would be his.

The queen was wishful that the shoe would fit her own daughter, and she put the daughter of the first queen in hiding, so that she should not be seen till she should try if the shoe should fit her own daughter.

When the prince came to try the shoe on her, her foot was too big, but she was very anxious that the shoe should fit her, and she spoke to the henwife about it. The henwife cut the points of her toes off that the shoe might fit her, and the shoe went on her when the points of the toes were cut.

When the wedding-day came the daughter of the first queen was set in hiding in a nook that was behind the fire.

When the people were all gathered together, a bird came to the window, and he cried—

"The blood's in the shoe, and the pretty foot's in the nook at the back of the fire."*

One of them said, "What is that creature saying?" And the queen said—"It's no matter what that creature is saying; it is but a nasty, beaky, lying creature." The bird came again to the window; and the third time he came, the prince said—"We will go and see what he is saying."

And he rose and he went out, and the bird cried—

"The blood's in the shoe, and the pretty foot's in the nook that is at the back of the fire."

He returned in, and he ordered the nook at the back of the fire to be searched. And they searched it, and they found the first queen's daughter there, and the golden shoe on the one foot. They cleaned the blood out of the other shoe, and they tried it on her, and the shoe fitted her, and its like was on the other foot. The prince left the daughter of the last queen, and he married the daughter of the first queen, and he took her from them with him, and she was rich and lucky after that.

A CHAORA BHIORACH, GHLAS.

Bha Righ agus Banrigh ann, agus bha nighean aca. Agus thuair a Bhanrigh bàs, agus phòs an Righ h-aon eile, agus bha Bhanrigh ma dheireadh dona ri nighean na ceud Bhanrigh, agus bhiodh i gabhail orra, agus ga cuir amach air an dorus. Chuir i a bhuachailleach nan caorach i, agus cha robh i tabhart dh' i na dh' fhoghnadh dh' i. Agus bha caora bhiorach 'glas 'san treud a bha

---

* The words in Gaelic have a sound that might be an imitation of the note of a singing bird; the vowel sounds are *ui* and *oi*, and there are many soft consonants.

tighinn le biadh a' h-ionsuidh. Bha a Bhanrigh a gabhail iongantas gun robh i fanach beo, agus nach robh i faotuinn biadh ni 's leoir uaipe fein ; agus dh' innis i do chailleach nan cearc e. Smuainich cailleach nan cearc gun cuireadh i a nighean fein a dh' fhaireachdainn ciamar a bha i faotinn biadh. Agus chaidh ni mhaol charach nighean chailleach nan cearc a bhuachailleachd nan caorach le nighean na Banrigh. Cha tigeadh a chaora d'a h-ionsuidh fhad 's bha an ni' mhaol charach an sin, 's bha ni' mhaol charach a' fanach fad an la' leatha. Bha nighean na Banrigh 'gabhail fadail arson a biadh, agus thubhairt i ri ni' mhaol charach. " Cuir do cheann air mo ghlùn agus fasgabhaidh mi thu." Agus chuir ni' mhaol charach a ceann air glun nighinn na Banrigh agus choidil i. Thainig a chaora le biadh a dh' ionsuidh nighinn na Banrigh.

Ach bha an t-sùil a bh' ann an cùl cinn nighean mhaol charach nighean chailleach nan cearc fosgailte, 's chunnaic i na bha dol air aghaidh. Agus an uair a dhuisg i dh' fhalbh i dhachaidh, agus dh' innis i e d'a mathair, agus chaidh cailleach nan cearc agus dh' innis i do'n Bhanrigh e. 'Nuair a thuig a Bhanrigh cia mar bha an nighean a faotuinn biadh cha'n fhoghnadh ni air bi dhi ach gun rachadh a chaora a mharbhadh. Thainig a chaora a dh' ionnsuidh nighinn na Banrigh agus thubhairt i ri, "Tha iad a dol gum' mharbhadh ; ach goid thusa mo chroicinn agus truis mo chnamhan agus rol 'n am' chroicionn iad, agus thig mi beo, agus thig mi a'd' ionsuidh a rìs." Chaidh a chaora a mharbhadh, agus ghoid nighean an Righ a croicinn agus thrus i a cnàmhan agus a crodbain, agus rol i iad 'sa chroicinn ; ach dhiochuimhnich i na crodhain bheaga. Thainig a chaora beo aris, ach bha i crùpach. Thainig i dh' ionsuidh nighean an Righ 's ceum crùpach aice 's thubhairt i rithe. "Rinn thu mar a dh' iarr mi ort, ach dhichuimhnich thu na crodhain bheaga." Is bha i cumail biadh rithe an deigh sin. Bha Prionnsa òg ann a bha sealgadh, 's a' tighinn tric seachad orra, agus chunnaic e cho boidheach 's bha i, 's fharaid e, "Co i?" agus dh' innis i dha. Agus ghabh e gaol d' i. Agus bha e 'tighinn bidheanta an rathad. Ach thug nighean mhaol charach nighean chailleach nan cearc an aire dha agus dh' innis i d'a mathair e. Agus chaidh cailleach nan cearc agus dh' innis i e do'n Bhanrigh. Bha 'Bhanrigh toileach fios fhaotuinn co am fear a bh' ann. Agus dh' iarr cailleach nan cearc gus an d' fhuair i mach co e, agus dh' innis i do'n Bhanrigh. 'N uair a chuala a Bhanrigh co bh' ann bha i toileach a nighean fein a chuir 'na rathad, agus thug i stigh nighean na ceud Bhanrigh, agus chuir i a nighean fein a bhuachailleachd na h' àite, agus bha i toirt air nighean na ceud Bhanrigh a chòcaireachd agus na h-uile seirbhis a dheanamh tiomchioll an tighe. Bha nighean na ceud Bhanrigh amach sgriob, agus choinnich am Prionnsa orra, agus thug e dh' i paidhir do bhrògan òir. Agus bha e toileach a faicinn aig an t-searmoin, ach cha leigeadh a muime leatha dol ann. Ach 'n uair a dh' fhalbhadh càch dheanadh ise deas, agus dh'fhalbhadh i 'n an deigh, agus shuidhibh i far am faicibh e i; ach dh' éireadh i agus dh' fhalbhadh i mun sgoileadh an sluagh, agus bhitheadh i aig an tigh, agus na h' uile nith an ordugh mun tigeadh a muime. Ach air an treas uair a bha i ann bha am Prionnsa toileach falbh leatha, agus shuidh e dluth do'n dorus, agus, 'n uair a dh' fhalbh ise, bha esan a cumail suil orra, agus dh' eirich e, agus dh' fhalbh e as a deigh. Bha ise 'ruidh dhachaidh, agus chaill i h-aon d'a brògan 's a pholl, agus thuair esan a bhròg. Agus a chionn nach b' urrainn dha a faicinn thubhart e gum b'e an te aig an robh cas a fhreagradh a bhrog dhi a bhean a bhitheadh aigesan. Bha a Bhanrigh toileach gu freagradh a bhrog a'n nighinn aice fein, agus chuir i nighean na ceud Bhanrigh am folach air alt 's nach biodh i r'a fhaicinn gus am faiceadh i am freagradh a bhròg a' nighinn fein. 'N uair a thainig am Pronnsa a dh' fheuchainn na broig orra bha a cas tuille 's mòr; ach bha i ro thoileach gu' freagradh a' bhròg i, agus bhruidhinn i ri cailleach nan cearc uime. Ghearr cailleach nan cearc bàrr nan laor d' i 's gun freagradh a bhròg, i, agus chaidh a bhròg orra 'n uair bha barr nan laor gearrta dhi. 'N uair a thainig la na bainnse chaidh nighean na ceud Bhanrigh chuir am folach an an cùil aig cùl an teine. 'N uair a bha an sluagh uile cruinn aig a bhanais, thainig eun chum na h' uinneig agus ghlaodh e. "Tha an fhuil 's a bhròig agus tha chos bhoidheach 'sa chùil aig cùl an teine." Thubhairt h-aon diubh, "Ciod e tha am beathach ud ag radh." Agus thubhairt a Bhanrigh, "'S comadh ciod tha am beathach ud ag radh cha 'n 'eil ann ach beathach mosach, gobach, breugach." Thainig an t-eun arìs chum na h' uinneig; agus an treas uair a thainig e thubhart am Prionnsa. "Theid sinn agus chi sinn ciod tha e ag radh." Agus dh' eirich e agus chaidh e mach agus ghlaodh an t-eun, "Tha'n fhuil 'sa bhròig 's tha chos bhoidheach sa' chùil aig cùl an teine." Phill e 'stigh agus dh' orduich e a chuil bh' aig cul an teine iarruidh. Agus dh' iarr iad i, agus thuair iad nighean na ceud Bhanrigh an sin, agus brògòir air a darna cois. Ghlan ian an fhuil as a bhròig eile, agus dh' fheuch iad orra i, agus bha a leith-bhreac air a chois eile. Dh' fhàg am Prionnsa nighean na Banrigh mu dheireadh, agus phòs e nighean na ceud Bhanrigh, agus thug e leis uapa i, agus bha i sona, saoibhir, na dheigh sin.

"He has an eye in the back of his head," is a common saying for some one preternaturally sharp.

This story has some resemblance to Argus, who had a hundred eyes, and slept with two at a time; and was set by Juno (a queen) to watch Io, a human being changed into a heifer.

The sheep that came alive and was lame, is like Norse mythology (*Edda*—Dasent's translation, p. 51). "Thorr took his he-goats and killed them both, and after that they were flain and borne to the kettle. . . . Then laid Thorr the goatskins away from the fire, and told the husband and his household they should cast the bones into the goatskins. . . . Thor . . hallowed the goatskins, then stood up the goats, and one of them was halt in one of his hind feet."

One of the people had broken the thigh for the marrow.

I know nothing in any story quite like the first part, but it is like Cinderella (Grimm, English, p. 81), where the birds and the shoe appear; but with a wholly different set of incidents. It is like One Eye, Two Eyes, and Three Eyes (p. 387); but in that story the church and the golden shoe do not appear.

See Grimm, vol. iii., p. 34, for numerous references to versions of Cinderella in books of all ages.

It has some resemblance to Bellin the Ram of the Countess Daulnoy.

The second part is closer to the Norse versions of Cinderella than to the English story, and may be compared with part of Katie Woodencloak, where the birds and the shoe appear; and where there is a going to church.

I have many Gaelic versions of the incidents, all of which resemble each other; the golden shoe is sometimes transferred to a man, which I take to be some confusion in the memory of the person who tells the story.

XLIV.

THE WIDOW'S SON.

From John MacPhie, South Uist, and Donald MacCraw, North Uist.

THERE was a poor fisher's widow in Eirinn, and she had one son; and one day he left his mother with a lump of a horse, and a man met him with a gun, a dog, and a falcon (gunna cu agus seobhag); and he said, "Wilt thou sell me the horse, son of the fisher in Eirinn?" and he said, "What wilt thou give me? Wilt thou give me thy gun and thy dog, and thy falcon?" And he said, "I will give them;" and the bargain was struck; and Iain, the fisher's son, went home. When his mother saw him she was enraged, and she beat him; and in the night he took the gun and went away to be a hunter.* He went and he went till he reached the house of a farmer, who was sitting there with his old wife. The farmer said, "It was fortune sent thee here with thy gun; there is a deer that comes every night to eat my corn, and she will not leave a straw." And they engaged Iain the fisherman's son to stay with them, and shoot the deer; and so he stayed; and on the morrow's day he went out, and when he saw the deer he put the gun to his eye to shoot her, and the lock was up; but when he would have fired, he saw the finest woman he ever

---

* MacCraw started him with a big bonnoch and a little one, and his mother's blessing.

saw before him, and he held his hand, and let down the gun, and let down the lock, and there was the deer eating the corn again.

Three times he did this, and then he ran after the deer to try to catch her.

(In the other version, he went out on three successive days. On the first, when he aimed he saw over the sight a woman's face and breast, while the rest remained a deer. "Don't fire at me, widow's son," said the deer; and he did not, and went home and did not tell what had happened. The next day when he aimed, the woman was free to the waist, but the rest was still deer; and on the third she was free; and she told the hunter that she was the king of Lochlin's daughter, enchanted by the old man, and that she would marry the hunter if he came to such a hill.)

The deer ran away, and he followed till they came to a house thatched with heather; and then the deer leaped on the house, and she said, "Go in now, thou fisher's son, and eat thy fill." He went in and there was a table spread with every kind of meat and drink, and no one within; for this was a robber's house, and they were away lifting spoil.

So the fisher's son went in, and as the deer had told him, he sat him down, and ate and drank; and when he had enough he went under a TOGSAID (hogshead).

He had not been long there when the twenty-four robbers came home, and they knew that some one had been at their food, and they began to grumble and dispute. Then the leader said, "Why will you dispute and quarrel? the man that has done this is here under the mouth of this hogshead, take him now, and let four of you go out and kill him."

So they took out Iain, the fisher's son, and four of

them killed him; and then they had their food and slept, and in the morning they went out as usual.

When they had gone the deer came where Iain was, and she shook SOL (wax) from her ear on the dead man, and he was alive and whole as he was before. "Now," said she, "trust me, go in and eat as thou didst yesterday."

So Iain, the fisher's son, went in and ate and drank as he had done; and when he had enough he went in under the mouth of the hogshead; and when the robbers came home, there was more of their food eaten than on the day before, and they had a worse dispute. Then the captain said, "The man that did it is there, go out now with him four of you, and kill him; and let those who went last night be killed also, because he is now alive." So the four robbers were slain, and Iain was killed again; and the rest of the robbers ate and drank, and slept; and on the morrow before dawn they were off again. Then the deer came, and she shook SOL from her right ear on Iain the fisher's son, and he was alive as well as before; in a burst of sweat.

That day Iain ate and drank, and hid as before; and when the robbers came home, the captain ordered the four who had gone out to be slain; and now there were eight dead; and four more killed Iain the fisher's son, and left him there. On the morrow the deer came as before, and Iain was brought alive; and the next day the robbers all killed each other.*

---

* I am sure this has been a numerical puzzle, such as "the shealing of Duan's men." As it now stands there would remain four robbers who had not earned death like the rest, and it must be wrong. Perhaps this is the problem :—

		Alive. Dead.
	John and 24 robbers . . .	= 25.
1.	John killed by 4 men	= 24 to 0, and has 2d life.

On that day the deer came, and Iain followed her to the white house of a window, where there lived an old hag, and Gille Caol dubh, a slender dark lad, her son, and the deer said, "Meet me to-morrow at eleven in yonder church," and she left him there.

On the morrow he went, but the carlin stuck a BIOR NIMH, spike of hurt, in the outside of the door post; and when he came to the church he fell asleep, and the black lad was watching him. Then they heard the sweetest music they ever heard coming, and the finest lady that ever was came and tried to waken him; and when she could not, she wrote her name under his arm, NIGHEAN RIGH RIOGHACHD BAILLE FO' THUINN, the daughter of the king of the kingdom of the town under waves; and she said that she would come to-morrow, and she went away. When she was gone he awoke, and the slim black lad told him what had happened, but did not tell him that her name was written under his arm.

On the next day it was the same, the sweetest of music was heard, and the lady came, and she laid his head on her knee and dressed his hair; and when she could not awaken him, she put a snuff-box in his pocket, and cried, and went away.

---

2. John and the 4 = 5 killed by 4 each = 20 to 4, and has 3d life.
3. The 20 have all earned death, and kill each other, and John remains, having had 2 lives in addition to the 1 which he first had, which makes up the usual mystic number 3. And so 3 lives dispose of 24.

Or this :—

		Alive. Dead.
	John and 24 robbers . . .	= 25.
1.	John killed once by 4 men . .	= 24 to 0, and has 2d life.
2.	John and the 4 by 2 each, 10 men	= 20 to 4, and has 3d life.

3. There are ten guilty and ten who should kill them ; they kill each other, and so the 3 lives dispose of the 24.

This, however, is but a guess.

On the third day she said she would never come again, and she went away home; and when she was gone he awoke.

("Now, John MacPhie," said I, "did she not come in a chariot with white horses?"

"Do thou put in what I tell thee," said the narrator.

"Did *she* put the box in his pocket?"

"Yes she did; now, go on, there is no one in Uist who can tell this story as I can; I have known it for more than sixty years.")

(MacCraw had said that the old woman gave the lad a great pin to stick in his coat; that he went to meet the lady on a hill, and then he slept. Then came the lady dressed all in white in a chariot, "CARBAD," drawn by four milk-white steeds; and she laid his head in her lap and dressed his hair, and tried to waken him, but in vain. Then she dragged him down the hill, but he slept on; and she left him, but bid the black rough-skinned lad tell him to be there on the morrow. When she was gone he awoke, and the lad told him. On the morrow he went as before, and the lad stuck the pin in his coat, and he slept; then came the lady with a sorrowful face, and she was dressed all in grey, and her chariot was drawn by grey steeds; and she did as before but could not rouse him. On the next day he would have none of the big pin; but the old wife gave the lad an apple, and when they sat on the hill thirst struck him, and the lad gave him the apple, and he ate it, and slept again. Then came the lady dressed all in black, with four black steeds in her chariot; and she laid his head in her lap and dressed his hair, and she put a ring on his finger, and she wept; and as she went away she said, "He will never see me again, for I must go home.")

When the lad awoke (said John MacPhie), Bha e falbh gus an robh dubhadh air a bhonan, toladh air a chasan, neoil dubha doracha na oidhche a tighinn neoil sithe seamh an latha ga fhagail gus an robh eoin bhega an t-shleibh a gabhail an am bun gach preas a b' fhaisge dhaibh na chéile.

He was going till there was blackening on his soles, holes in his feet, the dark black clouds of the night coming, the quiet peaceful clouds of day leaving him, till the little mountain birds were betaking themselves about the root of each bush that was nearest to them; and he went till he reached the house of a wife, who said, "All hail! son of the great fisher in Eirinn, I know thy journey and thine errand; come in and I will do what I can for thee (*and here came in a lot of queer language which I could not catch*). So he went in, and on the morrow she said, "I have a sister who dwells on the road; it is a walk of a year and a day, but here are a pair of old brown shoes with holes in them, put them on and thou wilt be there in an instant; and when thou art there, turn their toes to the known, and their heels to the unknown, and they will come home; and so he did.

The second sister did the very same; but she said, "I have a third sister, and she has a son, who is herd to the birds of the air, and sets them asleep, perhaps he can help thee;" and then she gave him another pair of shoes, and he went to the third sister.

The third said she did not know how to help him farther, but perhaps her son might, when he came home; and he, when he came, proposed that the cow should be killed; and after some talk, that was done, and the meat was cooked, and a bag made of the hide, red side out; and John, the fisher's son, was put in with his son, bnt he left the dog and the falcon. He had not been long in the bag when the Creveenach* came, for she had a nest in an island, and she raised the red bag; but she had not gone far when she dropped it in the sea. Then the other one came, and she gripped to it firmly with her claws; and at last they left the bag on the island where all the birds of the air were wont to sleep.† He came out of the bag; and he was for a day and year living on what he had, and on the birds which he killed with his gun; but at last there was nothing more to eat, and he thought he would die there. Then he searched his pockets for food, and found the box which the lady had put there; he opened it, and three came out, and they said, "Eege gu djeege,‡ master, good, what shall we do?" and he said, "Take me to the realm of the king under the waves;" and in a moment there he was.§

---

* This word is unknown to me. It was explained to mean a bird like a large eagle.

† MacCraw skipped all the old women and took him at once to an old man, who was herding a cow, and said he would rather do anything else, but his wife made him do it. He went home with him, and after much chaffering bought the cow for as much gold as would go from her nose to her tail. Then he and all that he had were put into the hide with the meat; and with the wind off the strand (traigh) he had himself thrown into the sea. The great birds pounced on the red bag, and carried him to their nest, where he killed the young ones, and rolled over the rock into the sea. He was lifted again by the birds and landed in Lochlinn.

‡ The explanation of these sounds was, that it was "as if they were asking." The sounds mean nothing that I know in any language.

§ MacCraw said that the box had been given to him by his grandfather. It first appeared in Lochlann; and "he" that was within said, "Good master, good master, what shall 'we' do?" The hunter had then been recognized by the king's daughter; so he ordered a palace to be built.

He went up to the house of a weaver; and after he had been there for some time, the weaver came home with flesh, and other things from the great town; and he gave him both meat and lodging.

On the morrow the weaver told him that there was to be a horse race in the town; and he bethought him of the box, and opened it; and three came out and said "Eege gu djeege, Master, good, what shall we do?" and he said, "Bring me the finest horse that ever was seen, and the grandest dress, and glass shoes;" and he had them all in a minute. Now he who won the races was to have the king's daughter to wife. Then he went, and won, and the king's daughter saw him; but he never stayed; he went back to the weaver, and threw three "mam" handsfull of gold into his apron, and said that a great gentleman, who won the race, had given him the gold; and then he broke the weaver's loom, and tore the cloth to bits.

Next day there was a dog race; and he got a finer dress, and a splendid dog, by the help of the box, and won, and threw handsfull of gold to the weaver, and did more mischief in his house.

On the third day it was a falcon race, and he did the very same; and he was the man who was to marry the princess, but he was nowhere to be found when the race was over.

Then (as happens in plenty of other stories) the whole kingdom was gathered, and the winner of the prize was nowhere to be found. At last they came to the weaver's house, and the hunter's beard was grown over his face, and he was dirty and travel-stained; and he had given all the gold to the weaver, and smashed everything; and he was so dirty and ugly, and good for nothing, that he was to be hanged. But when he was under the gallows. he was to make the gallows speech, SEARMOIN NA CROICHE; and he put up his arm, and the king's daughter saw the name which she had written there, and knew him; and she called out, "Hold your hands, for every one in the kingdom shall die if that man is hurt." And then she took him by the hand, and they were to be married.

Then she dressed him grandly, and asked how he had found her out; and he told her; and she asked where he had found the box; and he said, when he was in extremity in the island; and then she took him by the hand before her father, and all the kings, and she said she would marry the fisher's son, for he it was who had freed her from spells.*

"Oh kings," said she, "if one of you were killed

---

* Here, according to MacCraw, he built a palace; and one of the rivals stole the magic box, and carried off the princess and the palace to the realm of rats; and when the widow's son saw that the palace was gone he was very sorrowful, and went down to the shore; and there he met with an old man, who took pity on him, and offered to help him. He threw a rod into the sea, and it became a boat; and he said, "Here's for thee a he-cat, and he will sail with thee;" and the cat sat at the helm, and they hoisted the three tall towering sails, etc., etc. (*The old passage descriptive of the voyage.*) When they reached the realm of rats, the first rat that the cat saw he caught; and the rat said, "Thine is my lying down and rising up; let me go and I will serve thee." So the cat let him go; and the man said, "Now steal for me the snuff-box that the man in the castle has." "That," said the rat, "is easy, for it is on the window ledge;" and the rat stole the box. Then the man opened it, and "*they*" said "Good master, good master, what shall '*we*' do?" and he said, "Take me and my wife, and that castle, back to Lochlann; and be knocking each other's heads about till we arrive, for that you brought it here." So they were all carried back to Lochlann, and then the right wedding was held.

to-day, the rest would fly; but this man put his trust in me, and had his head cut off three times. Because he has done so much for me, I will marry him rather than any one of the great men who have come to marry me; for many kings have tried to free me from the spells, and none could do it but Iain here, the fisher's son."

Then a great war ship was fitted up, and sent for the old carlin who had done all the evil, and for her black slim son; and seven fiery furnaces were set in order, and they were burnt, and the ashes were let fly with the wind; and a great wedding was made, and "I left left them in the realm."

This story was first told to me on the 2d September 1859 by MacCraw, as we walked along the road. He said that he had learned it as a child from an old wife in North Uist, whose cottage was the resort of all the children for miles and miles. He has often gone himself six or seven miles in the snow, and he used to sit with dozens of other bairns about her fire, mute and motionless for the best part of the night. The children brought offerings of tobacco, which they got from older people, as best they could, and for each bit the old woman gave a story. He "never heard her like."

The story lasted for several miles, and my companion said that he had forgotten much of it. He had forgotten nearly all the measured prose phrases with which, as he said, the story was garnished, and he said he had not heard it for many years.

It seemed to resemble the story of Aladdin in some incidents, but my companion said that he had never heard of the Arabian Nights. He said that in Kinross and Perthshire it is the custom for the hinds and farm-labourers to assemble and repeat stories in broad Scotch, which closely resemble those told in the islands, but which are not garnished with measured prose. He thinks that as there are many Highland servants in the country, they tell the heads of their stories, and then others repeat them in Lowland Scotch. This may be, and in like manner the Highland servants may pick up and carry home, and repeat in Gaelic, scraps of such books as the Arabian Nights. Still, as such stories do resemble books quite beyond the reach of the people, the resemblance which this bore to the Arabian Nights *may* be due to common origin.

On the 5th I asked MacPhie if he knew the story. He did; and I got him to tell it twice over. It was vain to attempt to make him dictate, for he broke down directly he was stopped, or his pace altered; and I could not write Gaelic, at all events, fast enough to do any good; so I took notes in English. The Magic Box was in both versions, but the transport of the castle to a foreign country, and back by the help of the box, was not in old MacPhie's story.

There is a long story about the country of rats, of which I have only heard part as yet.

Bior Nimh, spike of hurt, and the big pin, may be "the thorn of sleep" referred to in the introduction to Norse Tales, as mentioned in the Volsung Tale.

The town under the waves is common in Gaelic stories; the phrase probably arose from the sinking of hills beneath the horizon as a boat sails away from the shore. In another story it is said, Thog eud Eilean—they "raised an Island"—when they were approaching one.

The bag of skin with the man inside, is remarkably like a tradition of the skin boats in which the old inhabitants of Caledonia used to invade England.

The great birds belong to popular tales of many lands, and are common in Gaelic. I have one story in which the hero is carried into a dragon's nest, and does much the same as this one did.

XLV.

MAC-A-RUSGAICH.

From John Dewar, April 1860.

THERE was (at) some time a tenant, and he was right bad to his servants, and there was a pranky man who was called Gille Neumh Mac-a-Rusgaich (holy lad son of Skinner), and he heard tell of him, and he went to the fair, and he took a straw in his mouth, to shew that he was for taking service.

The dour tenant came the way, and he asked Mac-a-Rusgaich if he would take service; and Mac-a-Rusgaich said that he would take it if he could find a good master; and Mac-a-Rusgaich said,

"What shall I have to do if I take with thee?"

And the dour tenant said, "Thou wilt have to herd the mountain moor."

And Mac-a-Rusgaich said, "I will do that."

And the tenant said, "And thou wilt have to hold the plough."*

And Mac-a-Rusgaich said, "I will do that."

"And thou wilt have ever so many other matters to do."

And Mac-a-Rusgaich said, "Will these matters be hard to do?"

And the other said, "They will not be (so), I will

---

* Crann, a tree.

but ask thee to do the thing that thou art able to do; but I will put into the covenant that if thou dost not answer, thou must pay me two wages."

And Mac-a-Rusgaich said, "I will put into the covenant, if thou askest me to do anything but the thing which I am able to do, thou must give me two wages."

And they agreed about that.

And the dour tenant said, "I am putting it into the covenant that if either one of us takes the rue, that a thong shall be taken out of his skin, from the back of his head to his heel."

And Mac-a-Rusgaich said, "Mind that thou hast said that, old carle."

And he took service with the hard tenant, and he went home to him.

The first work that Mac-a-Rusgaich was bidden to do, was to go to the moss to cast peats, and Mac-a-Rusgaich asked for his morning meal before he should

---

The following was omitted by the collector, and inserted by him in his revise of the Gaelic:—"There was (at) some time a tenant, and he was right bad to his servants; and when the time of service was nearly ended, he used to fix a pretext for quarrelling with them. He would cast out with them and send them away without their wages. And he sent away many of his servants in this way. And there was a pranky man whose name was Saints servant, son of the fleecer (Gilleneaomh Mac-a-Rusgaich), and he said that he would take service with the dour tenant, and that he would give him trick about,* that he would be as far north as the dour tenant might be south, Mac-a-Rusgaich went to the fair of Peevish fair, and he took a straw in his mouth, to shew that he was for taking service."

---

* The original meaning of the Gaelic phrase is to take a turn out of a man,—untwist his turns. The expression then conveys the idea of a man winding coils about another; and one with more craft unwinding them; and the next phrase is as metaphorical.

go, so that he need not come for it, and he got as much meat as they used to allow the servants at one meal, and he ate that; and he asked for his dinner, so that he need no stop at mid-day, and he got the allowance which there was for dinner, and he ate that; and he asked for his supper, so that he need not come home at night, and they gave him that, and he ate that; and he went where his master was, and he asked him,

"What are thy servants wont to do after their supper?"

And his master said to him, "It is their wont to put off their clothes and go to lie down."

And Mac-a-Rusgaich went where his bed was, and he put off his clothes, and he went to lie down.

The mistress went where the man of the town (the master) was and she asked him, "What sort of a servant he had got there, that he had eaten three meals at one meal, and had gone to lie down?" And the master went where Mac-a-Rusgaich was, and he said to him,

"Why art thou not at work?"

And Mac-a-Rusgaich said, "It is that thou thyself saidst to me that it was thy servants' wont, when they had got their supper, to put off their clothes and go to lie down."

And the master said, "And why didst thou eat the three meals together?"

And Mac-a-Rusgaich said, "It is that the three meals were little enough to make a man content."

And the master said, "Get up and go to thy work."

And Mac-a-Rusgaich said, "I will get up, but I must get meat as I need, or my work will accord. I am but to do as I am able. See! art thou taking the rue, old carle?"

"I am not, I am not," said the carle, and Mac-a-Rusgaich got his meat better after that.

And there was another day and the carle asked Mac-a-Rusgaich to go to hold the plough in a dale that was down from the house, and Mac-a-Rusgaich went away, and he reached (the place) where the plough was, and he caught the stilts in his hands and there he stood.

And his master came where he was, and his master said to him.

"Why art thou not making the red land?" * And Mac-a-Rusgaich said, "It is not my bargain to make a thraive, but to hold the plough; and thou seest that I am not letting her go away."

And his master said, "Adversity and calamities be upon thee!"

And Mac-a-Rusgaich said, "Adversity and calamities be on thyself, old carle! Art thou taking the rue of the bargain that thou madest?"

"Oh! I am not, I am not," said the old carle.

---

* Another way of telling this part:—Thainig an tuathanach do ionnsaidh, 's dh' fharraid e deth cia air-son nach eil thu a deanamh an deargadh: Agus Thubhairt Mac-a-Rusgaich ris, cha n è mo bhargansa deargadh a dheanamh, ach an crann a chumail, 's tha thu a faicinn nach eil mi e leigidh leatha falbh; na 'm bithinn a deargadh an talamh, cha b' ann a cu mail a chroinn a bhithinn.

The farmer came to him and asked him, why art thou not making the red land? And Mac-a-Rusgaich said, it was not my bargain to do the reddening, but to hold the plough; and thou seest that I am not letting her go away. If I were reddening the land, it would not be holding the plough that I would be.

In some districts, the farmers call the ploughed land the red land, and the unploughed land white land.

JOHN DEWAR.

"But if thou wilt give me another reward for it, I will make a ploughing," said Mac-a-Rusgaich.

"Oh, I will give, I will give it!" said the carle; and they made a bargain about the thraive.

And there was a day, and the hard tenant asked Mac-a-Rusgaich to go to the mountain moor to look if he could see anything wrong, and Mac-a-Rusgaich went up to the mountain.* And when he saw his own time he came home, and his master asked him,

"Was each thing right in the mountain?" and Mac-a-Rusgaich said,

"The mountain himself was all right."

And the hard tenant said, "That is not what I am asking; but were the neighbours' cattle on their own side?"

And Mac-a-Rusgaich said, "If they were they were, and if they were not let-a-be. It is my bargain to herd the mountain, and I will keep the mountain where it is."

And the carle said, "Adversity and calamities be upon thee, thou boy!"

And he said, "Adversity and calamities be on thyself, old carle! Art thou taking the rue that thou hast made such a bargain?"

"I am not, I am not!" said the dour tenant; "I will give thee another reward for herding the cattle."

And Mac-a-Rusgaich said, "If I get another reward, I will take in hand if I see the neighbours' cattle on thy ground that I will turn them back, and if I see thy cattle on the neighbours' ground I will turn them back to thine own ground; but though some of them should be lost, I will not take in hand to find them; but if thou

* Against, or at the mountain.

askest me to go to seek them, I will go, and if I get them I will bring them home."

"And the dour tenant had for it but to agree with Mac-a-Rusgaich, and to give Mac-a-Rusgaich another reward for herding his cattle.

Next day the carle himself went to the hill, and he could not see his heifers; he sought for them, but could not find them. He went home, and he said to Mac-a-Rusgaich,

"Thou must go thyself to search for the heifers, Mac-a-Rusgaich, I could not find them this day; and go thou to search for them, and search for them until thou find them?"

And Mac-a-Rusgaich said, "And where shall I go to seek them?"

The old carle said, "Go and search for them in the places where thou thinkest that they are; and search for them in places where thou dost not suppose them to be."

Mac-a-Rusgaich said, "Well, then, I will do that."

The old carle went into the house; and Mac-a-Rusgaich got a ladder, and set it up against the house; he went up upon the house, and he began at pulling the thatch off the house, and throwing it down. And before the carle came out again, the thatch was about to be all but a very little off the house, and the rafters bare; and Mac-a-Rusgaich was pulling the rest and throwing it down.

The old carle said, "Adversity and calamity be upon thee, boy; what made thee take the thatch off the house in that way?"

Mac-a-Rusgaich said, "It is because that I am searching for the heifers in the thatch of the house."

The old carle said, "How art thou seeking the heifers

in the thatch of the house, where thou art sure that they are not."

Mac-a-Rusgaich said, "Because thou thyself saidst to me to search for them in places where I thought that they were; and also in places where I did not suppose them to be; and there is no place where I have less notion that they might be in than in the thatch of the house."

And the carle said, "Adversity and calamity be upon thee, lad."

Mac-a-Rusgaich said, "Adversity and calamity be upon thyself, old carle; art thou taking the rue that thou desiredst me to search for the heifers in places where I did not suppose them to be?"

"I am not, I am not," said the carle. "Go now and seek them in places where it is likely that they may be."

"I will do so," said Mac-a-Rusgaich; and Mac-a-Rusgaich went to seek the heifers, and he found them, and brought them home.

Then his master desired Mac-a-Rusgaich to go to put the the thatch on the house, and to make the house as water-tight to keep out rain as he was able. Mac-a-Rusgaich did so, and they were pleasant for a while after that.

The dour tenant was going to a wedding, and he asked Mac-a-Rusgaich when the evening should come, to put a saddle on the horse, and to go to the house of the wedding to take him home; and he said to him,

"When it is near the twelfth hour, cast an ox eye on the side where I am, and I will know that it is near the time to go home."*

* Damh shuil—an ox eye. To cast an ox eye at any one means, according to Dewar, to look with a wry face, and open

"I will do that," said Mac-a-Rusgaich.

When the tenant went to the wedding, Mac-a-Rusgaich went to put the stots into the fang, and he took a knife and took their eyes out, and he put the eyes in his pocket: and when the night came, Mac-a-Rusgaich put the saddle on the horse, and he went to the wedding house to seek his master, and he reached the wedding house, and he went into the company, and he sat till it was near upon the twelfth hour.

And then he began at throwing the eye of a stot at the carle at the end of each while, and at last the old carle noticed him, and he said to him,

"What art thou doing?"

And Mac-a-Rusgaich said, "I am casting an ox-eye on the side that thou art, for that it is now near upon the twelfth hour."

And the old carle said, "Dost thou think thyself that thou hast gone to take the eyes out of the stots?"

And Mac-a-Rusgaich said, "It is not thinking it I am at all; I am sure of it. Thou didst ask me thyself to cast an ox eye the side thou mightest be when it was near upon the twelfth hour, and how could I do that unless I should have taken the eyes out of the stots?"

And the tenant said, "Adversity and calamities be upon thee, thou boy."

And Mac-a-Rusgaich said, "Adversity and calamities on thyself, old carle! Art thou taking the rue that thou didst ask me to do it?"

"I am not, I am not!" said the carle; and they went home together, and there was no more about it that night.

---

the eyes wide, and stare at a person—as a signal. The idiom, to cast an eye, is common to Gaelic and English; and so is the expression, to cast a sheep's eye.

And the end of a day or two after, his master asked asked Mac-a-Rugaich to go up to the gates at the top and make a sheep footpath.*

"I will do that," said Mac-a-Rusgaich; and he went, and he put the sheep into the fang, and he cut their feet off, and he made a stair with the sheeps' legs, and he went back where his master was, and his master said to him,

"Didst thou that?"

And Mac-a-Rusgaich said, "I did. Thou mayest go thyself and see."

And the master went to see the sheep footpath that Mac-a-Rusgaich had made, and when he arrived and saw the sheeps' legs in the path, he went into a rage, and he said, "Adversity and calamities be upon thee, boy; what made thee cut the legs off the sheep?"

And Mac-a-Rusgaich said, "Didst thou not ask me thyself to make a sheep footpath; and how should I make a sheep footpath unless I should cut the legs of the sheep? See! Art thou taking the rue that thou didst ask me to do it, old carle?"

"I am not, I am not!" said his master.

"What have I to do again?" said Mac-a-Rusgaich.

"It is," said his master, "to clean and to wash the horses and the stable, both without and within."

---

* STAIR, a path or causeway in a wet bog.

CHASA, for the feet, or of the feet. CHAORACH, of sheep.

According to Dewar, a path made over a bog, when a gate happens to be where the ground is soft, or where peat moss is. If sheep be often driven through such a gate, the pathway soon gets soft, so that the sheep sink in it. It is repaired by cutting brushwood or heather, and laying it on the soft place with a covering of gravel, and is called "Stair chasa caorach."

I know the kind of road meant, but I never heard the name.—J. F. C.

And Mac-a-Rushgaich went and he cleaned out the stable, and he washed the walls on the outside, and he washed the stable on the inside ; he washed the horses, and he killed them, and he took their insides out of them, and he washed their insides, and he went where his master was, and he asked him what he was to do again ; and his master said to him to put the horses in what concerned them (harness) in the plough, and to take a while at ploughing.

Mac-a-Rusgaich said, "The horses won't answer me."

"What ails them ?" said his master.

"They won't walk for me," said Mac-a-Rusgaich.

"Go and try* them," said his master.

And Mac-a-Rusgaich went where the horses were, and he put a morsel of one of them into his mouth, and he went back where his master was, and he said, "They have but a bad taste."

"What art thou saying ?" said his master.

The master went where his horses were, and when he saw them, and the inside taken out of them, and washed and cleaned, he said, "What is the reason of this ?"

"It is," said Mac-a-Rusgaich, "that thou thyself didst ask me to clean and to wash both the horses and the stable both without and within, and I did that. Art thou taking the rue ?" said Mac-a-Rusgaich.

"I had rather that I had never seen thee," said the master.

"Well, then," said Mac-a-Rusgaich "thou must give me three wages, or else a thong of thy skin shall be taken from the back of thy head down to thy heel."

The dour tenant said that he had rather the thong

*** Feuch, is either taste or try in the Gaelic.**

to be taken out of his skin, from the back of his head to his heel, than give the money to a filthy clown like Mac-a-Rusgaich.

And according to law the dour tenant was tied, and a broad thong taken from the back of his head down his back. And he cried out that he had rather give even the money away than that the thong should be cut any longer; and he paid the money, and he was forced to be a while under the leeches, and he was a dour man no longer.

After that Mac-a-Rusgaich was set to be a servant to a giant that was bad to his servants.

Mac-a-Rusgaich reached the giant, and he said, "Thy servant is come."

The giant said, "If thou be servant to me, thou must keep even work with me, or else I will break thy bones as fine as meal."*

Said Mac-a-Rusgaich, "What if I beat thee?"

"If thou beatest me," said the giant, "thou shalt have like wages."

"What are we going to do, then?" said Mac-a-Rusgaich.

"It is (this)," said the giant; "we will go to bring home faggots."

And they went and they reached the wood, and the giant began to gather every root that was thicker than the rest, and Mac-a-Rusgaich began to gather every top that was slenderer than the others.

The giant looked and he said,

"What art thou doing so?"

And Mac-a-Rusgaich said, "I am for that we should

---

* PRONNOIN, coarse, unsifted oatmeal; poundings.

take the whole wood with us instead of leaving a part of it useless behind us."

Said the giant, "We are long enough at this work; we will take home these burdens, but we will get other work again."

The next work they went to was to cut a swathe; and the giant asked Mac-a-Rusgaich to go first. Mac-a-Rusgaich would mow the swathe, and he began and he went round about short on the inner side, and the giant had to go a longer round on the outside of him.

"What art thou doing so?" said the giant.

"I," said Mac-a-Rusgaich, "am for that we should mow the park at one cut instead of turning back every time we cut the swathe, and we shall have no time lost at all."

The giant saw that his cut would be much longer than the cut of Mac-a-Rusgaich, and he said, "We are long enough at this work, we will go to another work. We will go and we will thresh the corn."

And they went to thresh the corn, and they got the flails, and they began to work. And when the giant would strike the sheaf, he would make it spring over the baulk (rafter), and when Mac-a-Rusgaich would strike it it would lie down on the floor.

He would strike, and Mac-a-Rusgaich would say to the giant,

"Thou art not half hitting it. Wilt thou not make it crouch as I am doing?"

But the stronger the giant struck, the higher leaped the sheaf, and Mac-a-Rusgaich was laughing at him; and the giant said,

"We are long enough at this work; I will try thee in another way. We will go and try which of us can cast a stone strongest in the face of a crag that is beyond the fall."

"I am willing," said Mac-a-Rusgaich; and the giant went and he gathered the hardest stones he could find. And Mac-a-Rusgaich went and he got clay, and he rolled it into little round balls, and they went to the side of the fall.

The giant threw a stone at the face of the crag, and the stone went in splinters, and he said to Mac-a-Rusgaich,

"Do that, boy."

Mac-a-Rusgaich threw a *dudan*, lump of the clay, and it stuck in the face of the crag, and he said to the giant, "Do that, old carl."

And the giant would throw as strongly as he could, but the more pith the giant would send with the stone he would throw, the smaller it would break. And Mac-a-Rusgaich would throw another little ball of the clay, and he would say,

"Thou art not half throwing it. Wilt thou not make the stone stick in the crag as I am doing?"

And the giant said, "We are long enough at this work; we will go and take our dinner, and then we will see which of us can best throw the stone of force (putting stone)."

"I am willing," said Mac-a-Rusgaich, and they went home.

They began at their dinner, and the giant said to Mac-a-Rusgaich,

"Unless thou eatest of bread and cheese as much as I eat, a thong shall be taken out of thy skin, from the back of thy head to thy heel."

"Make seven of it," said Mac-a-Rusgaich, "on covenant that seven thongs shall be taken out of thy skin, from the back of thy head to thy heel, unless thou eatest as much as I eat."

"Try thee, then," said the giant.

"Stop then till I get a drink," said Mac-a-Rusgaich; and he went out to get a drink, and he got a leathern bag, and he put the bag between his shirt and his skin, and he went in where the giant was, and he said to the giant, "Try thee now."

The two began to eat the bread and the cheese, and Mac-a-Rusgaich was putting the bread and the cheese into the bag that he had in under his shirt, but at last the giant said,

"It is better to cease than burst."

"It is better even to burst than to leave good meat," said Mac-a-Rusgaich.

"I will cease," said the giant.

"The seven thongs shall be taken from the back of thy head to thy heel," said Mac-a-Rusgaich.

"I will try thee yet," said the giant.

"Thou hast thy two choices," said Mac-a-Rusgaich.

The giant got curds and cream, and he filled a cup for himself and another cup for Mac-a-Rusgaich.

"Let's try who of us is best now," said the giant.

"It's not long till that is seen," said Mac-a-Rusgaich. "Let's try who can soonest drink what is in the cup."

And Mac-a-Rusgaich drank his fill, and he put the rest in the bag, and he was done before the giant.

And he said to the giant, "Thou art behind."

The giant looked at him, and he said, "Ceasing is better than bursting."

"Better is bursting itself than to leave good meat," said Mac-a-Rusgaich.

"We will go out and try which of us can throw the

stone of force the furthest, before we do more," said the giant.

"I am willing," said Mac-a-Rusgaich. And they went out where the stone was, but the giant was so full that he could not stoop to lift it.

"Lift that stone and throw it," said the giant.

"The honour of beginning the beginning is to be thine own," said Mac-a-Rusgaich.

The giant tried to lift the stone, but he could not stoop. Mac-a-Rusgaich tried to stoop, and he said,

"Such a belly as this shall not be hindering me," and he drew a knife from a sheath that was at his side, and he put the knife in the bag that was in front of him, and he let out all that was within, and he said, "There is more room without than within," and he lifted the stone and threw it, and he said to the giant, "Do that."

"Canst thou not throw it further than that?" said the giant.

"Thou has not thrown it as far as that same," said Mac-a-Rusgaich.

"Over here thy knife!" said the giant.

Mac-a-Rusgaich reached his knife to the giant. The giant took the knife, and he stabbed the knife into his belly, and he let out the meat; and the giant fell to earth, and Mac-a-Rusgaich laughed at him, and the giant found death.

Mac-a-Rusgaich went in to the giant's house, and he got his gold and silver, then he was rich, and then he went home fully pleased.

SGEULACHD MHAC A RUSGAICH.

BHA uaireiginn Tuathanach ann 's bha e ro dhona ri sheirbhisich, agus tra a bhiodh an tiom-seirbhis aca dlùth air a bhith aig crioiche, gheibhidh e leisgeul gu connsachadh a dheanamh riuth, thileadh e a mach riutha, s chuireadh e air falbh iad gun an tuarasdal. Agus chuir e air falbh moran do a sheirbhishich air an doigh sin. Agus bha fear pratail ann do b' ainm Gillenaomh Mac-a-Rusgaich, 's chual e iomradh air s thubhairt e, gun gabhadh easan tuarasdal aig an tuathanach dhoirbh, s gun tugadh e car man seach as, gum bitheadh esan cho fada ma thuath, is a bhiodh an tuathanach doirbh ma dheas. Chaidh Mac-a-Rusgaich chun faighir na feill groig, s ghabh e sràbh na bheul, mar chomharradh gu 'n robh e los muinntearas a ghabhail.

Thainig an Tuathanach doiribh an rathad agus dh' fharraid e do Mac-a-Rusgaich a' gabhadh e muinntearas, 's thubhairt Mac-a-Rusgaich ga ghabhadh nam faigheadh e maighistear math ; 's thubhairt Mac-a-Rusgaich, " Ga-dé a bhiodhs agum ri dheanamh ma ghabhas mi agut ? " 'S thubhairt an tuathanach doiribh, " Bithidh agut ris a monadh a bhuachailleachd," 's thuirt Mac-a-Rusgaich, " Ni mi sin," 's thuirt an tuathnach, " 'S bithidh agut ris a chrann a chumail," 's thuirt Mac-a-Rusgaich, " Ni mi sin." " 'S bithidh na thuibhire do gnothaichean eile agut ri dheanamh cuideachd," 's thuirt Mac-a-Rusgaich, " Am bi na gnothaichean sin duillich a dheanamh ? " 's thuirt am fear eile, " Cha bhì, cha 'n iarr mise ort a dheanamh ach rud a 's urrainn duit a dheanamh. Ach cuiridh mi 'sa chumhnant, mar freagair thu, gu 'm feum thu dà thuarasdal a phaigh dhomhsa," 's thuirt Mac-a-Rusgaich " Cuiridh mise ann sa chumhnant ma dh' iarras tu orm rud air bhithe a dheanamh ach rud a 's urrainn mi a dheanamh, gu 'm feum thusa dà thuarasdal a thoirt domhsa ; " 's chòirt iad uime a sin.

Agus thubhairt an tuathanach doirbh, " Tha mise a cuir ann 'sa chumhnant ma ghabhas a h-aon air bith againn an t-aithreachas, gu 'n teid iall a thobhairt as a chraicionn o chùl a chinn gu 'shàil," 's thubhairt Mac-a-Rusgaich, " Cuimhnich gun dubhairt thu sin a bhodaich," 's ghabh e tuarasdal aig an Tuathanach dhoirbh, 's chaidh e dachaidh d' a ionnsaidh.

'Se chiad obair a chaidh iarraidh air Mac-a-Rusgaich a dheanamh, e a dhol do 'n mhonadh a thilgeadh mòine, 's dh' iarr Mac-a-

Rusgaich a bhiadh-maidne ma'm falbhadh e, 's nach ruigeadh e a leas tighinn dachaidh air a shon, 's fhuair e na bha iad a luathsachadh do bhiadh air seirbheisich aig aon trà, 's dh' ith e sin, 's dh' iarr e a dhinneir 's nach ruigeadh e a leas stad aig meadhon latha, 's fhuair e an luathsacha a bha air son a dhinneir, s dh'ith e sin, 's dh'iarr e a shuipeir 's nach ruigeadh e a leas tighinn dachaidh aig an oidhche, 's thug iad sin da, 's dh'ith e sin ; 's chaidh e far an robh a mhaighistear, 's dh' fharraid e deth, "Ciod 's àbhaist do na seirbheisich agutsa a dheanadh an deigh an suipeir?" 'S thubhairt a mhaighistear ris, "Is àbhaist doibh an aodach a chuir diubh 's dol a luidh," 's dh' fhalbh Mac-a-Rusgaich far an robh a leaba, 's chuir e dheth aodach 's chaidh e a luidh.

Chaidh a bhana mhaighistear far an robh fear a bhaile, 's dh' fharraid i deth, "Gu-dé an seorsa gille a fhuair e an siud, gu'n d' ith e na tri tràithean a dh' aon trà, 's gu'n deachaidh e a luidh ?" 's chaidh a mhaighistear far an robh Mac-a-Rusgaich, 's thubhairt e ris, "Gar son nach eil thu aig obair?" 's thubhairt Mac-a-Rusgaich, "Tha gun dubhairt thu-fein rium, gu'm bè a b' àbhaist do d' sheirbheisich-sa dheanamh 'nuair gheibheadh iad an suipeir, an aodach a chuir diubh 's dol a luidh, 's thubhairt a a mhaighistear, "'S cia airson a dh' ith thu na trì trà 'n mar chomhla?" 's thuirt Mac-a-Rusgaich, "Thà gu'n robh na trì tràithean beag gu leoir gu duine a dheanamh sàthach," 's thubhairt am maighistear, "Eirich 's rach gu t' obair," 's thubhairt Mac-a-Rusgaich, "eiridh ach feumaidh mi mo bhiadh fhaotainn mar is cubhaidh dhomh, air neò bidh m' obair d'a reir, cha'n 'eil orm a dheanamh ach mar is urrainn mi, feuch a bheil thu a gabhail an aireachas a bhodaich?" "Cha'n 'eil, cha'n 'eil," orsa am bodach, 's fhuair Mac-a-Rusgaich a bhiadh na b' fhearr na dheigh sin.

'S bha latha eil' ann 's dh' iarr am bodach air Mac-a-Rusgaich e a dhol a chumail a chroinn ann 'n dail a bha shìos bho'n tigh, 's dh' fhalbh Mac-a-Rusgaich 's rainig e far an robh an crann, 's bheir e air na uaidnean na lamhan 's sheas e ann sin. 'S thainig a mhaighistear far an robh e, 's thuirt a mhaighistear ris, "Cia air son nach 'eil thu a deanamh an treabhadh?" 's thubhairt Mac-a-Rusgaich. "Cha'n e mo bhargan treabhadh a dheanamh, ach mi a chumail a chroinn, 's tha thu a faicinn, cha'n 'eil mi a leigeol leatha falbh," 's thubhairt a mhaighistear. "Na h-uire 's na h-uireandan ort!" 's thubhairt Mac-a-Rusgaich. "Na h-uire agus na h-uireandan ort fhein a bhodaich! a bheil thu a gabhail an aireachais do'n bhargan a rinn thu?" "O! cha'n eil, cha'n eil," thuirt am bodach, "ach ma bheir thu dhomh duais eil' air a shon, ni mi treabha," orsa Mac-a-Rusgaich. "O bheir, bheir," orsa am bodach. 'S rinn iad bargan ùr man treabhadh."

'S bha ann latha 's dh' iarr an tuathanach doiribh air Mac-a-Rusgaich, e a dhol ris a mhonadh, a shealtuinn am faicidh e nì air bith air an dochair, 's chaidh Mac-a-Rusgaich ris a mhonadh, 's an uair a chunnaic e a thiom fein thainig e dachaidh, s dh' fharraid a mhaighistear deth, "An robh gach nì ceart ann sa' mhonadh?" 's thuirt Mac-a-Rusgaich. "Bha am monadh e fhein ceart," 's thuirt an tuathanach doirbh, "Cha'n è sin a tha mise a farraid ach an robh crodh nan coimhearsnaich air an taobh fein?" 's thubhairt Mac-a-Rusgaich. "Mo bhà, bhà, 's mar robh leigear dà, 'se mo bhargansa a monadh a bhuachailleachd, s gleidhidh mise am monadh, far a bheil e," 's thubhairt am bodach. "Na h-uire s na h-uireandan ort a bhallaich," 's thuibh-airt esan, "Na h-uire 's na h-uireandan ort fein a bhodaich, a bheil thu a gabhail an aireachas gu'n do rinn thu a leithid do bhargan?" "Cha'n eil, cha'n eil," orsa an tuathanach doirbh, "bheir mi dhuit duais eile air son an crodh a bhuachailleachd," 's thubhairt Mac-a-Rusgaich, "Ma gheibh mise duais eile, gabhaidh mi os laimh mo chi mi crodh nan coimhearsnaich air a ghrunnd agadsa, gu'n till mi air an ais iad, agus ma chi mi do chrodhsa air grunnd nan coimhearsnaich tillidh mi air an ais iad thun do ghrunnd fein, ach ged do theid cuid diubh a chall, cha ghabh mi os laimh am faotainn, ach ma dh' iarras tu orm dol gu'n iarraidh theid mi ann, 's mo gheibh mi iad bheir mi dachaidh iad."

'S cha robh aig an tuathanach dhoirbh air ach cordadh ri Mac-a-Rusgaich, 's duais eile a thobhairt do Mac-a-Rusgaich, 's duais eile a thoirt da air son an crodh a bhuachailleachd. Agus bha iad reidh rè grathunn n'a dheigh sin.

An ath latha chaidh am bodach e fein ris a mhonadh, agus cha b' urrainn d'a na h-aighean aig fhaicinn. Dh iarr e air an son, ach cha b' urrainn d'a am faotuinn. Chaidh e dachaidh; s thubhairt e ri Mac-a-Rusgaich, "Is fheudar duit fein dol a dh iarraidh air son na 'n aighean a Mhic-a-Rusgaich, cha b' urrainn mise am faotuinn an diugh, agus rach thusa gu an iarraidh, s iarr iad gus gu m faigh thu iad."

Thubhairt Mac-a-Rusgaich, "Agus c'aite an teid mise ga'n iarraidh?"

Thubhairt am bodach, "Rach agus iarr iad anns na h-aiteachan ann san saoil thu iad a bhith, agus iarr iad ann an aiteachan ann is nach saoil thu iad a bhith."

Thubhairt Mac-a-Rusgaich, "Ni mise mar sin ma-ta."

Chaidh am bodach a stigh do 'n tigh, agus fhuair Mac-a-Rusgaich fàra, s chuir e ris an tigh e. Chaidh e a naird air an tigh, agus thòisich e air spionadh na tubhadh far an taigh, s ga thilgidh le leathad, agus ma'n d' thainig am bodach a mach a rithisd, bha an tubhadh gu ach ro bheagan far an taigh, s na cabair lom, agus Mac-a-Rusgaich a spionadh s a tilgidh le leathad a chorr.

Thubhairt am bodach, "Na h-unradh s na h-urchoidean ort a bhallaich cia-dé a thug ort an tubhadh a thoirt fàr an taigh mar sin ? "

Thubhair Mac-a-Rusgaich, " Tha gu m bheil mi a'g irraidh na'n aighean ann an tubhadh an taigh." Thubhairt am bodach, " cia mar a tha thu a'g iarraidh na'n aighean ann an tubha an taigh, far am bh'eil thu cinnteach nach eil iad ?"

Thubhairt Mac-a-Rusgaich. "Tha gun do iarr thu fhein orm, an iarraidh far an saoilinn iad a bhith. Agus cuideachd mi gu'n iarraidh ann an aiteachan far nach saoilinn iad a bhith. Agus cha 'n eil aite air bith far an lugh a tha do shaoilsinn agamsa iad a bhith ann, na ann an tubh an taigh."

Thubhairt am bodach, "Na h-unradh agus na h-urchoidean ort a bhallaich." Thubhairt Mac-a-Rusgaich, "Na h-unradh s na h-urchoidean ort fein a bhodaich. Am bh'eil thu a gabhail an aireachas gun d' iarr thu orm na h-aighean iarraidh far nach saoilinn iad a bhith?" "Cha n eil, cha 'n eil, thubhairt am bodach, rach a nise agus iarr iad ann an aiteachan far am bheil a coltach gu 'm faot iad a bhith ann." "Ni mise mar sin," orsa Mac-a-Rusgaich.

Dh fhalbh Mac-a-Rusgaich a dh iarraidh na'n aighean. Fhuair e iad, s thug e dachaidh iad. An sin, dh' iarr a mhaighstir air Mac-a-Rusgaich, e a dhol a chuir an tubhadh air an tigh, s e a dheanamh an taigh, cho dionach gu uisge a chumail a mach is a b urrainn d'a. Rinn Mac-a-Rusgaich sin, agus bha iad reidh rè grathunn na dheigh sin.

Bha an tuathanach doirbh a dol a dh' ionnsaidh banais, 's dh' iarr e air Mac-a-Rusgaich, tra thigeadh am feasgar, e a chuir diollaid air an each, 's e a dhol a dh' ionnsaidh tigh na bainnse, gus esan a thoirt dachaidh, 's thubhhirt e ris, " An uair a bhithis a dlù air dà-uair-dheug, tilg damh-shuil an taobh a bhitheas mi 's aithnaidh mi gu'm bheil e dlù air an am, gu dol dachaidh." "Nì mi sin," orsa Mac-a-Rùsgaich. Nuair a dh' fhalbh an tuathanach thun na banais, chaidh Mac-a-Rùsgaich 's chuir e na daimh a stigh do'n fhang, a 's ghabh e sgian 's thug e na sùilean asta, a's chuir e na phòc na sùilean, 's nuair a thainig an oidhche, chuir Mac-a-Rùsgaich an dìollaid air an each, 's chaidh e gu tigh na bainnse a dh' iarraidh a mhaighistear, a's rainig e tigh na bainnse, 's chaidh e a stigh do'n chuideachd 's shuidh e, gus an robh a dlù air dà-uair-dheug. A's an sin, thòisich e air tilgeadh sùil daimh air a bhodach, aig ceann gach tacan, a 's ma dheireadh thug am bodach an aire dha; a's thubhairt e ris, "Gu-dé a tha thu a deanamh?" 's thubhairt Mac-a-Rùsgaich, "Tha mi a tilgeadh sùil daimh an taobh a thà thu, thun a tha e dlù air an dà-uair-dheug a nis," a 's thubhairt am bodach, "An saoil thu fhein gun deachaidh thu a thoirt nan sùilean as na daimh!" a 's thubhairt Mac-a-Rùsgaich, "Cha'n ann ga shaoilsinn idir a tha mi. Tha mi cinnteach as; dh' iarr thu fein orm mi a thilgeadh suil daimh an taobh a bhitheadh tu, a nuair a bhithidh a dlù air an dà-uair-dheug, 's dé-mar a b' urrainn mi sin a dheanamh, mar tugainn na sùilean as na daimh," a 's thubhairt an tuathanach, "Na h-uire a 's na h-uraindean ort a bhallaich," a 's thuirt Mac-a-Rùsgaich, "na h-uire 's na h-uraindean ort fhein a bhodaich, a bheil thu a gabhail aireachas, gu'n d'iarr thu orm a dheanamh?" "Cha'n eil, cha'n 'eil," thuirt am bodach, 's chaidh iad dachaidh comhla, 's cha robh tuile ma dheibhinn an oidhche sin.

A's aig ceann latha na dhà na dheigh sin, dh'iarr a mhaighistear air Mac-a-Rùsgaich e a dhol an àirt thun na cath-chliathair mhullaich 's e a dheanamh stair chasa-caorach. "Ni mi sin," orsa Mac-a-Rùsgaich, 's dh' fhalbh e, a 's chuir e na caoirich a stigh do'n fhang a 's ghearr e na casan diubh, a's rinn e an stair le casan nan caorach, a 's chaidh e air ais far an robh a mhaighistear, 's thubhairt a mhaighistear ris, "An do rinn thu siod?" 'S thubhairt Mac-a-Rùsgaich, "Rinn, faodaidh tu fein dol gu fhaicinn." 'S chaidh am maighistear a dh' fhaicinn an stair chasa-caorach a rinn Mac-a-Rùsgaich, a 's a nuair a rainig e, 's a chunnaic e casan nan caorach ann 'san stair, chaidh e air a bhresadh 's thubhairt e, "Na huire 's na thuraindean ort a bhallaich, gu-dé a thug ort na casan a ghearradh fàrr nan caorach?" A's thubhairt Mac-a-Rùsgaich, "Nach d' iarr thu fein orm stair chasa-caorach a dheanamh, 's cia-dé mar a dheanainn stair chasa chaorach mar gearrainn na casan fàrr nan caoirich ; feuch am bheil thu a gabhaill an aireachas gun d' iarr thu orm a dheanamh, a bhodaich ?" "Cha'n eil, cha'n eil," thubhairt a mhaighistear. "Cia-dé a tha agam ri dheanamh a rithisd, " thuirt Mac-a-Rùsgaich. "Tha," orsa a' maighistear, "na h-eich 's an stàpull a ghlanadh, a 's a nigheadh an dà chuid a mach, agus a stigh." A's dh' fhalbh Mac-a-Rùsgaich, 's ghlan e a mach an stàpull, 's nigh e na balladhan air an taobh a mach, a's nigh e an stàpull air an taobh a stigh ; nigh e na h-eich, a's mharbh e iad, 's thug e an taobh a stigh ast', 's nigh e an taobh a stigh aca. 'S chaidh e far an robh a mhaigbistear, 's dh' fharraid e cia-dé a bha aige ri a dheanamh a rithisd, 's thubhairt a mhaighistear ris e a chuir nan each 'nan uime ann sa chrann, 's e thobhairt tacain air an treabhadh. Thubhairt Mac-a-Rùsgaich, "Cha fhreagair na h-eich mi." "Cia-dé a dh' airich iad ?" orsa a mhaighistear. "Cha choisich iad air mo shon," orsa Mac-a-Rùsgaich. "Falbh 's feuch iad," thuirt a mhaighistear. A 's dh' fhalbh Mac-a-Rùsgaich, 'far an robh na h-eich 's chuir e crioman do h-aon diubh na bheul, 's chaidh e air ais far an robh a mhaighistear, 's thubhairt e, "Cha'n 'eil ach droch bhlas orra." "Cia-dé a tha thu ag ràdh ?" thuirt a mhaighistear. Chaidh am maighistear, far an robh na h-eich, 's dra * chunna e iad a 's an taobh a stigh air a thoirt asta, 's iad nighte glante thubhairt e, "Cia-dé is ciall do so ?" "Tha," orsa Mac-a-Rùsgaich, "gu 'n d' iarr thu fhein orm, an dà chuid, na h-eich a 's an stàpull a ghlànadh agus an nigheadh an dà chuid a mach agus a stigh, 's rinn mi sin." "A bheil thu a gabhail an aireachais ?" thubhairt Mac-a-Rùsgaich. "B' fhearr leam nach fhaca mi riamh thu," thubhairt am maighistear. "Ma-ta," orsa Mac-a-Rùsgaich, "feumaidh tu trì tuarasdail a thobhairt domhsa ; air neo theid iall do d' chraicionn a thoirt o chùl do chinn, sìos gu do shàil." Thubhairt an tuathanach doirbh, gu'm fhearr leis iall a bhi air thobhairt as a chraicionn bho chùl a chinn gu shàil, na an t-airgiod thoirt do thrusdar coltach ri Mac-a-Rùsgaich. Agus do réir an lagh, chaidh an tuathanach doirbh a cheangal a 's iall leathan a thoirt o chùl a chinn sìos a dhruim 's ghlaoidh e gu'm fhearr leis an t-airgiod fhein a thoirt seachad, na an iall a ghearradh na b' fhaide, 's phaigh e an t-airgiod, 's b' eiginn d'a a bhith greis foigh na lighichean, a's cha robh e na dhuine doirbh tuile.

---

* Dra or tra is = when.

Na dheigh sìn, chaidh Mac-a-Rùsgaich a chuir gu bhith na ghille aig famhair, a bha dona ri a sheirbheisich.

Rainig Mac-a-Rùsgaich am famhair 's thubhairt e, "Tha do ghille air tighinn." Thubhairt am famhair, "Ma s gille dhomhsa thu, feumaidh tu comh obair a chumail rium. air neo bristidh mi do chnaimhean cho mìn ri pronnan." Thuirt Mac-a-Rùsgaich, "Gu-dé ma dh' fhairslichis mi ort?" "Ma dh' fhairslichis," thuirt am famhair, "gheibh thu do dhuais da réir." "De a tha sinn a dol a dheanamh ma ta?" orsa Mac-a-Rùsgaich. "Thà," orsa am famhair, "theid sinn a thobhairt dachaidh connaidh." 'S dh' fhalbh iad 's rainig iad a choille, a 's thòisich am famhair air trusadh na h-uile bun bu ghairbhe na cheile, 's thòisich Mac-a-Rùsgaich air na th-uile bharr bu chaoile na cheile a thrusadh. Sheall am famhair air 's thubhairt e, "Ciod a tha thu deanamh mar sin?" 's thubhairt Mac-a-Rùsgaich, "Tha mise a los gun toir sinn a' choille uile leinn seach a bhith a fàgail pairt d'i gun fheum 'nar deigh." Thuirt am famhair, "Tha sinn glé fhada aig an obair so, bheir sinn dachaidh na h-eallachan so, ach gheibh sinn obair eile a rithisd."

'Se an ath obair gus an deachaidh iad dol a bhuain saidhe, a's dh' iarr am famhair air Mac-a-Rùsgaich, esan a dhol air thoiseach. Gheuraich Mac-a-Rùsgaich an speal agus thòisich e 's chaidh e man chuairt ghoirid air an taobh a stigh, a 's bha aig an fhamhair ri dol cuairt a b' fhaide air an taobh a mach deth, "Gu-dé a thà a dheanamh mar sin?" thubhairt am famhair, "Thà," thuirt Mac-a-Rùsgaich, "mise a los gum buain sinn a phàiric a dh-aon spaogh, an àite a bhith a tilleadh air ar n-ais, na h-uile uair a gheuraichameaid an speal, a 's cha bhi tiom chaillte idir againn." Chunnaic am famhair gu'm bitheadh an spaogh aigsan mòran na b' fhaide na bhiodh spaogh Mhic-a-Rùsgaich, 's thuirt e, "Tha sinne glé fhada aig an obair so." Theid sinn a dh-ionnsaidh obair eile, theid sinn as buailidh sinn an t-arbhar. 'S dh' fhalbh iad a dh' ionnsaidh bualadh an arbhair, fhuair iad na suisteachan, thoisich iad air obair, 's dra a bhuaileadh am famhair an sguaib, bheireadh e urra leum an aird thair an spàrr, 's tra bhuaileadh Mac-a-Rùsgaich an sguab, laidheadh i sìos air an urlar bhualaidh, 's theireadh Mac-a-Rùsgaich ris an famhair, "Cha'n 'eil thusa ga leath bhualadh, nach toir thu urra crùban mar a tha mise a deanamh." Ach mar bu làidireadh a bhuaileadh am famhair, 'sann a b' airde a leumadh an sguab, 's bha Mac-a-Rùsgaich a' gàiriachdaich air, a thubhairt am famhair, "Tha sinn glé fhad aig an obair so, feuchaidh mi air doigh eile thu. Theid sinn 's feuchaidh sinn, cò againn is làidirich a thilgeas cloch an aodan creige, a tha air taobh thall an eas." "Tha mi toileach," orsa Mac-a-Rùsgaich. 'S dh' fhalbh am famhair 's thrus e na clachan bu chruaidh a b' urrainn d'a fhaotuinn, a 's chaidh Mac-a-Rusgaich 's fhuair e crèadh, 's rothail e na bhùill bheaga chruinn' e, agus chaidh iad a dh' ionnsaidh taobh an eas. Thilg am famhair clach an aodann na craige, 's chaidh a' chloich na criomagan, 's thuirt e ri Mac-a-Rùsgaich, "Dean sin a bhallaich." Thilg Mac-a-Rùsgaich dudan do an chrèadh, agus stic e ri aodan na craige, a 's thubhairt e ris an fhamhair, "Dean siod a bhodaich." 'S thilgeadh am famhair cho làidir is a b'urrainn e ; ach mar bu mhòmh' a chuireadh am famhair da neart leis a' chloich a thilgeadh e, 'sann a bu mheanbhadh a bhriseadh iad, 's ghàireadh Mac-a-Rùsgaich, 's thilgeadh e ball beag eile do an chrèadh 's theireadh e, "Cha'n 'eil thu 'ga leath thilgeadh, nach toir thu air a' chloich sticeadh ann sa' chraige mar a tha mise a deanamh." Agus thubhairt am famhair, "Tha sinn glé fhada aig an obair so, theid sinn a 's gabhaidh sinn air dinneir, 's an sin, feuchaidh sinn, cò againn is fhearr a thilgeas a' chloich neart." "Tha mi toileach," orsa Mac-a-Rusgaich, 's chaidh iad dachaidh. Thòisich iad air an dinneir, a's thubhairt am famhair ri Mac-a-Rùsgaich, "Mar ith thu do'n aran 's do'n chàise uibhir is a dh' ithis mise theid iall thoirt as do chraicionn bho chùl do chinn, gu do shàil." "Dean seachd dheth," orsa Mac-a-Rùsgaich, "air chumha 's gu'n teid seachd iallan a thoirt as a chraicionn agudsa, bho chùl do chinn gu d' shàil, mar ith thu uibhir a 's a dh' itheas mise." "Feuch riut* ma ta," orsa 'm famhair. "Stad ma ta gus am faigh mise deoch," thuirt Mac-a-Rusgaich, 's chaidh e a mach a dh' fhaotainn deoch, agus fhuair e balg leathraich, 's chuir e am bàlg eadar a léine 's a chraicinn, 's chaidh e a stigh far an robh am famhair, 's thuirt e ris an fhamhair, "Feuch riut a nise." Thòisich an dithis air itheadh an arain 's a chàise. Agus bha Mac-a-Rùsgaich a cuir an arain 's a cháise a stigh ann sa' bhàlg a bh' aige a stigh fo a léine ; ach ma dheireadh thuirt am famhair, "Is fearr sgur na sgàine." "Is fhearr sgàine fhein na biadh math fhàgail," orsa Mac-a-Rùsgaich. "Sguiridh mise," orsa am famhair. "Theid na seachd iallan

* Try thyself now.

thoirt o chùl do chinn gu do shàil," orsa Mac-a-Rùsgaich. "Feuchaidh mi fhathast thu," orsa am famhair. "Tha do dhà roghuinn agad," orsa Mac-a-Rùsgaich. Fhuair am famhair gruth 's cè, 's lìon e cuman d'a fhein, 's cuman eile do Mhac-a-Rùsgaich. "Feuchamaid cò againn is fhearradh an nise," orsa am famhair. "Cha'n fhada gus am faicir sin," orsa Mac-a-Rùsgaich. "Feuchamid cò againn is luaith a dh' òlas na tha ann 'sa chuman." A 's dh'òl Mac-a-Rùsgaich a dhaoithne † aige, 's chuir e a chuid eile ann 'sa bhalg, 's bha e ullamh air thoiseach air an fhamhair, 's thuirt e ris an fhamhair, "Tha thu air deireadh. "Sheall am famhair air 's thuirt e. "Is fearradh sgur na sgaineadh." "Is fearr sgàineadh fhein na biadh math fhàgail," orsa Mac-a-Rùsgaich. "Theid sinn a mach a dh' feuchainn cò againn is faide a thilgeas a chlach neart mu'n dean sinn tuile," orsa am famhair. "Tha mi toileach," orsa Mac-a-Rùsgaich. A 's chaidh iad am mach far an robh a chloich ; ach bha am famhair cho làn 's nach b' urrainn d'a cromadh gu a togail, "Tog a chloich sin agus tilg i," orsa am famhair. "Tha onair toiseach tòiseach gu bhith agad fhein," orsa Mac-a-Rùsgaich. Dh' fheuch am famhair ris a' chloich a thogail, ach cha b' urrainn da cromadh, dh' fheuch Mac-a-Rùsgaich ri cromadh 's thuirt e, "Cha bhì a leithid so do bhalg a cumail bacadh ormsa." 'S tharrainn e sgian a truaill a bha ri thaobh 's chuir e'n sgian sa' bhalg a bha air a bheulobh, a 's leig e a mach na bha ann sa' bhalg agus thuirt e, "Tha tuile rum a mach na tha stigh," agus thog e a chloich 's thilg e i, 's thuirt e ris an fhamhair, "Dean sin." "Nach tilg thu na's faide na sin i?" orsa am famhair. "Cha do thilg thusa cho fada ri sin fhein i," orsa Mac-a-Rùsgaich. "An nall an so da sgian," orsa am famhair. Shìn Mac-a-Rùsgaich an sgian aige do an fhamhair, ghabh am famhair an sgian, agus stop e a stigh na bhrù i, a 's leig e am mach am biadh, 's thuit am famhair gu làr, 's ghàir Mac-a-Rusgaich air, agus fhuair am famhair bàs. Chaidh Mac-a-Rusgaich a stigh do thigh an fhamhair, 's fhuair e an t-òr a 's an t-airgiod aige. Bha e an sin beartach, 's dh' fhalbh e an sin dachaidh làn thoilichte. JOHN DEWAR.

GILLE, the servant of. NEUMH, a holy man, a saint. MAC, the son of. RUSGAICH, the peeler, or a rough man, a ruffler.

Gille Neumh is a name usually translated in English, NIVEN.

---

† Until satisfied.

The whole might be rendered "The story of Saint's servant, Mac Skinner."

Mr. Dewar writes :—"Tradition says that Gille Neumh Mac Rusgaich disguised himself in woman's apparel, went to Iona, passed for a nun, and caused some of the sisters to become frail sisters. There is a long tale about him and his sister. She would get into service to attend ladies, and Mac-a-Rusgaich would disguise himself in his sister's clothes—but that part of the sgeulachd was so unbecoming that I did not write it. I heard the part which I did write as early as 1810, from an old man of the name of Alexander Dewar in Arrochar."

The story of MacRuslaig, as it is sometimes called, is very widely spread, and, as Dewar says, part of it is "unbecoming." I believe it is printed in Gaelic, but I have been unable hitherto to see the book.—J. F. C.

A very similar story is known in Sutherland.

2. The Erse version of Jack the Giant Killer.

"The opening of the tale, and the deaths of Cormoran and Blunderbore, as told in our children's books, are unknown here; and the whole thing, as found in Sutherland, more nearly resembles the Scandinavian story of the Giant and the Herd Boy, given in Thorpe's Yule-tide stories. (Bohn's Lib. edit.) I cannot get it in Gaelic (that is to say, written down in Gaelic); but am told that it happened in this wise :—

"The giant appeared to the little herd boy and threatened to kill him; but the boy gave him to understand that he had better not try, as he was very strong, though small; and that he was an enchanter, and that if the giant ate him he would make him very ill.

"The giant did not quite believe him; and taking up a stone, he ground it to powder by closing his hand over it, and bid the herd do the same, or he would make short work with him.

"The lad had a lump of curds in his pocket, which he contrived to roll in the dust till it looked like a stone, then pressing it between his fingers, a stream of whey ran through them, and the giant could not do that.

"The next trial was with the heavy hammer; the giant threw to a great distance, telling the would-be-enchanter that unless he could match that he would knock his brains out.

"'I suppose,' said the boy, 'you have no regard for the hammer, and don't care whether you ever see it again or not?'

"'What do you mean?' growled the giant.

"'I mean, that if I take up the hammer, it goes out of sight in the twinkling of an eye, and into the sea.'

"'I beg you will let the hammer alone, then, for it was my great-grandfather's hammer,' replied the giant; and they were both well pleased with the bargain.

"Then followed the hasty-pudding feat, called brose or brochan here; and the experiment with the black pudding which the boy had in his jacket, and which ran blood when he pierced it. The giant, trying to imitate him, plunged a knife into himself and died, as may be seen in all carefully compiled books for the use of young persons."—C. D.

XLVI.

MAC IAIN DIREACH.

From Angus Campbell, quarryman, Knockderry, Roseneath.

AT some time there was a king and a queen, and they had one son; but the queen died, and the king married another wife. The name of the son that the first queen had, was Iain Direach. He was a handsome lad; he was a hunter, and there was no bird at which he would cast his arrow, that he would not fell; and he would kill the deer and the roes at a great distance from him; there was no day that he would go out with his bow and his quiver, that he would not bring venison home.

He was one day in the hunting hill hunting, and he got no venison* at all; but there came a blue falcon past him, and he let an arrow at her, but he did but drive a feather from her wing. He raised the feather and he put it into his hunting bag, and he took it home; and when he came home his muime said to him, "Where is thy game to-day?" and he put his hand into the hunting bag, and he took out the feather and he gave it to her. And his muime took the feather in her hand, and she said, "I am setting it as crosses, and as spells, and as the decay of the year on thee; that thou be not without a pool in thy shoe, and that thou be

* The Gaelic word means rather game than venison.

wet, cold, and soiled, until thou gettest for me the bird from which that feather came."

And he said to his muime, "I am setting it as crosses and as spells, and as the decay of the year on thee; that thou be standing with the one foot on the great house, and the other foot on the castle; and that thy face be to the tempest whatever wind blows, until I return back."

And MacIain Direach went away as fast as he could to seek the bird from which the feather came, and his muime was standing with the one foot on the castle, and the other on the great house, till he should come back; and her front was to the face of the tempest, however long he might be without coming.

MacIain Direach was gone, travelling the waste to see if he could see the falcon, but the falcon he could not see; and much less than that, he could not get her; and he was going by himself through the waste, and it was coming near to the night. The little fluttering birds were going from the bush tops, from tuft to tuft, and to the briar roots, going to rest; and though they were, he was not going there, till the night came blind and dark; and he went and crouched at the root of a briar; and who came the way but AN GILLE MAIRTEAN, the fox; and he said to him, "Thou'rt down in the mouth a Mhic Iain Direach; thou camest on a bad night; I have myself but one wether's trotter and a sheep's cheek, but needs must do with it."

They kindled a fire, and they roasted flesh, and they ate the wether's trotter and the sheep's cheek; and in the morning Gille Mairtean said to the king's son, "Oh son of Iain Direach, the falcon thou seekest is by the great giant of the Five Heads, and the Five Humps, and the Five Throttles, and I will shew thee where his house is; and it is my advice to thee to go to be as his servant, and that thou be nimble and ready to do each thing that is asked of thee, and each thing that is trusted thee; and be very good to his birds, and it well may be that he will trust thee with the falcon to feed; and when thou gettest the falcon to feed be right good to her, till thou gettest a chance; at the time when the giant is not at home run away with her, but take care that so much as one feather of her does not touch any one thing that is within the house, or if it touches, it will not go (well) with thee."

MacIain Direach said "That he would take care of that;" and he went to the giant's house; he arrived, he struck at the door.

The giant shouted, "Who is there?"

"It is me," said MacIain Direach, "one coming to see if thou has hast need of a lad."

"What work canst thou do?" said the giant.

"It is (this)," said MacIain Direach, "I can feed birds and swine, and feed and milk a cow, or goats or sheep."

"It is the like of thee that I want," said the giant.

The giant came out and he settled wages on MacIain Direach; and he was taking right good care of everything that the giant had, and he was very kind to the hens and to the ducks; and the giant took notice how well he was doing; and he said that his table was so good since MacIain Direach had come, by what it was before; that he had rather one hen of those which he got now, than two of those he used to get before. "My lad is so good that I begin to think I may trust him the falcon to feed;" and the giant gave the falcon to MacIain Direach to feed, and he took exceeding care of the falcon; and when the giant saw how well MacIain

Direach was taking care of the falcon, he thought that he might trust her to him when he was (away) from the house; and the giant gave him the falcon to keep, and he was taking exceeding care of the falcon.

The giant thought each thing was going right, and he went from the house one day; and MacIain Direach thought that was the time to run away with the falcon, and he seized the falcon to go away with her; and when he opened the door and the falcon saw the light, she spread her wings to spring, and the point of one of the feathers of one of her wings touched one of the posts of the door, and the door post let out a screech. The giant came home running, and he caught MacIain Direach, and he took the falcon from him; and he said to him, "I would not give thee my falcon, unless thou shouldst get for me the White Glave of Light that the Big Women of Dhiurradh have;" and the giant sent MacIain away.

MacIain Direach went out again and through the waste, and the Gille Mairtean met with him, and he said—

"Thou art down in the mouth* MacIain Direach; thou didst not, and thou wilt not do as I tell thee; bad is the night on which thou hast come; I have but one wether's trotter and one sheep's cheek, but needs must do with that."

They roused a fire, and they made ready the wether's trotter and the sheep's cheek, and they took their meat and sleep; and on the next day the Gille Mairtean said, "We will go to the side of the ocean."

They went and they reached the side of the ocean, and the Gille Mairtean said,

---

* Dewar translates the phrase, "A down mouth on thee."

"I will grow into a boat, and go thou on board of her, and I will take thee over to Dhiurradh; and go to the seven great women of Dhurrah and ask service, that thou be a servant with them; and when they ask thee what thou canst do, say to them that thou art good at brightening iron and steel, gold and silver, and that thou canst make them bright, clear, and shiny; and take exceeding care that thou dost each thing right, till they trust thee the White Glave of Light; and when thou gettest a chance run away with it, but take care that the sheath does not touch a thing on the inner side of the house, or it will make a screech, and thy matter will not go with thee."*

The Gille Mairtean grew into a boat, and MacIain Direach went on board of her, and he came on shore at Creagan nan deargan,† on the northern side of Dhiurradh, and MacIain Direach leaped on shore, and he went to take service with the Seven Big Women of Dhiurradh. He reached, and he struck at the door; the Seven Big Women came out, and they asked what he was seeking. He said, "He could brighten, or make clear, white and shiny, gold and silver, or iron or steel." They said, "We have need of thy like;" and set wages on him. And he was right diligent for six weeks, and put everything in exceeding order; and the Big Women noticed it; and they kept saying to each other, "This is the best lad we have ever had; we may trust him the White Glave of Light."

They gave him the White Glave of Light to keep in order; and he was taking exceeding care of the

---

* This may be compared with the theft of the sword in No. 1.

† DEARGAN, a fish called a breàm (Dewar), from DEARG, red. Perhaps a flea, for there were mystical fleas in Jura.—J. F. C.

White Glave of Light, till one day that the Big Women were not at the house, he thought that was the time for him to run away with the White Glave of Light. He put it into the sheath, and he raised it on his shoulder; but when he was going out at the door the point of the sheath touched the lintel, and the lintel made a screech; and the Big Women ran home, and took the sword from him; and they said to him, "We would not give thee our White Glave of Light, unless thou shouldst get for us the Yellow (Bay) Filly of the King of Eirinn."

MacIan Direach went to the side of the ocean and the Gille Mairtean met him, and he said to him, "Thou'rt down in the mouth, MacIain Direach; thou didst not, and thou wilt not do as I ask thee; I have to-night but one wether's trotter and one sheep's cheek, but needs must do with it."

They kindled a fire, and they roasted flesh, and they were satisfied. On the next day the Gille Mairtean said to MacIain Direach, "I will grow into a barque, and go thou on board of her, and I will go to Eirinn with thee; and when we reach Eirinn go thou to the house of the king, and ask service to be a stable lad with him; and when thou gettest that, be nimble and ready to do each thing that is to be done, and keep the horses and the harness in right good order, till the king trusts the Yellow (Bay) Filly to thee; and when thou gettest a chance run away with her; but take care when thou art taking her out that no bit of her touches anything that is on the inner side of the gate, except the soles of her feet; or else thy matter will not prosper with thee."

And then the Gille Mairtean put himself into the form of a barque, MacIain Direach went on board, and the barque sailed with him to Eirinn. When they reached the shore of Eirinn, MacIain Direach leaped on land, and he went to the house of the king; and when he reached the gate, the gate-keeper asked where he was going; and he said "That he was going to see if the king had need of a stable lad;" and the gate-keeper let him past, and he reached the king's house; he struck at the door and the king came out; and the king said, "What art thou seeking here?"

Said he, "With your leave, I came to see if you had need of a stable lad."

The king asked, "What canst thou do?"

Said he, "I can clean and feed the horses, and clean the silver work, and the steel work, and make them shiny."

The king settled wages on him, and he went to the stable; and he put each thing in good order; he took good care of the horses, he fed them well, and he kept them clean, and their skin was looking SLIOM, sleek; and the silver work and the steel work shiny to look at; and the king never saw them so well in order before. And he said, "This is the best stable lad I have ever had, I may trust the Yellow (Bay) Filly to him."

The king gave the Yellow (Bay) Filly to MacIain Direach to keep; and MacIain Direach took very great care of the Yellow (Bay) Filly; and he kept her clean, till her skin was so sleek and slippery, and she so swift, that she would leave the one wind and catch the other. The king never saw her so good.

The king went one day to the hunting hill, and MacIain Direach thought that was the time to run away with the Yellow Bay Filly; and he set her in what belonged to her, with a bridle and saddle; and when he took her out of the stable, he was taking her through the gate, she gave a switch, SGUAISE, with her tail, and the point of her tail touched the post of the gate, and it let out a screech.

The king came running, and he took the filly from MacIain Direach; and he said to him, "I would not give thee the Yellow (Bay) Filly, unless thou shouldst get for me the daughter of the king of the Frainge.*

And MacIain Direach needs must go; and when he was within a little of the side of the sea the Gille Mairtean met him; and he said to him, "Thou art down in the mouth, oh son of Iain Direach; thou didst not, and thou wilt not do as I ask thee; we must now go to France, I will make myself a ship, and go thou on board, and I will not be long till I take thee to France."

The Gille Mairtean put himself in the shape of a ship, and MacIain Direach went on board of her, and the Gille Mairtean sailed to France with him, and he ran himself on high up the face of a rock, on dry land; and he said to MacIain Direach "to go up to the king's house and to ask help, and to say that his skipper had been lost, and his ship thrown on shore."

MacIain Direach went to the king's house, and he struck at the door; one came out to see who was there; he told his tale and he was taken into the fort. The king asked him whence he was, and what he was doing here.

He told them the tale of misery; "that a great storm had come on him, and the skipper he had was lost; and

---

* France is always meant by this word now—*The Frang*, AN FHRAING.

the ship he had thrown on dry land, and she was there, driven up on the face of a rock by the waves, and that he did not know how he should get her out."

The king and the queen, and the family together, went to the shore to see the ship; and when they were looking at the ship, exceeding sweet music began on board; and the King of France's daughter went on board to see the musical instrument, together with MacIain Direach; and when they were in one chamber, the music would be in another chamber; but at last they heard the music on the upper deck of the ship, and they went above on the upper deck of the ship, and (so) it was that the ship was out on the ocean, and out of sight of land.

And the King of France's daughter said, "Bad is the trick thou hast done to me. Where art thou for going with me?"

"I am," said MacIain Direach, "going with thee to Eirinn, to give thee as a wife to the King of Eirinn, so that I may get from him his Yellow (Bay) Filly, to give her to the Big Women of Dhiurradh, that I may get from them their White Glave of Light, to give it to the Great Giant of the Five Heads, and Five Humps, and Five Throttles, that I may get from him his Blue Falcon, to take her home to my muime, that I may be free from my crosses, and from my spells, and from the bad diseases of the year."

And the King of France's daughter said, "I had rather be as a wife to thyself."

And when they came to shore in Eirinn, the Gille Mairtean put himself in the shape of a fine woman, and he said to MacIain Direach, "Leave thou the King of France's daughter here till we return, and I will go with thee to the King of Eirinn; I will give him enough of a wife."

MacIain Direach went with the Gille Mairtean in the form of a fine maiden, with his hand in the oxter of MacIain Direach. When the King of Eirinn saw them coming he came to meet them; he took out the Yellow (Bay) Filly and a golden saddle on her back, and a silver bridle in her head.

MacIain Direach went with the filly where the King of France's daughter was. The King of Eirinn was right well pleased with the young wife he had got; . . but little did the King of Eirinn know that he had got Gille Mairtean; and they had not long been gone to rest, when the Gille Mairtean sprung on the king, and he did not leave a morsel of flesh between the back of his neck and his haunch that he did not take off him. And the Gille Mairtean left the King of Eirinn a pitiful wounded cripple; and he went running where MacIain Direach was, and the King of France's daughter, and the Yellow (Bay) Filly.

Said the Gille Mairtean, "I will go into the form of a ship, and go you on board of her, and I will take you to Diurradh; he grew into the form of a ship; and MacIain Direach put in the Yellow (Bay) Filly first, and he himself and the King of France's daughter went in after her; and the Gille Mairtean sailed with them to Diurradh, and they went on shore at Creagan nan deargan, at Cilla-mhoire, at the northern end of Diurradh; and when they went on shore, the Gille Mairtean said, "Leave thou the Yellow (Bay) Filly here, and the king's daughter, till thou return; and I will go in the form of a filly, and I will go with thee to the Big Women of Diurradh, and I will give them enough of filly-ing."

The Gille Mairtean went into the form of a filly, MacIain Direach put the golden saddle on his back, and the silver bridle in his head, and he went to the Seven Big Women of Diurradh with him. When the Seven Big Women saw him coming, they came to meet him with the White Glave of Light, and they gave it to him. MacIain Direach took the golden saddle off the back of the Gille Mairtean, and the silver bridle out of his head, and he left him with them: and he went away himself with the White Glave of Light, and he went where he left the King of France's daughter, and the Yellow Bay Filly which he got from the King of Eirinn; and the Big Women of Diurradh thought that it was the Yellow Bay Filly of the King of Eirinn that they had got, and they were in great haste to ride. They put a saddle on her back, and they bridled her head, and one of them went up on her back to ride her, another went up at the back of that one, and another at the back of that one, and there was always room for another one there, till one after one, the Seven Big Women went up on the back of the Gille Mairtean, thinking that they had got the Yellow Bay Filly.*

One of them gave a blow of a rod to the Gille Mairtean; and if she gave, he ran, and he raced backwards and forwards with them through the mountain moors; and at last he went bounding on high to the top of the MONADH mountain of Duirradh, and he reached the top of the face of the great crag, that is there, and he moved his front to the crag, and he put his two fore feet to the front of the crag, and he threw

* This incident is told of a bay water-horse in Sutherland. "The Seven Herds of Sollochie."

his aftermost end on high, and he threw the Seven Big women over the crag, and he went away laughing; and he reached where were MacIain Direach and the King of France's daughter, with the Yellow Bay Filly, and the White Glave of Light.

Said the Gille Mairtean, "I will put myself in the form of a boat, and go thyself, and the daughter of the King of France on board, and take with you the Yellow Baby Filly and the White Glave of Light, and I will take you to mainland."

The Gille Mairtean put himself in the shape of a boat; MacIain Direach put the White Glave of Light and the Yellow Bay Filly on board, and he went himself, and the King of France's daughter, in on board after them; and the Gille Mairtean went with them to the mainland. When they reached shore, the Gille Mairtean put himself into his own shape, and he said to MacIain Direach—

"Leave thou the King of France's daughter, the Yellow Bay Filly from the King of Eirinn, and the White Glave of Light there, and I will go into the shape of a White Glave of Light; and take thou me to the the giant and give thou me to him for the falcon, and I will give him enough of swords."

The Gille Mairtean put himself into the form of a sword, and MacIain Direach took him to the giant; and when the giant saw him coming he put the blue falcon into a MUIRLAG,* and he gave it to MacIain Direach, and he went away with it to where he had left the

* A basket, shaped like an egg, with a hole at the middle. (Dewer.) Such baskets, with hens in them, may be seen now-a-days.—J. F. C.

King of France's daughter, the Yellow Bay Filly, and the White Glave of Light.

The giant went in with the Gille Mairtean in his hand, himself thinking that it was the White Glave of Light of the Big Women of Diurradh that he had, and he began at FIONNSAIREACH, fencing, and at SGUAISEAL, slashing with it; but at last the Gille Mairtean bent himself, and he swept the five heads off the giant, and he went where MacIain Direach was, and he said to him, "Son of John the Upright, put the saddle of gold on the filly, and the silver bridle in her head, and go thyself riding her, and take the King of France's daughter at thy back, and the White Glave of Light with its back against thy nose; or else if thou be not so, when thy muime sees thee, she has a glance that is so deadly that she will bewitch thee, and thou wilt fall a faggot of firewood; but if the back of the sword is against thy nose, and its edge to her, when she tries to bewitch thee, she will fall down herself as a faggot of sticks.

MacIain Direach did as the Gille Mairtean asked him; and when he came in sight of the house, and his muime looked at him with a deadly bewitching eye, she fell as a faggot of sticks, and MacIain Direach set fire to her, and then he was free from fear; and he had got the Best Wife in Albainn; and the Yellow Bay Filly was so swift that she could leave the one wind and she would catch the other wind, and the Blue Falcon would keep him in plenty of game, and the White Glave of Light would keep off each foe; and MacIain Direach was steadily, luckily off.

Said MacIain Direach to the Gille Mairtean, "Thou art welcome, thou Lad of March, to go through my ground, and to take any beast thou dost desire thyself to take with thee; and I will give word to my servants that they do not let an arrow at thee, and that they do not kill thee, nor any of thy race, whatever one of the flock thou takest with thee."

Said the Gille Mairtean, "Keep thou thy herds to thyself; there is many a one who has wethers and sheep as well as thou hast, and I will get plenty of flesh in another place without coming to put trouble on thee; and the Fox gave a blessing to the son of Upright John, and he went away; and the tale was spent.

SGEULACHD MIC IAIN DIRICH.

Bha uaireiginn Righ agus Bannrigh ann, 's bha aca aona mhac, ach shiubhail a' Bhan-righ agus phòs an righ bean eile. B'è an t' ainm a bha air mac na ciad Bhannrigh Iain Direach. Bha è 'na ghille dreachmor. Bha è 'na shealgair 's cha robh eun air an tilgeadh è a shaighead nach leagadh e. Agus mharbhadh e na feidh 's na earbhaichean aig astar mòr uaidh. Cha robh latha a rachadh e a mach le bhogha 's a dhòrlach nach tugadh e dachaidh sithionn.

Bha e aon latha ann 'sa bheinn sheilg aig sealg, 's cha d' fhuair e sithionn air bhith ach thainig seabhag ghorm seachad air 's leig è saighead rithe, ach cha do rinn e ach aon iteag a chuir as a sgiath. Thog e an iteag, 's chuir è na bholg seilg i, 's thug e dachaidh i, 's a nuair a thainig e dachaidh, thubhairt a mhuime ris, "C' àite am bheil do shithionn an diugh?" 's chuir esan a lamh a stigh na bholg seilg, 's thug e a mach an iteag, 's thug è d'i i.

'S ghabh a muime an iteag 'na laimh, 's sheall i urra, 's thubhairt i, "Tha mise a' cuir mar chrosaibh 's mar gheasaibh 's mar eusaibh na bliadhna ortsa, nach bi thu gun loba a' d' bhròig, a's gum bì thu gu fliuch, fuar, salach, gus gu'm faigh thu dhomhsa, an t- eun as an d' thainig an iteag sin."

S thubhairt esan ri a mhuime; "Tha mise a cuir mar chros 'n 's mar gheas'n a's mar eusan na bliadhna ortsa, gum bìth thu a'd' seasamh 's an darna cas agad air an tigh mhòr 's a chas eile air a'

Chaisteal, agus gum bi t' aodann ri aghaidh nan siantaidhean, ga b'e gaoth a shéideas, gus gu'm pill mise air m' ais."

'S dh' fhalbh Mac Iain Dirich cho luath 'sa b' urrainn da, a dh' iarraidh an eoin as an d' thainig an iteag, 's bha 'mhuime, na seasamh a's an darna cas aic' air a' chaisteal, a's a' chas eile aic' air an tigh mhòr, gus an tigeadh e air ais, agus, cuideachd, bha a h-aodann ri aghaidh nan sian, ga b'e aird as an séideadh a ghaoth, gus an tigeadh esan air ais a rithisd, cia air bith co fada is a bhitheadh e gu'n tighinn.

Bha Mac Iain Dirich air falbh a' siubhal nam fàsach, a sheall am faiceadh e an t-seabhaig, ach an t-seabhag cha b' urrainn d'a fhaicinn, 's moran na bu lugha na sin cha b' urrainn da a faotuinn. A's bha e a' falbh leis fhein air feadh na fàsaich 's e a' tighinn dlùth air an oidhche, bha na h-eoin bheaga bhaidealach a' dol o bhàrr nam preas, o dhos gu dos, 's gu bun nan dris, a' dol gu tàmh, is gad bhà cha robh esan a' dol ann, gus an d' thainig an oidhche dhàll dhorcha, a's chaidh e 's chrùbain è aig bun pris, 's co a thainig an rathad ach an gille màirtein, 's thubhairt e ris, "Beul-sios ort a mhic Iain Dirich, is olc an oidhche an d' thainig thu ; cha 'eil agam fhein an nochd ach aon spàg muilt, 's aon leath-cheann caora, ach is éigin a bhith a deanadh leis." Bheothaich iad gealbhan 's ròist iad feoil, 's dh' ith iad an spòig muilt 's an leath-cheann caora, 's aig a' mhaduinn, thubhairt an gille-mairtein, ri mac an righ, "A Mhic Iain Dirich, tha an t-seabhag a tha thu ag iarraidh aig famhair mòr nan cuig cinn, nan cuig mill 's na'n cuig muineal, 's leigidh mise fhaicinn duit far am bheil an tigh aige, agus 's e mo chomhairle-sa dhuit thu a dhol gu a bhith nad' ghille aige, a's thu a bhith gu easgaidh, ealamh a dheanamh gach ni a theid iarraidh ort, a's gach ni a theid earbaidh riut, 's bith ra mhath ris na h-eoin aige, 's math a dh-fhaoidt' gun earb e riut an t-seabhag a bhiadh, 's a nuair a gheibh thusa an t-seabhaig ri bhiadhadh, bi ra mhath rithe, gus gu 'm faigh thu fàth, an uair nach bì am famhair aig an tigh, ruith air falbh leatha, ach thoir an aire, nach bean uibhir is aon ite dh' i do ni air bith, do na tha air taobh a stigh an taighe, air neo ma bheanas cha teid leat."

Thuirt Mac Iain Dirich gu'n thugadh e an fhaire air sin, a's dh' fhalbh e a dh' ionnsaidh tigh an fhamhair. Rainig e, 's bhuail e aig an dorus.

Ghlaodh am famhair, "Co a tha ann an sin ?" "Tha mise,"

thuirt Mac Iain Dirich, "fear a tha a' tighinn a sheall am bheil feum agad air gille."

"Dé an obair as urrainn duit a dheanamh?" orsa am famhair.

"Thà," orsa Mac Iain Dirich, "is urrainn domh eunlaidh 's mucan a bhiadhadh, 's bò, na gabhair, na caoirich a bhiadhadh a 's a bhleoghan."

"'S e do leithid a tha a dhìth orm," thuirt am famhair.

Thainig am famhair a mach 's chuir e tuarasdal air Mac Iain Dirich. A's bha e a' tobhairt aire ra mhath air gach nì a bha aig an fhamhair, 's bha e ra mhath ris na cearcan 's ris na tonnagan, a's thug am famhair an fhaire cho math is a bha e a deanamh, 's thubhairt e gu' m bu math a bhòrd fun a thainig Mac Iain Dirich seach mar a bha e a roimhe, gu 'm b' fhearr leis aona chearc, do na bha è a' faotainn an nise na dithis do na gheibheadh e roimhe, "Tha mo ghille co math, 's gum bheil dùil agam gu'm faot mi earbadh ris an t-seabhag a bhiadhadh." A's thug am famhair an t-seabhag do Mhac Iain Dirich ri bhiadhadh, 's thug e an fhaire shònraichte air an t-seabhag.

'S a nuair a chunnaic am famhair cho math is a bha Mac Iain Dirich a' toirt aire air an t-seabhaig; bha leis gu 'm faotadh e a h-earbadh ris a nuair a bhitheadh e fhein bho 'n tigh. S thug am famhair da an t-seabhag ri gleidh, 's bha Mac Iain Dirich a' tobhairt an fhaire shònraichte air an t-seabhaig.

Bha leis an fhamhair, gu 'n robh gach nì a' dol gu ceart. Agus dh' fhalbh e o'n tigh aon latha; a 's smuaintich Mac Iain Dirich, gu 'm b'e sin an t-am gu ruith air falbh leis an t-seabhag, 's bheir e air an t-seabhaig gu falbh leatha. A's a nuair a bha e a' fosgladh an doruis, is a chunnaic an t-seabhag an solus, sgaoil i a sgiathan gu leum 's bhean barr h-aon da na itean, aig aon do na sgiathan aice do aon do ursainnean an doruis, 's leig an ursainn sgreach as. Thainig am famhair dachaidh 'na ruith, 's bheir e air Mac Iain Dirich, 's thug e uaidh an t-seabhag, a's thubhairt e ris, "Cha tugainnsa dhuit mo sheabhag, mar faighidh tu domh an claidheamh geal soluis a tha aig seachd mnathan mòra Dhiurath," 's chuir am famhair Mac Iain Dìrich air falbh.

Chaidh Mac Iain Dìrich a rithisd troimhe an fhàsaich, 's choinnich an gille-màirtein air, 's thubhairt e; "Beul sios ort a Mhic Iain Dirich, cha do rinn, 's cha dean thu mar a dh' iarras misidh ort, is olc an oidhche an d' thainig thu an nochd, cha 'n'eil agam ach aon spoig muilt, agus aon leth-cheann caorach, is eiginn a bhith deanamh leis."

Bheothaich iad gealbhan, 's rinn iad deis an spàg muilte 's an leth-cheann caora, 's ghabh iad biadh 's chadal. Agus an ath latha, thubhairt an gille-màirtean, theid sinn gu taobh a' chuain.

Chaidh iad 's rainig iad taobh a chuain ; 's thuirt an gille-màirtean, "Cinnidh mise ann a'm' bhàta, 's rach thusa air bòrt orra, 's bheir mi a null gu Diurath thu, 's rach a dh' ionnsaidh seachd mnathan mòra Dhiurath, 's iarr seirbhis, gu thu a bhith nad' ghille aca, 's tra a dh' fharraidies iad d' ìot, gu-dé is urrainn duit a dheanamh, abair riutha, gu'm bheil thu math air glanadh iarunn agus stàilinn, òr agus airgiod, agus gu 'n dean thu gu glan, soillear, deàrlach iad, a's thoir an fhaire shònraichte gu 'n dean thu gach nì gu ceart, gus gu 'n earb iad an claidheamh geal-soluis riut, 's an uair a gheibh thu fàth, ruith air falbh leis, ach thoir an fhaire, nach bean an truaill do nì air bith air taobh a stigh an taighe, air neo ni e sgread 's cha teid do ghnothach leat."

Chinn an gille mairtean 'na bhàta, 's chaidh Mac Iain Dirich air bòrd urra, 's thainig i air tìr aig creagan nan deargan aig taobh ma thuath Dhiùrath, 's leum Mac Iain Dìrich air tìr, 's chaidh e a ghabhail muintireas aig seachd mnathan mòra Dhiùrath. Rainig e a's bhuail e aig an dorus, thainig na seachd mnathan mòr a mach, 's dh' fharraid iad gu-dé a bha e ag iarraidh. Thubhairt e, gu 'n thainig e a sheall an robh feum aca air gille ; dh' fharraid iad deth, ciod a b' urrainn d'a a dheanamh. Thuirt e, gu 'm b' urrainn d'a òr 's airgiod, na iarunn na stàilinn, a ghlanadh, 's an deanamh gu soilleir, geal, dearrsgnuidh. Thuirt iad "Tha do leithid a dhìth oirnn," 's chuir iad tuarasdal air.

Agus bha e ra dhichiollach rè sè seachdainean, 's chuir e na h-uile nì an an ordugh anbharra. A's thug na mnathan mòr an fhaire dh' a, 's bha iad ag radh ri cheile. "'S e so an gille is fhearr a bha againn riamh, faotaidh sinn an claidheamh geal soluis earbadh ris."

Thug iad d'a an claidheamh geal-soluis ri ghleidh an ordugh, agus bha esan a' toirt aire shònraichte air a' chlaidheamh gheal-sholuis gus aon latha nach robh na mnathan mòr aig an tigh. Smuainich esan gu 'm b' è sin an t-am dh'àsan gu ruith air falbh leis a' chlaidheamh gheal sholuis ; chuir e ann 'san truaill e, 's thog e air a ghualainn e ; ach a nuair a bha e a' dol a mach air an dorus, bhean barr an truaill do an ard-dorus, 's rinn an t-ard-dorus sgread, 's ruidh na mnathan mòr dachaidh, 's thug iad uaidh an claidheamh, 's thuirt iad ris. Cha tugamaid duit nair claidheamh geal-soluis, mar faigheadh tu dhùinne an fhalaire bhuidh aig righ Eirinn.

Dh' fhalbh Mac Iain Dirich gu taobh a' chuain, 's choinnich an gille-màirtean air, 's thuirt e ris, "Beul sios ort a Mhic Iain Dirich, cha do rinn 's cha dean thu mar a dh' iarras mis' ort; cha 'n 'eil agam an nochd ach aon spog muilte, 's aon leth-cheann caora, ach is eiginn a bhith a' deanamh leis." Bheothaich iad gealbhan, 's roist iad feoil, ghabh iad biadh 's bha iad subhach. An ath latha thubhairt an gille-màirtean ri Mac Iain Dirich. "Cinnidh mise ann 'm bhàrca 's rach thusa air bòrt urra, 's theid mi a dh' Eirinn leat, 's a nuair a ruigeas sinn Eirinn rach thusa 'dh' ionnsaidh tigh an righ, as iarr seirbhis gu a bhith ann a' d' ghille stàpuil aige, 's a nuair a gheibh thu sin, bith gu easgaidh, ealamb a dheanamh gach ni a tha ri dheanamh, a's gleidh na h-eich agus an usair ann 'n òrdugh ra mhath, gus gu 'n earb an righ an fhalaire bhuidh riut, a 's a nuair a gheibh thu fàth ruith air falbh leatha.

"Ach thoir an fhaire tra a bhitheas tu ga toirt a mach, nach bean mìr air bith dh' i, do nì air bith air taobh a stigh a' gheata, ach bonnaibh nan cas aice, air neo cha soirbhich do ghnothach leat."

Agus an sin, chuir an gille-màirtean e fhein ann an riochd bàrca, chaidh Mac Iain Dirich air bòrd, 's sheol a' bhàrca leis do dh' Eirinn, Tra a rainig iad tìr na h-Eirionn, leum Mac Iain Dirich air tìr, 's chaidh e gu tigh an righ; 's a nuair a rainig e an geata, dh' fharraid fear gleidh a' gheata d'e c'aite an robh e a' dol, 's thubhairt esan, gu 'n robh e a' dol a shealltinn an robh gille stàpuil a dhìth air an righ, 's leig fear gleidh a' gheata seachad e, 's rainig e tigh an righ, bhuail e aig an dorus, 's thainig an righ a mach; agus thubhairt an righ, "De a tha thu ag iarraidh ann an so?"

Thuirt esan, "Le n' air cead, 'sann a thainig mi a shealltuinn, an robh feum agaibh air gille stàpuil."

Dh' fharraid an righ, "Ciod a's urrainn duit a dheanamh?"

Thuirt esan, "Is urrainn mi na h-eich a ghlanadh 's am biadh-adh, a's an usair aca ghlanadh, a's an obair airgiod a's an obair stàilinn a ghlanadh, agus an deanadh dearrsgnuidh."

Chuir an righ tuarasdal air; 's chaidh e do an stàpull. 'S chuir e gach nì an òrdugh math, thug e aire mhath air na eich, bhiadh e gu math iad, 's ghleidh e glan iad, 's bha an craicionn aca ag amhrac slìom a's an obair airgiod 's an obair stailinn gu dearrsgnuidh ag amhrac, 's cha'n fhaca an righ iad cho math an ordugh riamh roimh. Agus thubhairt e, "'S e so an gille stàpuil is fhearr a bha agam riamh, faotaidh mi an fhàlaire bhuidh earbadh ris."

Thug an righ an fhàlaire bhuidh do Mhac Iain Dìrich ri ghleidh, agus thug Mac Iain Dìrich an fhaire shònraichte air an fhàlaire bhuidh, bhiadh e, 's ghleidh e glan i, gus an robh an craicionn aice gu slìom sleamhainn, 's i cho luath a's gu'm fagadh i an darna gaoth, 's gu'm beireadh i air a' ghaoth eile. Cha'n fhaca an righ i riamh cho math.

Chaidh an righ aon latha do'n bheinn sheilg ; agus smuaintich Mac Iain Dìrich, gu'm b'e sin an t-am gu ruith air falbh leis an fhàlaire, chuir e na h-uìm i le srian 's diolaid, 's 'tra thug e a mach as an stàpull i, 's a bha e ga toirt a mach troimhe'n gheata, thug i sguaise le a h-earbull 's bhean barr a h-earbaill do ursainn a' gheata, a's leig i sgread aiste.

Thainig an righ 'na ruith 's thug e o Mhac Iain Direach an fhàlaire, agus thubhairt e ris, "Cha tugainnsa dhuit an fhàlaire bhuidh, mar faigheadh tu dhomh nighean righ na Frainge."

Agus b' eiginn do Mhac Iain Dìrich falbh, 's a nuair a bha e mar bheagan do thaobh na mara, choinnich an gille màirtean air, 's thubhairt e ris, "Beul sios ort a Mhic Iain Dìrich, cha do rinn 's cha dean thu mar a dh'iarras mise ort, is eiginn duinne an nis dol do'n Fhraing. Ni mise mi fhein ann a'm' lòng, 's rach thusa air bòrd, a's cha'n fhada a bhithis mise gus an toir mi do'n Fhraing thu."

Chuir an gille-màirtean e fhein ann 'n riochd long, 's chaidh Mac Iain Dìrich air bòrd urra, 's sheol an gille màirtein do'n Fhraing leis, 's ruith e a fhein an aird ri aodann craige air tìr tioram, 's thubhairt e ri Mac Iain Dìrich e a dhol an aird gu tigh an righ a dh' iarraidh cobhair a's e a gh' radh, gu 'n deachaidh an sgioba a chall, a's an long aige a thilgeadh air tìr. Chaidh Mac Iain Dìrich gu tigh an righ, 's bhuail e aig an dorus, thainig a h-aon a mach a dh' fhaicinn co a bha ann, dh' innis e a sgeul, 's chaidh a thobhairt a stigh do 'n lùchairt ; dh' fharraid an righ dheth, cia as a bhà e, 's gu-dé a bha e deanamh an so. Dh' innis e sgeul na truaighe dhaibh, gu 'n d' thainig stoirm mhòr air, 's gun deachaidh an sgioba a bh' aige a chall, a's an long a bh' aige, a thilgeadh air tìr tioram, 's gu 'n robh i an siod, air a cuir an aird ri aodann creige, leis na tonnan, 's nach robh fios aige, gu-dé mar a gheibheadh e as i.

Chaidh an righ a's a' Bhanrigh, 's an teaghlach gu leir, gus a chladach, a dh' fhaicinn na long, 's tra bha iad ag amhrac na luing, thòisich ceol anbharra bìnn air bòrd. Agus chaidh nighean righ na Frainge, air bòrd, a dh' fhaicinn an inneal chiùil, comhla ri Mac Iain Dìreach ; 'S an uair a bhitheadh iadsan ann an aon seombar, bhitheadh an ceol ann an seombar eile ; ach ma dheireadh, chualadh an ceol air clair uachdair na luinge, 's chaidh iad an aird, air a clar uachdair na long ; agus 'sann a bha an long, a mach air a' chuan a sealladh tìr.

'S thubhairt nighean righ na Frainge, "Is olc an cleas a rinn thu orm, c'àite am bh'eil thu los dol leam?" "Thà," thubhairt Mac Iain Dìrich, "mi a' dol leat do dh' Eirinn, gus do thoirt mar mhnaoidh do righ Eirinn, 's gu'm faigh mise uaidhsan an fhàlaire bhuidh aige, gus a tobhairt do mhnathan mòra Dhiùrath, 's gum faigh mi uapsan an claidheamh geal soluis aca, gus a thoirt do fhamhair mòr nan coig cinn, nan coig mill, 's nan coig muinealan, 's gu'm faigh mi uaidhsan an t-seabhag ghorm aige, gus a tobhairt dachaidh a dh' ionnsaidh mo mhuime, 's gu'm faigh mi saor o m' chrosan, a's o m' gheasan, 's bho dhroch eusaibh na bliadhna."

'S thubhairt nighean righ na Frainge, "B' fhearr leamsa, a bhith mar mhnaoidh agad fein."

Agus tra thainig iad gu tìr aig Eirinn, chuir an gille-màirtean e fein ann an riochd mnaoidh bhriagh, 's thuirt e ri Mac Iain Dìrich, "Fàg thusa nighean righ na Frainge ann an so gus gu'n till sinn ; 's theid mise leat gu righ na h-Eirionn ; 'S bheir mise a dhìol mnatha dh'a."

Chaidh Mac Iain Dìrich a's an gille-màirtean gu tigh righ na h-Eirionn, 's an gille-màirtean ann an riochd nighean bhriagh, 's a laimh ann an asgailt Mhic Iain Dìrich. Tra chunnaic righ na h-Eirionn iad a' tighinn, thainig e 'nan coinnimh, thug e a mach an fhàlaire bhuidh agus dìolaid òir air a druim, 's srian airgiod as a ceann. Dh' fhalbh Mac Iain Dìrich leis an fhàlaire, far an robh nighean righ na Frainge. Bha righ Eirinn ra thoilichte leis a' mhnaoidh òg a fhuair e ; 's bha cho beag foighidin aige, is gu'n robh e a los dol a luidh leatha, ma'n d' thainig an oidhche. Chaidh leaba a dheanamh deas daibh, 's chaidh iad a luidh, ach is beag fios a bha aig righ Eirinn gu'm b'e an gille màirtean a bha aige. 'S cha robh iad fada nan luidh, gus an do leum an gille màirtean air an righ, 's cha d' fhàg e mìre feoil eadar cùl a mhuineil a's a bhunamhàs, nach tug e dheth.

'S dh' fhalbh an gille-mairtean, 's dh' fhàg e righ na h-Eirionn na abalach truagh leònta, 's chaidh e 'na ruith far an robh Mac Iain Dìrich 's nighean righ na Frainge, 's an fhàlaire bhuidh. Thuirt an gille-màirtean, "Theid mise an riochd long, 's rachadh sibhse air bòrd urra, 's bheir mi gu Diùrath sibh.

Dh' fhàs e ann an riochd long, 's chuir Mac Iain Dirich an fhàlaire bhuidh a stigh an toiseach, 's chaidh e fhein 's nighean righ na Frainge a stigh as a déigh. Agus sheol an gille-màirtean leo gu Diùrath 's chaidh iad air tìr aig creagan nan deargan, aig Cille-mhoire, aig ceann mo thuath Dhiùrath. 'S tra chaidh iad air tir, thubhairt an gille-màirtean, "Fag thusa an fhàlaire bhuidh, 's nighean an righ ann an so, gus gun till thu, 's theid mise ann an riochd fàlaire, 's theid mi leat gu mnathan mòra Dhiùrath, 's bheir mis' an diòl falaireachd dhaibh."

Chaidh an gille-màirtean ann an riochd falaire, chuir Mac Iain Dìrich an diolaid òir air a dhrim, 's an t srian airgiod na cheann, 's chaidh e a dh' ionnsaidh seachd mnathan mòr Dhiùrath leis. Nuair a chunnaic na seachd mnathan mòr e a' tighinn, thainig iad na choineamh leis a chlaidheamh gheal-sholais, 's thug iad d'a e. Thug Mac Iain Dìrich an diolaid òir far druim a' ghille-mhàirtean, 's an t-srian airgiod a a cheann, 's dh' fhàg s-e aca e, a's dh' fhalbh e fhein leis a chlaidheamh gheal-sholuis, 's chaidh e far an d' fhàg e nighean righ na Frainge, 's an fhalaire bhuidh a fhuair e o righ na h-Eirionn. Agus shaoil mnathan mòr Dhiùrath, gu'm b'e falaire bhuidh righ na h-Eirionn a fhuair iadsan, 's bha cabhaig mhòr urra gu dol g'a marcachd. Chuir iad diolaid air a druim, 's shrianaich iad a ceann, 's chaidh té dhiubh an aird air a drim, gus a marcachd, chaidh té eile an aird air cùlabh na té sin, 's té eile aig cùlamh na te sin, 's bha daonnan rum air son té eile ann, gus h-aon an deigh h-aon, gu'n deachaidh na seachd mnathan mòr air druim a' ghille-mhàirtain, 's dùil aca gu'm b'e an fhàlaire bhuidh a bhà aca.

Thug té dhiubh buille le slait do'n ghille mhàirtean, 's ma thug, ruith, 's roideasairich e air ais, 's air aghaidh, leo, air feadh a mhonaidh, 's ma dheireadh chaidh e 'na leum-ruich, an aird thun mullach monadh Dhiùrath, 's rainig e mullach aodann na creige mòr' a tha ann an sin, 's chàraich e aghaidh ris a' chreige, 's chuir e a dhà chas toisich ri beulaobh na creige, 's thilg e an aird a cheann deiridh 's thilg e na seachd mnathan mòr thair a' chreige. 'S dh fhalbh e a' gàrachdaich, 's rainig e far an robh Iain Direach 's nighean righ na Frainge, leis an fhàlaire bhuidh, agus an claidheamh geal-soluis.

Thubhairt an gille-mairtean, "Cuiridh mise mi fhein ann an riochd bàta, 's rach fein agus nighean righ na Frainge air bòrd, a' s thugaibh leibh an fhàlaire bhuidh, 's an claidheamh geal soluis, 's bheir mise gu tìr mòr sibh."

Chuir an gille mairtean e fhein ann an riochd bàta, chuir Mac Iain Dirich an claidheamh geal-soluis, 's an fhàlaire bhuidh air bòrd, 's chaidh e fhein 's nighean righ na Frainge a stigh air bòrd as an deigh, 's chaidh an gille màirtean gu tìr mòr leo. Nuair a rainig iad tìr, chuir an gille-mairtein e fhein na riochd fein, 's thubhairt e ri Mac Iain Dirich.

"Fàg thusa nighean righ na Frainge, an fhalaire bhuidh o righ Eirinn, 's an claidheamh geal soluis, ann an sin, 's theid mise ann an riochd claidheamh geal soluis, 's thoir thusa a dh' ionnsaidh an fhamhair mi, 's thoir thusa dh' a mi air son na seabhaig, 's bheir mise 'dhìol claidheamh dh'a.

Chuir an gille màirtean e fein an riochd claidheamh geal soluis, 's thug Mac Iain Dirich leis e a dh' ionnsaidh an fhamhair. 'S tra a chunnaic am famhair e a' tighinn chuir e an t-seabhag ghorm ann am mùrlag, 's thug e do Mac Iain Dirich i, 's dh' fhalbh e leatha gus far an d' fhàg e nighean righ na Frainge, an fhalaire bhuidh, 's an claidheamh geal soluis.

Chaidh am famhair a stigh leis a' ghille-mhairtean 'na laimh, 's e fhein a' saoilsinm gu'm b' e claidheamh geal soluis mnathan mòra Dhiùrath a bha aige. 'S thòisich e air fionnsaireachd 's air sguaiseal leis ; ach ma dheireadh, lùb an gille màirtein fhein, agus sguids e na còig cinn fàrr an fhamhair, 's chaidh e far an robh Mac Iain Dìrich, 's thubhairt e ris.

"A Mhic Iain Dìrich, cuir an dìolaid òir air an fhàlaire, a's an t-srian airgiod na ceann ; 's rach fein ga marcachd, a's thoir nighean righ na Frainge aig do cùlaobh a's an claidheamh geal soluis, 's a chùl ri d' shròin. Air neò mar bì thu mar sin, tra chì do mhùime thu, tha sealladh aic' a tha cho nimh is gu'n gon i thu, 's tuitidh tu ann a'd' chùal chrìonaich ; ach ma bitheas cùl a chlaidheimh ri d' shròin, 's am faobhar rithse, a nuair a dh' fheuchas i ri do ghonadh, tuitidh i fein 'na cùal chrìonaich."

Rinn Mac Iain Dìrich mar a dh' iarr an gille-màirtean air, 's a nuair a thainig e an sealladh an taigh, 's a sheall a mhuime air le sùil nimheil, ghoimheill, thuit i 'na cùal chrìonaich ; 's chuir Mac Iain Dìrich teine rithe, 's bha e an sin saor o eagal, 's bha aige a' bhean a b' fhearr an Albainn, 's bha an fhàlaire bhuidh cho luath is gu'm fàgadh i an darna gaoith, 's bheireadh i air a' ghaoith eile, 's chumadh an t-seabhag ghorm am pailteas sithinn ris, 's chumadh, an claidheamh geal-soluis air falbh gach nàmhaid, 's bha Mac Iain Dìrich gu sochdrach sona dheth.

Thuirt Mac Iain Dìrich ris a' ghilie mhàirtean, "'S è do bheatha 'ille-mhàirtean gu dol feadh mo ghrùnd 's beothach air bith a shandaicheas tu fein a ghabhail a thoirt leat, 's bheir mise àithne do m' ghillean, nach tilg iad saithead, 's nach marbh iad thu fhein na gin do d àl, ga b'e aon do an treud a bheir thu leat.

Thubhairt an gille-màirtean, "Gleidh thusa do threud dhuit fhein, is iomadh fear aig am bheil muilt a's caoirich cho math is a tha agadsa, 's gheibh mise am pailteas feoil an àite eile gun tighinn a chuir dradh ortsa, 's thug an gille-màirtean beannachd le Mac Iain Dìrich 's dh' fhàlbh e, 's theirig an sgeul.

Told by Angus Campbell, quarryman, Knockderry, Roseneath. Written by John Dewar, whose language has been strictly followed. This dialect of Gaelic seems to contain English idioms; and varies from the island Gaelic, especially in grammatical construction.

In this form the intention of the story seems to be the same as that of Murchag or Mionachag, No. 8. Every incident gives rise to another till the whole unwinds as a chain of cause and effect; a single feather is the first link, and a Princess the last, and then the whole is run back again and the chain wound up, and it ends with Theirig an sgeul, which means that the story came to an end because there was no more of it.

It is worth remark, that the objects sought are those which have been valued from the very earliest of times; a Falcon, a Sword, a Horse, and a fair Lady. The story might belong to any country and to any age. The scene is as usual laid to the westward, as far as it will go, and then it turns back to the nearest and best known foreign country.

Only two spots are specified—one is close to the Gulf of Corrie Bhreacan, the most remarkable place in the Highlands; the other the most conspicuous rock on the top of one of the most conspicuous and peculiar mountains in the West Highlands.

It seems hopeless to speculate who these seven great women who guarded a shining sword may have been, but the worship of the scimitar may have some bearing on the incident. The wicked muime fell a faggot of sticks before the sword, and the temple of the Scythian sword-god was a heap of faggots, from which human victims were thrown when thcy were sacrificed.

People who are beaten to death, or enchanted in these Gaelic legends, are always falling like a faggot of sticks or twigs, CUAL CHRIONACH ; so the expression here may be simply an illustration, but still the analogy is worth remark.

The language is peculiar in the absence of pronouns ; the names are repeated over and over again, but this belongs rather to the writer than to the telling of stories in general. It is the way in which Dewar expresses himself with precision and accuracy. There can be no mistake about the meaning of anything which he has written for me. The effect is rather too much repetition, but a story so told would not be easily forgotten by those into whose heads the incidents had been so hammered.

The following stories may throw some light on the Big Women of Jura. The first I have known all my life. They were sent to me by Mrs. MacTavish from Islay.

2. CHAILEACH BHEINE MHORE lived in Jura, at Largic Breac, and had a ball of thread by which she could draw towards her any person or thing, if she could throw the ball beyond them.

She got MacPhie of Colonsay into her toils, and would not part with him. Every time he attempted to leave her, she used to intercept him, and even after he got into his BIORLINN, or barge, and got off from the shore, she would get him ashore again, by throwing the ball into the boat. (The giant in the story of Black White-red had a like magic clue). At last he pretended perfect contentment in his bondage, and got the secret from her that she had a hatchet which would cut the thread on the enchanting clue. He watched an opportunity and stole the hatchet, having previously ordered his boat to be in waiting at Cnoc Breac at the foot of Bean a Chaolis. He set out by the dawn of day, and was seated in his boat before the Caileach got to the top of the hill, which she had climbed with speed, as soon as she missed him. When she saw him in the boat, she cried out most piteously—

A Mhic a Phie
A Ghaoils' thasgaidh
An d' fhag thu air a chladach mi ?

Oh! Mac Phie
My love and treasure,
Hast thou left me on the strand?

And this she often repeated throwing at the same time the Cearsla dhruidheachd, magic clue, into the boat, and drawing it towards the shore. But when she saw the thread cut and the boat rowing off beyond her reach, she got desperate, and slid down what is called SGRIOB NA CAILICH, crying out,

A Mhic a Phie
Charrich, granda
'An d' fhag thu air a chladach mi?

Oh! Mac Phie
Rough skinned and foul
Hast thou left me on the strand?

Sgriob na Cailich is a very curious and conspicuous mark on the north-western side of the highest of the Jura hills. Two rocky gorges begin at the very top of the hill, which were made by the Carlin's heels, and two strips of bare grey boulders extend across the side of lower hills almost to the sea. Unless these last are the marks of lightning, I cannot account for them. This is the place where Dewar's fox threw the big women over the rock.

In her time the Island of Jura was under the sway of MacDonald of Islay, but this Carlin was so powerful, that she would not allow the Islay post to pass through Jura, for she killed him as soon as he crossed the ferry.

MacDonald spoke to a Jura man of the name of Buie, who lived at the Ferry and promised the farm of Largie Breac where the Caileach lived, to him and his heirs for ever, if he would kill her.

He told his wife the offer that MacDonald had made him, remarking at the same time, that he never would attempt to encounter the giantess.

Their eldest son, however, overheard his father, and set off the next day to offer battle to the Caileach.

They had wrestled hard and long, when at length she brought him on his knees, and she said "Thou art in extremity, a Mhic Meadh Bhuie, and pity it is so." "My grandmother, on the hinderside of Alba, is here, and will come to help me if I be," said he, as he put his hand on his dirk.

They engaged again, and she brought him on his knees again, saying the same words, Tha thu at eigin a Mhic Meadh Bhuie s' b olc an arraidh e, when he drew his dirk and stabbed her to the heart.

MacDonald performed his promise of giving the Buies Largie Breac, which they held for centuries after.

3. There is a song about the same personage, whoever she may have been. I give it, though I do not quite understand it.

Caileach Bheinna Bhric horo
Bhric horo Bhric horo
Caileach Bheinna Bhric horo
Caileach mhor leathan ard
Cha deachaidh mo bhuidheann fhiadh
Bhuidheann fhiadh bhuidheann fhiadh
Cha deachaidh mo bhuidheann riamh
A dh'iarraidh chlaba do 'n traigh

Carlin of Ben Breac horo, &c.,
Carlin great broad high,
There went not my troop of deer, &c.
There went not my troop ever
To seek her clack to the strand.

Now this old woman, or set of old women guarding a sword, or owning magic clues, and living in an island, are surely the same as the Groach, of whom so many stories are told in Brittany, and these are presumed to have been a college of Druidesses. See Foyer Breton, vol. i. p. 157 ; and if so, the Carlin may be a fiction founded upon fact.

The spelling Diura and Diurath for the Island of Jura, does not change the sound, but seems to indicate a reasonable derivation for the name which is common to the "Jura" mountains, and may well be an old Celtic name preserved, AN DIU RATH, the waste steep, the Jura.

There is a local rhyme in support of this view, said to have been composed by a poetess who was a native of some other island.

Dhiu Rath an domhain,
'S diu dath an domhain ann,
Buidhe Dugh a's Riabhach.

Waste steep of the world,
And waste hue of the world in it,
Yellow, black, and brindled.

These three colours being the most common family names, until very lately, in the island, as well as the distinguishing colours of the landscape, according to the eye of the discontented lady.

4. I have another version of this, which gives such a very different view of the same incidents that I translate it, giving such bits of the Gaelic as seem best worth preservation.

AN SIONNACH, THE FOX, from John the tinker, Inveraray, written by Hector Urquhart, 1859.

Brian, the son of the king of Greece, fell in love with the hen-wife's daughter, and he would marry no other but she. His father said to him on a day of days, before that should happen that he must get first for him the most marvellous bird that there was in the world.

Then here went Brian, and he put the world under his head, till he went much farther than I can tell, or you can think, till he reached the house of CAILLEACH NAN CUARAN, the carlin of buskins. (A sock, a brogue of untanned leather or skin, commonly worn with the hairy side outward; *Lat.*, Cothurnus; *Welsh*, Cwaran; *Fr.*, Cothurne.) He got well taken to by the carlin that night, and in the morning she said to him, "It is time for thee to arise, the journey is far."

When he rose to the door, what was it but sowing and winnowing snow; he looked hither and thither, and what should he see but a fox drawing on his shoes and stockings.

"SHA! BHEATHAICH, Sha! beast," said Brian, "Thou hadst best leave my lot of shoes and stockings for myself."

"Och," said the fox, "it's long since a shoe or a stocking was on me; and I am thinking that I shall put them to use this day itself."

"Thou ugly LADAMA (?) beast, art thou thinking to steal my foot webs, CHAISBEART, and I myself looking at thee?"

"Well," said the fox, "if thou wilt take me to be thy servant, thou shalt get thy set of shoes and stockings."

"Oh, poor beast," said he, "thou wouldst find death with me from hunger."

"O hoth!" said the fox, "there's little good in the gille that will not do for his ownself, and for his master at times."

"Yes! yes," said he, "I don't mind, at all events; thou mayest follow me."*

They had not gone far on their journey when the fox asked him if he was good at riding. He said he was, if it could be known what on.

"Come on top of me a turn of a while," said the fox.

"On top of thee! poor beast, I would break thy back."

"Ho! huth! son of the King of Greece," said the fox, "thou didst not know me so well as I knew thee; take no care but that I am able to carry thee."

But never mind; when Brian went on the top of the fox, CUIREADH IAD SAD AS GACH LODAN AGUS SRAD AS GACH CREAGAN S' CHA DO GHABH IAD TAMH NA FOIS GUS AN D' RAINIG IAD TIGH FAMHAIR NAN COIG CINN S' NAN COIG MÌLL S' NAN COIG MUINEAIL. They would drive spray from each puddle, spark from each pebble; and they took no halt nor rest till they reached the house of the Giant of Five Heads, Five Humps, and Five Throttles.

"Here's for thee," said the fox, "the house of the giant who has the marvellous bird, AN T EUN IONGANTACH; and what wilt thou say to him when thou goest in?"

"What should I say, but that I came to steal the marvellous bird?"

"Hu! hu! said the fox, "thou wilt not return; but," said the fox, "take thou (service) with this giant to be a stable lad, and there is no sort of bird FO SHEACHD RONAGAN RUADH AN T SAOGHAIL, under the seven russet rungs of the world (from RONG, a joining spar, a hoop, perhaps ring) that he has not got; and when he brings out the marvellous bird, say thou 'Fuith! fuith!' the nasty bird, throw it out of my sight, I could find braver birds than that on the middens at home."

Brian did thus.

"S' tia!" said the big one, "then I must go to thy country to gather a part of them."

---

* So far, this is somewhat like the opening of Puss in Boots, mixed up with something else.

But Brian was pleasing the giant well; but on a night of the nights, Brian steals the marvellous bird, and drags himself out with it. When he was a good bit from the giant's house, "S'tia!" said Brian to himself, "I don't know if it is the right bird I have after every turn." Brian lifts the covering off the bird's head, and he lets out one screech, and the screech roused the giant.

"O! O! son of the King of Greece," said the giant, "that I have coming to steal the marvellous bird; the prophet FAIDH was saying that he would come to his GIRD."

Then here the giant put on the shoes that could make nine miles at every step, and he was'nt long catching poor Brian. They returned home to the giant's house, and the giant laid the binding of the three smalls on him, and he threw Brian into the peat corner, and he was there till the morning on the morrow's day.

"Now," said the giant, "son of the King of Greece, thou hast thy two rathers; whether wouldst thou rather thy head to be yonder stake, or go to steal for me the White Glave of Light that is in the realm of Big Women?"

"S' BAIGHEIL DUINE RI BHEATHA, a man is kind to his life," said Brian, "I will go to steal the White Glave of Light."

But never mind; Brian had not gone far from the giant's house when the fox met him.

"O DHUINE GUN TUR GUN TOINSG, Oh man, without mind or sense, thou didst not take my counsel, and what will now arise against thee! Thou art going to the realm of Big Women to steal the White Glave of Light; that is twenty times as hard for thee as the marvellous bird of that carl of a giant."

"But what help for it now, but that I must, IONNSAIDH A THUBHAIRT AIR, betake myself to it," said poor Brian.

"Well, then," said the fox, "come thou on top of me, and I am in hopes thou wilt be wiser the next time."

They went then farther than I can remember, till they reached CNOCAN NA 'N AOINE AIR CUL GAOITHE 'S AIR AODAN GREINE, the knoll of the country at the back of the wind and the face of the sun, that was in the realm of big women.

"Now," said the Fox, "thou shalt sit here, and thou shalt begin at BURRALAICH blubbering, and CAOINEADH crying, and when the big women come out where thou art, they will lift thee N'AN ACHLAIS in their oxters, and when they reach the house with thee, they will try to coax thee, but never thou cease of crying until thou get the White Glave of Light, and they will leave it with thee in the cradle the length of the night, to keep thee quiet."

Worthy Brian was not long blubbering and crying when the big women came, and they took Brian with them as the fox had said, and when Brian found the house quiet, he went away with the White Glave of Light, and when he thought he was a good way from the house, he thought he would see if he had the right sword. He took it out of the sheath, and the sword gave out BINN, a ring. This awoke the big women, and they were on their soles. "Whom have we here," said they, "but the son of the King of Greece coming to steal the White Glave of Light."

They took after Brian, and they were not long bringing him back. CHEANGAIL IAD GU CRUIN E, they tied him roundly (like a ball), and they threw him into the peat corner, till the white morrow's day was. When the morning came they asked him CO B FHEARR LEIS A BHI FO SHRADAN A BHUILG SHEIDIDH * to be under the sparks of the bellows, or to go to steal AN DIA GREINE † NIGHEAN RIGH FEILL FIONN, the Sun Goddess, daughter of the King of the gathering of Fioun.

"A man is kind to his life," said Brian, "I will go steal the Sun Goddess."

Never mind. Brian went, but he was not long on the path AIR AN T SLIGHE when the fox met him.

"Oh! poor fool," said the fox, "thou art as FAOIN silly as thou wert ever. What good for me to be giving thee counsel, thou

---

* BOLG SEIDIDH, bag of blowing. The bellows used for melting copper in the mint at Tangiers in 1841, consisted of two sheepskins worked by two men. The neck of the hide was fastened to the end of an iron tube, and the legs sewn up. The end of each bag opened with two flat sticks, and the workmen, by a skilful action of the hand, filled the bag with air as he raised it, and then squeezed it out by pressing downwards. By working the two bags turn about, a constant steady blast was kept on a crucible on the furnace, and the copper was soon melted. The Gaelic word clearly points to the use of some such apparatus. I believe something of the kind is used in India; but I saw the Tangier mint at work.

† DIA GREINE may perhaps be DEO GREINE, the sunbeam, the name given to Fionn's banner, and here applied to his daughter.

art now going to steal the Sun Goddess. Many a better thief than thou went on the same journey ; but ever a man came never back. There are nine guards guarding her, and there is no dress under the seven russet rungs of the world that is like the dress that is on her but one other dress, and here is that dress for thee. And mind, said the fox, that thou dost as I ask thee, or, if thou dost not, thou wilt not come to the next SGEULA tale."

Never mind. They went, and when they were near the guard the fox put the dress on Brian, and he said to him to go forward straight through them, and when he reached the Sun Goddess to do as he bid him. And, Brian, if thou gettest her out I will not be far from you.

But never mind. Brian took courage, and he went on, and each guard made way for him, till he went in where the Sun Goddess, daughter of the King of the Gathering of Fionn, was. She put all hail and good luck on him, and she it was who was pleased to see him, for her father was not letting man come near her.

And there they were ; but how shall we get away at all at all, said she, in the morning. Brian lifted the window, and he put out the Sun Goddess through it.

The fox met them. "Thou wilt do yet," said he ; "leap you on top of me."

And when they were far, far away, and near the country of big women,

"Now, Brian," said the fox, "is it not a great pity for thyself to give away this Sun Goddess for the White Glave of Light?"

"Is it not that which is wounding me at this very time?" said Brian.

"It is that I will make a Sun Goddess of myself, and thou shalt give me to the big women," said the fox.

"I had rather part with the Sun Goddess herself than thee."

"But never thou mind, Brian, they wont keep me long."

Here Brian went in with the fox as a Sun Goddess, and he got the White Glave of Light. Brian left the fox with the big women, and he went forward.

In a day or two the fox overtook them, and they got on him, and when they were nearing the house of the big giant,

"Is it not a great pity for thyself, oh Brian, to part with the White Glave of Light for that filth of a marvellous bird."

"There is no help for it," said Brian.

"I will make myself a White Glave of Light," said the fox; "it may be that thou wilt yet find a use for the White Glave of Light."

Brian was not so much against the fox this time, since he saw that he had got off from the big women.

"Thou art come with it," said the big man. "It was in the prophecies that I should cut this great oak tree, at one blow, which my father cut two hundred years ago with the same sword."

Brian got the marvellous bird, and he went away.

He had gone but a short distance from the giant's house, when the fox made up to him with his pad to his mouth.

"What's this that befel thee," said Brian. "Oh, the son of the great one!" said the fox, "when he seized me, with the first blow he cut the tree all but a small bit of bark; and look thyself there is no tooth in the door of my mouth which that filth of a Bodach has not broken."

Brian was exceedingly sorrowful that the fox had lost the teeth, but there was no help for it.

They were going forward, walking at times, and at times riding, till they came to a spring that there was by the side of the road.

"Now, Brian," said the fox, "unless thou dost strike off my head with one blow of the White Glave of Light into this spring, I will strike off thine."

"S'tia!" said Brian, "a man is kind to his own life," and he swept the head off him with one blow, and it fell into the well; and in the wink of an eye, what should rise up out of the well, but the son of the King that was father of the Sun Goddess?

They went on till they reached his father's house, and his father made a great wedding with joy and gladness that lasted a day and a year, and there was no word about marrying the hen-wife daughter when I parted from them.

There can be no doubt that this is the same legend as the Golden Bird in Grimm, and it is evident that it is not derived from the printed story. From the notes in Grimm's third volume, it appears to be very old and very widely spread. I am told that even now there is some trace of a veneration for birds amongst the Turks, who secretly worship parrots even at Constantinople.

The giant of many heads and ornithological tastes is not in

the German version, and the tinker has omitted the horse, which seems to belong to the story.

On the 25th of April, 1859, John the tinker gave the beginning of this as part of his contribution to the evening's entertainment. He not only told the story, but acted it, dandling a fancied baby when it came to the adventure of the big women, and rolling his eyes wildly. The story which he told varied from that which he dictated in several particulars. It began :—

BHA RIGH ANN AGUS BHA RIGHDEIRE MAR A BHA S MAR A BHITHIS S' MAR A CHÌNNIS AN GHIUTHAS, CUID DHE CAM S' CUID DHE DIREACH AGUS SE RIGH EIRINN A BH' ANN.

"There was a king and a knight, as there was and will be, and as grows the fir tree, some of it crooked and some of it straight, and it was the King of Eirinn, it was ; and the Queen died with her first son, and the King married another woman. And the henwife came to her, and she said—A BHANRIGH DONA GHOLACH CHA NEIL THUSA COSAIL RIS A BHANRIGH SHONA SHÒLACH A BH' AGAIN ROIMHE SO. Oh ! bad straddleing Queen, thou art not like the sonsy, cheery Queen that we had ere now. And here came a long bit which the tinker put into another story, and which he seems to have condensed into the first sentence in the version which I have got and transiated. He has also transferred the scene from Ireland to Greece, perhaps because the latter country sounds better, and is farther off, or perhaps he had got the original form of the story from his old father in the meantime."

Some of the things mentioned in the tinker's version have to do with Druidical worship—the magic well, the oak tree, the bird ; for the Celtic tribes, as it is said, were all guided in their wanderings by the flight of birds. The Sun Goddess : for the Druids are supposed to have worshipped the sun, and the sun is feminine in Gaelic. These are all mixed up with Fionn, and the sword of light, and the big women, personages and things which do not appear out of the Highlands. Perhaps this is one of "the sermons" to which Dewar refers. (See introduction.)

XLVII.

FEARACHUR LEIGH.

From Sutherland.

NOW Farquhar was one time a drover in the Reay country, and he went from Glen Gollich to England (some say Falkirk), to sell cattle; and the staff that he had in his hand was hazel (caltuinn). One day a doctor met him. "What's that," said he, "that ye have got in y'r hand?" "It is a staff of hazel." "And where did ye cut that?" "In Glen Gollig: north, in Lord Reay's country. "Do ye mind the place and the tree?" "That do I." "Could ye get the tree?" "Easy." "Well, I will give ye gold more than ye can lift, if ye will go back there and bring me a wand off that hazel tree; and take this bottle and bring me something more, and I will give you as much gold again. Watch at the hole at the foot, and put the bottle to it; let the six serpents go that come out first, and put the seventh one into the bottle, and tell no man, but come back straight with it here.

So Farquhar went back to the hazel glen, and when he had cut some boughs off the tree he looked about for the hole that the doctor had spoken of. And what should come out but six serpents, brown and barred like adders. These he let go, and clapped the bottle to the hole's mouth, to see would any more come out. By and by a white snake came rolling through. Farquhar had him in the bottle in a minute, tied him down, and hurried back to England with him.

The doctor gave him siller enough to buy the Reay country, but asked him to stay and help him with the white snake. They lit a fire with the hazel sticks, and put the snake into a pot to boil. The doctor bid Farquhar watch it, and not let any one touch it, and not to let the steam escape, "for fear," he said, "folk might know what they were at."

He wrapped up paper round the pot lid, but he had not made all straight when the water began to boil, and the steam began to come out at one place.

Well, Farquhar saw this, and thought he would push the paper down round the thing; so he put his finger to the bit, and then his finger into his mouth, for it was wet with the bree.

Lo! he knew everything, and the eyes of his mind were opened. "I will keep it quiet though," said he to himself.

Presently the doctor came back, and took the pot from the fire. He lifted the lid, and dipping his finger in the steam drops he sucked it; but the virtue had gone out of it, and it was no more than water to him.

"Who has done this!" he cried, and he saw in Farquhar's face that it was he. "Since you have taken the bree of it, take the flesh too," he said in a rage, and threw the pot at him—(ma dh' ol thu 'n sugh ith an fheoil). Now Farquhar had become allwise, and he set up as a doctor. [The collector who took this down, grammar and all, here remarks, that Michael Scott got his knowledge by serpent's bree (brigh); and the wisdom of the mouth is said to have belonged to Fingal, who began life as a herd boy on the Shin. Some giants came to him one day and bade him roast a fish for them, threatening to kill him if he burnt it. He did so, all but one small spot. On this spot he quickly put his finger, and as quickly transferred the hot finger to his mouth, putting it under his teeth : a gift of omniscience was the result, and this became the foundation of his future greatness.

The very same incident with a dragon's heart is in the Volsung tale, see Dasent's introduction, p. 65. It is told in Chambers' Nursery Songs, of some laird in Scotland. Mrs. MacTavish tells it, and I have heard it in the west in various shapes ever since I can remember. Grimm found it in Germany in the story of the White Snake ; and there are varieties of the same incident scattered throughout Grimm ; for instance in the Two Brothers, where children eat the heart and liver of a golden bird, and find gold under their pillows ; and this story has a relation in Gaelic also. But to return to Farquhar Leech.]

He set up as a doctor, and there was no secret hid from him, and nothing that he could not cure.

He went from place to place and healed men, and so they called him Farquhar Leigheach (the healer). Now he heard that the king was sick, and he went to the city of the king to know what would ail him. "It was his knee," said all the folk, "and he has many doctors, and pays them all greatly; and whiles they can give him relief, but not for long, and then it is worse than ever with him, and you may hear him roar and cry with the pain that is in his knee, in the bones of it." One day Farquhar walked up and down before the king's house. And he cried—

"An daol dubh ris a chnamh gheal."
The black beetle to the white bone.

And the people looked at him, and said that the strange man from the Reay country was through-other.

The next day Farquhar stood at the gate and cried, "The black beetle to the white bone!" and the king sent to know who it was that cried outside, and what was his business. The man, they said, was a stranger, and men called him the Physician. So the king, who was wild with pain, called him in; and Farquhar stood before the king, and aye "The black beetle to the white bone!" said he. And so it was proved. The doctors, to keep the king ill, and get their money, put at whiles a black beetle into the wound in the knee, and the beast was eating the bone and his flesh, and made him cry day and night. Then the doctors took it out again, for fear he should die; and when he was better they put it back again. This Farquhar knew by the serpent's wisdom that he had, when he laid his finger under his teeth; and the king was cured, and had all his doctors hung.

Then the king said that he would give Farquhar lands or gold, or whatever he asked. Then Farquhar asked to have the king's daughter, and all the isles that the sea runs round, from point of Storr to Stromness in the Orkneys; so the king gave him a grant of all the isles. But Farquhar the physician never came to be Farquhar the king,* for he had an ill-wisher that poisoned him, and he died.

I am indebted to the kindness of Mr. Cosmo Innes for the following note, which joins a legend to an historical fact.

The names given are a curious instance of old Gaelic spelling. They are evidently spelt by ear, and so spelt as to be easily understood; but they are not spelt according to modern rule.

---

* There is a kind of rhyme here, in Gaelic,—Fearachur Leigh, and Fearachur Righ.

It is not often we can connect these wild legends with record or charter, but Farchar Leech receives a local habitation from authentic writs.

The "Reay country" of the legend is Strathnaver. One race of Mackays who inhabit it are called by their countrymen clan vic Farquhar—from what Farquhar, was unknown to Sir Robert Gordon and the local historians. The legend points to the man. In 1379 Farquhar, the King's physician *(medicus Regis)* had a grant from the Prince Alexander Stuart (the wolf of Badenoch) of the lands of Mellenes and hope in that district; and in 1386 King Robert II. granted to the same person, styled Ferchard Leech, in heritage, the islands of Jura (now Alderney), Calwa Sanda *(Handa)*, Elangawne, Elanewillighe, Elanerone, Elanehoga, between Rowestorenastynghe *(i.e., the Rowe or point of Store, in Assynt)*, and Rowearmadale *(i.e., Armidale Head in Farr)*.

The writer of the old statistical account of the parish, speaking of these grants from hearsay or tradition, names the grantee "Ferchard Beton, a native of Isla, and a famous physician." Perhaps he was misled by the celebrity of the Isla Betons, several generations of whom were "mediciners," famous through all the Islands and West Highlands.

Whether Farchar Leech died by poison or otherwise, he seems to have left descendants who inherited his lands; for, so late as 1511, Donald M'Donacy M'Corrochie described as "descendit frae Farquhar Leiche;" resigned Melness, Hope, and all his lands of Strathnaver in favour of the chief family of the Mackays.

The marriage with the King's daughter, as well as the black beetle, want confirmation.

There is a west country version of this story which I have known all my life in part; and which agrees with the account of the writer who spoke from tradition long ago.

Mrs. MacTavish writes :—

2. The OLLADH ILEACH (Islay Doctor).

There were three brothers of the name of Beaton, natives of Islay, famed for their skill in medicine. One of the brothers, called John, went to Mull, and was known as the *Olladh Muilleach*, or Mull doctor. His tomb is to be seen in Iona. Another called Fergus remained in Islay, and was known as the OLLADH ILEACH. The third, GILLEADHA, was in the end the most famed of the tree ; he was the herbalist, and employed by his brother Fergus to gather herbs and prepare them for use.

When boiling a cauldron of herbs, in which a white snake had been put, in stirring, it bubbled up and spattered on his hand, this he licked off, and at once he got such a view of his profession as to make him unrivalled. He was summoned to attend one of the Scotch Kings, who was cured by him ; but through the jealousy of other doctors, he never returned to Islay, having been poisoned.

(So far the Islay tradition very nearly accords with the Sutherland account of Farquhar Leech). He was called to see a young lady, daughter of Mackay of Kilmahumaig, near Crinan. When approaching the house, attended by a servant, the latter remarked a sweet female voice which he heard singing a song :—

"'S binn an guth cinn sin" ars' an gilleadh.
"'S binn" ars' an t-Olladh, "air uachdar Losguin."

"Sweet is that head's voice," said the lad ;
"Sweet," said the doctor, "above a Toad."

The poor young woman had an enormous appetite, which could not be satisfied, but she was reduced to a skeleton. The doctor, on hearing her voice, knew what her disease was, and ordered a sheep to be killed and roasted.

The lady was prevented from getting any food, from which she was in great agony.

She was made to sit by the sheep while it was being roasted, and the flavour of the meat tempted the toad she had swallowed to come up her throat and out of her mouth, when she was completely cured. The reptile she had swallowed was called Lon Craois.

Now, something very like this part was told me in Norway as a fact by a Norwegian, the travelling interpreter of an English companion. My old friend Juil has since become a flourishing contractor. He had seen a young woman on board a steamer going with her friends to Christiania for advice. She had been reaping, and had fallen asleep on a sheaf of corn in the field. She slept with her mouth open, and a serpent had run down her throat. She had been in a state of terror and horror ever since, and they were taking her to the capital. "I saw her myself," said my informant ; "I heard that the doctors could not cure her at Christiania, and that she went to Copenhagen. There all the great doctors were beat; but a young doctor made them put her in a dark room, lying on her side on the floor, with a saucer of milk before her. 'Serpents are very fond of milk you see.' The first time they opened the door the serpent had only put his head up, and he drew it in again when he heard the noise. The second time they moved the saucer a little further away, and he came out altogether, and the young doctor killed the serpent and shewed it to the young 'womans,'" and thus she got quite well. "And that is quite true."

Every word of it might be true, if we suppose a clever man and a woman possessed with an idea which had to be coaxed out of her; but the question is, when did that clever man live, and where?—in Copenhagen—in the West Highlands—or in Africa, where the creature swallowed was a baboon, and the bait a banana skilfully administered by a doctor to Anansi (Dasent, Norse Tales, p. 502); or in London, where a clever doctor tempted a serpent out of a patient with a mutton chop, according to a story told to a friend of mine in his childhood; or have there been many doctors and patients who have gone through the same adventure? But to go on with the west country wise men.

"The wife of a man who was suffering from rheumatism consulted the Olladh Muileach. He went to see him, bringing a birch rod, and having got his patient out of bed, ordered his wife to lay the birch rod smartly on his back, and chase him till the doctor would say it was enough. He would not allow her to cease till the poor man perspired freely and became supple, and free from pain."

This again might be true, every word; but when did the doctor live, and where? Was it in the country of King Voonan?

A learned doctor in the Arabian Nights, the sage Dooban, makes King Voonan play at ball till he perspires and absorbs some medicaments from the handle of the "Golfstick."

"Another man went to him for a cure for sore eyes. The doctor examined his eyes, but told him he was likely to suffer in a more serious manner from horns that would soon appear on his knees. The man seemed much alarmed, and asked if there was any way in which he could prevent such a calamity. 'No way,' said the doctor, 'but by keeping your hands on your knees for three weeks. At the end of that period come to me, that I may see how you get on.' The man did as he was advised, and went to the doctor."

"Well," said the doctor, "have the horns made their appearance?" "No," said the man.

"Have you attended to my advice?" said the doctor. "Oh, yes," said the patient, "I have kept my hands continually, night and day, on my knees."

"How are your eyes?" said the doctor. "My eyes are quite well," said the man. "Very well," said the doctor, "go home and keep your mind easy about the horns, and don't rub your eyes."

"The descendants of both Fergus and Gilleadh are still in Islay."

The name of Malcolm Bethune is written on a curious old manuscript in the Advocates' Library. It is described at page 295 of the report of the Highland Society on the poems of Ossian, 1805, with this note on the name:—"He was one of a family eminent for learning that supplied the Western Isles for many ages with physicians, whose diligence and skill are gratefully remembered in the traditionary record of their country."

It seems, then, that fifty-five years have not obliterated the popular tales clustered about the name of Bethune or Beaton, stored in the mind of one lady who may well remember the publication of the report, and to whose excellent memory this collection of stories owes so much.

Is the whole of this a remnant of Serpent worship and supposed possession by the god? In the Highlands now, as elsewhere, and from the earliest of times, serpents have something to do with healing. From the brazen serpent in the wilderness, to Æsculapius, and from Æsculapius to Farquhar Leech and Dr. Beaton, is a long stretch of time and space; but snakes are still associated with healing amongst Spartan shepherds, as well as Highland peasants, as the following extract from my journal will show:—

"1852, May 10.—Having turned some Indian corn out of a loft, took up our quarters for the night at a half-ruined house not far from Sparta. At the door were a lot of fellows in shaggy capotes drinking sour wine and making a row. One of them, dressed in a kind of sheepskin cloak, with a long crook in his hand, astonished me by pulling out a serpent a yard long, which he handled with perfect coolness.

"I rattled down the ladder, to the risk of my neck, and found that he had a bag full. There might have been half a dozen. I made him turn them all out, and set the Greeks to catch them again. My friend ended by producing a number of white powders, which made the swallower independent of snake bites. I bought a dozen, and proceeded to test them in the candle. They were vegetable, and I suspect flour."

In Ceylon, according to Sir Emerson Tennent (page 193), it is the same.

"There is a rare variety (of snakes) which the natives fancifully designate the King of the Cobras. It has the head and the anterior half of the body of so light a colour that at a distance it seems like a silvery white." . . . "Raja or King."

In the same page it appears that the snake charmers use a certain *stone* to cure snake bites, and that they also use a certain *root*. I do not know the word for snake, but Raja is not unlike RIGH, King. Snake charmers are also common in Northern Africa.

The serpent creed then is very widely spread, and the belief in the Highlands is worth illustration.

Widow Mary Calder (in Sutherland) tells, that "The great white snake is not uncommon in Sutherland, and has been sometimes, but not often, killed. It never rests by day or by night, and besides running along the ground, has a revolving motion peculiar to itself, turning over and over through an ivory ring which is loose on its body. This is formed from its own slime, and sometimes slips off,—in which case the snake makes another, and the finder of the ring is safe against all diseases and enchantments,"—Vide adder beads in the Gallovidian Encyclopædia.

"Another great serpent has been seen by the natives. The last was nine feet long, and covered with hair; it had a mane, and was a bodily manifestation of the evil one."

It was a common belief in the West that "snakes' eggs" were lucky. I once owned one, but lost it. It was a bead of various colours, blue and white, apparently of glass, very like those figured in Wilson's Prehistoric Annals of Scotland, page 304. These are commonly found in tumuli, and are the adder stones of the Lowlands, and Druid's glass in Ireland. They are supposed by Mr. Wilson to have been worn as charms by women of that unknown prehistoric race which once inhabited Scotland. At all events, the idea that they were produced by snakes is common.

Mr. Wilson suggests "the probable means of accounting for their introduction into Britain is by the Phœnicians, or by traders in direct communication with that people." If so, the same people may have brought the belief and the tales from the East, where a serpent has had to do with mythology from the earliest of times. (See Rawlinson's Herodotus, under the head Serpent). But besides this white king of snakes, who has a brother Raja in Ceylon, there is the great eel which is always appearing in lakes and in the sea, and which is firmly believed to exist. It has no peculiarity that I know of but enormous size. A keeper used to tell me that he saw it repeatedly in a small but very deep lake. "It was as big as a saik" (sack). I am quite sure the man believed what he said, though I believe his eyes had but realized an old legend.

Mrs. MacTavish writes:—"An old man in Lorn used to tell that he went one summer morning to fish on a rock; he was not long there when he saw the head of an eel pass. He continued fishing for an hour, and the eel was still passing. He went home, worked in the field all day, and having returned to the same rock in the evening, the eel was still passing, and about dusk he saw her tail disappearing behind the rock on which he stood fishing." The old man was nicknamed Donul n' ro; Donald of the reef.

That eel was a bouncer, but not so big as the sea-serpent of the Edda, which went round the world.

A gentleman, in whose house I dined at Tromsoe, near the Arctic circle, told me that "the fishermen often saw the sea-worm in Salten Fjord." All the world have heard of Capt. MacQuae's sea-snake. I have a drawing of him done by a gentleman who was a midshipman on board the Dœdulus and saw him. I lately saw a master of a merchant vessel at Liverpool, who calmly and deliberately assured a royal commission that he had seen a large serpent "in the sea about the same place." He said nothing about it in the papers, for no one would believe him; but he had no doubt about it—he saw the sea-snake.

I have no doubt that these men all believed what they said to be true. It is hard to believe that they were all mistaken. Few of them can have heard of Pontoppidan, Bishop of Bergen; but his book gives pictures of the sea-snake, and tells how it was seen and shot at in Norwegian Fjords in his day. There surely are some such creatures in the sea. Highland stories are full of sea monsters which are called Uille bheist and Draygan, and which have numerous heads. Surely there must be some foundation for so many fictions. St. George killed a Dragon; Perseus a sea monster; Bellerophon the Chimera; Hercules the Hydra; Apollo killed Pytho; Fraoch killed, and was killed by, a Behir (great snake); Vishnoo killed a serpent in India. "Sin, the giant Aphophis, as 'the great serpent,' often with a human head," was represented pierced by the spear of Horus or of Atmoo (as Re the Sun) in Egypt.* In short, I believe that the Gaelic serpent-stories, and the Highland beliefs concerning them, are old myths, a part of the history of the oldest feud in the world; the feud with the serpent who was "more subtle than any beast of the field that the Lord had made," for the leading idea seems always to be that the holy, healing power overcomes the subtle destroyer. Thus Mrs. M'Tavish tells that St. Patrick coaxed the last Irish snake into a chest by the promise that he would let him out "to-morrow," and then he put him into Lough Neagh, and there he is still. The serpent is always asking, "is it to-morrow?" but a "to-morrow" is never come; and no serpents are to be found on any place belonging to Ireland to this day.

The same belief extends to numerous small islands on the coast of Scotland, and old ruined chapels with sculptured grave-stones are generally to be found in them. I know one such island where some boys (as I was told) once took a living serpent, and it died. It is named Texa, and this legend is attached to it:— "It is a portion of Ireland which a giant's wife took a fancy to carry across the Channel in her apron. From a rent in the apron, Tarsgier fell through, and the rent getting larger, Texa fell from her, and so by degrees did all the other rocks and islets between Texa and the point of Ardmore, where she left Eillan a chuirn, which she did not think worth taking any further, being so much annoyed at having lost the rest. Certain it is that neither serpents nor toads are found in these islands, though both are numerous in Islay. It is said that neither can live in any place which St. Columba blessed, or where he built chapels and monasteries, such as in Eillach a Naomh and Iona."

So then, in the West Highlands now, the holy power overcomes the snake, as in mythology over great part of the world, and as it seems to me the belief may perhaps be traced to holy writ.

---

* Rawlinson's Herod., vol. ii., p. 261.

XLVIII.

THE TALE OF SGIRE MO CHEALAG.

From John Campbell, Strath Gairloch, Ross.

THERE was once a young lad, and he went to seek a wife to Sgire mo Chealag; and he married a farmer's daughter, and her father had but herself. And when the time of cutting the peats came on, they went to the peat hag, the four.

And the young wife was sent home to seek the food; and when she had gone in she saw the speckled filly's packsaddle over her head, and she began to cry, and to say to herself,—

"What should she do if the packsaddle should fall, and kill herself and all that were to follow."

When the people who were gathering the peats found that she was long without coming, they sent her mother away to see what was keeping her, and when the carlin arrived she found the bride crying,

"That it should come to me!"—Said she, "What came to thee?"

"Oh," said she, "when I came in I saw the speckled filly's packsaddle over my head, and what should I do if it should fall and kill myself and all that are to follow!"

The old woman struck her palms. "It came to me this day! If that should happen, what shouldst thou do, or I with thee!"

The men who were in the peat-hag were thinking it long that one of the women was not coming, for hunger had struck them. So it was that the old man went home to see what was keeping the women, and when he went in it was so that he found the two crying, and beating their palms.

"O, uvon!" said he, "what came upon you?"

"O!" said the old woman, "when thy daughter came home, did she not see the speckled filly's pack-saddle over her head, and what should she do if it should fall and kill herself and all that were to follow!"

"It came upon me!" said the old man, as he struck his palms, "If that should happen!"

The young man came at the mouth of night, full of hunger, and he found a leash crying together.

"Oovoo!" said he, "what came upon you?" and when the old man told him;

"But," said he, "the packsaddle did not fall."

When he took his meat he went to lie down; and in the morning he said, "My foot shall not stay till I see other three as silly as ye."

Then he went through Sgire mo Chealag, and he went into a house in it, and there was no man within but a leash of women, and they were spinning on five wheels.

"I myself will not believe," said he, "that it is of the people of this place that you are."

"Well, then," said they, "it is not. We ourselves will not believe that it is of the people of the place that thou art thyself."

"It is not," said he.

"Weel," said they, "the men that there are in this

place are so silly, that we can make them believe anything that we please ourselves."

"Weel," said he, "I have here a gold ring, and I will give it to the one amongst you who will best make her husband believe."

The first one that came home of the men, his wife said to him, "Thou art sick."

"Am I," said he.

"Oh thou art," said she, "put off thee thy lot of clothes, and be going to lie down."

He did this, and when he was in the bed she said to him, "Thou art now dead."

"Oh, am I?" said he.

"Thou art," said she, "shut thine eyes and stir not hand or foot."

And now he was dead.

Then there came the second one home, and his wife said to him, "It is not thou."

"O, is it not me?" said he.

And he went away and betook himself to the wood.

Then here came the third to his own house, and he and his wife went to lie down, and a summons went out on the morrow for the burial of the dead man, but this wife would not let her husband get up to go there.

When they saw the funeral going past the window, she told him to be rising. He arose in great haste, and he was seeking his set of lost clothes, and his wife said to him that his clothes were about him.

"Are they?" said he.

"They are," said she: "Haste thee that thou mayest catch them."

Here, then, he went, running hard. And when the funeral company saw the man who was stripped coming, they thought it was a man who was out of his reason, and they themselves fled away, and they left the funeral. And the naked man stood at the end of the dead-chest. And there came down a man out of the wood, and he said to the man who was naked,—

"Dost thou know me?"

"Not I," said he, "I do not know thee."

"Oh, thou dost not! if I were TOMAS my own wife would know me."

"But why," said he, "art thou naked?"

"Am I naked? If I am, my wife told me that the clothes were about me."

"It was my wife that said to me that I myself was dead," said the man in the chest.

And when the men heard the dead speaking, they took their soles out (of that), and the wives came and they took them home, and it was the wife of the man who was dead that got the ring.

And then he saw three as silly as the three he left at home, and returned home.

And then he saw a boat going to fish, and there were twelve men counted going into the boat, and when she came to land, there was within her but eleven men, and there was no knowing which one was lost, for the one who was counting was not counting himself at all. And he was beholding this.

"What reward would you give me if I should find you the man that is lost by you?"

"Thou shalt get any reward if thou wilt find the man," said they.

"Sit there," said he, "beside each other;" and he seized a rung of a stick, and he struck the first one a sharp stroke.

"Mind thou that thou wert in her" (the boat).

He kept on striking them, till he had roused twelve men, and made them bleed on the grass.

And though they were pounded and wounded, it was no matter, they were pleased, because the man who was lost was found, and after the payment they made a feast for the one who had found the man who was lost.

The tenants of Sgire mo Chealag had a loch on which they used to put fish, and so it was that they needs must drain the loch, to get fresh fish for the feast; and when the loch was drained, there was not a single fish found on the loch but one great eel. Then they said,—

"This is the monster that ate our fish." Then they caught her, and they went away with her to drown her in the sea. And when he saw this he went home; and on the way he saw four men putting a cow up to the top of a house that she might eat the grass that was growing on the house-top. Then he saw that the people of Sgire mo Chealag were men without intelligence; but said he, "What reward will you give me, and I will bring the grass down?"

He went and he cut the grass, and he gave it to the cow, and went on before him.

Then he saw a man coming with a cow in a cart, and the people of the town had found out that the man had stolen the cow, and that MOD a court should be held upon him, and so they did; and the justice they did was to put the horse to death for carrying the cow.

And to shew you that this tale is true, it was this that made Iain Lom the bard say:

"As law of ages that are not
As was Sgire mo Cheallag,
When doomed they the garron in mote."

SGEULACHD SGIRE MO CHEALAG.

Bha Gille og ann uair 's chaidh e dh' iarraidh mna do Sgire ma Chealag, agus phos e nighean tuathanaich 's cha robh aig a h-athair ach i fhein, agus dar a thainig am buain na mòine, chaidh iad do'n bhlar mhòine 'nan ceathrar. 'S chuiradh a' bhean og dhachaidh air thòir na diathad, agus air dol a stigh dhi chunnaic i strathair na làroch brice fos a cionn, agus thòisich i air caoineadh 's air gradha rithe fhein, de dheanag ise na 'tuiteag an t-srathair, 's gum marbhag e i fhein 's na bheir a siubhal. Dar a b' fhada le luchd buain na moine a bha e gun tighinn chuir iad a màthair air falbh a shealltainn de bha ga cumail. Nuair a ranig a' chailleach fhuair i 'bhean og a caoine a steach, "Air tighinn ormsa," ars' ise, "de thainig riut?" "O," as ise, "dar a thainig mi steach chunnaic mi strathair na làroch brice fos mo chionn 's de dheanainn-sa na'n tuiteadh i 's gu marbhag i mi fhein 's na th'air mo shiubhal!" Bhuail an t-seana bhean a basan. "Thainig ormsa an diugh! na'n tachradh sin, de dheanadh tu, na mise leat!" Bha na daoine a bha 'sa bhlar mhòin' a gabhail fadachd nach robh a h-aon do na Boireanaich a tighinn, bho'n bhuail an t-acras iad. 'Sann a dh' fhalbh an seann duine dhachaidh, a dh' fhaican de bha cumail nam boireannach, agus dar a chaidh e steach 'sann a fhuair e 'n dithis a' caoineadh sa' bas bhualadh. "Ochon," ars' easan, de a thainig oirbh." "O," arsa 'n t-seana bhean, "dar a thainig do nighean dachaidh, nach faca i strathair na làiroch brice fos a cionn, 's de dhianag ise na 'n tuiteag i 's gum marbhag i i fhein 's na bheir a siubhal. "Thainig ormsa," arsa ann seann duine 'se buala nam bas, "nan tachradh sin." Thainig an duine og am beul na h-oidhche làn acrais, 's thuair e triur a' comh chaoiniadh. "Ubh, ubh," ars' esan, "gu de thainig oirbh." Agus an uair a dh' innis an seann duine dha. "Ach," ars' esan, "cha do thuit an t-srathair." Nuair a ghabh e biadh chaidh e luidhe, agus anns a mhaduinn thubhairt easan, "Cha stad mo chas ach gu faic mi triur eile cho gòrrach ruibh. Dh' fhalbh e so air feadh Sgire mo Chealag, agus chaidh e steach do thigh ann, agus cha robh duine a steach ach triur bhan, 's iad a' sniamh air coig cuigealan. "Cha chreid mi fhein," ars' easan, "gur h-ann a' mhuintir an àite so tha sibh. "Ta," ars' iadsan, "cha 'n ann; cha chreid sin fhein gur ann a mhuintir an àite sinn fhein. "'S ann cha 'n ann," ars' easan. "Will," ars' iadsan, tha na daoine tha 'san àite so cho faoin 's gun dobhair sinn a chreidsinn orra na h-uile ni a thoileachas sinn fhein." "Will," ars' easan, "tha fàinne òir agam an so agus bheir mi e do'n te agaibh a's fearr a bheir a chreidsin air an duine." A cheud fhear a thainig dhachaidh do na daoine thuirt a bhean ris, "Tha thu tinn." "Am bheil?" as eise. "O tha," thuirt ise. "Cuir dhiot do chuid aodaich 's bi dol a luidh." Rinn e so; agus dar a bha e anns a' leabaidh, thuirt i ris, "Tha thu nise marbh." "O am bheil?" as eise. "Tha," as ise, "dùin do shuilean 's na gluais lamh na cas." Agus bha e so marbh. Thainig an so an darna fear dhachaidh, agus thubhairt a bhean ris, "Cha tu th'ann." "O nach mi," as eise. "O cha tu," as ise. 'S dh' fhalbh e 's thug e choille air. Thainig an so an trithumh fear a dh'ionnsaidh a thighe fhein, agus chaidh e fhein 'sa bhean a luidhe, 's chaidh gairm a mach am mairoch chum an duine marbh thiolagag; ach cha robh a bhean-san a leigeil leisean eiridh dho dhol ann. Dar a chunnaic iad an giulan a' dol seachad air an uineig dh' fhiar i air e bhi 'g eiridh. Dh' eirich e 'so le cabhaig mhoir 's bha e 'g iarraidh a chuid aodaich 's e air chall, 's thubhairt, a bhean ris gun robh a chuid aodaich uime. "Am bheil?" as eise. "Tha," as ise. "Greas thusa ort achd gu beir thu orra." Dh' fhalbh e 'so 'na chruaidh ruith, agus an uair a chunnaic cuideachd a' ghiulain an duine lomnochd a' tighinn, smaoinich iad gur duine e a bha as a chiall, 's theich iad fhein air falbh, 's dh' fhag iad an giulan, agus sheas an duine lomnochd aig ceann na ciste mhairbh, agus thainig duine nuas as a' choille, agus thubhairt e ris an duine bha lomnochd, "Am bheil thu dha m' ainmin?" "Cha 'n 'eil mise," as easan, "dha 'd tainin." "O cha 'n 'eil; na bo mbi Tomas dh' ainichag mo bhean fhein mi." "Ach carson," as easan, a tha thusa lomnochd?" "Am bheil mi lomnochd? Ma tha thubhairt mo bhean rium gun robh an t-aodach umam." "'Se mo bhean a thubhairt riumsa gun robh mi fhein marbh," arsa a' fear a bha 'sa chiste. Agus an uair a chuala na daoine am marbh a' bruidhinn thug iad na buinn asta 's thainig na mnathan 's thug iad dhachaidh iad, agus 'se bean an duine a bha marbh a fhuair am fàinne, agus chunnaic easan an sin triur cho gòrrach ris an triur a dh' fhag e aig an tigh, agus thill easan dhachaidh.

Agus chunnaic easan an sin bàta 'dol a dh' iasgach, agus chunntadh da dhuine dheug a' dol a steach do'n bhàta, agus an uair a thainig i gho tìr cha robh innte ach aon duine deug. 'S cha robh fios co 'a fear a bha air chall. Agus a' fear a bha gha'n cunntag cha robh e gha chuntag fhein idir, agus bha easan a' coimhead so. "Gu de an duais a bheir sibh dhomhsa na 'faoighinn a' fear a tha air chall oirbh?" "Gheamh thu duais air bhith mo gheamh thu 'n duine," thubhairt iadsan. "Dianaibh," as easan, "suidhe ri taobh a cheile ma tha." Agus rug e air siulpan maide, agus bhuail e 'cheud fhear, "Biadhag cuimhne agadsa gu robh thu fhein innte." Lean e air am bualadh gus an d' fhuair e naire da dhuine dheag 'se cuir fuil gu feur orra, agus ged a bha iad pronnte agus leòinte cha robh comas air, bha iad toilichte air son gu 'n d' fhuarag an duine bha air chall, agus air chùl paigheag 's ann a rinn iad cuirm d'on duine a fhuair a' fear a bha air chall.

Bha loch aig tuath Sgire mo Chealag air am bitheag iad a' cur iasg, agus 'ars esan, "'sann bo chòir dhuibh a' loch a' thràig gus am faigheag iad iasg ùr dhon na cuirme;" agus dar a thraog an loch cha d' fhuarag diarg éisg air an loch ach aon Easgann mhor. Thubhairt iad an so gu 'm b'e siud a' bhiast a dhìth an t-iasg oirra. Rug iad orra an so agus dh' fhalbh iad leatha gu bathag 'sa mhuir; agus a nuair a chunnaic easan so, dh' fhalbh e dhachaidh, agus air a' rathad, chunnaic e ceathrar dhaoine a' cur suas mart gho mullach tighe gus an itheag e feur a bha cinntin air mullach an tighe. Chunnaic e 'so gu mo daoine gun tamhuil sluagh Sgire mo Chealag. "Ach," as easan, "de 'n duais a bheir sibh dhomhsa 's bheir mi nuas am feur?" Chaidh e 's dh' iarr e feur 's thug e do 'n mhart e agus dh' imich e roimhe. Chunnaic e 'so duine a' tighinn 's mart aige ann an cairt, agus dh' aithnich daoine a' bhaile gur e 'goid a' mhairt a rinn a' fear so, agus 's e bo chòir mòd a chur air. Mar so rinn iad, agus 's e 'n ceartas a rinn iad an t-each a chuir gu bàs airson a bhith giùlan a' mhairt.

Agus gu diarbhag a thoir dhuibhsa gu 'm bheil an sgeulachd so fior 'se so a thug air *Iain Lom am Bard a chantainn.*

"Mar lagh na linnibh nach mairionn
A bha 'Sgire Mo Cheallag
Dar a dhit iad an gearran"
'Sa mhòd.

H. Urquhart.

This story was written by Hector Urquhart, from the telling of John Campbell in Strathgairloch, in Ross-shire, in June 1859. The narrator is sixty-three, and he says he learned the story from his father about forty years ago. Iain Lom, the bard quoted was a famous Highland poet, and lived in the reigns of Charles the First and Second; he died at a very advanced age about 1710. His name was Macdonald; his country, Lochaber; and his nickname, Lom, means bare or keen, for it is applied to a beardless man like the poet, or a biting keen wind like his sarcastic genius.

He was pensioned by Charles the Second as his bard, brought Montrose and the Campbells together at Inverlochy, and kept out of the fight, saying to the commander of the Irish auxiliaries, "If I fall, who will sing thy praises?" He did sing the battle, in which the Campbells got the worst; and the story goes, that Argyll was so nettled by the song that he offered a reward for his head.

He came himself and claimed the reward, and was courteously received, and conducted through the castle. On entering a room hung round with black-cocks' heads, Argyll said, "Hast thou ever, John, seen so many black-cocks in one place?" "I have seen them," said John. "Where?" "At Inmher Lochaidh." "Ah! John, John, thou wilt never cease gnawing the Campbells." "The worst for me is that I cannot swallow them," said John.

This story, a short biography, and a selection from the poems of Iain Lom, will be found in John Mackenzie's "Beauties of Gaelic Poetry," 1841 (Glasgow: MacGregor, Polson, & Co., 75 Argyll Street), a work which deserves to be better known. The verse quoted from memory by John Campbell, is in a song dedicated to the Macdugalds, and is this:—

> "Cleas na binne nach mairean
> Bha 'n sgìre Cille-ma- Cheallaig
> 'Nuair a dhit iad an gearran 'sa mhòd;"

and the story told in the note is, that some women, as judges, doomed a horse to be hanged. The thief who stole him first got off, because it was his first offence; the horse went back to the house of the thief, because he was the better master, and was condemned for stealing himself the second time.

There is an ingenuity in this unreasonable decision, which proves the inventor of that story to be no fool.

The story had passed into a saying long ago:—

CHA TUGADH AN CILLE-MA-CHEALLAIG BREATH BU CHLAOINE.

There would not be given in Cille ma Cheallaig judgment more squint or perverted.

Part of this story, then, has a Gaelic pedigree of about 200 years. Part of it is nearly the same as the beginning of No. 20, and is like "Die kluge Else" in German, which has a German pedigree in Grimm's third volume, which dates from 1588. The story belongs to the same class as an old English rhyme, of which a version is given in Old Nurse's book, by C. Bennet, 1857.

"There was a little woman
As I've heard tell,
And she went to market
Her eggs for to sell," etc., etc.

She goes through adventures,—

"And she met a pedlar,
And his name was Stout,
And he cut her petticoats
All round about."

The little old woman got very cold, and when she awoke doubted her identity, and when her little dog at home barked at her, she ran away, sure it was not her (and this is like the Norse tale, "Goosy Grizzle.")

A lot of similar stories are common in the Highlands. The following are from Sutherland, and form part of the collections already referred to :—

2. The Assynt man's mistakes.

Assynt is looked on in Sutherland and Ross-shire as being in a state of barbarism resembling that which the people south of Stirling supposed to prevail north of it ; and the mistakes of the Assyndiach are the groundwork of half the children's stories. I have seen nearly all these, and more, ascribed in German to two children, Kördel. und Michel, whose stupidity has become proverbial in their own land. I am told that schoolboys are conversant with a Greek version, and that they construe a tale of the man who, when asked if his house was a good one, brought one of the stones as a sample.

The Assyndiach was once sent by his wife to take her spinning-wheel to the turner's to get it mended. In coming back the wind set the wheel in motion, so he threw the whole thing down, saying, "Go, and welcome."

He struck across the hills, and reaching home, asked his wife if she had got her wheel yet.

"No," said she.

"Well, I thought not," said he, "for I took the short cut."

3. A very similar story was told me by an old Highlander in London.

An Inverness wife went to market with a creelful of balls of worsted, which she had spent a long time in spinning. As she walked along, one of the balls fell out, and the end being fast to the others, the ball followed, rolling and bumping along the road.

The wife turned round, and seeing the ball said, "Oh, you can go alone! Then you may all walk." And she emptied her creel, and tied the ends of the thread to it, and marched into Inverness without ever looking behind her; but when she got there, she had but a ravelled hesp.

4. A traveller stopped at his (the Assynt man) house to ask the hour. He lifted a large sun-dial from its stand, and put it into his lap, that he might see for himself.

5. Seeing a four-wheeled carriage, he exclaimed "Well done the little wheels, the big ones won't overtake them to-day." (Which story is told of Sir Andrew Wylie in Galt's novel).

6. He once took his child to be baptized; the minister said he doubted if he were fit to hold the child for baptism.

"Oh, to be sure I am, though it was as heavy as a stirk."

This answer shewing little wit, the minister asked him how many commandments there were.

"Twenty," he said boldly.

"Oh, that will never do; go back and learn your questions" (Shorter Catechism).

Half way home he met a man.

"How many commandments will there be? There must be thirty, for the minister was not content with twenty."

He was set to rights on this point, and turning back (it was winter), he thought the clergyman would not refuse him this time.

He had slipped the child into his great-coat sleeve, and tied up the cuff with a string; but the string got loose, and the bairn fell out, and the clever father never heard it, for it fell into a snow wreath. In the church he discovered his loss, and said to the clergyman, "I am very sorry, but not a bit of Kenneth have I" (no wise man will ever name an unchristened child). The unlucky infant nearly died in the snow, and I do not know that the sacrament was administered to it.

7. The Assynt man once went to Tain to buy meal. Outside the town, a man asked him if he knew what o'clock it was. "Last time it was 12. If it is striking still, it must be at 50."

8. His wife, like the Mütter in the story of Michel and Cordelia, had all the wit of the family, and was much distressed at his stupidity and simplicity.

He was carrying two bags of cheeses to market for her one day; one bag burst, and he saw all the cheeses rolling fast down hill. Pleased at their newly discovered power of locomotion, he undid the second bag, and sent its contents after the first, and walked on himself to market. When he got there, he asked if his dairy stuff had not turned up yet?

"No," said the neighbours. So he waited all day, and then returned to tell his wife, who, guessing his mistake, bid him look at the bottom of the hill, where he was enchanted to find the missing cheeses.

9. Seeing a hare for the first time, he backed from it, repeating the Lord's Prayer, till he fell into a duck pond, from which his wife drew him with difficulty.

This last adventure is like the "Seven Swabians" in Grimm, and that is like the Hunting of the Hare, a very old ballad; and all this was gathered from people whose names are not given, but who belong to Sutherland, and whose occupations generally are such as to make it probable that their stories are what they profess to be—traditions.

They are a people whose native language is Gaelic, but who generally speak English.

10. I have another version of the story in Gaelic, from Islay, called "FIGHEADAIR MOR BAILE NA GAILLEARAIN," "The Big Weaver of the Strangers' Town," written by Hector MacLean,

from which I translate the following extracts, told by Alexander Macalister, Bowmore :—

There was a poor woman before now, and she had a son, and he was reckoned a kind of LEITH-BHURRAIDH—half booby.

A ship was broken on the shore, and it was a cargo of wood that was on board, and he stole some PLANCAICHEN (planks, made into Gaelic), out of her, and he hid them in the sand. Much of the wood was stolen and there was RANNSACHADH, a ransacking going on. The carlin knew, NAM FEORACHADH EUD, if they should ask her son if he had stolen the planks, that he would say he had stolen them ; so in the morning before he awoke, she put on a pot, and she made milk porridge, and she took the porridge with her, and she sprinkled it on the doors and the door-posts. When her son got up he went out, and he saw the porridge on the door.

"What is here?" said he.

"Is it thus thou art?" said his mother; "didst thou not notice the shower of milk porridge at all?"

"I did not notice it ; this is a marvellous thing. A shower of milk porridge !" said the son.

On a day after that, all about the place was called on to be questioned about the wood. They asked him if he had stolen much ; and he said that he had.

"When didst thou steal it?"

"Have you any knowledge of the day that the porridge shower was?"

"There is enough ! there need not be any more speaking made to thee, be thou gone."

At the end of a while, when all talk was past, he went and he took the wood and he made INNSREABH (?) for the house, and CREADHAL, a cradle, so that when he should marry and he should have children, that the cradle might be ready. He married, and he was a while married, and he had no children at all.

His wife, and his mother, and his mother-in-law were in with him. On a day that there was, he was weaving, and what should SPAL, the shuttle, do, but cast MEID (?) a weight into the cradle. His wife got up, and she belaboured her palms, and she roared and she cried. His mother got up, and his mother-in-law, and they belaboured their palms, and they roared and they cried, "The booby ! without reason. If he were there he were dead ; was there ever heard tell of a man GUN MOHATHACHADH without perception like him !"

He got up at last, when he was SEARBH, worn out, with the roaring and the scolding. "There shall not come a stop on my foot, or rest on my head, till I hit upon three more silly than you." And he went away.

The first fools he met were the same as in the Ross-shire version, a man and a woman trying to put a cow on a house top to eat GOIRT, corn, which was growing on the roof. He asked what they would give him if he would make the cow eat it below; and when they said that could not be done, he cut the corn with his knife and threw it down, and got fifty marks.

And here let me point out that there is nothing *impossible* in this nonsense. In the first place, corn and hay do grow on thatched houses in the West Highlands, in Norway, and in Lapland, and it is by no means uncommon to see goats browsing there. I have seen a Lapp mowing his crop of hay on the top of the best house in the village of Karasjok, a log-house which is occupied in winter and deserted in summer.

I helped the people at their hay harvest one day, and tried to teach them the use of a fork. Their manner was to gather as much of the short grass as they could grasp in their arms, and carry it to the end of the field. I and my comrade cut two forked sticks, and, beginning at the end of the swathe, pushed the heap before us, doing as much at one journey as the Lapps at half-a-dozen trips. But we had fallen in with one of the old school. He was an old fellow with long tangled elf-locks and a scanty beard, dressed in a deerskin shirt full of holes, and exceedingly mangy, for the hair had been worn off in patches all over. He realized my idea of a seedy brownie, a gruagach with long hair on his head; an old wrinkled face, and his body covered with hair. He gave us one glance of sovereign contempt, his daughter a condescending smile, and then they each gathered another armful of grass, and toddled away, leaving the forked sticks where they were, as new-fangled contrivances, unworthy of the notice of sensible men.

And let any inventor say whether this is not human nature all over the world: but to go on.

He went on till he came to some men who were building a dyke, with their feet bare. There came a shower of rain, and he sat in the shelter of a dyke, and when it was clear they sat there, and there was no talk of getting up.

"It is astonishing to me," said he, "that you should keep on sitting, now that it is dry. It did not astonish me that you should go to shelter in the rain, but it must be that you are not diligent for your master when you are sitting while you ought to be working."

"That is not it," said they; "it is that our legs are all mingled together, and not one of us can recognize our own legs."

"What will you give me if I make you recognize your own legs.

"What wilt thou ask?"

"Half a hundred MARG, marks."

"Thou shalt have that CHA BU GHEAMHA DHUINN AIR MORAN BARRACHD. It were no pledge for us by much more to be thus away from our work."

He went down to a bramble bush, and he cut one as long and as strong as he could see. He came up and THUG E RALLSADH GU MATH TEANN ORRA, and he gave a good tight raking at them about their legs, and it was not long till every one knew his own legs.

(There is a double meaning in this which cannot be translated. To know means also to feel).

"Though our legs are sore and scratched," said they, "it is well for us to be able to go to our work rather than be seated thus."

"You are strange enough," said he, "but I will go further."

And then he goes on to a house, and plays tricks to some people there, and says his name is SAW YE EVER MY LIKE. And when the old man of the house came home, he found his people tied upon tables, and said, "What's the reason of this?" "Saw ye ever my like?" said the first. "No, never," said he. And went to the second, "What's the reason of this?" said he.

"Saw ye ever my like?" said the second.

"I saw thy like in the kitchen," said he; and he went to the third. "What is the reason of this?" said he. "Saw ye ever my like?" said the other. "I have seen plenty of thy likes," said he, "but never before this day." And then he understood that some one had been playing tricks on his people, and pursued; but the weaver played him a trick, which is almost the same as that which is given in Norse Tales as part of the adventures of the Master Thief, at page 286, second edition.

And so here, as in almost every case, the popular tales of the

West Highlands join in with those of other countries, and turn out to be as old as the hills.

Now surely this has some reason and some foundation in fact. When so many popular tales agree in describing a set of strangers, who were fools, does it not seem as if each land had once been occupied by a race who appeared to the new comers as foolish as the old Lapp haymaker seemed to me.

XLIX.

THE CAT AND THE MOUSE.*

From Hector MacLean, Islay.

1.

THUIRT an luch bheag 's i 'san toll,
" Dé 'm fonn a th' air a' chat ghlas ? "
" Fonn math is deagh shaod
Gum faodadh thusa tighinn a mach."

2.

" 'S mor m' eagal romh na dubhain chrom,
A th' agad ann am bonn do chas
Mharbh thu mo phiuthrag an dé
'S fhuair mi fein air eigin as."

3.

" Cha mhis' a bha 'sin ach cat mhic Iain Ruaigh
A b' àbhaist a bhi ruagadh chearc,
Ghoid i 'n caise 'bha 's a' chliabh,
'S dh'ith i 'n t-iasg a bha 's a' phreas."

TRANSLATION.

1.

Said the mousie in the hole,
" What *is* that purr of the grey cat ?"
" A good purr and a pleasant mood,
That thou mightest come out of that."

---

* You speak of Nursery Rhymes. The following is a very trifling one, which I remember myself, and have never been able to forget.

HECTOR MACLEAN, Islay.

2.

"Great is my fear for the crooked hooks
That thou hast got in the sole of thy feet;
Thou killedst my sister yesterday,
And I myself got hardly quit."

3.

"That was not me, but John Roy's cat,
That used to be the hen's distress:
She stole the cheese that was in the creel,
And ate the fish that was in the press."

This old rhyme has become proverbial. A part of it was sent as a proverb from Inverary. J. F. C.

L.

THE THREE QUESTIONS.

From the Brothers MacCraw, North Uist, 1859.

THERE was once, long ago, a scholar; and when he had done learning, his master said that he must now answer three questions, or have his head taken off. The scholar was to have time to make ready, and being in a great fright, he went to a miller who was the master's brother, and asked his aid.

The miller disguised himself and went instead of the scholar, and the first question put to him was this:—"How many ladders would reach the sky?"

"Now," said the narrator, "can *you* answer that?"

"One, if it were long enough."

"That's right." The second was:—

"Where is the middle of the world?"

So the miller laid down a rod, and he said:—"Here, set a hoop about the world, and thou will find the middle here."

The third was:—"What is the world's worth?"

"Well," said the miller, "the Saviour was sold for thirty pieces of silver, I am sure the world is worth no more."

"Oh," said the brother who was riding beside us, "that's not the way I have heard it. The second was,"

"How long will it take to go round the world?"
And the miller said:—

"If I were as swift as the sun and moon, I would run it in twenty-four hours."

And the third was:—

"What is my thought?"

And the miller answered:—

"I can tell: Thou thinkest that I am thy scholar, but I am thy brother, the miller."

This was told to me September 1, 1859, in North Uist, as I walked along the road. There are a great many similar wise saws current, which are generally fathered on George Buchanan, the tutor of James VI.

The following are a few riddles of the same kind, collected at Gairloch, for Osgood Mackenzie, Esq., by Mr. Donald MacDonald:

1. Whether is older, the man or the beard?

The beard is the older, for the work of creation was all finished before the man, and the beard was on the goat before the man was.

2. What is the wood that is not bent nor straight?

Sawdust. It is neither bent nor straight.

This riddle forms part of a very long and curious story which I heard told at Inverary, at Easter, 1859, and which is written down.

3. What is the thing which the Creator never saw, and that kings see but seldom, and that I see every day?

There is but one Creator, for that he never saw his like. Kings are but scarce, for that they see each other but rarely; but I see my own like every day that I get up,—other sinners like myself.

The riddle is very well known; but this is another view of it.

4. There were three soldiers coming home on furlough, and their three wives with them; they came to a river over which there was a ferry, but the boat would take with it but two together. The question is, how did they make the passage, for no one of them would trust his wife with another man, unless he was himself beside her?

Two women went over first, one went on shore, and the other came back with the boat, and she took the third with her, one of them went back and she stood beside her own husband, and the two husbands of the women who were over went back with the boat; one of them went on shore, and the wife of the man who was in the boat went into her along with him, and they went to the other side. His wife went on shore, and the man who was yonder came in the boat; then the two men went over; then there were three men over, and a woman; this woman took over the other women by the way of one and one; and there seem to be more solutions than one for the problem.

This puzzle, in various shapes, is well known, *e.g.* the Fox, the Goose, and the Bag of Corn.

TOIMHSEACHAIN.

1. *C.* Co dhiubh is sine an duine na an fheusag?

F. Is sine an fheusag; oir bha obair a chruthachaidh uile deanta roimh an duine, agus bha feusag air na gabhair mun robh an duine ann.

2, *C.* Ciod e am fiodh nach 'eil cuagach no direach?

F. Min an t-saibh; cha'n 'eil i cuagach no direach.

3. *C.* Ciod e an rud nach fac an Cruithfhear riamh; is nach faic righrean ach anminic; agus a chi mise na h'uile latha?

F. Cha'n 'eil Cruithfhear ann ach a h'aon; uime sin cha'n fhaic e coimeas da fein; cha'n eil righrean ach tearc, uime sin cha'n fhaic iad a cheile ach anminic; ach mise chimi mo choimeas fein na h'uile latha dh'eirears mi,—peacaich eile mar mi fein.

4. *C.* Bha triuir shaighdearan a tighin dachaidh air forlach, agus an triuir mhnathan aca maille riu. Thainig iad gu abhainn air an robh aisig—ach cha tugadh am bata leatha comhla ach dithis. Se a cheisd cionnus a rinn iad an t-aisig, 's nach faodadh duine dhiu a bhean earbsa ris an duine eile gun e fein a bhi lamh rithe?

F. Chaidh dithis bhan a null an toiseach; chaidh te dhiu air tir agus thainig an te 'eile air a h-ais leis a bhàta agus thug i leatha an tritheamh te. Chaidh te dhiu air a h-ais agus sheas i lamh ri 'duine fein agus thainig dithis dhaoine nam ban a bha thall air an ais leis a bhàta; chaidh fear dhiu air tir agus chaidh bean an duine a bh'anns a bhàta a steach innte maille ris agus chaidh iad gus an taobh eile. Chaidh a bhean air tir agus thainig an duine a bha thall anns a bhata; chaidh an dithis dhaoine an sin a null. Bha an sin an triuir dhaoine thall agus bean; thug a bhean so a lion te is te a null na mnathan eile.

DONALD M'DONALD.

The following are a few riddles, collected by Hector MacLean; most of them from a little school-girl in Islay:—

1.

Row and noise and racket
About the market town,
It is no bigger than a flea,
An' money it brings home.
Lint seed.

St-ioram starum starararaich
Air feadh a bhaile mhargaidh
Cha mhoth' e na deargann
Is bheir e dhachaidh airgiod.
Fras lìn—Linseed.

2.

Two feet down and three feet up,
And the head of the living in the mouth of the dead.
A man with a porridge pot on his head.

Da 'chas shìos 's tri chasan shuas
'S ceann a' bheo am beul a' mhairbh.
H-aon agus poit air a cheann.

3.

I see to me, over the hill,
A little one with a cut in his nose,
Two very long teeth in his jaw,
And a tatter of tow about his tail.
A hare.

Chi mi thugam thar a' bheinn
Fear beag 's beum as a shròin
Da fhiacaill fhada 'na chìr
'S cirb de bhlaigh lìn ma thòin.
Gearraidh.

4.

I see to me, over the fall,
A little curly hasty one;
A tuck of his shirt under his belt,
And the full of the world under his power.

Death.—This portrait varies from the usual sketches.

Chi mi thugam thar an eas
Fear beag cuirneanach cas
Cirb d'a léine fo a chrios
'S làn an t-saoghail fo a los.
Am bàs.

5.

I see to me, I see from me,
Two miles and ten over the sea,
The man of the green boatie,
And his shirt sewn with a thread of red.
The rainbow.

Chi mi thugam, chi mi bhuam,
Da mhìle dheug thar a' chuain,
Fear a' choitilein uaine,
Is snàthainn dearg a' fuaghal a léine.

Am bogha frois.

6.

Sheep small, and very small,
That have been thrice shorn of all,
On the hill that is farthest out,
Where every little saint will be.

The stars.

Caora mhion, mhionachag,
Air an treas lomachag,
Air an t-sliabh is fhaide muigh,
Far am bi gach ionachag.

Na reultan.

7.

The bard, the bard, the Frenchman,
Behind the house a wheezing.

The nettle.

(The meaning of this is not very clear.)

An fhile 'n fhile Fhrangach
Cul an tighe 's sreann aice.

An fheanndagach.

8.

A bent crooked stick between two glens,
When moves the crooked bent stick
Then move the two glens.

Scales and balance.

Maide crom cam eadar da ghleánn,
Ma charachas am maide crom cam
Carachaidh an da ghleann.

Meidh is sgàlain.

9.

Three red kinè on the bank of the sea,
That never drank a drop of the water of Alba.

Three dogrose-hips.

Tri ba dearga 'chois na fairge,
Nach d' òl deur do dh' uisg' Alba riabh.

Tri mucagan failm.

There seems to be a pun in this Alba of Scotland or wandering.

10.

Three spotted kine under a stone,
A drop of their milk never was milked.

Three snakes.

Tri ba breaca chois na leaca,
Nach do bhleodhnadh deur d'am bainne riabh.

Tri nathraichean.

11.

Four shaking and four running,
Two finding the way,
And one roaring.

A cow—feet udder, eyes, and mouth.

Ceathrar air chrith 's ceathrar 'nan riuth,
Dithisd a' deanadh an rathaid
'S h-aon a' glaodhaich.

A' bhò. Ceithir casan, ceithir ballain, da shuil 's a beul.

12.

A little clear house, and its two doors shut.

An egg.

Tigh beag soillear 's a dha dhorusd dùinte.
Ubh.

13.

Two strings as long as each other.
A river's banks.

Da thaod cho fhada.
Da thaobh na h-abhann.

14.

Rounder than a ball, longer than a ship.
A clew.

'S cruinn' e na ball 's fhaid' e na long.
Ceairsle.

15.

I can hold it myself in my fist,
And twelve men with a rope cannot hold it.
An egg.

Cumaidh mi fein a'm' dhorn e,
'S cha chum da fhear dheug air ròp' e.
Ubh.

16.

A great crooked stick in yonder wood,
And not a thing in it,
But clang bo clang.
A weaving loom.

Maide mor cam 's a' choill ud thall
'S gun aona mhìr ann
Ach gliong bo gliong.
Beairt fhighte.

17.

It travels on the little meads,
It travels on the midden steads,
It travels on the lengthened riggs,
And home it cometh late at night.
The reaping hook.

Siubhlaidh e na leunagan,
Siubhlaidh e na breunagan,
Siubhlaidh e 'n t-imire fada,
'S thig e dhachaidh anmoch.
An corran buana.

18.

Clean sour (salt or of the field) water without brine or salt.

Water in a field.—There is a pun which cannot be rendered.

Uisge glan goirt gun sàile gun salann.
Uisg' ann an claiseachan a' ghoirt.

19.

A rod in the wood of MacAlister,
And neither yew nor ivory,
Nor tree of wood in the universe,
And the deuce take him that it measures not.
A snake.

Slat an coill Mhic Alasdair,
'S cha 'n iubhar i 's cha n' eabhar i,
'S cha chraobh de dh' fhiodh an domhain i,
'S an deomhan air an fhear nach tomhais i.
Nathair.

20.

A black cock is in yonder town,
Feather black, feather brown,
Feathers twelve in the point of his wing,
And more than threescore (thirsts) in his back.

A bottle of whisky.—The pun is on "ite," a feather —or thirst.

Coileach dubh 's a' bhail' ud thall,
Ite dhubh is ite dhonn
Da ite dheug am bàrr a sgeith
'S corr is tri fichead 'na dhriom.

Botall uisge bheatha.

21.

Guess-guess, whelp, son of the son of guessing,
Twelve chains in the very middle,
Four ties, guess-guess.

A team of horses.

Tomh tomh a chuilean 'ic 'ic Thomh.
Da shlabhraidh dheug 'san teis meadhoin
Ceìthir cheanghail tomh tomh.

An t-seisreach.

(Seisreach means, literally, a team of six horses; and this seems to be the sense of the puzzle.)

22.

A little bit cogie in yonder wood,
Its mouth below, and it spills no drop.

A cow's udder.

Miodaran beag 's a choill ud thall,
'S a bheul foidhe, 's cha doirt e deur.

Uth na boine.

23.

A little gold well in the midst of this town,
Three golden ends and a cover of glass.

A watch.

Tobaran òir am meadhon a bhaile so
Trì chinn oìr is comhla ghloine ris.

Uaireadair.

24.

Clattering without, clattering within,
A box four-cornered, and brimful of clattering.

A weaver's shuttle.

Gliogaran a muigh, gliogaran a stigh,
Bocsa ceithir chearnach 's e làn ghliogaran.

Spàl figheadair.

25.

No bigger it is than a barleycorn,
And it will cover the board of the king.

The stone (apple) of the eye.

Cha mhoth' e na grainean eorna
'S comhdachaidh e bord an righ.

Clach na suil.

26.

A small wife come to this town,
And well she makes a "drandan;"
A cap of the chochullainn on,
And yellow coat of blanket.

A bee.

Bean bheag a' tigh 'n do 'n bhaile so,
'S gur math a ni i dranndan,

Currachd do 'n cho chullainn urra,
'S còta buidhe plangaid.
Seillean.

27.

A small wife coming to this town,
And creagada creag an her back,
Feet on her, and she handless,
And loads of chaff in her chest.
A hen.

Bean bheag a' tigh 'n do 'n bhaile so,
'S creagada creag air a muin,
Casan urra 's i gun làmhan
'S ultachan càthadh 'na h-uchd.
Cearc.

28.

A shaving upon the floor,
And well it makes a humming,
A yard of the Saxon yew,
And bow of the yew of France.
The Fiddle.

Sliseag air an urlar,
'S gur math a ni i dranndan,
Slat 'n iubhar Shasunnach,
A 's bogha 'n iubhar Fhrangach.
An fhidheal.

29.

It came out of flesh, and has no flesh within,
It tells a story without ever a tongue.
A pen.

Thainig e a feoil 's cha n' eil feoil ann
Innsidh e naigheachd 's gun teanga 'na cheann.
Peann.

30.

A golden candlestick on a two-leaved board,
Guess it now, come quickly guess it.

Death.

Coinnlear òir air bord da shliseig,
Tomhais a nis e, 's tomhais gu clis e.

Am Bàs.

31.

A black horse and a brown horse, sole to sole,
Swifter is the black horse than the brown.

Water and the mill wheel.

Each dubh is each donn bonn ri bonn,
'S luaithe 'n t-each dubh na 'n t-each donn.

An t-uisge 's roth a' mhuilinn.

32.

Twelve brethren in one bed,
And no one of them at the front or the wall.

Spokes of the spinning-wheel.

Da bhrathair dheug 'san aon leaba,
'S gun h-aon diu aig a' bheingidh na aig a bhalla.

Roth na cuibhealach.

33.

Three whales so black, so black, three whales coloured, coloured,
Whale in the east, whale in the west, and punish him that guesses not.

Waves.

Tri mucan dubha, dubha, tri mucan datha, datha ;
Muc an ear, 's muc an iar, 's pian air an fhear nach tomhais e.

Na tonnan.

34.

A small house out in the West,
And five hundred doors in it.

A sieve.

Tigh beag 'san aird an iar
'S coig ciad dorus air.

Ruideal.

35.

It is higher than the king's house,
It is finer than silk.

Smoke.

'S aird e na tigh an righ,
'S min' e na'n sioda.

An toit.

36.

The son on the house top,
And the father unborn,

Smoke before flame.

Am mac air muin an tighe
'San t-athair gun bhreith.

An toit ma'n gabh an gealbhan.

37.

A man went eyeless to a tree where there were apples,
He didn't leave apples on it, and he didn't take apples off.

There were two, and he took one.

Chaidh fear gun suilean 'ionnsuidh craobh air an robh ubhlan
Cha d' fhag e ubhlan urra 's cha d' thug e ubhlan dith.

'Se da ubhal a bh' air a' chraoibh 's thug e h-aon leis.

38.

Totaman, totaman, little black man,
Three feet under, and bonnet of wood,

(A potato) pot with the lid in.

Totaman, totaman, duine beag dugh,
Tri chasan foidhe, agus boinneid air de dh' fhiodh.

Poit agus brod innte.

39.

I went to the wood and I sought it not,
I sat on a hill and I found it not,
And because I found it not, I took it home with me.

A thorn in the foot.

Chaidh mi 'n choille 's cha d' iarr mi e,
Shuidh mi air cnoc 's cha d' fhuair mi e,
'S o'n nach d' fhuair mi e thug mi leam dachaidh e.

Bior ann an cois.

40.

A waveless well, it holds its fill of flesh and blood.

A tailor's thimble.

Tobar gun tonn, cumaidh e 'làn de dh' fhuil 's de dh' fheoil.

Meuran tailleir.

41.

Blacky, blacky, out at the door and a human bone in her mouth.

A shoe on a foot.

Dubhag, dubhag mach an dorusd 's cnaimh duine 'na beul.

Bròg air cois.

42.

Red below, black in the middle, and white above.

Fire, griddle, and oatcake.

Dearg foidhe, dugh 'na mheadhon, 's geal as a chionn.
An gealbhan, a' ghreideal, 's an t-aran.

43.

I can go over on a bridge of glass,
And I can come over on a bridge of glass,
And if the glass bridge break,
There's none in Islay, nor in Eirinn,
Who can mend the bridge of glass.
Ice.

Theid mi nunn air drochaid ghloine,
'S thig mi nall air drochaid ghloine
'S ma bhrisdeas an drochaid ghloine
Cha 'n 'eil an Ile na 'n Eirinn
Na chàras an drochaid ghloine.
Eitheandach.

44.

A brown stag in the hill, and his ear on fire.
The gun.

Damh donn 's a' bheinn 's a chluas ra theinidh.
An gunna.

45.

I will go out between two woods,
And I will come in between two lochs.
A pair of pails.

Theid mi mach eadar dha fhiodh,
'S thig mi stigh eadar dha loch.
Na cuinneagan.

46.

A green gentlewoman behind the door.
A broom, usually made of a bunch of some plant.

Bean uasal uaine cùl an doruisd.
An gais sguabaidh.

47.

Wiggle waggle about the river,
Iron its head, horse its neck,
Man its tail.
A fishing-rod.

Driobhal drabhal feadh na h-abhann, iarunn a cheann each a mhuineal duin' a thòn.
Slat iasgaich.

48.

A sharp sharp sheep, and her entrails trailing.
A big needle.

Caora bhiorach bhiorach, 's a mionach slaodadh rithe.
Snathad mhor.

49.

A red red sheep, red mad.
The tongue.

Caora dhearg dhearg, air an dearg choitheach.
An teanga.

50.

I have a puzzle for thee:
It isn't thy hair, and it isn't thy locks,
It isn't a bit of the bits of thy trunk,
It is upon thee, and thou art no heavier.
The man's name.—The Gaelic expression being, "What name is upon thee?"

Tha toimhseagan agam ort,
Cha n' e t-fhionna 's cha 'n e t-fhalt,
Cha n' e ball de bhallaibh do chuirp,
S tha e ort 's cha truimid thu e.
Ainm duine.

Got these puzzles, riddles, or toimseagain, from Flora MacIntyre, and a little girl, Catherine MacArthur, at Ballygrant, twelve years of age.

GLOSSARY.

AIR AN T-SLIABH IS FHAIDE MUIGH, the farthest off hill or mountain.

BEUM, a piece or bit.

BLAIGH LIN, linen cloth.

BREUNAGAN; this word may mean every filthy piece of ground over which the sickle passes.

CATHADH, gen. of càith, corn seeds.

CIR, the fore-part of the jams.

COITILEAN, a garment somewhat of one piece, serving as the whole clothes; or perhaps a little boat or skiff, which suggests the form of the rainbow.

CAS, fast.

CUIRNEANACH, curled in ringlets.

FHILE or Ile, or perhaps eibheal or eibhle, an ember.

IONACHAG may be aonachag, from aon, a solitary little thing.

LOMACHAG, a bareness, from lom.

LOS, power of destruction.

It will be observed that these riddles are all of a peculiar kind, such as the well known—

> "Polly with a white pettiecoat and a red nose,
> The longer she stands, the shorter she grows."

J. F. C.

LI.

THE FAIR GRUAGACH, SON OF THE KING OF EIRINN.

From Alexander MacNeill, fisherman, Ten Tangval, Barra.

THE Fair Chief, son of the King of Eirinn, went away with his great company to hold court, and keep company with him. A woman met him, whom they called the Dame of the Fine Green Kirtle; she asked him to sit a while to play at the cards; and they sat to play the cards, and the Fair Chief drove the game against the Dame of the Fine Green Kirtle.

"Ask the fruit of the game," said the Wife of the Fine Green Kirtle.

"I think that thou hast not got a fruit; I know not of it," said the Fair Chief, son of the King of Eirinn.

"On the morrow be thou here, and I will meet thee," said the Dame of the Fine green Kirtle.

"I will be (here)," said the Fair Chief.

On the morrow he met her, and they began at the cards, and she won the game.

"Ask the fruit of the game," said the Fair Chief.

"I," said the Dame of the Fine Green Kirtle, "am laying thee under spells, and under crosses, under holy herdsmen of quiet travelling, wandering women, the little calf, most feeble and powerless, to take thy head and thine ear and thy wearing of life from off thee, if thou takest rest by night or day; where thou takest thy breakfast that thou take not thy dinner, and where thou takest thy dinner that thou take not thy supper, in whatsoever place thou be, until thou findest out in what place I may be under the four brown quarters of the world."*

She took a napkin from her pocket, and she shook it, and there was no knowing what side she had taken, or whence she came.

He went home heavily-minded, black sorrowfully; he put his elbow on the board, and his hand under his cheek, and he let out a sigh.

"What is it that ails thee, son?" said the king of Eirinn; "Is it under spells that thou art?—but notice them not; I will raise thy spells off thee. I have a smithy on shore, and ships on sea; so long as gold or silver lasts me, stock or dwelling, I will set it to thy losing till I raise these spells off thee."

"Thou shalt not set them," said he; "and, father, thou art high-minded. Thou wouldst set that away from thyself, and thou wilt lose all that might be there. Thou wilt not raise the spells; thy kingdom will go to want and to poverty, and that will not raise the spells; and thou wilt lose thy lot of men; but keep thou thy lot of men by thyself, and if I go I shall but lose myself."

So it was in the morning of the morrow's day he went away without dog, without man, without calf, without child.

He was going, and going, and journeying; there was blackening on his soles, and holes in his shoes; the black clouds of night coming, and the bright, quiet

* This sort of incantation is common, and I am not certain that it is quite correctly rendered.

clouds of the day going away, and without his finding a place of staying, or rest for him. He spent a week from end to end without seeing house or castle, or any one thing. He was grown sick; sleepless, restless, meatless, drinkless, walking all the week. He gave a glance from him, and what should he see but a castle. He took towards it, and round about it, and there was not so much as an auger hole in the house. His "DUDAM" and his "DADAM" fell with trouble and wandering, and he turned back, heavily-minded, black sorrowfully. He was taking up before him, and what should he hear behind him but a shout.

"Fair Chief, son of the king of Eirinn, return: there is the feast of a day and year awaiting thee; the meat thou thinkest not (of), and the drink thou thinkest not of; the meat thou thinkest on, and the drink thou thinkest on," and he returned.

There was a door for every day in the year in the house; and there was a window for every day in the year in it. It was a great marvel for him, the house that he himself had gone round about, and without so much as an auger hole in it, that door and window should be in it for every day in the year when he came back.

He took in to it. Meat was set in its place for using, drink in its place of drinking, music in its place for hearing, and they were plying the feast and the company with solace and pleasure of mind, himself and the fine damsel that cried after him in the palace.

A bed was made for him in the castle, with pillows, with a hollow in the middle; warm water was put on his feet, and he went to lie down. When he rose up in the morning, the board was set over with each meat that was best; and he was thus for a time without his feeling the time pass by.

She stood in the door. "Fair Chief, son of the king of Eirinn, in what state dost thou find thyself, or how art thou?" said the damsel of the castle.

"I am well," said he.

"Dost thou know at what time thou camest here?" said she.

"I think I shall complete a week, if I be here this day," said he.

"A quarter is just out to-day," said she. "Thy meat, thy drink, or thy bed will not grow a bit the worse than they are till it pleases thyself to return home."

There he was by himself till he was thinking that he had a month out. At this time she stood in the door.

"Yes! Fair Chief, how dost thou find thyself this day?" said she.

"Right well," said he.

In what mind dost thou find thyself?" said she.

"I will tell thee that," said he; "if my two hands could reach yonder peaked hill, that I would set it on yon other bluff hill."

"Dost thou know at what time thou camest hither?" said she.

"I am thinking that I have completed a month here," said he.

"The end of the two years is out just this day," said she.

"I will not believe that the man ever came on the surface of the world that would gain victory of myself in strength or lightness," said he.

"Thou art silly," said she; "there is a little band

here which they call An Fhinn, the Een, and they will get victory of thee. The man never came of whom they would not get victory."

"Morsel I will not eat, draught I will not drink, sleep there will not come on my eye, till I reach where they are, and I know who they are," said he.

"Fair Chief be not so silly, and let that lightness pass from thy head; stay as thou art, for I know thou wilt return," said she.

"I will not make stay by night or day, until I reach them," said he.

"The day is soft and misty," said she, "and thou art setting it before thee that thou wilt go. The Feen are in such a place, and they have a net fishing trout. Thou shalt go over where they are. Thou wilt see the Feen on one side, and Fionn alone on the other side. Thou shalt go where he is, and thou shalt bless him. Fionn will bless thee in the same way; thou shalt ask service from him; he will say that he has no service for thee, now that the Feen are strong enough, and he will not put a man out. He will say, 'What name is upon thee?' Thou shalt answer, the name thou didst never hide, An Gruagach ban Mac Righ Eireann. Fionn will say then, 'Though I should not want of a man, why should I not give service to the son of thy father.' Be not high minded amongst the Feeantan. Come now, and thou shalt have a napkin that is here, and thou shalt say to Fionn, whether thou be alive or dead to put thee in it when comes its need."

He went away, and he reached the (place) where the Feen were; he saw them there fishing trout, the rest on the one side, and Fionn on the other side alone. He went where Fionn was, and he blessed him. Fionn blessed him in words that were no worse.

"I heard that there were such men, and I came to you to seek hire from you," said the Fair Chief.

"Well, then, I have no need of a man at the time," said Fionn. "What name is upon thee?"

"My name I never hid. The Gruagach Ban, son of the king of Eireann," said he.

"Bad! bad! for all the ill luck that befel me! where I got my nourishment young, and my dwelling for my old age; who should get service unless thy father's son should get it; but be not high minded amongst the Feentan," said Fionn. "Come hither and catch the end of the net, and drag it along with me."

He began dragging the net with the Feen. He cast an eye above him, and what should he see but a deer.

"Were it not better for the like of you, such swift, strong, light, young men to be hunting yonder deer, than to be fishing any one pert trout that is here, and that a morsel of fish or a mouthful of juice will not satisfy you rather than yonder creature up above you—a morsel of whose flesh, and a mouthful of whose broth will suffice you," said the Fair Chief, son of the king of Eirinn.

"If yonder beast is good, we are seven times tired of him," said Fionn, "and we know him well enough."

"Well, I heard myself that there was one man of you called LUATHAS (Swiftness) that could catch the swift March wind, and the swift March wind could not catch," said the Fair Chief.

"Since it is thy first request, we will send to seek him," said Fionn.

He was sent for, and CAOILTE came. The Fair Chief shouted to him.

"There is the matter I have for thee," said the Gruagach, "to run the deer that I saw yonder above."

"The Fair Chief came amongst our company this day, and his advice may be taken the first day. He gave a glance from him, and he saw a deer standing above us; he said it was better for our like of swift, strong, light men to be hunting the deer, than to be fishing any one pert trout that is here; and thou Caoilte go and chase the deer."

"Well, then, many is the day that I have given to chasing him, and it is little I have for it but my grief that I never got a hold of him," said Caoilte.

Caoilte went away, and he took to speed.

"How will Caoilte be when he is at his full speed?" said the Fair Chief.

"There will be three heads on Caoilte when he is at his full speed," said Fionn.

"And how many heads will there be on the deer?" said the Chief.

"There will be seven heads on him when he is at full swiftness," said Fionn.*

"What distance has he before he reaches the end of his journey?" said the Chief.

"It is seven glens and seven hills, and seven summer seats," said Fionn; "he has that to make before he reaches a place of rest."

"Let us take a hand at dragging the net," said the Chief.

The Fair Chief gave a glance from him, and he said to Fionn, "Een, son of Cumhail, put thy finger under

---

* What this means I do not know. Perhaps a head may be the height of a man, a fathom—three and seven fathoms at a stride.

thy knowledge tooth, to see what distance Caoilte is from the deer."

Fionn put his finger under his knowledge tooth. "There are two heads on Caoilte, and on the deer there are but two heads yet," said Fionn.

"How much distance have they put past?" said the Fair Chief.

"Two glens and two hills; they have five unpassed still," said Fionn.

"Let us take a hand at fishing the trout," said the Fair Chief.

"When they had been working a while, the Fair Chief gave a glance from him. "Fionn, son of Cumal," said he, "put thy finger under thy knowledge tooth to see what distance Caoilte is from the deer."

"There are three heads on Caoilte, and four heads on the deer, and Caoilte is at full speed," said Fionn.

"How many glens and hills and summer seats are before them," said the Chief.

"There are four behind them, and three before them," said Fionn.

"Let us take a hand at fishing the trout," said the Fair Chief.

They took a while at fishing the trout.

"Fionn, son of Cumal," said the Chief, "what distance is still before the deer before he reaches the end of his journey?"

"One glen and one hill, and one summer seat," said Fionn.

He threw the net from him, and he took to speed. He would catch the swift March wind, and the swift March wind could not catch him, till he caught Caoilte; he took past him, and he left his blessing with him. Going over by the ford of Sruth Ruadh, the deer gave a spring—the Fair Chief gave the next spring, and he caught the deer by the hinder shank, and the deer gave a roar, and the Carlin cried—

"Who seized the beast of my love?"

"It is I," said the Fair Chief, "the son of the king of Eirinn."

"Oh, Gruagach ban, son of the king of Eirinn, let him go," said the Carlin.

"I will not let (him go); he is my own beast now," said the Gruagach.

"Give me the full of my fist of his bristles, or a handful of his food, or a mouthful of his broth, or a morsel of his flesh," said the Carlin.

"Any one share thou gettest not," said he.

"The Feen are coming," said she, "and Fionn at their head, and there shall not be one of them that I do not bind back to back."

"Do that," said he, "but I am going away."

He went away, and he took the deer with him, and he was taking on before him till the Een met him.

"Een, son of Cumal, keep that," said he, as he left the deer with Fionn.

Fionn, son of Cumal, sat at the deer, and the Fair Chief went away. He reached the smithy of the seven and twenty smiths. He took out three iron hoops out of it for every man that was in the Een (Fhinn); he took with him a hand hammer, and he put three hoops about the head of every man that was in the Een, and he tightened them with the hammer.

The Carlin came out, and let out a great screech.

"Een, son of Cumal, let hither to me the creature of my love."

The highest hoop that was on the Feeantan burst with the screech. She came out the second time, and she let out the next yell, and the second hoop burst. (Was not the Carlin terrible!) She went home, and she was not long within when she came the third time, and she let out the third yell, and the third hoop burst. She went and she betook herself to a wood; she twisted a withy from the wood; she took it with her; she went over, and she bound every man of the Feeantaichean back to back, but Fionn.

The Fair Chief laid his hand on the deer, and he flayed it. He took out the GAORR, and every bit of the inside; he cut a turf, and he buried them under the earth. He set a caldron in order, and he put the deer in the caldron, and fire at it to cook it.

"Een, son of Cumal," said the fair Chief, "whether wouldst thou rather go to fight the Carlin, or stay to boil the caldron?"

"Well, then," said Fionn, "the caldron is hard enough to boil. If there be a morsel of the flesh uncooked, the deer will get up as he was before; and if a drop of the broth goes into the fire, he will arise as he was before. I would rather stay and boil the caldron."

The Carlin came. "Een, son of Cumal," said she "give me my fist full of bristles, or a squeeze of my fist of GAORR, or else a morsel of his flesh, or else a gulp of the broth."

"I myself did not do a thing about it, and with that I have no order to give it away," said Fionn.

Here then the Fair Chief and the Carlin began at each other; they would make a bog on the rock and a rock on the bog. In the place where the least they would sink, they would sink to the knees; in the place where the most they would sink, they would sink to the eyes.

"Art thou satisfied with the sport, Een, son of Cumal?" said the Fair Chief.

"It is long since I was satiated with that," said Fionn.

"There will be a chance to return it now," said the Chief.

He seized the Carlin, and he struck her a blow of his foot in the crook of the hough, and he felled her.

"Een, son of Cumal, shall I take her head off?" said the Chief.

"I don't know," said Fionn.

"Een, son of Cumal," said she, "I am laying thee under crosses, and under spells, and under holy herdsman of quiet travelling, wandering woman, the little calf, most powerless, most uncouth, to take thy head and thine ear, and thy life's wearing off, unless thou be as a husband, three hours before the day comes, with the wife of the Tree Lion.*

"I," said the Fair Chief, "am laying thee under crosses and under spells, under holy herdsman of quiet travelling, wandering woman, the little calf most powerless and most uncouth, to take thy head and thine ear, and thy life's wearing off, unless thou be with a foot on either side of the ford of Struth Ruadh, and every drop of the water flowing through thee."

He arose, and he let her stand up.

"Raise thy spells from off me, and I will raise them from off him," said the Carlin. "Neither will I lift nor lay down, but so; howsoever we may be, thou comest not."

---

* Leòmhan chraobh. This, I presume, is a griffin; I have often heard the name though it is not in dictionaries. The word griffin is also omitted from some.

The fair Chief went and he took off the caldron; he seized a fork and a knife, and he put the fork into the deer; he seized the knife and he cut a morsel out of it, and he ate it. He caught a turf, and cut it, and he laid that on the mouth of the caldron.

"Een, son of Cumal, it is time for us to be going," said he; "art thou good at horsemanship?"

"I could hit upon it," said Fionn.

He caught hold of a rod, and he gave it to Fionn. "Strike that on me," said he.

Fionn struck the rod on him and made him a brown ambler.

"Now, get on top of me," said the Chief. Fionn got on him.

"Be pretty watchful; I am at thee."

He gave that spring and he went past nine ridges, and Fionn stood (fast) on him. "She" gave the next spring and "she" went past nine other ridges and Fionn stood fast on "her." He took to speed. He would catch the swift March wind, and the swift March wind could not catch him.

"There is a little town down here," said the ambler, and go down and take with thee three stoups of wine and three wheaten loaves, and thou shalt give me a stoup of wine and a wheaten loaf, and thou shalt comb me against the hair, and with the hair."

Fionn got that and they reached the wall of the Tree Lion.

"Come on the ground, Een, son of Cumal, and give me a stoup of wine and a wheaten loaf."

Fionn came down and he gave him a stoup of wine and a wheaten loaf.

"Comb me now against the hair, and comb me with the hair."

He did that.

"Take care of thyself," said the ambler.

Then "she" leaped, and she put a third of the wall below her, and there were two-thirds above, and she returned.

"Give me another stoup of wine and another wheaten loaf, and comb me against the hair, and comb me with the hair."

He did that.

"Take care of thyself, for I am for thee now," said the ambler.

She took the second spring, and she put two-thirds of the wall below her, and there was a third over her head, and she returned.

"Give me another stoup of wine and a wheaten loaf, and comb me against the hair, and with the hair."

He did that.

"Take care of thyself, for I am for thee now," said she.

She took a spring, and she was on the top of the wall.

"The matter is well before thee, Een," said the ambler, "the Tree Lion is from home."

He went home. My Chief, and all hail! were before him: meat and drink were set before him; he rested that night, and he was with the wife of the Tree Lion three hours before the day.

So early as his eye saw the day, earlier than that he arose, and he reached the ambler, the Gruagach Ban, and they went away.

Said the Fair Chief, "The Tree Lion is from home; anything that passed she will not hide; he is coming after us, and he will not remember his book of witchcraft; and since he does not remember the book of witchcraft, it will go with me against him; but if he should remember the book, the people of the world could not withstand him. He has every DRAOCHD magic, and he will spring as a bull when he comes, and I will spring as a bull before him, and the first blow I give him, I will lay his head on his side, and I will make him roar. Then he will spring as an AISEAL, (ass), and I will spring as an ass before him, and the first thrust I give him I will take a mouthful out of him, between flesh and hide as it may be. Then he will spring as a hawk in the heavens; I will spring as a hawk in the wood, and the first stroke I give him, I will take his heart and his liver out. I will come down afterwards, and thou shalt seize that napkin yonder, and thou shalt put me in the napkin, and thou shalt cut a turf, and thou shalt put the napkin under the earth, and thou shalt stand upon it. Then the wife of the Tree Lion will come, and thou standing on the top of the turf, and I under thy feet; and she with the book of witchcraft on her back in a hay band, and she will say—Een, son of Cumal, man that never told a lie, tell me who of the people of the world killed my comrade, and thou shalt say I know not above the earth who killed thy comrade. She will go away and take to speed with her weeping cry."

When they were on forward a short distance, whom saw they coming but the Tree Lion.

He became a bull; the Fair chief became a bull before him, and the first blow he struck him he laid his head on his side, and the Tree Lion gave out a roar. Then he sprung as an ass, the Fair Chief sprung as an ass before him, and at the first rush he gave towards him he took a mouthful between flesh and skin. The Tree Lion then sprang as a hawk in the heavens, the Fair Chief sprang as a hawk in the wood, and he took the heart and liver out of him. The Fair Chief fell down afterwards, Fionn seized him and he put him into the napkin, and he cut a turf, and he put the napkin under the earth, and the turf upon it, and he stood on the turf. The wife of the Tree Lion came, and the book of witchcraft was on her back in a hay band.

"Een, son of Cumal, man that never told a lie, who killed my comrade?"

"I know not above the earth, who killed thy comrade," said Fionn.

And she went away in her weeping cry, and she betook herself to distance.

He caught hold of the Fair Chief and he lifted him with him, and he reached the castle in which was the dame of the Fine Green Kirtle. He reached her that into her hand. She went down with it, and she was not long down when she came up where he was.

"Een, son of Cumal, the Gruagach Ban, son of the king of Eirinn, is asking for thee."

"That is the news I like best of all I ever heard, that the Fair Chief is asking for me," said Fionn.

She set meat and drink before them, and they would not eat a morsel nor drink a drop till they should eat their share of the deer with the rest at Sruth Ruaidh.

They reached (the place) where the Een were bound, and they loosed every single one of them, and they were hungry enough. The Fair Chief set the deer before them, and they left of the deer thrice as much as they ate.

"I should go to tell my tale," said the Fair Chief. He reached the carlin at the ford of Sruth Ruaidh, and he began to tell the tale how it befel him. Every tale he would tell her she would begin to rise; every time she would begin to rise he would seize her, and he would crush her bones, and he would break them until he told his lot of tales to her.

When he had told them he returned, and he reached the Een back again.

Fionn went with him to the Castle of the Dame of the Fine Green Kirtle.

"Blessing be with thee, Een, son of Cumal," said the Fair Chief, son of the king of Eirinn, "I have found all I sought—a sight of each matter and of each thing, and now I will be returning home to the palace of my own father."

"It is thus thou art about to leave me, after each thing I have done for thee; thou wilt take another one, and I shall be left alone."

"Is that what thou sayest?" said he, "If I thought that might be done, I never saw of married women or maidens that I would take rather than thee, but I will not make wedding or marrying here with thee, but thou shalt do to the palace of my father with me."

They went to the palace of his father, himself and the Dame of the Fine Green Kirtle, and Fionn. A churchman was got, and the Fair Chief and the dame of the Fine Green Kirtle married. A hearty, jolly, joyful wedding was made for them; music was raised and lament laid down; meat was set in the place for using, and drink in the place for drinking, and music in the place for hearing, and they were plying the feast and the company until that wedding was kept up for a day and a year, with solace and pleasure of mind.

AN GRUAGACH BAN, MAC RIGH EIREANN.

DH' FHALBH an Gruagach bàn, Mac Rìgh Eireann, le mhòr-chuideachd, a chumail cùirt agus cuideachd ris fhìn. Choinnich boireannach e ris an canadh eud, bean a chaol chot' uaine. Dh' iarr i air treis suidhe dh' iomairt air chairtean, agus shuidh eud a dh' iomairt air na cairtean, agus chuir an Gruagach bàn an cluichd air bean a chaol chòt uaine. "Iarr toradh de chluichd," ursa bean a chaol chot' uaine. "Cha 'n 'eil mi smaointeachadh gom bheil toradh agad—cha 'n 'eil mi fhin fiosrach air," urs' an Gruagach bàn, Mac Rìgh Eireann. "Am màireach bidh thu aunn an so, agus coinneachaidh mis' thu," ursa bean a chòta chaoil uaine. "Bithidh," urs' an Gruagach bàn. An la 'r na mhàireach choinnich e i. Agus thòisich eud air na cairtean, agus bhuidhinn is' an cluichd. "Iarr toradh de chluichd," urs' an Gruagach bàn. "Tha mi," ursa bean a chaol chòt' uaine, "'ga d' chur fo gheasan agus fo chroisean, fo naoidh buaraiche mnatha sìthe, siùbhlaiche, seachranaiche; an laogh beag is meata 's is mi-threòraiche 'thoirt do chinn, 's do chluas, 's do chaitheadh-beatha dhìot; mu ni thu tamh oidhche na latha, far an gabh thu do bhraiceas nach gabh thu do dhinneir, agus far an gabh thu do dhinneir nach gabh thu do shuipeir, ge b'e àit 'am bi thu, gos am faigh thu 'mach ge b'e àit am bi mise fo cheithir ranna ruadha 'm t-saoghail. Thug i nèapaigin as a pòca, 's chrath i e, 's cha robh fhios co'n taobh a ghabh i na as an d' thàinig i.

Chaidh esan dachaidh go trom-inntinneach, dugh-bhrònach. Chuir e uileann air a' bhòrd 's a làmh fo a leithcheann, 's lig e osann as. "Dé sin ort a mhic;" ursa Rìgh Eireann. "An aunn fo gheasan a tha thu? Ach na biodh umhail agad diu, togaidh mise do gheasan diat. Tha ceàrdach air tìr agam agus luingeas air muir. Fad 's a mhaireas òr na airgiod domhsa, stochd na iondas, cuiridh mi g'a t' fhuasgladh e, gos an tog mi na geasan so diat." "Cha chuir," urs' esan; "agus m' athair tha thu gòrrach. Cuiridh tusa sin air falbh uait fhìn, agus caillidh tu na bhios an sin. Cha tog thu na geasan. Théid do rìoghachd go dìth 's go bochdainn, agus cha tog sin na geasan, agus caillidh tu do chuid daoine. Ach gléidh thusa do chuid daoin' agad fhin; 's ma dh' fhalbhas mise cha bhi dhìth orm ach mi-fhìn."

'Se bh' aunn aunns a' mhadainn an la 'r na mhàireach, dh' fhalbh e gon chù, gon duine, gon laogh, gon leanabh. Bha e' falbh agus a' falbh, 's ag astarachadh. Bha dughadh air a bhonnaibh agus tolladh air a bhrògan ; neòil dhugha na h-oidhch' a' tighinn, agus nèoil gheala, shéimhidh an latha 'falbh, 's gon e faighinn aite stad na tàmh da. Thug e seachduin o cheaunn go ceaunn gon tigh na caisteal fhaicinn, na gon sgath. Bha e air fàs dona, gon chadal, gon tàmh, gon bhiadh, gon deoch, a' coise-achd fad na seachduin. Thug e sealladh uaidh, 's de chnnnaic e ach caisteal ! Ghabh e a 'ionnsuidh, 's ghabh e mu 'n cuairt air. Cha d' fhuair e urad ri toll tora de dh' fhosgladh air an tigh. Thuit a dhudam agus a dhadam air le trioblaid agus le allaban ; agus thill e go trom-inntinneach, dugh-bhrònach. Bha e 'gabh-ail suas roimhe, agus de chual e ach eubh as a dhéigh—" A Ghruagach bhàn, Mhic Righ Eireann till ; tha cuirm la a's bliadhna feitheamh ort, am biadh nach smaointich thu 's an deoch nach smaointich thu ! am biadh a smaointeachas thu 's an deoch a smaointeachas thu ! " Thìll e. Bha dorusd mu choinneamh a h-uile latha 's a' bhliadhn air an tigh, 's bha uinneag mu choin-neamh h-uile latha 's a' bhliadhna air ; bha e 'na ioghnadh mòr leis, an tigh a chaidh e fhìn mu 'n cuairt air, 's gon urad agus toll tora de dh' fhosgladh air, uinneag agus dorusd a bhith air mu choinneamh h-uile latha 's a' bhliadhna, nur a thill e ! Thug e stigh air. Chuireadh biadh an àit' a chaitheadh, deoch an ait' a h-òl, agus ceòl an ait' éisdeachd. Agus bha eud a' caitheadh na cuirm agus na cuideachd, e fhin agus an nighean bhriagh a dh' eubh as a dhéigh, aunns a' phàileas. Rinneadh leaba le ceaunn adhart dha aunns a' chaisteal, 's lag 'na builsgein. Chuireadh burn blàth air a chasan, 's chaidh e 'laidhe. Nur a dh' éiridh e 'n la 'r na mhàireach bha 'm bòrd air cur thairis leis gach biadh a b' fheàrr, agus bha e mur so ri ùine, 's gon e 'mòth'chainn na h-ùine 'dol seachad. Sheas is' aunns an dorusd. " A Ghruagach bhàn, Mhic Rìgh Eireann, de 'n staid aunns am bheil thu' ga t' fhaotainn fhìn na démur tha thu ?" urs' ise. "Nighean a chaisteil, tha mì go math," urs' esan. "Am bheil fios agad de 'n uin' o thàinig thu 'n so ? " urs' ise. " Tha mi smaointeachadh go 'n slànaich mi seachduin, mu bhios mi aunn an diugh," urs' esan. " Tha ràithe mach dìreach an diugh," urs' ise. "Cha d' théid do bhiadh, no do dheoch, na do leaba, mìr na 's miosa na tha eud gos an togair thu tilleadh dhachaidh." Bha e 'n sin leis fhìn gos an robh e smaointeachadh gon robh mias aige 'mach. Aig an am so sheas ise 'san dorusd. "Seadh a Ghruagach bhàn, demur a tha thu' ga t' fhaighinn an diugh?" urs' ise. "Gle mhath," urs' esan. "De 'n inntinn aunns am bheil thu 'ga t' fhaotainn fhìn?" urs' ise. "Innsidh mi sin duit," urs' esan. "Na'm b' urrainn mo dhà làmh ruighinn air a' bheinn bhioraich 'ud shuas, gon cuirinn air muin na beinn mhaoil 'ud eil' i." "Am bheil fios agad de 'u ùin' o' thàinig thu 'n so?" urs' ise. "Tha mi smaointeachadh gon do shlànaich mi mias aunn," urs' esan. "Tha ceaunn an da bhliadhna dìreach a mach," urs' ise. "Cha chreid mi e, air uachdar an t-saoghail, gon d' thàinig aon duine 'gheibheadh buaidh orm fhin ann an spionnadh na 'n aotromachd," urs' esan. "Tha thu gòrrach," urs' ise, "Tha buidheann bheag an so ris an can eud an Fhìnn, 's gheibh eud buaidh ort; cha d' thàinig am fear air nach fhaigh eud buaidh." "Gréim cha 'n ith mi, deoch cha 'n òl mi, cadal cha d' théid air mo shùil, gos an ruig mi far am bheil eud, 's gos am bi fhios agam cò eud," urs' esan. "A Ghruagach bhàn na bi cho gòrrach, agus lig seachad an fhaoineis sin as do cheaunn. Fan mur a tha thu, 's fios agam gon till eud thu," urs' ise. "Tàmh oidhche na latha cha dian mi gos an ruig mi eud," urs' esan. "Tha latha bog, ceòthar aunn an diugh," urs' ise, "agus tha thu 'cur romhad gom falbh thu. Tha 'n Fhìnn 'na leithid so de dh' àite, agus lian ac ag iasgach bric. Gabhaidh tu null far am bi eud. Chi thu 'n Fhìnn air an darna taobh, 's Fionn na ònrachd air an taobh eile. Gabhaidh tu far am bi e, agus beannachaidh tu dhà. Beannachaidh Fionn duit aunns an dòigh chiadhna. Iarraidh tu cosnadh air. Abraidh e nach 'eil cosuadh aige dhuit an dràsd, gom bheil an Fhìnn glé làidir, 's nach cuir e duine 'mach. Abraidh e de 'n t-ainm a th' ort. Freagraidh tus' an sin, t' ainm nach do cheil thu riabh, an Gruagach bàn, Mac Rìgh Eireann. Abraidh Fionn an sin, Gad a bhithinn-sa gon duine dhìth démur nach d' thugainn cosnadh do mhac t' athar sa; ach na bi mòr-fhaclach am miosg nam Fianntan. Thalla nis agus gheibh thu nèapaigin a tha 'n so, agus bheir thu leat e, agus abraidh tu ri Fionn, co 'ca bhios thusa beò na marbh do chur aunn nur a thig feum air."

Dh' fhalbh e agus ràinig e far an robh 'n Fhìnn. Chunnaic e eud an sin ag iasgach bric, càch air an darna taobh, 's Fionn air an taobh eile na ònrachd. Chaidh e far an robh Fionn, agus bheannaich e dha. Bheannaich Fionn dàsan aunn am briathran nach bo mhiosa. "Chuala mi gon robh 'ur leithidean de dhaoin' aunn, agus thàinig mi g' 'ur ionnsuidh airson cosnadh iarraidh oirbh," urs' an Gruagach bàn. "Mata cha 'n 'eil duin' a dhìth òirnn 'san am," ursa Fionn. Dé n t-ainm a th' ort?" "M' ainm cha do cheil mi riabh, an Gruagach bàn Mac Rìgh Eireann," urs' esan. "Dona! dona! mur a dh' éiridh de thubaist domh! Far an d' fhuair mi mo thogail go h-òg, agus m' àrach gom' shine. Co gheibheadh cosnadh mur am faigheadh mac t' athar e; ach na bi mor-fhaclach am miosg nam Fianntan," ursa Fionn. "Teaunn a naull agus beir air ceaunn an lìn, agus tarruinn leis an Fhìnn. Thug e sùil as a chionn, agus dé 'chunnaic e ach fiadh. "Nach b fheàrra d' ur leithidean-sa de dhaoine luath, làidir, aotrom, òg, a bhith 'g ianach an fhéidh 'ud shuas; seach a bhith 'g iasgach aona bhreac beadaidh an so, agus nach ruig greim dh' a iasg sibh, na balgam dh' a shùgh; seach am beathach 'ud shuas as 'ur cionn, a ruigeas gréim d' a fheoil sibh agus balgam d'a eanruith," urs' an Gruagach bàn, Mac Rìgh Eireann. "Mu 's math am beathach sin," ursa Fionn, "tha sinne seachd sgìth dheth 's tha sinn eòlach na leòir air." "Mata chuala mi fhìn gon robh aon duin' agaibh ris an canadh eud Luathas, a bheireadh air a' ghaoth luath Mhàrt, agus nach beireadh a ghaoth luath Mhart air," urs, an Gruagach bàn. "O 'n is e do chiad iarradas e cuiridh sinn a 'iarraidh," ursa Fionn. Chuireadh air a shon, 's thainig Caoilte. Dh' eubh an Gruagach bàn air. "Siud an gnothach a bh' agam duit," urs' an Gruagach. "Dol a ruith an fhéidh a chunnaic mi shuas 'ud." "Thàinig an Gruagach bàn an diugh 'nar cuideachd, agus faodar a chomhairl' a ghabhail a' chiad latha. Thug e sùil uaidh, agus chunnaic e fiadh 'na sheasamh as ar cionn. Thuirt e gom b' fheàrr d'ar leithidean-sa de dhaoine luath, làidir, aotrom, a bhith sealg an fhéidh, na bhith 'g iasgach aona bhreac beadaidh an so; agus a Chaoilte falbh thus' agus ruith am fiadh," ursa Fionn. "Mata 's ioma latha 'thug mis' air a ruith, agus 's beag a bh' agam air a shon ach mo thrioblaid nach d' fhuair mi gréim riabh air," ursa Caoilte. Dh' fhalbh Caoilt' agus thug e go h-astar.

"Démur a bhios Caoilte nur a bhios e 'na làn luathas," urs' an Gruagach bàn. "Bidh tri chinn air Caoilte nur a bhios e aig a làn luathas," ursa Fionn. "'S co mhiad ceaunn a bhios air an fhiadh," urs' an Gruagach. "Bidh seachd cinn air nur a bhios e 'na làn luathas" ursa Fionn. "De 'n t-astar a th' aige mu 'n ruig e' cheaunn uidhe?" urs an Gruagach. "Tha seachd glinn, agus seachd mill, agus seachd aiteacha suidhe samhraidh," ursa

Fionn. "Tha sinn aige r' a dhianadh mu 'n ruig e àite tàimh." "Thugamaid làmh air tarruinn an lìn," urs' an Gruagach. Thug an Gruagach bàn sealladh uaidh, 's thuirt e ri Fionn. "Fhinn Mhic Cumhail cuir do mhiar fo d' dheud fios fiach de 'n t-astar 's am bheil Caoilte dha 'n fhiadh." Chuir Fionn a mhiar fo a dheud fios. "Tha da cheaunn air Caoilte, 's cha 'n 'eil air an fhiadh ach an da cheaunn fhathasd," ursa Fionn. "Dé chuir eud seachad de dh' astar," urs' an Gruagach bàn. "Da ghleann agus da mheaull; tha coig aca gon chur seachad fhathasad," ursa Fionn. "Thugamaid làmh air iasgach a' bhric," urs' an Gruagach bàn. Thòisich eud air iasgach a' bhric. Air treis daibh a bhith 'g obair thug an Gruagach bàn suil uaidh. "Fhinn Mhic Cumhail," urs' esan, "cuir do mhiar fo d' dheud fios fiach de 'n t-astar a tha Caoilt' o 'n fhiadh." "Tha tri chinn air Caoilte 's tha ceithir chinn air an fhiadh, 's tha Caoilte 'na làn luathas," ursa Fionn. Co mhiad gleaunn, agus meaull, agus àite suidhe samhraidh a tha romhpa," urs' an Gruagach. Tha ceithir as an déigh agus tri rompa," ursa Fionn. "Bheireamaid làmh air iasgach a' bhric," urs' an Gruagach bàn. Thug eud treis air iasgach a bhric. "Fhinn Mhic Cumhail," urs' an Gruagach, "dé 'n t-astar a tha romh 'n fhiadh fhathasd mu 'n ruig e cheaunn uidhe." "Aona ghleaunn, agus aona mheaull, agus aon àite suidhe samhraidh," ursa Fionn.

Thilg e uaidh an lian, agus ghabh e go h-astar. Bheireadh e air' a' ghaoth luath Mhàrt, 's cha bheireadh a' ghaoth luath Mhàrt air, gos an d' rug e air Caoilte. Ghabh e seachad air, 's dh' fhàg e beannachd aige. A' dol a null ri clachan Struth ruaidh thug am fiadh leum as. Thug an Gruagach bàn an ath leum as, 's rug e air chalpa deiridh air an fhiadh, 's thug am fiadh ràn as, 's dh' eubh a' Chailleach. "Co 'rug air mo bheathach gaoil?" "Tha mis," urs' an Gruagach bàn, Mac Rìgh Eireann. "A Ghruagach bhàn, Mhic Rìgh Eireann lig as e," urs' a' Chailleach. "Cha lig mi, mo bheathach fhìn a nis a th' aunn," urs' an Gruagach bàn. "Thoir dhomh làn mo dhùirn d' a chalg, no taosg mo dhùirn d' a ghaorr, air neo balgam dh' a shùgh, airneo gréim dh' a fheòil," urs' a' Chailleach. Aona chuid cha 'n fhaigh thu," urs' esan. "Tha 'n Fhìnn a' tighinn," urs' ise, "agus Fionn air an ceann; cha bhi h-aon aca nach ceanghail mi cùl ri cùl." "Dian sin," urs' esan, "ach tha mis' a' falbh."

Dh' fhalbh e, 's thug e leis am fiadh, 's bha e 'gabhail roimhe gos an do choinnich an Fhìnn e. "Fhinn Mhic Cumhail gléidh siud," urs' esan, 's e fàgail an fhéidh aig Fionn. Shuidh Fionn Mac Cumhail aig an fhiadh, 's dh' fhalbh an Gruagach bàn. Ràinig e ceàrdach nan seachd goibhne fichead. Thug e tri chearcaill iarruinn aisde mu choinneamh h-uile duine 'bha 'san Fhìnn. Thug e leis làmh-òrd, agus chuir e tri chearcaill mu cheann a h-uile duine 'bha 'san Fhìnn, agus theannaich e leis an òrd eud. Thàinig a' Chailleach a mach, 's lig i sgairt mhòr. "Fhinn Mhic Cumhail lig thugam mo bheathach gaoil." Bhrist an cearcall a b' airde 'bh' air na Fianntan leis an sgairt. Thàinig i 'mach an darna 'uair, 's lig i 'n ath sgairt, 's bhrist i 'n darna cearcall. ("Nach b' uamhasach a Chailleach.") Chaidh i dachaidh, 's cha b' fhad' a bha i stigh nur a thàinig i 'n treas uair, 's lig i 'n treas sgairt, 's bhrist i 'n treas cearcall. Dh' fhalbh i; ghabh i go ruige coille; shniamh i gad coille; thug i leath e; ghabh i 'null agus cheanghail i h-uile fear dha na Fiantaichean cul ri cul, ach Fionn.

Thug an Gruagach bàn làmh air an fhiadh 's dh' fheaunn e e. Thug e 'n gaorr as. Rug e air a h-uile sgath dha 'n mhionach 's dha 'n ghaorr, ghearr e plochd, agus thìodhlaic e fo 'n talamh eud. Chuir e coir' air dòigh, agus chuir e 'm fiadh 's a' choire, agus teine ris a 'bhruich. "Fhinn Mhic Cumhail," urs' an Gruagach bàn ri Fionn, "cò 'ca 's fheàrr leatsa dol a chòmhrag na Caillich, na fantail a' bruich a' choire?" "Matà," ursa Fionn, "tha 'n coire glé dhoirbh a bhruich. Mu bhios bìdeag de 'n fheòil gon an lìth 'bhith thairis, eireachaidh am fiadh mur a bha e roimhid; agus mu théid boinne dha 'n lìthe mu 'n teine, éireachaidh e mur a bha e roimhid. 'S fheàrr leamsa fantail a' bruich a' choire."

Thàinig a' Chailleach "Fhinn Mhic Cumhail," urs' ise, "bheir domh làn mo dhùirn dh' an chalg, airneo taosg mo dhuirn dh' a ghaorr, airneo greim dh' a fheòil, airneo balgam dh' a eanruith." "Cha d' rinn mi fhìn dad timchioll air, agus, leis an sin, cha 'n 'eil ordan agam air a thoirt seachad," ursa Fionn. Thòisich an Gruagach bàn 's a' Chailleach air a' chéile an so. Dhianadh eud bogan air a' chreagan, agus creagan air a' bhogan; an t-àite 'bo lugha 'rachadh eud fodha, rachadh eud fodha g' an glùinean; 's an t-àite 'bo mhoth' a rachadh eud fodha, rachadh eud fodha g' an sùilean. "Am bheil thu buidheach aighir Fhinn Mhic Cumhail?" urs' an Gruagach bàn. "S fhad o 'n a bha mise buidheach dheth sin," ursa Fionn. "Bidh cothrom air a thoirt seachad a nis," urs' an Gruagach. Rug e air a' Chailleach, 's bhuail e breab urr' aunn am bacan na heasgaid, 's leag e i. "An d' thoir mi 'n ceaunn di Fhinn Mhic Cumhail," urs' an Gruagach. "Cha 'n 'eil fhios' am," ursa Fionn. "Fhinn Mhic Cumhail," urs' ise, "tha mi 'gad' chur fo chroisean 's fo gheasan, 's fo naodh buaraiche mnatha sithe, siùbhlaiche, seachranaiche; an laogh beag is meata 's is mi-threòirich a thoirt do chinn, 's do do chluas, 's do chaitheadh-beatha dhiòt, mur am bi thu mur fhear pòsd' tri uairean mu 'n d' thig an latha aig bean an leòmhan chraobh." "Tha mis'," urs' an Gruagach bàn, "'gad' chur-sa fo chroisean agus fo gheasan, fo naodh buaraiche mnatha sìthe, siùbhlaiche, seachranaiche; an laogh beag is meata 's is mi-threoiriche thoirt do chinn, 's do chaitheadh-beatha dhiot, mur am bi thus' agus cas air gach taobh do chlachan Struth ruadh agad, agus a h-uile diar uisge 'dol a stigh air an darna ceaunn, 's a' dol a mach air a' cheaunn eile dìot." Dh' éiridh e agus lig e 'na seasamh i. "Tog dhìom do gheasan, agus togaidh mise dheth-san eud," urs' a' Chailleach. "Cha tog agus cha leag ach mur siud. Ge b' e air bith mur a thilleas sinne cha d' thig thusa."

Dh' fhalbh an Gruagach bàn 's thug e deth an coire. Rug e air forc agus air sgian, 's chuir e 'n fhorc aunns' an fhiadh. Rug e air an sgithinn, agus gheàrr e gréim as, 's dh' ith e. Rug e air plochd, 's ghearr e e, 's chuir e siud air ceaunn a' choire. "Fhinn Mhic Cumhail tha 'n t-am againn a bhith 'falbh," ursa esan, "am bheil thu math go marcachd?" "Dh' aimisinn orra," ursa Fionn. Rug e air slataig, 's thug do dh' Fhionn i. "Buail siud orms'," urs' esan. Bhuail Fionn an t-slatag air, 's rinn e falaire dhonn dheth. "Theirig a nis air mo mhuinn-sa," urs' an Gruagach. Chaidh Fionn air a mhuinn." Bi go math furachar, tha mise g' a' t' ionnsuidh." Thug e 'n leum sin as 's chaidhe seachad air naoidh iomairean, agus sheas Fionn air a mhuinn. Thug i 'n darna leum aisde, 's chaidh i seachad air naoidh iomairean eile, 's sheas Fionn air a muinn. Thug i 'n treas leum aisde, 's chaidh i seachad air naoidh iomairean eile, 's sheas esan air a muinn. Thug e go astar. Bheireadh e air a' ghaoth luath Mhàirt, 's cha bheireadh a' ghaoth luath Mhàirt air. "Tha baile beag shios an so," urs' an fhàlaire, "agus theirig sìos 's bheir leat tri stòpannan fian agus tri muilnean crionachd, agus bheir thu dhòmhsa stòp fian agus muileana crionachd, agus cìoraidh thu 'n aghaidh an fhionna agus leis an fhionna mi." Fhuair Fionn siud agus ràinig eud ball' an leòmhan chraobh. "Thalla air làr Fhinn Mhic Cumhail agus thoir dhomh stòpa fian agus muileann crionachd. Cìor a nis an aghaidh an fhionna mi, agus cìor leis an fhionna mi." Rinn e siud. "Bheir an aire dhuit fhìn," urs' an fhàlaire. Leum i 'n sin ; agus chuir i trian fòiche dha 'n bhalla, 's bha da thrian as a cionn, 's thill i. "Bheir dhomh stòp fian agus muileann crionachd eile, agus cìor an aghaidh an fhionna mi, agus cìor an aghaidh an fhionna mi, agus cìor leis an fhionna mi." Rinn e siud. "Thoir an aire dhuit fhin 's mise dha t' ionnsuidh a nis," urs' an fhàlaire. Thug ì 'n darna leum aisde ; agus chuir i da thrian de 'n bhalla fòiche, 's bha thrian as a cionn, agus thill i. "Thoir domh stòp fian agus muileann crionachd eile, agus cìor an aghaidh an fhionna mi, agus cìor leis an fhionna mi," urs' ise. Rinn e siud, "Thoir an aire dhuit fhìn 's mise dha t' ionnsuìdh a nis," urs' ise. Thug i leum aisde 's bha i air bàrr a' bhalla. "Tha 'n gnothach go math romhad Fhinn," urs' an fhàlaire ; "tha 'n leòmhan craobh o 'n tigh." Ghabh e dhachaidh. Bha flath agus fàilte roimhe. Chuireadh biadh agus deoch air a bhialthaobh. Ghabh e mu thàmh an oidhche sin. Mu 'n d' thàinig an latha bha e tri uairean mur fhear pòsd' aig bean an leòmhan craobh.

Cho moch 's a chunnaic a shùil an latha, 's moiche na sin a dh' éiridh e, 's a ràinig e 'n fhàlaire, an Gruagach bàn, agus dh' fhalbh eud. Urs' an Gruagach bàn, "Tha 'n leòmhan craobh o 'n tigh. Dad sam bith mur a bha cha cheil ise. Tha e 'falbh as ar déighne, 's cha chuimhnich e air an leobhar bhuidseachais, théid agams' air ; ach na 'n cuimhneachadh e air an leobhar cha chuireadh sluagh an t-saoghail ris. Tha h-uile draochd aigesan, agus leumaidh e 'na tharbh nur a thig e, agus leumaidh mis a' m' tharbh mu choinneamh, agus a' chiad bhuill' a bheir mise dha, leagaidh mi cheaunn air a shlinnean, 's bheir mi ràn air. Leumaidh e 'n sin 'na aiseal, 's leumaidh mise 'nam aiseil mu choinneamh ; agus a' chiad speach a bheir mise dha, bheir mi làn mo bheòil as eadar feòil agus craicionn mur a bhitheas e. Leumaidh e 'n sin 'na sheobhag aunns a' choille, 's a chiad speach a bheir mi dhà bheìr mi 'n cridh' agus an gruan as. Thig mis' a nuas as a dhéigh, agus beiridh tus' air an nèapaigin 'ud an siud, agus cuiridh tu aunns an nèapaigin mi, agus gearraidh tu plochd, 's cuiridh tu 'n nèapaigin fo 'n talamh, agus seasaidh tu air. Thig bean an leòmhan chraobh an sin, agus thusa 'nad' sheasamh air muinn a' phluichd, agus mise fo d' chasan, agus an leobhar buidseachais aic' air a muinn aunn an sùgan, agus their i, "Fhinn Mhic Cumhail, fhir nach d' innis briag riabh, innis domh co 'mharbh mo chompanach a shluagh an t-saoghail ?" Their thusa, "Cha 'n aithne dòmhs' as cionn an talanta co 'mharbh do chompanach." Falbhaidh is' agus bheir i go astar urra 'na gaoire guil."

Nur a bha eud treis air an aghaidh co 'chunnaic eud a' tighinn ach an leòmhan craobh. Chaidh e 'na tharbh. Chaidh an Gruagach bàn 'na tharbh mu 'choinneamh, agus a' chiad bhuill' a thug e dha leag e' cheaunn air a shlinnean, agus thug an leòmhan craobh ràn as. Leum e 'n so 'na aiseal. Leum an Gruagach bàn 'na aiseal mu 'choinneamh, 's air a' chiad speach a thug e làn a' bheoil as eadar fheoil agus chraicionn. Leum an leòmhan craobh an so 'na sheobhag aunns na speuran. Leum an Gruagach bàn 'na sheobhag aunns a' choille, agus thug e 'n cridh' agus an gruan as. Thuit an Gruagach bàn a nuas as a dhéigh. Rug Fionn air, agus chuir e aunns an nèapaigin e, agus gheàrr e plochd, agus chuir e 'n nèapaigin fo 'n talamh agus am plochd air a mhuinn, agus sheas e air muinn a' phluichd. Thàinig bean an leòmhan craobh, agus an leobhar buidseachais leath' air a muinn aunn an sùgan. "Fhinn Mhic Cumhail, fhir nach d' innis briag riabh, 'co' mharbh mo chompanach ?" "Cha 'n aithne dòmhs' as cionn an talanta co mharbh do chompanach," ursa Fionn agus 'dh fhalbh i 'na gaoire guil, agus thug i go h-astar urra.

Rug e air a Ghruagach bhàn agus thog e leis e, agus ràinig e 'n caisteal 's an robh bean a chaol-chot' uaine. Shìn e dhi siud 'na làimh. Ghabh i 'sias leis, agus cha b' fhada 'bha i shias nur a thàinig i nias far an robh esan. "Fhinn Mhic Cumhail," urs' ise, "tha 'n Gruagach bàn, Mac Rìgh Eireann, 'ga t' iarraidh." "'S e sin naigheachd is fhearr leom a chuala mi riabh fhathasd, gom bheil an Gruagach bàn' gam' iarraidh," ursa Fionn. Chuir i biadh agus deoch air am bialthaobh. Cha 'n itheadh eud greim, 's cha 'n òladh eud diar, gos an itheadh eud an cuid de 'n fhiadh le càch aig Struth ruaidh. Ràinig eud far an robh 'n Fhinn ceanghailte, agus dh' fhuasgail eud a h-uile h-aon riabh aca, 's bha acras go leòir orra. Chuir an Gruagach bàn am fiadh air am bialthaobh, 's dh' fhàg eud dha 'n fhiadh tri urad 's a dh' ith eud. "S còir dòmhsa dol a dh' innseadh mo sgéil," urs' an Gruagach bàn. Ràinig e 'Chailleach aig clachan Struth ruaidh. Thòisich e aìr innseadh a sgeil mur a dh' éiridh dha. H-uile sgial a dh' innseadh esan dise, thòiseachadh ise ri éiridh. H-uile h-uair a thòiseachadh ise ri éiridh, bheireadh esan urra, agus phronnadh e na cnàmhan aice, agus bhristeadh e eud, gos an d' innis e chuid sgialachdan di. Nur a dh' innis e eud thill e, agus ràinig e 'n Fhìnn air ais. Chaidh Fionn leis go caisteal bean a chaol-chot' uaine. "Beannachd leat Fhinn Mhic Cumhail," urs' an Gruagach bàn, Mac Rìgh Eireann. "Fhuair mise na bha mi 'g iarraidh, fradharc air gach cùis agus air gach gnothach, agus bidh mi 'nis a' tilleadh dhachaidh go pàileas m' athar fhìn." "'S an aunn mur so a tha thu 'brath mis' fhagail an déis gach rud a rinn mi riut,—thu 'bhith aig té eile, agus mise falamh!" "An e sin a tha thu 'ràdh?" urs' esan. "Na 'n saoilinnsa gon gabhadh sin dianadh, cha 'n fhaca mi 'mhnathan pòsda na diallainn riabh na ghabhainn a roighinn ort! Ach cha dian mise banais na pòsadh leat an so, ach falbhaidh tu go pàileas m' athar leam." Chaidh eud go pàileas athar, e fhin, agus bean a chaol-chòt' uaine, agus Fionn. Fhuaradh pears' eaglais, agus phòs an Gruagach bàn agus bean a chaol-chòt' uaine. Rinneadh banais shunndach, éibhinn, aighearach daibh. Thogadh ceòl agus leagadh bròn. Chuireadh biadh an àit' a chaitheadh, agus deoch an àit' a h-òl agus ceòl an àit' éisdeachd. Bha eud a' caitheadh na cuirm agus na cuideachd gos an do chumadh suas a' bhanais sin la agus bliadhna le sòlas agus toileachas-inntinn.

ALEXANDER MACNEILL, Fisherman.

Ten Tangval, Barra.

This is another specimen of what is called Seanachas—one of those old Highland stories which in their telling resemble no others. Fionn and his comrades are mentioned as England is by Americans. They are the greatest of heroes, but only act as foils to one still greater. "The Britishers wop the world, and we wop the Britishers," says the Americans. And Gruagach Ban, the Irish chief, beats the Fingalians, who beat the world. It seems hopeless to search for the original of this, unless it is to be found in mythology. The history of the Island of Barra, and the name of the place where the story was told, suggest a mixture of Norse and Celtic mythology as the most probable.

Fionn and his comrades are clearly Celtic worthies, and though they are usually brought down to be "militia" raised in Ireland by a particular Irish king, at a certain date, I strongly suspect them to be divinities in disguise. The leader at one end of the net and all his comrades at the other, has a parallel in the Edda (page 76, Dasent's translation).

"When the net was made ready, then fared the Asa to the

river, and cast the net into the force; Thorr held one end and the other held all the Asa, and so they drew the net."

And in other stories Fionn has part of the gear of Thorr in the shape of a hammer, whose stroke was heard over Eirinn and Lochlann, and which surely was a thunderbolt rather than the whistle of a militiaman.

Fionn, too, has the character of the leader in all the old Western romances; and in all mythology of which I know anything, he is the chief, but he is not the strongest; he is the wisest, but there is always some power wiser and stronger than him.

The dame of the Fine Green Kirtle, and the carlin with the wonderful deer, were both able to perform feats which the Feen could not equal, and they with their magic arts overcame the heroes, as the Fates ruled Jupiter and the Nornir ruled men, though there were Greek and Norse gods and goddesses in plenty. So King Arthur was chief but not the most valiant, the wisest but not the best of his time. And so in the Niebelungen Lied there was always a hero greater than the great man. And here seems to be something of the same kind in this Gaelic story.

The wife of the Tree Lion in her magic castle, and the leaping man in disguise, who carries the wooer, are characters which may be traced in the old German romance, and the incidents have a parallel in the Volsung tale, as its outline is given in the Norse Tales. There, too, is a lady to be won, and an obstacle to be surmounted, and a steed which springs over it, and a disguised worthy, more valiant than the chief.

The transformation into many shapes is a very common incident in Gaelic tales. It is common to Norse, to Mr. Peter Buchan's Scotch MS. Collection; and is somewhat like a story in the Arabian Nights where a princess fights a genius.

The dame of the Fine Green Kirtle is a common character in Gaelic tales. In Sutherland she was mentioned as seen about hills. She is always possessed of magic powers; and I know nothing like her in other collections. The carlin with the deer is to be traced in the Irish tales published by Mr. Simpson, and in Breton tales and poems, and in Welsh stories; and she is at least as old as Diana and the Sacred Hind with golden horns and brazen feet, which Hercules caught after a year's chase, which Diana snatched from him, reprimanding him severely for molesting an animal sacred to her.

LII.

THE KNIGHT OF THE RED SHIELD.

From John MacGilvray, Colonsay.

THERE was before now a king of Eirinn, and he went himself, and his people, and his warriors, and his nobles, and his great gentles, to the hill of hunting and game. They sat on a hillock coloured green colour, where the sun would rise early, and where she would set late. Said the one of swifter mouth than the rest.

"Who now in the four brown * quarters of the universe would have the heart to put an affront and disgrace on the King of Eirinn, and he in the midst of the people, and the warriors, great gentles, and nobles of his own realm."

"Are ye not silly," said the king; "he might come, one who should put an affront and disgrace on me, and that ye could not pluck the worst hair in his beard out of it."

It was thus it was. They saw the shadow of a shower coming from the western airt, and going to the eastern airt; † and a rider of a black filly coming cheerily after it.

---

* Probably a corruption, ruadh for roth, the four quarters of the wheel or circle of the universe.

† That is against the sun, which is unlucky according to all popular mythology.

As it were a warrior on the mountain shore,
As a star over sparklings,*
As a great sea over little pools,
As a smith's smithy coal
Being quenched at the river side ;
So would seem the men and women of the world beside him,
In figure, in shape, in form, and in visage.

Then he spoke to them in the understanding, quieting, truly wise words of real knowledge; and before there was any more talk between them, he put over the fist and he struck the king between the mouth and the nose, and he drove out three of his teeth, and he caught them in his fist, and he put them in his pouch, and he went away.

"Did not I say to you," said the king, "that one might come who should put an affront and disgrace on me, and that you could not pluck the worst hair in his beard out of it!"

Then his big son, the Knight of the Cairn, swore that he wouldn't eat meat, and that he wouldn't drink draught, and that he would not hearken to music, until he should take off the warrior that struck the fist on the king, the head that designed to do it.

"Well," said the Knight of the Sword, the very same for me, until I take the hand that struck the fist on the king from off the shoulder.

There was one man with them there in the company, whose name was Mac an Earraich uaine ri Gaisge, The Son of the Green Spring by Valour. "The very same for me," said he, "until I take out of the warrior who struck the fist on the king, the heart that thought on doing it."

---

* Roineagan, small stars, minute points of light.

"Thou nasty creature!" said the Knight of the Cairn, "what should bring thee with us? When we should go to valour, thou wouldst turn to weakness; thou wouldst find death in boggy moss, or in rifts of rock, or in a land of holes, or in the shadow of a wall, or in some place."

"Be that as it will, but I will go," said the Son of the Green Spring by Valour.

The king's two sons went away. Glance that the Knight of the Cairn gave behind him, he sees the Son of the Green Spring by Valour following them.

"What," said the Knight of the Cairn to the Knight of the Sword, "shall we do to him?"

"Do," said the Knight of the Sword, "sweep his head off."

"Well," said the Knight of the Cairn, "we will not do that; but there is a great crag of stone up here, and we will bind him to it."

"I am willing to do that same," said the other.

They bound him to the crag of stone to leave him till he should die, and they went away. Glance that the Knight of the Cairn gave behind him again, he sees him coming and the crag upon him.

"Dost thou not see that one coming again, and the crag upon him!" said the Knight of the Cairn to the Knight of the Sword; "what shall we do to him?"

"It is to sweep the head off him, and not let him (come) further," said the Knight of the Sword.

"We will not do that," said the Knight of the Cairn; but we will turn back and loose the crag off him. It is but a sorry matter for two full heroes like us; though he should be with us, he will make a man to polish a shield, or blow a fire heap or something."

They loosed him, and they let him come with them. Then they went down to the shore; then they got the ship, which was called AN IUBHRACH BHALLACH, The speckled barge.*

They put her out, and they gave her prow to sea, and her stern to shore.
They hoisted the speckled, flapping, bare-topped sails
Up against the tall, tough, splintery masts.
They had a pleasant little breeze as they might choose themselves,
Would bring heather from the hill, leaf from grove, willow from its roots,
Would put thatch of the houses in furrows of the ridges.
The day that neither the son nor the father could do it,
That same was neither little nor much for them,
But using it and taking it as it might come,
The sea plunging and surging,
The red sea the blue sea lashing
And striking hither and thither about her planks.
The whorled dun whelk that was down on the ground of the ocean,
Would give a SNAG on her gunwale and crack on her floor,
She would cut a slender oaten straw with the excellence of her going.

They gave three days driving her thus. "I myself am growing tired of this," said the Knight of the Cairn to the Knight of the Sword, "It seems to me time to get news from the mast."

"Thou thyself are the most greatly beloved here, oh Knight of the Cairn, and shew that thou wilt have

* These words would bear many translations according to dictionaries, such as the spotted stately woman, the variegated abounding in bows. The meaning seems to be a gaily painted boat.

honour going up; and if thou goest not up, we will have the more sport with thee," said the Son of the Green Spring by Valour.

Up went the Knight of the Cairn with a rush, and he fell down clatter in a faint on the deck of the ship.

"It is ill thou hast done," said the Knight of the Sword.

"Let us see if thyself be better; and if thou be better, it will be shewn that thou wilt have more will to go on; or else we will have the more sport with thee," said the Son of the Green Spring by Valour.

Up went the Knight of the Sword, and before he had reached but half the mast, he began squealing and squealing, and he could neither go up nor come down.

"Thou hast done as thou wert asked; and thou hast shewed that thou hadst the more respect for going up; and now thou canst not go up, neither canst thou come down! No warrior was I nor half a warrior, and the esteem of a warrior was not mine at the time of leaving; I was to find death in boggy moss, or in rifts of rock, or in the shade of a wall, or in some place; and it were no effort for me to bring news from the mast."

"Thou great hero!" said the Knight of the Cairn, "try it."

"A great hero am I this day, but not when leaving the town," said the Son of the Green Spring by Valour.

He measured a spring from the ends of his spear to the points of his toes, and he was up in the cross-trees in a twinkling.

"What art thou seeing?" said the Knight of the Cairn.

"It is too big for a crow, and it is too little for land," said he.

"Stay, as thou hast to try if thou canst know what it is," said they to him; and he stayed so for a while.*

"What art thou seeing now?" said they to him.

"It is an island and a hoop of fire about it, flaming at either end; and I think that there is not one warrior in the great world that will go over the fire," said he.

"Unless two heroes such as we go over it," said they.

"I think that it was easier for you to bring news from the mast than to go in there," said he.

"It is no reproach!" said the Knight of the Cairn.

"It is not; it is truth," said the Son of the Green Spring by Valour.

They reached the windward side of the fire, and they went on shore; and they drew the speckled barge up her own seven lengths on grey grass, with her mouth under her, where the scholars of a big town could neither make ridicule, scoffing, or mockery of her. They blew up a fire heap, and they gave three days and three nights resting their weariness.

At the end of the three days they began at sharpening their arms.

"I," said the Knight of the Cairn, "am getting tired of this; it seems to me time to get news from the isle."

"Thou art thyself the most greatly beloved here,"

---

* The whole of this is drawn from the life of boatmen. The feat of climbing the mast of an open boat under sail is far from easy, and I have seen it done as a feat of strength and skill.

said the Son of the Green Spring by Valour, and go the first and try what is the best news that thou canst bring to us."

The Knight of the Cairn went and he reached the fire; and he tried to leap over it, and down he went into it to his knees, and he turned back, and there was not a slender hair or skin between his knees and his ankles, that was not in a crumpled fold about the mouth of the shoes.

"He's bad, he's bad," said the Knight of the Sword.

"Let us see if thou art better thyself," said the Son of the Green Spring by Valour. "Shew that thou wilt have the greater honour going on, or else we will have the more sport with thee."

The Knight of the Sword went, and he reached the fire; and he tried to leap over it, and down he went into it to the thick end of the thigh; and he turned back, and there was no slender hair or skin between the thick end of the thigh and the ankle that was not in a crumpled fold about the mouth of the shoes.

"Well," said the Son of the Green Spring by Valour, "no warrior was I leaving the town, in your esteem; and if I had my choice of arms and armour of all that there are in the great world, it were no effort for me to bring news from the isle."

"If we had that thou shouldst have it," said the Knight of the Cairn.

"Knight of the Cairn, thine own arms and armour are the second that I would rather be mine (of all) in the great world, although thou thyself art not the second best warrior in it," said the Son of the Green Spring by Valour.

"It is my own arms and array that are easiest to

get," said the Knight of the Cairn, "and thou shalt have them; but I should like that thou wouldst be so good as to tell me what other arms or array are better than mine."

There are the arms and array of the Great Son of the sons of the universe,* who struck the fist on thy father," said the Son of the Green Spring by Valour.

The Knight of the Cairn put off his arms and array; and the Son of the Green Spring by Valour went into his arms and his array.

He went into his harness of battle and hard combat,
As was a shirt of smooth yellow silk and gauze stretched on his breast;
His coat, his kindly coat, above the kindly covering;
His boss covered; hindering sharp-pointed shield on his left hand,
His head-dress a helm of hard combat,
To cover his crown and his head top,
To go in the front of the fray and the fray long lasting;
His heroes hard slasher in his right hand,
A sharp surety knife against his waist.

He raised himself up to the top of the shore; and there was no turf he would cast behind his heels, that was not as deep as a turf that the bread covering tree† would cast when deepest it would be ploughing. He reached the circle of fire; he leaped from the points of his spear to the points of his toes over the fire.

Then there was the very finest isle that ever was seen from the beginning of the universe to the end of eternity; he went up about the island, and he saw a yellow bare hill in the midst. He raised himself up

* MHACAIBH MHOIR MHACHAIBH AN DOMHAIN; who this personage may be I cannot even guess.

† DALLA CHRANN ARAIN, a plough.

against the hill; there was a treasure of a woman sitting on the hill, and a great youth with his head on her knee, and asleep. He spoke to her in instructed, eloquent, true, wise, soft maiden words of true knowledge. She answered in like words; and if they were no better, they were not a whit worse, for the time.

"A man of thy seeming is a treasure for me; and if I had a right to thee, thou shouldst not leave the island," said the little treasure.

"If a man of my seeming were a treasure for thee, thou wouldst tell me what were waking for that youth," said the Son of the Green Spring by Valour.

"It is to take off the point of his little finger," said she.

He laid a hand on the sharp surety knife that was against his waist, and he took the little finger off him from the root. That made the youth neither shrink nor stir.

"Tell me what is waking for the youth, or else there are two off whom I will take the heads, thyself and the youth," said the Son of the Green Spring by Valour.

"Waking for him," said she, "is a thing that thou canst not do, nor any one warrior in the great world, but the warrior of the red shield, of whom it was in the prophecies that he should come to this island, and strike yonder crag of stone on this man in the rock of his chest; and he is unbaptized till he does that.

He heard this that such was in the prophecy for him, and he unnamed. A fist upon manhood, a fist upon strengthening, and a fist upon power went into him. He raised the crag in his two hands, and he struck it on the youth in the rock of his chest. The one who was asleep gave a slow stare of his two eyes and he looked at him.

"Aha!" said the one who was asleep, "hast thou come, warrior of the Red Shield. It is this day that thou has the name; thou wilt not stand long to me."

"Two thirds of thy fear be on thyself, and one on me," said the Warrior of the Red Shield; "thou wilt not stand long to me."

In each other's grips they went, and they were hard belabouring each other till the mouth of dusk and lateness was. The Warrior of the Red Shield thought that he was far from his friends and near his foe; he gave him that little light lift, and he struck him against the earth; the thumb of his foot gave a warning to the root of his ear, and he swept the head off him.

"Though it be I who have done this, it was not I who promised it," said he.

He took the hand off him from the shoulder, and he took the heart from his chest, and he took the head off the neck; he put his hand in the dead warrior's pouch, and he found three teeth of an old horse in it, and with the hurry took them for the king's teeth, and he took them with him; and he went to a tuft of wood, and he gathered a withy, and he tied on it the hand and the heart and the head.

"Whether wouldst thou rather stay here on this island by thyself, or go with me?" said he to the little treasure.

"I would rather go with thee thyself, than with all the men of earth's mould together," said the little treasure.

He raised her with him on the shower top of his shoulders, and on the burden (bearing) part of his back, and he went to the fire. He sprang over with the little treasure upon him. He sees the Knight of the Cairn and the Knight of the Sword coming to meet him; rage and fury in their eyes.

"What great warrior," said they, "was that after thee there, and returned when he saw two heroes like us?"

"Here's for you," said he, "this little treasure of a woman, and the three teeth of your father; and the head, and hand, and heart of the one who struck the fist on him. Make a little stay and I will return, and I will not leave a shred of a tale in the island."

He went away back; and at the end of a while he cast an eye behind him, and he sees them and the speckled barge playing him ocean hiding.

"Death wrappings upon yourselves!" said he, "a tempest of blood about your eyes, the ghost of your hanging be upon you! to leave me in an island by myself, without the seed of Adam in it, and that I should not know this night what I shall do."

He went forward about the island, and was seeing neither house nor tower in any place, low or high. At last he saw an old castle in the lower ground of the island, and he took (his way) towards it. He saw three youths coming heavily, wearily, tired to the castle. He spoke to them in instructed, eloquent, true, wise words of true wisdom. They spoke in return in like words.

They came in words of the olden time on each other; and who were here but his three true foster brothers. They went in right good pleasure of mind to the big town.

They raised up music and laid down woe;
There were soft drunken draughts
And harsh, stammering drinks,
Tranquil, easy toasts

Between himself and his foster brethren,
Music between fiddles, with which would sleep
Wounded men and travailing women
Withering away for ever ; with the sound of that music
Which was ever continuing sweetly that night.

They went to lie down. In the morning of the morrow he arose right well pleased, and he took his meat. What should he hear but the GLIOGARSAICH, clashing of arms and men going into their array. Who were these but his foster brethren.

"Where are you going?" said he to them.

"We are from the end of a day and a year in this island," said they, "holding battle against MacDorcha MacDoilleir, the Son of Darkness Son of Dimness, and a hundred of his people: and every one we kill to-day they will be alive to-morrow. Spells are on us that we may not leave this for ever until we kill them."

"I will go with you this day; you will be the better for me," said he.

"Spells are on us," said they, "that no man may go with us unless he goes there alone."

"Stay you within this day, and I will go there by myself," said he.

He went away, and he hit upon the people of the Son of Darkness Son of Dimness, and he did not leave a head on a trunk of theirs.

He hit upon MacDorcha MacDoilleir himself, and MacDorcha MacDoilleir said to him,

"Art thou here, Warrior of the Red Shield?"

"I am," said the Warrior of the Red Shield.

"Well then," said MacDorcha MacDoilleir, "thou wilt not stand long for me."

In each other's grips they went, and were hard belabouring each other till the mouth of dusk and lateness was. At last the Knight of the Red Shield gave that cheery little light lift to the Son of Darkness Son of Dimness, and he put him under, and he cast the head off him.

Now there was MacDorcha MacDoilleir dead, and his thirteen sons; and the battle of a hundred on the hand of each one of them.

Then he was spoilt and torn so much that he could not leave the battle-field; and he did but let himself down, laid amongst the dead the length of the day. There was a great strand under him down below; and what should he hear but the sea coming as a blazing brand of fire, as a destroying serpent, as a bellowing bull; he looked from him, and what saw he coming on shore on the midst of the strand, but a great toothy carlin, whose like was never seen. There was the tooth that was longer than a staff in her fist, and the one that was shorter than a stocking wire in her lap. She came up to the battle-field, and there were two between her and him. She put her finger in their mouths, and she brought them alive; and they rose up whole as best they ever were. She reached him and she put her finger in his mouth, and he snapped it off her from the joint. She struck him a blow of the point of her foot, and she cast him over seven ridges.

"Thou pert little wretch," said she, "thou art the last I will next-live * in the battle field."

The carlin went over another, and he was above her; he did not know how he should put an end to the

---

* ATH BHEOTHAICHEAS; there is no such verb in English, but to next-live expresses the meaning.

carlin; he thought of throwing the short spear that her son had at her, and if the head should fall off her that was well. He threw the spear, and he drove the head off the carlin. Then he was stretched on the battle-field, blood and sinews and flesh in pain, but that he had whole bones. What should he see bnt a musical harper about the field.

"What art thou seeking?" said he to the harper.

"I am sure thou art wearied," said the harper; "come up and set thy head on this little hillock and sleep."

He went up and he laid down; he drew a snore, pretending that he was asleep, and on his soles he was brisk, swift, and active.

"Thou art dreaming," said the harper.

"I am," said he.

"What sawest thou?" said the harper.

"A musical harper," he said, "drawing a rusty old sword to take off my head."

Then he seized the harper, and he drove the brain in fiery shivers through the back of his head.

Then he was under spells that he should not kill a musical harper for ever, but with his own harp.

Then he heard weeping about the field. "Who is that?" said he.

"Here are thy three true foster brothers, seeking thee from place to place to-day," said they.

"I am stretched here," said he, "blood and sinews, and bones in torture."

"If we had the little vessel of balsam that the great carlin has, the mother of MacDorcha MacDoilleir, we would not be long in healing thee," said they.

"She is dead herself up there," said he, "and she has nothing that ye may not get."

"We are out of her spells forever," said they.

They brought down the little vessel of balsam, and they washed and bathed him with the thing that was in the vessel; then he arose up as whole and healthy as he ever was. He went home with them, and they passed the night in great pleasure.

They went out the next day in great pleasure to play at shinty. He went against the three, and he would drive a half hail down, and a half hail up, in against them.

They perceived the Great Son of the Sons of the World coming to the town; that was their true foster brother* also. They went out where he was, and they said to him—

"Man of my love, avoid us and the town this day."

"What is the cause?" said he.

"The Knight of the Red Shield is within, and it is thou he is seeking," said they.

"Go you home, and say to him to go away and to flee, or else that I will take the head off him," said the Great Son of the Sons of the Universe.

Though this was in secret the Knight of the Red Shield perceived it; and he went out on the other side of the house, and he struck a shield blow, and a fight kindling.

The great warrior went out after him, and they began at each other.

There was no trick that is done by shield man or skiff man,
Or with cheater's dice box,
Or with organ of the monks,
That the heroes could not do;

---

* DEARBH CHOMHALTA; this must mean something besides true *foster brother*.

As was the trick of CLEITEAM, trick of OIGEAM,*
The apple of the juggler throwing it and catching it
Into each other's laps
Frightfully, furiously,
Bloodily, groaning, hurtfully.
Mind's desire ! umpire's choice !
They would drive three red sparks of fire from their armour,
Driving from the shield wall, and flesh
Of their breasts and tender bodies,
As they hardly belaboured each other.

"Art thou not silly, Warrior of the Red Shield, when thou art holding wrestling and had battle against me?" said Macabh Mhacaibh an Domhain.

"How is this?" said the hero of the Red Shield.

"It is, that there is no warrior in the great world that will kill me till I am struck above the covering of the trews," said Macabh Mor.†

"The victory blessing of that be thine, telling it to me! If thou hadst told me that a long time ago, it is long since I had swept the head off thee," said the Warrior of the Red Shield.

"There is in that more than thou canst do; the king's three teeth are in my pouch, and try if it be that thou will take them out," said Macabh Mor.

When the Warrior of the Red Shield heard where the death of Macabh Mor was, he had two blows given for the blow, two thrusts for the thrust, two stabs for the stab; and the third was into the earth, till he had dug a hole; then he sprung backwards. The great warrior sprung towards him, and he did not notice the

* These may mean the pen trick—the trick of writing; but I am not certain.

† From which it appears that he was too tall to be reached by the other.

hole, and he went down into it to the covering of the trews. Then he reached him, and he cast off his head. He put his hand in his pouch, and he found the king's three teeth in it, and he took them with him and he reached the castle.

"Make a way for me for leaving this island," said he to his foster brethren, "as soon as you can."

"We have no way," said they, "by which thou canst leave it; but stay with us forever, and thou shalt not want for meat or drink."

"The matter shall not be so; but unless you make a way for letting me go, I will take the heads and necks out of you," said he.

"A coracle that thy foster mother and thy foster father had, is here; and we will send it with thee till thou goest on shore in Eirinn. The side that thou settest her prow she will go with thee, and she will return back again by herself; here are three pigeons for thee, and they will keep company with thee on the way," said his foster brothers to him.

He set the coracle out, and he sat in her, and he made no stop, no stay, till he went on shore in Eirinn. He turned her prow outwards; and if she was swift coming, she was swifter returning. He let away the three pigeons, as he left the strange country; and he was sorry that he had led them away, so beautiful was the music that they had.*

There was a great river between him and the king's house. When he reached the river, he saw a hoary man coming with all his might, and shouting, "Oh, gentleman, stay yonder until I take you over on my back, in case you should wet yourself."

---

* In another version pigeons were his foster brothers transformed.

"Poor man, it seems as if thou wert a porter on the river," said he.

"It is (so)," said the hoary old man.

"And what set thee there?" said he.

"I will tell you that," said the hoary old man; "a big warrior struck a fist on the King of Eirinn, and he drove out three of his teeth, and his two sons went to take out vengeance; there went with them a foolish little young boy that was son to me; and when they went to manhood, he went to faintness. It was but sorry vengeance for them to set me as porter on the river for it."

"Poor man," said he, "that is no reproach; before I leave the town thou wilt be well."

He seized him, and he lifted him with him: and he set him sitting in the chair against the king's shoulder.

"Thou art but a saucy man that came to the town; thou hast set that old carl sitting at my father's shoulder; and thou shalt not get it with thee," said the Knight of the Cairn, as he rose and seized him.

"By my hand, and by my two hands' redemption, it were as well for thee to seize Cnoc Leothaid as to seize me," said the Warrior of the Red Shield to him, as he threw him down against the earth.

He laid on him the binding of the three smalls, straitly and painfully. He struck him a blow of the point of his foot, and he cast him over the seven highest spars that were in the court, under the drippings of the lamps, and under the feet of the big dogs; and he did the very same to the Knight of the Sword; and the little treasure gave a laugh.

"Death wrappings be upon thyself!" said the king to her. "Thou art from a year's end meat companion, and drink companion for me, and I never saw smile or laugh being made by thee, until my two sons are being disgraced."

"Oh, king," said she, "I have knowledge of my own reason."

"What, oh king, is the screeching and screaming that I am hearing since I came to the town? I never got time to ask till now," said the hero of the Red Shield.

"My sons have three horses' teeth, driving them into my head, since the beginning of a year, with a hammer, until my head has gone through other with heartbreak and torment, and pain," said the king.

"What wouldst thou give to a man that would put thy own teeth into thy head, without hurt, without pain," said he.

"Half my state so long as I may be alive, and my state altogether when I may go," said the king.

He asked for a can of water, and he put the teeth into the water.

"Drink a draught," said he to the king.

The king drank a draught, and his own teeth went into his head, firmly and strongly, quite as well as they ever were, and every one in her own place.

"Aha!" said the king, "I am at rest. It is thou that didst the valiant deeds; and it was not my set of sons!"

"It is he," said the little treasure to the king, "that could do the valiant deeds; and it was not thy set of shambling sons, that would be stretched as seaweed seekers when he was gone to heroism."

"I will not eat meat, and I will not drink draught," said the king, "until I see my two sons being burnt to-morrow. I will send some to seek faggots of grey oak for burning them."

On the morning of the morrow, who was earliest on his knee at the the king's bed, but the Warrior of the Red Shield.

"Rise from that, warrior; what single thing mightest thou be asking that thou shouldst not get," said the king.

"The thing I am asking is, that thy two sons should be let go; I cannot be in any one place where I may see them spoiled," said he. "It were better to do bird and fool clipping to them, and to let them go."

The king was pleased to do that. Bird and fool clipping was done to them. They were put out of their place, and dogs and big town vagabonds after them.

The little treasure and the Warrior of the Red Shield married, and agreed. A great wedding was made, that lasted a day and a year; and the last day of it was as good as the first day.

RIDIRE NA SGIATHA DEIRGE.

Bha ann roimhe seo Righ Eireann 's dh' fholbh e fhéin, 'sa shluagh agus a laochraidh, 's a mhaithean, 's a mhòruaislean do 'n bheinn shithinn agus sheilg. Shuidh ad air cnocan dath-uaine daite, far an éireadh grian gu moch agus an laidheadh i gu h-anmoch. Thuirt am fear a bu luaithe beul na 'chéile.

"Co 'neis, ann an ceithir ranna ruath an domhain, aig am biodh a chridhe tàr, agus tailceas a dhèanadh air Righ Eireann, 's e am meadhon slòigh agus laochraidh, mòruaislean a's maithean a rioghachd fhéin."

"Nach amaideach sibh," ars' an righ, "dh' fhaodadh e tighinn fear a dheanadh tàir agus tailceas armsa 's nach b' urrainn sibh an rioba 'bu mheasa 'na fheusaig a thoirt aisde."

'S ann mar seo a bha. Chunnaic ad dubhradh frois' a' tighinn bho 'n aird an iar, 's a' triall do 'n aird an ear,—'s marcaiche falaire duighe 'tighinn gu sunndach 'na déigh.

Mar a bu churaidh air tir na sléibhte,
Mar reul air na rionnagan,
Mar mhuir mòr air lodannan,
Mar ghual guibhne gobha
'Ga bhàthadh aig taobh na h-abhann ;
'S ann mar sean a dh' amhairceadh fir agus mnathan an
domhain làmh ris,
An dealbh, 's an dreach, san cruth, agus an aogas.

Labhair e dhaibh, an sean, ann am briathra fiosneacha, foisneacha, fìor-ghlic, fior-eòlais ; 's ma 'n robh tuillidh seanachais eatorra chuir e thairis an dorn, 's bhuail e 'n righ eadar am beul 's an t-sròn 's chuir e tri fiaclan as, 's cheap e 'na dhorn ad, 's chuir e 'na phòc ad, 's dh' fhalbh e.

" Nach d' thubhairt mi, ruibh," urs' an righ, " gum faodadh e tighinn fear a dheanadh tàir agus tailceas ormsa, 's nach b' urrainn sibh an rioba 'bu mheasa 'na fheusaig a thoirt aisde." Bhòidich an seo a mhac mòr, ridir' a' chùirn, nach itheadh e biadh, a's nach òladh e deoch, a's nach éisdeadh e ceòl, gus an d' thugadh e bhàr a' ghaisgich a bhuail an dorn air an righ, an ceann a dhealbh a dhèanadh.

" Mata," orsa ridir' a' chlaidhimh, " an t-aon ciadhna dhomhsa gus an d' thoir mi 'n làmh a bhuail an dorn air an righ, o'n ghualainn deth."

Bha aon fhear leo, an sean, 's a' chuideachd d' am b' ainm Mac an Earraich uaine ri Gaisge, " An t-aon ciadhna domhsa," ars' esan, " gus an d' thoir mi, as a' ghaisgeach a bhuail an dorn air an righ, an cridhe 'smaointich air a dhèanadh."

" Thus' a bheathaich mhosaich," orsa Ridire Chùirn, " dé 'bheir thusa leinn ? Nur a rachamaidne air thapadh, rachadh tus' 'air mhithapadh. Geobhadh tu bàs am mòintich bhuig, na 'n sgeilpe chreag, na 'n talamh toll, na 'n sgàth gàrraidh, na 'n àit-eigin."

" Biodh sin 's a roghainn da ach falbhaidh mi," orsa Mac an Earraich uaine ri Gaisge.

Dh' fhalbh da mhac an rìgh. Suìl gu 'n dug Ridire a Chùirn as a dhéigh as faicear Mac an Earraich uaine ri Gaisge 'gan leantuinn.

"Gu-dé," orsa Ridire 'Chuirn ri Ridire 'Chlaidhimh, "a ni sinn ris."

"Ni," orsa Ridire 'Chlaidhimh, "an ceann a sgathadh dheth."

"Mata," orsa Ridire 'Chùirn, "cha dèan sinn sean; ach tha carragh mòr cloiche shuas an seo agus ceanghlaidh sinn ris e."

"Tha mi toileach sean fhéin a dheanadh," ors' am fear eile.

Cheanghail ad ris a' charragh chloich' e, an los fhàgail gus am bàsaicheadh e, 's ghabh ad air falbh. Sùil gun d' thug Ridire 'Chùirn a rithisd as a dhéigh, 's faicear a' tighinn e, 's an carragh air a mhuin.

"Nach fhaic thu, neis, am fear sean a' tighinn a rithisd, 's an carragh air a mhuin," orsa Ridire 'Chùirn ri Ridire Chlaidhimh. "Dé 'ni sin ris?"

"Tha 'n ceann a sgathadh dheth 's gun a leigeil na 's fhaide," orsa Ridire 'Chlaidhimh.

"Cha dean sinn sean," orsa Ridire 'Chùirn, "ach tillidh sinn agus fuasglaidh sinn an carragh dheth. Is suarrach d' ar leithidne do dha làn-ghaisgeach gad a bhiodh e leinn; ni e fear ghlanadh sgiath, na sheideach thùrlach, na rud-eigin."

Dh' fhuasgail ad e agus leig ad leo e. Ghabh ad a sìos an seo thun a' chladaich. Fhuair ad an sean an long ris an abradh ad, an Iubhrach bhallach.

Chuir ad a mach i, 's thug ad a toiseach do mhuir, 's a deireadh
do thìr.
Thog ad na siuil bhreaca, bhaidealacha, bhàrr-rùisgte,
An aodann nan crann fada, fulannach, fiùghaidh.
Bha soirbheas beag, laghach aca mar a thaghadh ad fhé'
'Bheireadh fraghach * a beinn, duilleach a coill, seileach a a
fhreumhaichan.
'Chuireadh tutha nan taighean ann an claisean nan iomairean,
An latha nach deanadh am mac na 'n t-athair e.
Cha bu bheag 's cha bu mhor leòsan sean fhé'
Ach 'ga caitheadh, 's 'ga ghabhail mar a thigeadh e.
An fhairge 'fulpanaich 's a' falpanaich ;—
An lear dearg 's an lear uaine 'lachannaich,
'S a' bualadh thall 's a bhos ma bòrdaibh.
An fhaochag chrom chiar a bha shìos an grunnd an aigein,

* Fraghach, same as fraoch, heather.

Bheireadh i snag air a beul-mòr agus cnag air a h-urlar.
Ghearradh i cuinnlein caol coirce le fheobhas 's a dh' fhalbhadh i.

Thug ad tri lathan 'ga caitheadh mar sean.

"Tha mi fhéin a' fàs sgìth dheth seo," orsa Ridire Chùirn ri Ridire Chlaidhimh; "bu mhithidh leam sgeul fhaotainn as a' chrann."

"'S tu fhéin a 's mòr-ionmhmuneach ann, a Ridire Chùirn, agus leig fhaicinn gu 'm bi spéis agad a dhol suas; agus mar an d' théid thu suas bidh am barrachd spòrs againn ort," orsa Mac an Earraich uaine ri Gaisge. Suas a ghabh Ridìre Chùirn le roid, 's thuit e nuas 'na ghlag paiseanaidh air clàr-uachrach na luinge.

"'S dona 'fhuaras tu," orsa Ridire Chlaidhimh.

"Faiceam an tu fhéin 'is fèarr; 's ma 's tu 's feàrr leigear fhaicinn gum bi barrachd toil agad dol air t' aghaidh, air-neo bidh am barrachd spòrs againn ort," orsa Mac an Earraich uaine ri Gaisge.

Suas a ghabh Ridire 'Chlaidhimh, 's ma 'n d' ràinig e ach leith a' chroinn thòisich e air sgiamhail 's air sgreadail, 's cha b' urrainn e dol a suas na tighinn a nuas.

"Rinn thu mar a dh' iarradh ort, 's leig thu fhaicinn gun robh am barrachd speis agad a dhol suas; 's a neis cha d' theid thusa suas, 's cha mhotha 'thig thu nuas! Cha ghaisgeach mise, 's cha leith ghaisgeach mi, 's cha robh meas gaisgich orm an am fagoil." Gheobhainn bàs am mòintich bhoig na 'n sgeilpe chreag, na 'n sgàth gàrraidh, na 'n àit-eiginn, "agus cha bu spàirn orm sgeul a thoirt as a' chrann," orsa Mac an Earraich uaine ri Gaisge.

"A shaoidh mhòir," orsa Ridire 'Chùirn, "feuch ris."

"Is saoidh mòr mi 'n diugh; ach cha b' eadh a' fàgail a' bhaile," orsa Mac an Earraich uaine ri Gaisge.

Thomhais e leum bho cheannaibh a shleagh gu barraibh ordag, 's bha e shuas a chlisgeadh anns a' chrannaig.

"Gu-dé 'tha thu 'faicinn?" orsa Ridire 'Chuirn.

"Tha e ro mhòr do dh' fheannaig 's tha e ro bheag do dh' fhearann," ors' esan.

"Fan mar a th' agad feuch an aithnich thu dé 'th' ann," ors' ad ris, 's dh' fhan e mar seo treis.

"Dé 'tha thu 'faicinn a neis?" ors' ad ris.

"Tha eilean agus cearcall teine ma 'n cuairt air, a' lasadh an ceann a chéile; 's tha mi 'smaointeachadh nach 'eil aon ghaisgeach anns an domhan mhòr a theid thairis air an teine," ars' esan.

"Mar an d' théid ar leithidne de dha ghaisgeach thairis air," ors àdsan.

"Tha dùil' am gum b' fhasa dhuibh sgeul a thoirt as a' chrann na dol a staigh an siod," ars' eisean.

"Cha'n athais e ?" orsa Ridire Chùirn.

"Cha'n eadh, 's fìrinn e!" orsa Mac an Earraich uaine ri Gaisge. Ràinig ad an taobh muin de 'n teine, 's chaidh ad air tìr, 's tharruinn ad an Iubhrach bhallach suas a seachd fad fhéin air feur glas, 's a beul fòiche, far nach deanadh sgoilearan baile-mhòir bùirt, na fochaid, na magadh urra. Shéid ad tùrlach, 's thug ad tri oidhchean a's tri lathan a' leigeil an sgìos.

An ceann nan tri lathan thòisich ad air lìobhadh nan arm.

"Tha mi," orsa Ridire Chùirn, "a' fàs sgìth dheth seo, bu mhithich leam sgeul fhaotainn as an eilean."

"'S tu fhéin," orsa Mac an Earraich uaine ri Gaisge, is mòr-ionmhuinneach ann, agus folbh an toiseach feuch dé 'n sgeul a's fhèarr a bheir thu a'r ionnsuidh."

Dh' fhalbh Ridire Chùirn, 's ràinig e 'n teine, 's thug e làmh air leum thairte, 's a sìos a ghabh e innte g'a ghlùinean ; 's thill e air ais, 's cha robh rioba caoille na craicinn eadar a ghlùinean 's a mhuthairnean nach robh 'na chuaran ma bheul nam bròg.

"'S don' e, 's don' e," orsa Ridire 'Chlaidhimh.

"Feiceam an tu fhéin a's fhèarr," orsa Mac an Earraich uaine ri Gaisge. "Leig fhaicinn gum bi barrachd spéis agad a' dhol air t' aghaidh, air-neo bidh am barrachd spòrs againn ort."

Dh' fhalbh Ridire 'Chlaidhimh, 's ràinig e 'n teine, 's thug e làmh air leum thairte, 's chaidh e sìos innte gu ceann ramhar na sléisde, 's thill e air ais, 's cha robh rioba caoille na craicinn eadar ceann ramhar na sléisde 's am muthairn nach robh 'na chuaran ma bheul nam bròg.

"Mata," orsa Mac an Earraich uaine ri Gaisge, "cha bu ghaisgeach mise an am fàgail a' bhaile 'nur beachd-sa ; 's na 'm biodh mo rogha arm a's éididh agam de na 'bheil anns an domhan mhòr, cha bu spàirn orm sgeul a thoirt as an eilean."

"Na'm biodh sean againn gheobhadh tus' e," orsa Ridire 'Chùirn.

"A Ridire 'Chùirn, b' e t' airm agus t' éideadh fhéin darna airm agus éideadh a b' fhèarr leam agam anns an domhan mhor ;

gad nach tu fhéin darna gaisgeach a 's fhèarr a th' ann," arsa Mac an Earraich uaine ri Gaisge.

"'Se m' airm agus m' éideadh fhéin a 's fhasa fhaotainn," orsa Ridire 'Chùirn, "agus gheobh thus' ad; ach b' fhèarr leam gum biodh tu cho math 's gun innseadh tu dhomh co na h-airm agus an t-éideadh eile 's fhèarr na m' fheadhainn-sa."

Tha airm agus éideadh Mhacaibh mhoir Mhacaibh an Domhain a bhuail an dorn air t' athair," orsa Mac an Earraich uaine ri Gaisge.

Chuir Ridire Chùirn dheth airm agus èididh, 's ghabh Mac an Earraich ri Gaisge na h-airm agus na h-éididh.

Ghabh e 'na threallaichean cath agus cruaidh-chòmhraig.

Mar a bha 'leine 'n t-sròl 's a'n t-sìoda shleamhuinn bhuidhe sìnte r'a chneas,

A' chòtainn caomh cotain air uachdar na caomh chotaige,
A sgiath bhucaideach, bhacaideach, bharra-chaol air a làimh chlì,
A cheanna-bheart, clogada cruaidh-chòmhraig
A' coimhead a chinn, 's a cheanna-mhullaich,
An toiseach na h-iorguill,—'san iorguill an-diomain,
A shlacanta cruaidh curaidh 'na làimh dheis,
Urra-sgithinn gheur an taice r'a chneas.

Thog e suas bràigh a' chladaich, 's cha robh fòid a thilgeadh e'n déigh a shàlach nach robh cho domhainn ri fòid a thilgeadh dallachrann arain nur a bu doimhne 'bhiodh e 'treobhadh. Ràinig e'n cearcall teine. Leum e o bharraibh a shleagh gu borraibh òrdag thar na teine. Bha 'n sean an aon eilean a bu bhòibhche 'chunncas o thus an domhain gu deireadh na dìlinn. Ghabh e suas feadh an eilean 's chunnaic e cnoc maol buidhe 'na mheadhon. Thog e ris a' chnoc. Bha Ionmhuinn mhnatha 'na suidhe air a' chnoc, 's òglach mòr 's a cheann air a glùn, 's e 'na chadal. Labhair e rithe ann am briathra fisneacha, foisneacha, fìor-ghlic, mìne, maighdeana, fìor-eolais. Fhreagair ise anns na briathra ciadhna; 's mar am b' àd a b' fhèarr, cha b' àd dad a bu mheasa 's an am.

"'S ionmhuinn leam fhéin fear do choltais, 's na'm biodh còir agam ort dh' fhàgadh tu'n t-eilean," ors' an Ionmhuinn.

"Nam b' ionmhuinn leat fear mo choslais dh' innseadh tu domh dé 'bu dùsgadh do 'n òlach seo," orsa Mac an Earraich uaine ri Gaisge.

"Tha bàrr na laodaig a thoirt deth " ors' ise.

Thug e làmh air an urra-sgithinn ghéir a bha 'n taice r' a chneas, 's thug e'n laodag deth o'n bhun. Cha d' thug siod smoisleachadh na gluasad air an òglach.

"Innis domh dé 's dùsgadh do'n òglach;—air neo 's dithisd deth an d' thoir mi na cinn thu fhèin 's an t-òglach!" orsa Mac an Earraich uaine ri Gaisge.

"'S dùsgadh dha," ors' ise, "rud nach dèan thusa, na aon ghaisgeach anns an domhan mhòr, ach gaisgeach na sgiatha deirge, do'n robh e' s an tairgneachd tighinn do'n eilean seo, agus an carragh cloich' ud thall a bhualadh air an duine seo ann an carraig an uchd; 's tha e gun bhaisteadh gus an dèan e sean."

Chual eisean seo, gu' robh 'leithid anns an tairgneachd dha, 's e gun bhaisteadh. Chaidh dorn air thapadh, 's dòrn air ghleus-adh, 's dorn air spionnadh ann. Thog e 'na dha làimh an carragh 's bhuail e air an òlach mhòr an carraig an uchd e. Thug am fear a bha 'na chadal blaomadh air a dha shuil 's dh' amharc e air. "Aha," ors' am fear a bha 'na chadal, "an d' thainig thu 'ghaisgich na sgiatha deirge? 's ann an diugh a tha 'n t-ainm ort. Cha'n fhada 'sheasas thu dhomhsa."

"Da thrian de t' eagal ort fhéin, 's a' h-aon ormsa," arsa Gaisgeach na Sgiatha deirge, "cha 'n fhad' a sheasas thusa domhsa."

An caraibh a chéile ghabh ad, 's bha ad a' cruaidh leadairt a chéile gus an robh an beul ath-dhath 'san anmoich ann. Smao-intich Gaisgeach na Sgiatha deirge gun robh e fad' o a chairdean 's fagus d'a naimhdean 's thug e'n togail bheag, shoilleir ud air, 's bhuail e ris an talamh e. Thug ordag a choise sanus do bhun a chluaise, agus sgath e dheth an ceann.

"Gad is mi 'rinn seo cha mhi 'gheall e," ors' esan. Thug e'n làmh o'n ghuallainn deth, 's thug e'n cridhe a a chom, 's thug e'n ceann bhar a mhuineil. Chuir e 'làmh am pòc' a' ghaisgich mhairbh, 's fhuair e tri fiaclan seann eich ann, 's, leis an deifir, ghabh e'n àite fiaclan an righ ad, 's thug e leis ad. Chaidh e gu tom coille, 's bhuain e gad, 's cheanghail e air an làmh, 's an cridhe, 's an ceann.

"Co'ca 's fhèarr leatsa fantail an seo, air an eilean seo leat fhéin, na falbh leamsa," ors' e ris an Ionmhuinn.

"'S fhèarr leamsa folbh leat fhéin, na le fir na h-ùir thalmhanta gu léir," ors' an Ionmhuinn.

Thog e leis i air fras-mhullach a ghuailne 's air uallach a

dhroma 's ghabh e gus an teine. Leum e thairis 'san Ionmhuinn air a mhuin. Faicidh e Ridire 'Chùirn 's Ridire 'Chlaidhimh a' tighinn 'na chomhdhail, 's boil a's buaireas 'nan 'sùilean.

"Dé 'n gaisgeach mòr," ars' àdsan, "a bha as do dheaghainn an siod, 's a thill nur a chunnaic e ar leithidnean do dha ghaisgeach a' tighinn."

"Seo duibhse." ors' esan, "an Ionmhuinn mhnatha seo, agus tri fiaclan bhur n-athar, agus ceann, agus làmh, agus cridhe an fhir a bhuail an dorn air. Deanaibh fuireach beag, 's tillidh mise, 's cha 'n fhàg mi fuigheall sgeoil anns an eilean."

Ghabh e air falbh air ais, 's an ceann treis, thug e sùil as a dhéigh, 's faicear àdsan agus a' Bhreacach a' deanadh falach cuain air.

"Marbh-phaisg oirbh féin," ors' esan; "sian fala ma'r sùilean; manadh 'ur crochaidh oirbh! m' fhagail an eilean leam fhéin, gun duine 'shìol Adhaimh ann, 's gun fhios'am a nochd dé 'ni mi."

Ghabh e air aghaidh feadh an eilean, 's cha robh e 'faicinn taigh na tùrais an àite 'sam bith, iseal na ard. Ma dheireadh chunnaic e seana chaisteal an ìochdar an eilean, 's gabh e a 'ionnsuidh. Chunnaic e tri òganaich a' tighinn gu trom, airtnealach, sgìth thun a' chaisteil. Labhair e dhaibh ann am briathra fisneacha, foisneacha, fiorghlic fior-eolais. Labhair àdsan an comain nam briathra ciadhna. Thainig ad ann am briathra seanachais air a chéile; 's co 'bha 'seo ach a thriuir dhearbh chomhdhaltan. Ghabh ad a staigh an deagh thoil-inntinn air a' mhọr-bhaile.

Thog ad ceòl 's leag ad bròn
Bha deochanna mìne, meisgeach,
'S deochanna garga, gachannach,
Beathanna saora, socharach,
Eadar e fhéin 's a chomhdhaltan;
Ceòl eadar fhidhlean leis an caidleadh fir ghointe 's mnathan
siubhla;
Searganaich a' sìor ghabhail le farum a chiuil sean,
A bha shìorrachd gu sìor-bhinn an oidhche sean.

Chaidh ad a laidhe. Anns a' mhaidinn an la'r na mhàireach dh' éiridh e ann an deagh thoil-inntinn 's ghabh e 'bhiadh. Dé 'chual e ach gliogarsaich arm 's daoine 'dol 'nan eideadh. Co 'bha 'so ach a chomhdhaltan.

"Ca' bheil sibh a' dol?" ars' esan riu.

"Tha sinn o cheann la a's bliadhna 'san eilean seo," ors' àdsan, "a' cumail cogaidh ri Mac Dorcha, Mac Doilleir, 's ciad sluaigh aige, 's a' h-uile h-aon mharbh as sinn an diugh bidh e beo am màireach. Tha 'gheasan oirnn nach fhaod sinn seo fhàgail gu bràch gus am marbh sinn ad."

"Théid mise leibh an diugh ; 's fhèairde sibh mi," ors' esan.

"Tha 'gheasan oirnn," ors' adsan, "nach fhaod duin' a dhol leinn, mar an d' théid e ann leis fhéin."

Fanadh sibhse staigh an diugh, 's théid mis' ann leam fhéin," ors' esan.

Thog e air falbh 's dh' amais e air sluagh Mhic Dorcha Mhic Doilleir, 's cha d' fhàg e ceann air colainn aca. Dh' amais e air Mac Dorcha Mac Doilleir fhéin, 's thuirt Mac Dorcha Mac Doilleir ris, "An tu 'seo a Ghaisgich na Sgiatha deirge."

"'S mi," orsa Gaisgeach na Sgiatha deirge.

"Mata," orsa Mac Dorcha Mac Doilleir, "cha 'n fhada sheasas thu dhomhsa."

An caraibh a chéile ghabh ad, 's bha ad a' cruaidh leadairt a chéile gus an robh beul an ath-dhath 's an anmoich ann. Mu dheireadh thug Ridire na Sgiatha deirge an togail bheag, shunndach, shoilleir ud air Mac Dorcha Mac Doilleir, 's chuir e foidhe e, 's thilg e dheth an ceann. Bha 'n seo Mac Dorcha Mac Doilleir marbh, 's a thri mic dheug, 's comhrag ceud air làimh gach fir dhiu. Bha eisean, an seo, air a mhilleadh 's air a reubadh cho mòr 's nach b' urrainn e 'n àrach fhàgail, 's cha d' rinn e ach e fhéin a leigeil 'na laidhe 'measg nam marbh fad an latha. Bha tràigh mhór fodha gu h-ìseal ; 's dé 'chual e ach an fhairge 'tighinn 'na caora teine teinteach,—'na nathair bheumannach,— 'na tarbh truid. Dh' amhairc e uaidhe 's de chunnaic e 'tighinn air tìr air meadhon na tràgha ach cailleach mhòr fhiaclach nach facas riabh a leithid. Bha 'n fhiacaill a b' fhaide 'na bata 'na dorn, 's an té bu ghiorra 'na dealg 'n a h-uchd.

Ghabh i nìos gus an àraich, 's bha dithisd eadar i agus esan. Chuir i 'meur 'nam beul 's thug i beo ad, 's dh' éiridh ad suas slàn mur a b' fhèarr a bha ad riabh. Rainig i eisean, 's chuir i 'meur 'na bheul, agus sgath e dhith o'n alt i. Bhuail i buille de bhàrr a cois' air agus thilg i thar seachd iomairean e. "A bheadagain," ors' ise, "'s tu fear ma dheireadh a dh' ath-bheothaicheas mi 'san àraich."

Chrom a' chailleach air fear eile 's bha eisean an taobh shuas dith. Cha robh fhios aige dé mur a chuireadh e as do 'n chaillich.

Smaointich e air an t-sleagh ghèarr a bh' aig a mac a thilgeil urra 's na 'n tuiteadh an ceann dith gum bu mhath. Thilg e'n t-sleagh 's chuir e'n ceann de 'n chaillich. Bha e'n seo 'na shìneadh air an àraich; fuil, a's féithean, a's feoil air an dochann, ach gun robh cnàmhan slàn aige. Dé 'mhothaich e ach cruitire ciuil feadh na h-àrach.

"Dé 'tha thu 'g iarraidh?" ors' e ris a' chruitire.

"Tha mi cinnteach gu 'bheil u sgìth," ors' an cruitire.

"Thig a nìos 's cuir do cheann air an tulmsaig seo, 's dean cadal."

Chaidh e suas 's laidh e. Tharruinn e sreann a' leigeil air gu'n robh e na chadal. Air a bhonn a bha e gu brisg, ealamh, èasgaidh.

"Tha thu bruadar," ors' an cruitear ris.

"Tha," ors' eisean.

"Dé 'chunnaic thu?" ors' an cruitear.

"Cruitire ciuil," ors' eisean, "a' tarruinn seana chlaidheamh meirgeach an los an ceann a thoirt diom."

Rug e'n seo air a' chruitire chiuil, 's chuir e'n ionachainn 'na cùibeanan teine trìd chùl a chinn. Bha e'n seo fo gheasan nach marbhadh e cruitire ciuil gu brathach ach le a chruit fhéin.

Chuail e 'n seo caoineadh feàdh na h-àraich.

"Co siod?" ors' eisean.

"Tha 'n seo do thriuir dhearbh-chomhdhaltan ga t' iarraidh o àite gu h-àite an diugh," ors' àdsan.

"Tha mise am shìneadh an seo," ors' eisean, "'s fuil, a's féithean, a's cnàmhan air an dochann."

"Na'm biodh againn an stòpan ìoc-shlaint a th' aig a chaillich mhòir, màthhair Mhic Dorcha Mhic Doilleir cha b' fhada 'bhitheamaid gad' leigheas," ors àdsan.

"Tha i fhéin marbh shuas an sean," ors' eisean, "'s cha 'n 'eil ni aice nach fhaod sibh fhaotainn."

"Tha sinne as a geasan gu bràthach," ors' àdsan.

Thug ad a nuas an stòpan ìoc-shlaint, 's nigh agus dh' fhailc ad e leis an rud a bh' anns' an stòp. Dh' eiridh e, 'n sean, suas cho slàn, fallan 's a bha e riabh. Chaidh e dachaidh leo, 's chuir ad an oidhche seachad ann an deagh thoil-inntinn.

Chaidh ad a mach an la'r na mhàireach ann an deogh thoil-inntinn a dh' iomain. Chaidh eisean ris an triuir, 's chuireadh e leathbhàir, sìos, 's leath-bhair suas, a staigh orra. Mhothaich ad do Mhacabh mòr Mhacaibh an Domhain a' tighinn do'n bhaile.

B'e seo an dearbh-chomhdhalta cuideachd. Chaidh ad a mach far an robh e 's thuirt ad ris.

"Fhir mo ghaoil seachainn sinne 's am baile an diugh."

"Gu-dé 's coireach ?" ors' eisean.

"Tha Gaisgeach na Sgiatha deirge staigh, agus 's tu a tha e 'g iarraidh," ors' adsan.

"Folbhadh sibhse dachaidh, 's abraibh ris falbh agus teicheadh, air-neo gu'n d' thoir mis' an ceann deth," orsa Macabh mòr Mhacaibh an Domhain.

Gad a bha seo uaigneach mhothaich Gaisgeach na Sgiatha deirge dha, 's chaidh e mach air an taobh eile de 'n taigh, agus bhuail e beum-sgéithe, agus fàd comhraig. Ghabh an gaisgeach mòr a mach as a dhéigh. Thòisich ad air a chéile.

Cha robh cleas a dhèante le sgithich na le sgothaich,
Na le disnein ghillean-feall,
Na le organ nam manach,
Nach dèanadh na gaisgich ;
Mur a bha cleas a' chleiteam, cleas an òigeam,
Ubhal a' chleasaiche 'ga thilgeil 's 'ga cheapail
An uchdannaibh a chéil.
Gu déisinneach, dàsunnach,
Fuilteach, cneadhach, creuchdanta.
Toil-inntinn ! toil-eadraiginn !
Chuireadh ad tri ditheannan dearga teine d' an armaibh
A cailceadh, d' an sgiathan, fal' agus feòla
De 'n cneas agus de 'n caoimh-cholainn,
'S ad a' cruaidh leadairt a chéile.

"Nach amaideach thusa 'Ghaisgich na Sgiatha deirge, nur a tha thu 'cumail gleichd na cruaidh chomhraig riumsa," arsa Macabh Mhacaibh an Domhain.

"Dé mar seo ?" orsa Gaisgeach na Sgiatha deirge.

"Tha nach 'eil gaisgeach anns an domhan mhòr a mharbhas mise gus am buailear mi as cionn teach mo thriubhais," orsa Macabh mòr.

"A bhuaidh bheannachd sean duit 'ga innseadh domhsa ! Na 'n innseadh tu sean domh o chionn fada, 's fhada o'n sgrìob mi 'n ceann diot," orsa Gaisgeach na Sgiatha deirge.

"Tha 'n sean barrachd 's is urrainn thu 'dheanadh."

"Tha tri fiaclan an righ ann a'm' phoca, 's feuch an tusa bheir as ad," orsa Macabh mòr.

Nur a chuala Gaisgeach na Sgiatha deirge ca' 'n robh bàs Mhac-abh mhòir, bha da dhuille aige air a thoirt seachad ma 'n bhuille, da shàthadh ma 'n shàthadh, da fhriochdadh ma'n fhriochdadh, 's bha 'n treas aon anns an talamh, gus an do chlaghaich e toll. Leum e'n sean an coimhir a chùil. Leum an gaisgeach mòr a 'ionnsuidh, 's cha d' thug e'n aire do'n toll, 's chaidh e sìos ann gu teach an triubhais. Ràinig eisean air au seo, 's thilg e dheth an ceann. Chuir e 'làmh 'na phòca, 's fhuair e tri fiaclan an righ ann, 's thug e leis ad, agus ràinig e'n caisteal.

"Deanaibh saod domhs' air an eilean seo fhàgail," ors' e r'a chomhdhaltan, "cho luath 's is urrainn duibh."

"Cha 'n 'eil saod againn," ors' àdsan, "air am fàg thu e; ach fan leinn fhéin gu bràch, 's cha bhi dìth bithidh na dibhe ort."

"Cha bhi 'chùis mar sean; ach mar an dean sibh saod air mo leigeil air falbh, bheir mi na tri cinn as na h-amhaichean agaibh," ors' eisean.

"Tha curachan a bh' aig do mhuime 's aig t' oide an seo, 's cuiridh sinn leat i gus an d' théid thu air tìr an Eirinn. An taobh a chuireas tu h-aghaidh falbhaidh i leat, 's tillidh i air a h-ais a rithisd leatha fhé'. Tha 'n seo tri chalmain 's cumaidh ad airdeachd riut air an rathad," ars' a chomhdhaltan ris.

Chuir e'n curachan a mach, 's shuidh e innte, 's cha d' rinn e stad na fois gus an deachaidh e air tìr an Eirinn. Thionndaidh e 'h-aghaidh a mach, 's ma bha i luath 'tighinn, bha i na bu luaithe tilleadh. Leig e air folbh na tri chalmain a' fàgail na h-eilthire. Bha duilichinn air gun do leig e air falbh ad leis cho bòidheach 's a bha 'n ceòl a bh' aca.

Bha abhainn mhòr eadar e agus tigh an righ. Nur a ràinig e 'n abhainn chunnaic e duine liath 'tighinn 'na dheann, 's e glaodh-ach, "A dhuin' uasail fanaibh thall, gus an d' thoir mise 'nall air mo mhuin sibh, ma'm fliuch sibh sibh péin."

"A dhuine bhochd, 's cosail gur h-ann a'd' phortair air an abhainn a tha thu," ors' eisean.

"'S ann," ors' an seann duine liath.

"Agus dé 'chuir ann thu?" ors' eisean.

"Innsidh mi sean duibh," ors' an seann duine liath.

"Bhuail gaisgeach mòr dorn air righ Eireann, 's chuir e tri fiaclan as, 's dh' fhalbh a dha mhac a thoirt a mach dioghlaidh. Dh' fholbh balachan òg, amaideach a bu mhac dhomhsa leo, 's nur a chaidh àdsan air thapadh chaidh eisean air mhiapadh.

Bu shuarrach an dioghaltas leotha mise 'chur a'm' phortair air an abhainn air a shon."

"A dhuine bhochd," ors' eisean, "cha 'n athais sean. Ma'm fàg mis' am baile bidh thusa gu math."

Rug e air, 's thog e leis e, 's chuir e e 'na shuidhe anns a' cha-thair a bha ri gualainn an righ e.

"Cha 'n 'eil annad ach duine mìomh'ail a thàinig a'n bhaile. Chuir thu 'm bodach sin 'na shuidhe ri gualainn m' athhar, 's cha 'n fhaigh thu leat e," orsa Ridire Chùirn, 's e 'g éireachd 's a' breith air.

"Air mo làimhsa, 's air mo dha làimh a 'shaoradh, gum bu cho math dhuit breith air Cnoc Leothaid 's breith ormsa," orsa Gaisgeach na Sgiatha deirge ris 's e 'ga leagail ris an talamh.

Chuir e ceanghal nan tri chaoil air gu daor agus gu docair. Bhuail e buille de bhàrr a chois' air, 's thilg e thar nan seachd sparrannan a b' airde 'bha 's a' chùirt e, fo shileadh nan lòchran 's fo chasan nan con mòra. Rinn e 'leithid eil air Ridire Chlaidh-eimh 's rinn an Ionmhuinn gàire.

"Marbh-phaisg ort fhé," ors' an righ rithe, "tha thu o cheann bliadhna air chomh-biadh, air chomh-deoch rium, 's cha 'n fhaca mi gean na gàire agad ga dheanadh gus am bheil mo mhic air am maslachadh."

"O righ!" ors' ise, "tha fios mo riasain agam fhé."

"Gu dé, a righ, an sgreadail 's an sgreuchail a tha mi 'cluinn-tinn o 'n a thàinig mi 'n bhaile; cha d' fhuair mi fhaighneachd gus an seo," arsa Gaisgeach na Sgiatha deirge.

"Tha, tri fiaclan eich aig mo mhic 'gan sparrann a' m' cheann o cheann bliadhna le ord, gus am bheil mo cheann air dol roimhe chéile le brisdeadh cridhe, 's le cràdh, 's le dòruinn," ars' an righ.

"Gu dé 'bheireadh thusa do dhuine 'chuireadh ann a'd' cheann t' fhiaclan fhéin gun neamh gun dòruinn," ors' eisean.

"Leith mo staid fhad 's a bhithinn beo, 's mo staid air fad nur a dh' fholbhainn," ors' an righ. Dh' iarr e cann' uisge, 's chuir e na fiaclan anns an uisge.

"Ol deoch," ars' e ris an righ.

Dh' òl an righ deoch, 's chaidh fhiaclan fhéin 'na cheann, gu làidir daingheann, a chearta cho math 's a bha ad riabh, 's a' h-uile té 'na h-àite fhéin. "Aha," ars' an rìgh, "tha mis' aig socair. 'S tusa 'rinn an tapadh, 's cha b'e mo chuid macsa!"

"'S e," ors' an Ionmhuinn ris an rìgh, "a b' urrain an tapadh a dheanadh, 's cha b'e do chuid mac leibideach-sa, a bhiodh 'nan sìneadh an siùrra feamann nur a bhiodh eisean a' dol air ghaisge."

"Cha 'n ith mi biadh 's cha 'n òl mi deoch," ors' an righ, "gus am faic mi mo dha mhac 'gan losgadh am màireach. Cuiridh mi feadhainn a dh' iarraidh cuallan glas-daraich airson an losgadh."

Anns a' mhaidinn an la'r na mhàireach co 'bu mhoiche bh' air a ghlùn aig leabaidh an righ, ach gaisgeach na sgiatha deirge.

"Eirich as an sean a ghaisgich; de 'n aon ni 'bhiodh tu 'g iarraidh nach faigheagh tu?" ors' an righ.

"'Se 'n rud a tha mi 'g iarraidh do dha mhac a leigeil air folbh; cha 'n urrainn mi 'bhith an aon àite am faic mi 'gam milleadh ad," ors' eisean; "b' fhèarr bearradh eoin agus amadain a dheanadh orra 's an leigeil air folbh."

Thoilich an righ siod a dheanadh. Rinneadh bearradh eoin agus amadain orra. Chuireadh a mach as an àit' ad, 's coin a's geocaich baile-mhòir as an déigh. Phôs agus chord an Ionmhuinn agus Gaisgeach na Sgiatha deirge. Rinneadh banais a mhair lath' agus bliadhna, 's bha 'n latha ma dheireadh dhi cho math ris a' chiad latha.

From John M'Gilvray, labourer, Baile Raomainn, Colonsay, aged seventy-two years. Says he learnt it from his father, Farquhar M'Gilvray, and that he heard him tell it since he remembers anything.

Farquhar M'Gilvray, his father, was a native of Mull, and there learnt this tale in his boyhood. He served nine years in the army, in North America, and subsequently settled in Colonsay. He died near about forty years ago, about seventy-five years of age.

Ballygrant, Islay, July 7, 1860.

I was uncertain how to class this story—whether to consider it as a mock heroic or a romance—and if the latter, to what period it belongs.

The island with fire about it might be a tradition of Iceland. There is something of the same kind in the Volsung tale, as given in the introduction to Norse Tales; but that also might be founded on the wonders of Iceland when they were first discovered.

The language of the story is a good example of the way in which these tales are repeated in the Highlands. Words all but synonymous, and beginning with the same letter, or one like it, are strung together; there are strange names for the heroes, roundabout phrases to express simple ideas, and words used which are seldom heard in conversation, and which are hard to translate.

The story is a good illustration of the manner in which such popular tales are preserved by tradition—how they change and decay. Its history may throw some light on the subject; so I give it.

The first incident was first sent to me by my kind friend Mrs. MacTavish from Port Ellen, in Islay, and may be taken to represent that portion of a popular tale which fixes itself in the minds of the well educated, and which would be transferred from one language to another. It is the beginning of Ursgeul Righ Eilean a Bhacruidh, and is thus told :—

"This king was out hunting with a number of attendants, when his son said, 'Where is there the man in Ireland, Scotland, or the four quarters of the *globe* that would dare strike my father with his fist in the midst of the company who now surround him;' or in Gaelic, 'Caite am bheil am fear an Erin no an Albuin no an *ceitheir ranna ruadh an domhain,*' etc., etc. (the words translated *four quarters of the globe* literally mean the four reddish brown divisions of the universe. This phrase, therefore, in translation fits itself to the knowledge of the person who uses it, and loses its originality in the new language).

"He had scarcely uttered these words when a dark cloud appeared in the north, and a rider on a black horse, who struck the king with his fist, and knocked out one of his front teeth, and took the tooth away with him. The king was downcast at the loss of his tooth, when his son said, '*Let it cost me what it will, but I will not rest* till I recover your lost tooth;' or, as it is expressed in Gaelic, 'Cha d' theid ruith as mo chois, na lodan, as mo bhroig, gas am faigh me t' fhiacil' (literally, running shall not go out of my foot, nor puddle out of my shoe, till I get thy tooth). Having said this he went off and travelled a great way."

So here again the original is better than the translation.

The incidents which follow are not the same as in the Knight of the Red Shield, but they end in the recovery of the lost tooth. The king's son goes to three houses, where he finds three sisters, each of whom gives him a pair of magic shoes, which return home when they have carried him seven years' journey in one day. The last sister is young and lovely; she lowers him over a rock in a basket to fight her brother, who is a giant with three heads. He cuts off a head each day; fires *a pistol shot* at the foot of the rock as a signal to be hauled up each evening, for this giant never fought after sunset; he is cured with magic balsam by the lady each night, and goes out fresh each morning. The giant's third head leaps on as often as it is cut off, but an eagle comes over the prince, and tells him to hold the sword on the neck till the marrow freezes, which he does, and the giant is killed. He takes his spoil from a castle, finds the tooth in a drawer, returns home with the beautiful lady, and marries her. "And the festivities on the occasion continued for a year and three days, and they lived long and happily together."

Two of the teeth and two of the adventurers have dropped out of sight, the island with fire about it is exchanged for a high rock, and the magic shoes, which are so common in all popular tales, take the place of the magic boat.

The story then in this form is wholly different from the Knight of the Red Shield, and yet its groundwork is manifestly the same. Incidents remain, and style and accessories change.

The incident of the king on the hill and the rider in the shower has come to me from a great many sources, and is followed by adventures which very with every narrator, but which have a general resemblance.

John MacDonald, travelling tinker, gives the incident as the beginning of a story called Loircean na luaith—Little Shanks in the Ashes, which was written down by Hector Urquhart. It is very like the Colonsay version; but instead of the rider on the black horse—

"One looked hither and one thither, and they saw a head coming in a flame of fire, and another head coming singing the song of songs (or? St. Oran). A fist was struck on the door of the mouth of the king, and a tooth was knocked out of him, and there was no button of gold or silver on the coat of the king but showered off him with the shame. The head did this three years after each other, and then it went home."

This then is the view of the incident taken by a wild harum-scarum strolling character, without any education at all, but with a great deal of natural wit; and his father, aged about eighty, told me a story with the incident of three old men who lived on separate islands, and sent a wandering hero on his way, with what I then took to be CURRACHD, a cap, but which I now believe to be CURRACH a corracle, which did the same as the magic shoes. Here again are the incidents, but told in a different manner.

The remainder of the story of Loircean is nearly the same as the Knight of the Red Shield, but with great variations. The king's son, who is a knight, RIDERE; COCAIRE CLAON RUADH, a red skulled cook; and SHANKS IN THE ASHES go off together, and play the part of the king's two sons and the son of the Green Spring.

They climb the mast. The despised one succeeds. The voyage is there, but only two or three lines of the descriptive passage, the first and the last. "They set her prow to sea and her stern to shore; and she would split a grain of hard corn with the excellence of the steering." But while much is left out, much is preserved which is lost elsewhere.

"When Loircean leaped on board the barge, and shook the ashes off him, he all but blinded the five fifths of Eirinn, and there fell seven bolls of ashes on the floor of the barge."

"They sailed further than I can tell you or you can tell me."

"'Oh, lads,' said Loircean (from the top of the mast), 'there is an island here before, and it is in a red blaze of fire. It is not in our power to go nearer it than seven miles, for the barge will go on fire if we do; and it is in this island that my father's teeth are, and you must leap on shore.'"

When he leaps on shore. "'Now, lads,' said Loircean, 'if you see the fire growing smaller at the end of nine days and nine nights, you may come on shore; but if you do not see it'——

And saying this he gave a dark spring (DUILEUM) on shore, and every handful he drove out was scorching those who were in the ship."

And then follow a wholly different set of adventures which are very curious, and give glimpses of forgotten manners with the same characters appearing. The fearful old woman, with the marvellous teeth; the gigantic warriors, of whom there are three with many heads; and three lovely ladies, who are found under ground, and carried off by the cowards. The story ends with the replacement of the king's lost teeth, and the punishment of the knight and the cook; and Loircean married the three ladies at once.

Again the very same incident is the beginning of Iullar og Armailteach Mac Righ na Greige, Young Heavenly Eagle, Son of the King of Greece, which was sent by John Dewar, and which he got, in Glendaruail, from J. Leitch, shoemaker, in 1860, and in 1817 from "one Duncan Campbell on Lochlong side, who is now working there as a roadman."

The three adventurers who go after the king's two teeth and *a bit of his jaw* are UBHAR, ATHAIRT, and IULLAR, and they go through a vast number of adventures with giants, monsters, and magical people of various sorts, which are also very curious. But still they set off in a boat, and for the same reason. The descriptive passage of the voyage is there in nearly the same words, but with variations; two are cowards; the one whom they despise is the true hero, and poetical justice is done at the end. The king's teeth are restored and his jaw mended; the brave lad marries a beautiful Greek lady whom he has rescued, and he turns out to be the king's only legitimate son, and he gets the kingdom, while the others are degraded—one to be a swineherd and the other a groom.

It is clearly the same story, but a different part of it; except the sailing passage, which is almost identical, it is told in different words. The names are all different, the scene is different, the adventures are different, but yet it is a remnant of the same story without doubt.

John Mackenzie, Fisherman, near Inverary, repeated another story to Hector Urquhart, in which the plot is much the same, in which a bit of the sailing passage occurs, in which the three adventurers are IULLIN, IUAR, and ARST, sons of the king of Greece, and their object the possession of the daughter of the king under the waves. The adventures which follow are again different, but like the rest, and they link the story to another set of adventures, which generally belong to the story of "Nighean Righ Fuidh Thuinn,"—adventures and exploits some of which are attributed to Fionn and Ossian and Conan in Mr. Simpson's book of Irish stories.

Many other versions of the story have been sent, or told, or mentioned to me. A gentleman in South Uist repeated some of the descriptive passages with variations, and said he remembered a man who came to his native island, Tyree, and who used to repeat the story to admiring audiences, about thirty years ago. Old Donald MacPhie, at the Sound of Benbecula, repeated part of the descriptive passages, and gave me the outline of a very similar story. On repeating the boat passage to a native of Can-tyre whom I found as assistant light-keeper at the point of Ayre, in the Isle of Man, he first stared in dumb astonishment at the unexpected sound of his own language; and then exclaimed—"Well, I have heard those very words said by my father when I was a child!" In short, the incidents and the measured prose passages with which they are garnished are scattered in fragments over the whole West Highlands of Scotland, and the less instructed the narrator the more quaint and complete his version is.

The conclusion seems unavoidable that these are the fragments of some old romance traditionally preserved, and rapidly fading away before the light of modern times.

If further evidence were required, it is not wanting. The very words of the boat passage, and a great deal that is not in any version of it which I have got, is in the "Fragment of a Tale, page 17th," lent me by my friend Mr. Bain, and referred to in the Introduction. It proves that the passage was in existence about the beginning of this century at all events, and that it was then thought worthy of preservation.

There are many other similar passages in the manuscript tale of which I have found no trace hitherto amongst the people, and which have probably died out with the old race, or emigrated with them to America.

I have been permitted to have access to other manuscripts belonging to the Highland Society. They are nearly all poetry. One is marked MS. poems collected in the Western Highlands and Islands by Dr. John Smith; and from it I copy this

"ADVERTISEMENT.

"The following poems being compiled from various editions "will often appear inelegant and abrupt, it being sometimes "necessary to take half a stanza or perhaps half a line from one "to join to as much of another edition.

"In order to complete the sense, and to supply many defects "in the versification, recourse has frequently been had to the "tales or *ursgeuls* which generally accompany the poems. As "these tales, although they have the appearance of prose, were "composed in a particular kind of measure, they are set down "in the form of verse, but without any alteration in the arrange-"ment of the words. This, it was thought, would give the "work a more uniform appearance than if it had been a mixture "of prose and verse, as one is apt to suppose it on hearing some "parts of it repeated.

"As these pieces were, for the most part, taken down from "oral recitation, frequent mistakes may have been made in the "proper division of the lines, and in the assigning of its due "quantity to each. A matter to which the poets themselves do "not always seem to have been very attentive, their measure "often varying as their subject changes.

"As those who recited ancient poems took frequently the "liberty of substituting such words as they were best acquainted "with, in room of such as were foreign or obsolete, a few words "that may perhaps be considered as modern or provincial may "occur in the course of these compositions. To expunge these "words, when none of the editions in the editor's hands supplied "him with better, was a task which he did not consider as any "part of his province. He hopes that, with all their imperfec- "tions, the poems have still so much merit as to give the reader "some idea of what they had once been. We have only the "fragments of the ruin, but they may serve to give an idea of "the grandeur of the edifice."

This then is the statement of the collector's plan of action.

The following note shews the spirit in which the best of them worked in these days. I think it was a mistaken spirit that caused the Ossianic controversy, and threw discredit on Highland literature. Still, as it is openly and fairly stated, it is fair to believe what is asserted by a gentleman and a clergyman, and for my part I implicitly believe that Dr. Smith of Campbeltown really did what he tells us, and that these poems are what they purport to be,—patched versions of oral recitations, with portions left out.

"DIARMAID.—This poem is generally interlarded with so much "of the ursgeuls or later tales as to render the most common "editions of it absurd and extravagant. But the fabulous dross "of the fifteenth century is easily separated from the more "precious ore of the ancient bards."

Of part of this same story of Diarmaid, Mrs. MacTavish writes in 1859 :—

"A dan or song which I heard an old ploughman of my father's sing very near sixty years since. He had a great collection of tales and songs, and often have I stood or sat by him in winter when kiln-drying corn, or in summer when building a peat stack, listening to what was to me so fascinating in those days. And then follows the story of how Diarmaid was killed by pacing bare-footed against the bristles of a boar which he had killed, and the lament of Diarmaid's love, and the music to which it used to be sung; and this same story of Diarmaid and the boar was sung to me by Alexander MacDonald in Barra, in September 1860, together with other long Gaelic poems. And whatever may be said or thought of MacPherson's collection, this at least is genuine old poetry, and still known to many in the Highlands.

The story, then, of the Knight of the Red Shield, or whatever its real name may be, seems to be one of the tales which were despised by the collectors of former days, and which have survived many of the poems which were fading away about eighty years ago, and which are now very nearly but not quite extinct.

Hector MacLean sent me first a version which he got from an Islay man, Alexander Campbell, farmer at Mulreas. He named his authority, "an old man still living in Colonsay, who frequently comes to Islay, and is welcome for the tales he recites."

The old man did come, and his version of the story being more complete, is given, though Campbell's version was the same shortened. It is said that it was written down by desire of the late Captain Stewart of Colonsay, and that it was noticed amongst his papers after his death.

I might have tried to reconstruct this tale from the materials which I have, but I have given without alteration the best version which came to me. I may some day try to fuse what I have into a whole; at all events, here is the clew for any other who may be disposed to work out the subject, and the best account I can give of the story.

"BEARRADH EOIN AGUS AMADAIN." This phrase is explained to mean clipping the hair and beard off one side of the head. The idea is taken from clipping one wing of a bird, and the punishment was probably inflicted at some period, for the phase occurs several times in Gaelic tales.

Another phrase, which occurs in this and other stories, probably gives a true picture of the hall of a chief in former days. A man is said to be bound with the binding of the three smalls (wrists, ancles, and small of the back), and cast under the board, under the dripping of torches, and the feet of big dogs, and there was not one in the company but cast a bone at him as he lay, and the wicked knight is kicked over the rafters. The hall meant, then, would seem to have been a large room without a ceiling, full of men and big dogs, and lighted with dripping torches; the scene of feasts, which consisted of flesh rather than potatoes; while the prisoners, bound hand and foot, lay on the floor.

In this, as in the great majority of Gaelic stories, the scene is laid in Ireland, but it seems probable that the customs of the Western Isles of Scotland and of Ireland were once nearly identical.

A version of this story, under the name of "The Son of the Green Spring by Valour," was repeated to me by an old man, Alexander MacNeill, in Barra, on the 10th of September, 1860.

The story contained less of the measured prose, and more incident than the Colonsay version. The hero is represented as sitting with his feet in the ashes, like "Boots" of the Norse Tales. He is the son of the Red Ridere, and goes off in the boat with the king's two sons to recover the king's teeth. When the feat of climbing the mast occurs, he runs up "faster than a mad woman's tongue." He has CLACH BHUAIDH, a stone of victory, with which he slays his foes. There is the magic island with fire about it, the lady and the sleeping warrior; he is left by the king's sons, goes to a small house where he finds no man, but food for three—wine and wheaten loaves. He takes a little from each portion, like the hero of many popular tales in many languages, and gets into one of three beds. Three sorely wounded men come in, and cure themselves with magic balsam, and discover him, and on the morrow he goes to fight for them. These warriors are enchanted princes, the rightful heirs of this fiery island, compelled for twenty years to contend daily with armies, and giants, and monsters. They have lost their mother, and some one has stolen their sister, who turns out to be the lady whom the hero had already rescued. They tell him what he will have to encounter, but he goes on and overcomes everytning, and his coming had been foretold. Armies of enchanted warriors fall, six hundred full heroes; three giants with several heads; "tri cruitairean na cruite bige;" the three harpers of the little harps, who could set the whole world asleep; the son of darkness, son of dimness; and a terrible old carlin, who as usual was the worst of all.

He takes a warrior by the legs and kills the others with his head; he drives his victory stone through the heads of the giants, and of MacDorcha MacDoilleir. When the harpers come, he gnaws his fingers till his mouth is full of blood, to keep himself awake, and at last he kills the magic harpers with their own harps. When the old carlin arrives she comes over the sea with a magic cup to revive her dead warriors and her sons; she puts her finger into his mouth and he bites it off. She has a tooth for a staff, and a tooth as, brod griosach, a poker, one eye in the midst of her face, one leg; and her heart, her liver, and her lungs could be seen through her mouth when it was opened. She is, in short, the same mythical carlin who so often appears, on whom the tellers of stories expend their powers in describing all that is hideous and monstrous. The hero cuts her head off, it leaps on again, he cuts it off again, and it flies up into the skies; he holds the sword on the neck, and looks up, and sees the head coming down and aiming at him; he leaps to one side, and the head goes four feet into the earth, and the victory is gained. The three warriors carry him home and bathe him in balsam, and he recovers. He raises their father and mother from the dead, and they promise him their daughter and realm. He gets a brown mare, recovers the king's teeth, returns to Ireland with a magic shoe, rides into the hall, presents the magic cup with the teeth in it to the king, saying, "I have travelled Christendom with my brown mare, and I have found out the king's teeth." He looses his father, the Red Knight, in whose stead he had set off, ties the knights to his shoe-ties and marries the fair lady, who is the daughter of the king of the town under the waves.

In short, it is manifest that this Gaelic story, now told by the poorest of the inhabitants of the western coasts and isles of Scotland, and very widely spread, is the ruin of some old romance, similar to those of the middle ages.

It is surely worth attention, though it is not strictly "true."

Certain persons, in a place which I abstain from naming, were so zealous in the cause of "truth," that they assured a simple old man, who had repeated a number of stories to one of my collectors, that he would have to substantiate every word he had uttered, or suffer punishment for telling falsehoods. I found him in great perturbation, evidently expecting that I had arrived for the purpose of calling him to account, and I had some trouble in setting his mind at rest. He repeatedly assured me that he only told what others had told him. In this instance, as it seems to me, "truth" might well say, "keep me from my friends."

LVII.

THE TAIL.

Told about thirty years ago by John Campbell, piper to his pupil, J. F. Campbell.

THERE was a shepherd once who went out to the hill to look after his sheep. It was misty and cold, and he had much trouble to find them. At last he had them all but one; and after much searching he found that one too in a peat hag half drowned; so he took off his plaid, and bent down and took hold of the sheep's tail, and he pulled! The sheep was heavy with water, and he could not lift her, so he took off his coat and he *pulled!!* but it was too much for him, so he spit on his hands, and took a good hold of the tail and he PULLED!! and the tail broke! and if it had not been for that this tale would have been a great deal longer.

This may be compared with Grimm's Golden Key. I have not given it in Gaelic, because, so far as I remember, the story was never told twice in the same words; and it can be told quite as well in any language. It is very well known in many districts in various shapes. I have a second version, which is called—

2. Ursgeal a' Ghamhna dhuinn, an aill leibh as a thoiseach e, The tale of the Brown Stirk. Do you wish from the beginning? It has nothing but a beginning; for the stirk fell over a rock and left his tail in the herdsman's hands; and the story comes to an untimely end with the Gaelic proverbial phrase—had the

tail been tougher the story had been longer. NA 'M BIODH AN T-URBALL NA BU RUIGHNE BHIODH AN T-URSGEUL NA B' FHAIDE.

3. According to a Skye version, a man put the stirk on a house top to eat a tuft of grass ; the beast fell down the chimney, and the rupture of the tail was

FINIS.